Alberto Giacometti

MYTH, MAGIC, AND THE MAN

LAURIE WILSON

Alberto

Giacometti

Yale
University
Press
New Haven
and
London

*I dedicate this book to the wisest, sanest, and smartest
gentle man I have ever met, my beloved husband,
Alfred Strasser. — LJW*

Page iii: Marc Vaux photograph of plaster
heads and figures, 1946 (destroyed)
Page vi: Ernst Scheidegger photograph of
Bust of Man, c. 1950, plaster (destroyed)

Designed by Richard Hendel
Set in Champion and Quadraat types by
B. Williams & Associates
Printed in the United States of America by

Library of Congress
Cataloging-in-Publication Data
Wilson, Laurie.
  Alberto Giacometti : myth, magic, and the man / Laurie Wilson
      p. cm.
Includes bibliographic references and index.
  ISBN 0-300-09037-4 (hardcover : alk. paper)
  1. Giacometti, Alberto, 1901–1966.   2. Artists—France—
Biography.   I.
Title.
  N6853.G5 W55 2003
  730'.92—dc21

                                        2002155620

A catalogue record for this book is available
from the British Library.

The paper in this book meets the guidelines for permanence and
durability of the Committee on Production Guidelines for Book
Longevity of the Council on Library Resources.

10 9 8 7 6 5 4 3 2 1

Contents

Preface

My first encounter with Giacometti's work was as a young sculptor in New York who found his art deeply challenging and inspirational. Giacometti has always been an artist's artist. He never compromised to please; he explored endlessly and he balanced himself and his work on the edge. He did not disdain the idea of beauty, but he hid his methods of achieving it. Like every art student, I learned the story of Giacometti's overriding dedication to his art and endless quest—if not for perfection, then for something he believed was more important—"aliveness."

My next encounter with Giacometti was as a doctoral student in art history with a specialty in modern art. The milieu in which he worked and the ways in which his art both expressed and defied prevailing currents in twentieth century European art became my focus. As an artist and art historian I learned to look at his sculpture and drawings, to let them speak for themselves with minimal interference from preconceived ideas.

Eventually I returned to him as a psychoanalyst and art therapist, believing that a psychoanalytic perspective would provide a fuller understanding of what he had created. Psychoanalysts are trained to look beyond (or beneath) the surface of conscious behavior and thought, to follow hunches, to examine "insignificant" details, and to question the received wisdom of family myths. That is the approach I have taken in this book, though I have never thought of him as a patient. Thus, I have gone more deeply into Giacometti's early childhood and have assigned more weight to certain crucial experiences from that faraway time than art historians usually do. Clinical experience has taught me that some such forgotten moments keep their power throughout an individual's life, subtly shaping character and personality. Difficult, even traumatic, events may color a personality over an entire lifetime, but of course they are never the whole story. So much depends on the talents and emotional gifts (as well as the luck) of the individual, who can either be crippled by them or transform them into art or, in some instances, both.

In addition to being a great artist, Giacometti was also a great friend to many. I have gone extensively into the lives and thoughts of some of his closest associates—Leiris, Breton, Ernst, Bataille, Sartre—because I believe their personalities echoed his own.

Scholars and poets—many of them in Giacometti's inner circle—have tried and failed to explain the great surrealist sculptures he produced between 1929 and 1934, which all agree hold the keys to his inner life. In 1931 or 1932 he wrote: "I can be myself only in objects, in sculpture, in drawing (perhaps in painting) and much less well through poetry. Nothing else."[1]

My hypotheses about the work done in this period can never be fully validated, because Giacometti will never lie on my analytic couch, responding to my interpretations, keeping us both on the track of his true self. But I can still question him and look to his work and words (and to the words of those who knew him or wrote about him) for answers: Why do the figures in groups feel so frozen in place? Why are so many of them androgynous? Why are the eye and the act of gazing so fraught with tension and erotic meaning? Why is sexuality depicted as dangerous, disagreeable, or painful? Why did a man who allegedly did not want and could not have children make so many references to pregnancy and childbirth? How can we better understand the frequent sculptural references linking life and death?

In the three chapters on surrealism I try to answer these questions by following the thematic clues as they appear chronologically in his sculptures and texts. I have separated out the themes artificially, one from the other, for clarity.[2] This method violates Giacometti's synthetic way of working, but it is the only way to disentangle the tightly woven threads that have camouflaged his complex purposes for so long. If we were to leave his art and writing undisturbed as objects to be appreciated and admired, we might never discover the deepest meaning of his genius.

The last great enigma of Giacometti's work is why his filiform postwar figures are so thin and so eloquently moving. Nothing he did before the war adequately prepares us for his leap into novelty and greatness. But the seeds were always there—growing slowly inside him. The accidental events of his life forced him to repeatedly confront the links between birth and death and the narrow ledge of existence that separates the two. The process of self-discovery and emotional growth began with early childhood experiences around which he wove fantasies that gradually became convictions and finally had to be expressed in painting and sculpture. This book is a study of that process, through which acts of life can be transformed into works of art—a process so deeply connected with the human condition that, in a certain way, it is part of each of us.

Acknowledgments

Like all authors who work on long projects, I owe much to many and have tried to be inclusive in expressing my gratitude. Whatever factual errors remain are mine.

James Lord offered generous assistance at the outset of my research fourteen years ago when he answered my every question. He also opened his archives at the Beinecke Rare Book and Manuscript Library at Yale University so that scholars could study the documents he had gathered in the course of his meticulous biographical research, and he subsequently shared with me further interview material not yet in the public domain. The publication of this book can be seen as testimony of the widening scope that his richly detailed biography has generated for later scholars. I thank Bruno Giacometti, who graciously met with me for a long interview early in my research and whose answers, both then and later, to many questions about the Giacometti family contributed importantly to the picture I have drawn. Many others of Giacometti's family and friends with whom I met have added crucial pieces to the puzzle, including Yves Bonnefoy, Henri Cartier-Bresson, Sina Dolfi-Giacometti, Jacques Dupin, Nina Engel, Elizabeth Geissbuhler, Françoise Gilot, Diego Giovanoli, E. W. Kornfeld, Michel Leiris, Herbert Lust, Raymond Mason, Pierre Matisse, Mercedes Matter, Isabel Rawsthorne, Henri Rol-Tanguy, Ernst Scheidegger, and Laura Semadeni.

Three individuals have contributed significantly throughout to the final outcome of this book. Joann Turo, my psychoanalytic colleague and friend, perceptively and patiently listened to, and looked at (as well as read), every hypothesis and speculation I explored along the way during this long journey. Her wise and deeply psychodynamic counsel contributed greatly to the constructions and reconstructions I have proposed about the artist. Valerie Fletcher, an art historian whose twenty-five years of expertise on Giacometti have earned her the premier position in Giacometti scholarship in the United States, generously shared her own research. She read and discussed my manuscript and candidly critiqued my controversial hypotheses. All scholars eagerly look forward to her forthcoming book on Giacometti's paintings. I have had the exceptional good fortune of working with an editor extraordinaire—Kitty Ross. With grace and patience she helped me with the seemingly impossible task of translating complex ideas and sometimes contradictory approaches into orderly, straightforward prose.

Michael Brenson was particularly generous and encouraging both early and throughout my long voyage with Giacometti. Other Giacometti scholars for whose help I am especially grateful include Christian Klemm and Veronique Wiesinger. My thanks to Anna Balakian, a scholar whose work on André Breton and surrealism was foundational, who read and commented on my surrealist chapters. Thanks also to Elizabeth Baker, another exceptional editor whose sterling questions invariably led to greater clarity and depth. A special thanks to Mary Gedo for her initial inspiration and wise counsel and support throughout this project, and to Hans Hitz, former art teacher at the Evangelical Secondary School at Schiers; to George Mauner, who is the foremost scholar of Cuno Amiet and who was unfailing in his assistance; and to James Romano, distinguished Egyptologist at the Brooklyn Museum, who was a superb guide to that vast and complex field. Other scholars, art historians, and artists who generously gave their time and encouragement include Ziva Amishai-Maisels, Ted Carpenter, Bradley Collins, Hansjacob Diggelmann, Patrick Elliot, Martin Green, Milly Heyd, David Hopkins, Martin James, Donald Kuspit, Gottlieb Leinz, Rose-Carol Washton Long, Evan Maurer, Krishna Reddy, John Rewald, Laurie Schneider Adams, Peter Selz, Jack Spector, Jewel Stern, and M. E. Warlick. To Steven Zucker I owe thanks and great appreciation for his meticulous research skills when I was gathering the bibliography.

I am also grateful to Drs. John Gedo, Jules Glenn, and Leonard Shengold for their careful reading of the entire manuscript and astute observations about my psychoanalytic formulations. Other psychoanalysts individually and in study groups to which I have presented have been very helpful, including the Colloquium on Psychoanalysis and the Humanities at New York University and the study group on Art and Psychoanalysis. Psychoanalytic colleagues with whom I discussed key ideas and from whom I received astute feedback, include: Renato Almansi, Anna Balas, Leonard Barkin, Frank Baudry, Harvey Bezahler, Harold Blum, Joseph Coltrera, Charles Goodstein, Eugene Halpert, James Hamilton, William Jeffrey, Louise Kaplan, Luba and Richard Kessler, Myunghee Kim, Graziella Magherini, Patricia Nachman, Peter Neubauer, Jerome Oremland, Shelley Orgel, Paul Schwaber, Herbert Stein, Alan Stern, and Jenny Stuart. Barry Opatow and Joel Whitebook not only offered psycho-analytic insights but also helped me understand some of the philosophical arguments swirling around Giacometti in the 1940s.

Thanks also to the friends who cheered me on while the slings and arrows of outrageous fortune were flying by: Linda Amster, Susan Caldwell, Cathy and Eric Hardman, Carol Neuman de Vegwar, Peninah Petruck, Kirsten Rohr-mann, Pam Schirmeister, Elizabeth Vercoe, and Charlie Sprague.

New York University provided several grants that helped me with travel and research, and a research grant from the American Psychoanalytic Association provided a generous sum over three years and proved crucial in freeing me from some academic obligations so I could complete the research. I bene-fited from discussions in which I presented various portions of the book at The New York Psychoanalytic Society, The New Jersey Psychoanalytic Society, The Psychoanalytic Association of New York, The Lucy Daniels Foundation, Sigmund Freud Center at the Hebrew University of Jerusalem, two interdisci-plinary symposia in Florence sponsored by the International Psychoanalytic Association, The Gardner Seminar in Psychiatry and the Humanities at Yale University, the North Carolina Museum of Art, The Society for Art and Psy-choanalysis, Florence, Italy, The American Art Therapy Association, and The American Psychoanalytic Association.

Premier art therapist and old friend Edith Kramer was especially helpful in deciphering some family myths as well as assisting me in making initial psychodynamic formulations about the artist. Art therapists Barbara Ball, Ani Buk, Rebecca Di Sunno, Judith Rubin, Michelle Spark, and Elizabeth Stone served as thoughtful and thought-provoking readers at various stages in the process. And I shall always be grateful to my students at New York University who responded so intelligently to the lectures in which I tested my hypotheses.

Thanks for help with translations to Terri Gordon, Rumi Ito Purcell, Edith Kramer, Vera Mueller, Dennis Perreira-Egan, and Alfred Strasser.

At the Morgan Library, where the Pierre Matisse Gallery Archives are stored, I wish to thank Sylvie Merin, Inge Dupont, and McKenna Lebens for their unfailing courtesy and meticulous assistance; at the Beinecke Library, Vincent Giroux; at the Kunsthaus Zürich, Ursula Perucchi, Cécile Brunner, and Romi Storer; at Museum Chur, Beat Stutzer; at Museo Stampa, Remo Maurizio; at Swiss Institute for Art Research, Simonetta Noseda; at the Mu-seum of Modern Art in New York, Judith Cousins and Anne Umland; at the Centre Georges Pompidou, Brigitte Vincens; at the Musée nationale d'art moderne in Paris, Isabelle Mounod-Fontane and Christian Derouet; at the National Gallery of Art in Washington, D.C., Nan Rosenthal and Jeremy

Strick; at the Guggenheim Museum, Ward Jackson; at the Musée de la ville de Paris, Danielle Molinari. Thanks also to gallerists Carroll Janis, Duncan MacGuigan, Albert Loeb, Ernst Beyeler, and Michel Soskine.

I have had the good fortune of working with several excellent editors at Yale University Press: Judy Metro, whose enthusiasm for my project brought me to Yale in the first place; and then Patricia Fidler, who has been instrumental in bringing the book to completion. Thanks also at Yale to the skillful, close work of manuscript editor Jeffrey Schier, photo editor John Long, Mary Mayer, as well as Michelle Komie for her careful and cheerful attention to detail during the final steps of the process.

Finally, I dedicate this book to the wisest, sanest, and smartest hedonist I have ever met, my beloved husband, Alfred Strasser, who has traveled cheerfully, translated, read, and listened endlessly to and for me and Giacometti.

ACKNOWLEDGMENTS

CHAPTER 1

1901-1914

DOWN IN THE VALLEY

Alberto Giacometti, one of the great artists of the twentieth century, grew up in an exquisite Alpine valley on the Italian edge of Switzerland. All his life he was wrapped firmly in the folds of a glowing family myth—that his had been the best of all possible childhoods, that he was the favored eldest son of an artist father who generously supported his son's talent, and a strong mother who provided a warm, stable base for her family. "I can't imagine any happier childhood or youth than those I passed with my father and all my family, my mother and my sister and my brothers."[1]

Yet, all who knew him—family, friends, and acquaintances—recognized that he was endlessly obsessed by thoughts of death. His cousin recalled that "Giacometti was always tormented and trapped by true anguish. He suffered continually and maybe most at the height of his fame. I, who knew him from childhood, don't ever remember having heard him laugh from the heart, except maybe once."[2] A friend who saw him regularly during the 1940s and 1950s reported that "he was haunted as if someone were chasing him; like a wanderer in exile, cursed. His anxiety level was terrible. . . . It was more than fear, it was terror. His only moments of peace, seemed to be at his studio where there would be a lull, as if the wind stopped."[3]

Why did this celebrated and gifted man suffer so much? Why did someone so apparently blessed by fortunate circumstances become so anxiety ridden and preoccupied with death? The usual explanation is that when he was nineteen he witnessed the death of an elderly man, a mere acquaintance with whom he was traveling. "Everything became fragile for me and since then I have never been able to sleep without a lamp, nor go to bed without thinking I might never wake up. From then on, death became a constant possibility, for myself, and for everyone. It was like a warning."⁴ But this single event in his young adulthood does not suffice—even for so sensitive a person as Giacometti. The power and persistence of his unhappiness obliges us to search for a more complex truth and to question, despite its seductive appeal, the myth of his "happy childhood." Though Giacometti and many others have been invested in maintaining this story, even to this day, we must now unravel it.⁵ Only by uncovering the source of his suffering can we can fully understand Giacometti's goals as an artist and the undisputed power of his artistic achievement.*

Alberto's father, Giovanni Ulrico, the third of eight children of Ottilia and Alberto Giacometti, was born March 7, 1868, in the tiny community of Stampa in the Bregaglia valley. He grew up at the center of a warm family in an old inn, the Piz Duan—named for one of the peaks towering above the deep Alpine valley—which had been his mother's family home for generations (fig. 1.1). From early on Giovanni's family saw him as different: "[At my birth] my mother was a bit anxious to see my red hair (the color of the devil). I was much admired as a handsome boy . . . and a boy who was a bit special, dreamy—so much that my elder brother . . . called me Sonderling [odd one]—and so I remained."⁶

Giovanni was a curious and creative child, constantly making toys and drawing. Both his parents encouraged his interest in art, an unlikely career for a son of the Bregaglia valley but in keeping with their interests in contemporary culture. As innkeepers in a community commanding a principal pass between northern and southern Europe, their contacts with the capitals of the larger world were infrequent but continuous. And they were willing to make sacrifices to send their talented son out of the valley to study art.

After two years of secondary school in Chur, capital of the canton, Giovanni Giacometti surprised his classmates by announcing he wanted to go to Munich to study art. But when he arrived in the beautiful German city in 1887 he was not accepted into the Munich Academy as he had hoped and went instead to the School of Decorative Arts. He met Cuno Amiet, a fellow Swiss art student in Munich, and the two young men quickly formed a close friendship, which deepened when they later went together to Paris to study for three years with the academic artists Bougereau and Fleury. By the time they left France,

---

*Because of copyright restrictions I have had to omit illustrations of certain works discussed in the text. For these illustrations readers are referred either to the source immediately following the first mention of one of these works or to its corresponding source note.

FIGURE 1.1 *Giacometti family home, Piz Duan, Stampa (author photograph).*

the two young artists saw themselves as revolutionaries, attracted to the new movements inspired by Gauguin and van Gogh.[7] Giovanni returned to the Bregaglia valley in 1891, broke and discouraged, and after two stagnant years there he took off again for "new horizons" in Italy using, as his traveling money, the fee he had earned from selling a portrait.

In Rome his living conditions were bleak, but he pursued his passions— studying Rembrandt, Velásquez, and Titian in the museums, and painting landscapes from dawn to dusk. By summer, he headed further south to Torre del Greco, a village on the Bay of Naples between Pompeii and Herculaneum. He painted outdoors by the sea every possible moment, using his last few lire for paint and canvas. The exceptionally lyrical canvas *Boys on the Beach at Torre del Greco* (1893) (Bündner Kunstmuseum, Chur) was the result. Each child glows with differently hued flesh, and the violet sky meets a turquoise sea in a vibrant work that presages his later joyous use of color and expresses his talent for painting nudes. Giovanni kept this painting for the rest of his life and often spoke of the suffering he had experienced in order to complete it. When he finally got back to Rome, he was so undernourished that he had to be cared for by relatives until he was physically strong enough to return to Switzerland.[8]

Giovanni was again dejected and disillusioned after his return from Italy. Fortunately, by 1895 he found a mentor nearby in Maloja, a small village on

Lake Sils in the upper valley of the Engadine, 2,500 feet above the Bregaglia valley. Giovanni Segantini was a celebrated painter who had moved recently from Italy seeking subjects for his monumental Neo-Impressionist landscapes. Segantini's popularity at the turn of the century was immense, and his support heartened the discouraged young painter.

At the end of October 1899, Segantini died unexpectedly in the mountains they had often painted together. The next night, alone with Segantini's corpse in a small candlelit chapel, Giovanni painted the dead man's portrait. Segantini's death was a professional setback as well as a terrible personal loss. The older artist's works were to have been exhibited at the 1900 Paris World's Fair, and Giovanni's paintings would have been shown at the same time—a big step for an unknown young painter—which could have gained him instant entrée into the international art world and early renown.

On January 31, 1900, four months after Segantini's death, Giovanni's father died. Exactly one month later, "on the same day, at the same hour," his younger brother, Sammuele, expired unexpectedly in his sleep. "First I lost my friend and teacher, then my father, and finally my brother. These are truly sad times," he wrote to a friend.[9] The death of his father, though expected, deprived Giovanni of a critically important source of support and inspiration, movingly described in Amiet's condolence letter: "Your real consolation can only be brought by work; your father left you an immense treasure which I envy; the desire and love of work as well as perseverance. I remember when we were painting up in the mountains with how much energy and speed he got up the mountain bringing wood for the fire. This toughness is the best thing a father can leave a son. The one other thing which makes your loss easier to bear is his great love for you which I often saw shining in his eyes."[10]

Seven months later, on October 4, 1900, Giovanni Giacometti married Annetta Stampa, the cool and distant daughter of the valley's secondary school teacher. Her family was old and well connected, more successful than many others in the region. In temperament Giovanni and Annetta were opposites. He was warm and openly affectionate, a romantic idealist and a gentle man who stood by his friends and rarely imposed his will on another living being.[11] Annetta, by contrast, held herself apart and made certain that the differences were noticed. She was, for example, the only woman of her age who did not carry water from the village fountain to her home; she had servant girls do such work. She also dressed differently, wearing a small, lacy apron for decoration only. She was "signorile"—Stampa aristocracy. Her values—bourgeois to the core—involved the appearance of gentility, the maintenance of her family's high status in the small compact community, correct behavior, scrupulous neatness, and Spartan fiscal household management in all things. Unlike her husband, Annetta was a regular churchgoer, and the local Protestantism reinforced her already rigorous asceticism.[12] The couple's life together was tempered by his more flexible artistic nature.

Annetta Giacometti's remarkable strengths are best understood in the context of a childhood that must have seemed to her like prolonged mourning. She was the second youngest child of her father's second marriage and was very close to her two sisters, Anna Cornelia (three years older) and Santina (two years younger). Her mother died when Annetta was four and a half years old, and she was raised by her father with help from a succession of female relatives. Four of these women—three aunts and one grandmother—died by the time she was fourteen.[13] In the Bregaglia valley of that era, custom prescribed a long period of black or dark clothing for women in mourning. And Annetta often recalled wearing black for four years.[14] She developed a characteristic response to repeated losses, which was to retreat behind a facade of toughness. Identifying with a father who believed in Spartan discipline, she lived in a culture obliged by weather and geography to be strong in order to survive. In Annetta Giacometti's Switzerland, her toughness was natural even if it hid a profound vulnerability.

A few months after their wedding, with Annetta pregnant with their first child, the couple moved to Borgonuovo, her village just up the road from Stampa. There they set up housekeeping with Annetta's father (also named Giovanni) and sisters as near neighbors in the tiny community.[15] Over the next six years Annetta gave birth to four children: Alberto (October 10, 1901), Diego (November 15, 1902), Ottilia (May 31, 1904), and, finally, Bruno (August 24, 1907).[16] Aided at first in the household by her older sister, Cornelia, Annetta soon employed "Lombardin," Italian girls from the communities just across the border, because they were known to be good with children. Daily visits from her father as well as marriage to a husband who worked at home ensured Annetta regular close contact with familiar loving adults. As the frequent subject of Giovanni's work, Annetta experienced a unique closeness with him, a silent togetherness echoing the intimacy with the mother she had lost in early childhood. To be lovingly regarded for hours on end must have felt profoundly comforting to a woman proud both of her ability to endure loneliness, and of her fortitude. His gaze completed her, making her feel strong and whole—reflecting back to her a beautiful and stable self. Furthermore, by giving her four children in quick succession and by covering the walls of his home and studio with family portraits, Giovanni literally surrounded his wife with relatives who could never abandon her.

Giovanni Giacometti was uninterested in the fiscal side of being an artist, and his marriage to Annetta freed him from financial uncertainty. Her small inheritance provided the means for their modest lifestyle, especially in the early years of their union. Eventually it allowed them to buy a home. Throughout their marriage, her prudence freed him to devote himself to art. She was his rock and anchor—keeping her eye fixed on the security and stability of her family. A capable manager, she took charge of everything, from setting prices and collecting fees for his artwork to assuming responsibility for the household finances, which she oversaw with an iron will.

That Annetta was warmed and charmed by her gentle husband was never in doubt. Her letters and the recollection of people who knew her testify to her undying love and affection for her "Caro Giovanin," whom she described as unfailingly kind, loving, gentle, and supportive.[17] From the time of his death in 1933 until the end of her long life in 1964, she never stopped thinking or talking about the good times they had together, his wonderful skill as an artist, and the happy years she passed as his wife.

Eleven days before Alberto, their joyously awaited first baby, came into the world, the Giacomettis were preparing to congratulate Giovanni's closest friend and fellow artist, Cuno Amiet, on the birth of his first child. Tragically, the Amiets' son was stillborn.[18] In an attempt to comfort their friends in their grief, the Giacomettis asked the Amiets to be their son's godparents. It was a fateful choice. The Amiets' tragic loss became part of the complex inner life of this gifted and very visual boy. It remained etched in his imagination for more than three decades, when he was finally able to transform it into his art.

A year after his birth Alberto lost his prime position with his mother when Diego was born—a withdrawal he must have keenly felt. A year and a half later, when his sister was born, Annetta was busy, maybe even overwhelmed, by the responsibility of two younger children to tend. Whenever she could, she sent Alberto into her husband's studio.[19] That, at least, is one of the Giacometti family stories. We know, however, that Annetta had at least one female servant to help her with the children and that Giovanni was traveling extensively during this period. This may be one of those family myths that contains little factual veracity but significant emotional truth.[20]

But the birth of Annetta's third child, Ottilia, was marked by an unfortunate coincidence. It preceded by five days the death of Giovanni's mother, Ottilia Santi Giacometti, the only grandmother Alberto had known. It seems likely that in April or May, near to the time of her daughter's birth, Annetta Giacometti moved with her family to the Piz Duan to help nurse the dying woman.[21] Given the small scale of the living space and the forced intimacy that would have resulted, the precociously observant young boy could not have remained untouched by the exciting and traumatic events that were taking place around him. I propose that Alberto witnessed some or all of the raw physicality of his sister's birth and his grandmother's death and stored away these experiences for later expression in his art (see Chapter 4).

Thus Alberto Giacometti was born under the pall of a tragic conjunction of birth and death. A second such conjunction just a few years later—the birth and death of his sister and grandmother, respectively, both named Ottilia—was to have an equally profound effect, setting him on a path that seemed magically to link the two phenomena. The effects of these events might not have been so severe had his mother been more resilient. Unfortunately her response—silent, cold withdrawal—due to her own early childhood losses, prevented her from cushioning her young children from the fatal blows. Annetta Giacometti was not really *there* to hold them when they most needed her. To her son this must have made each death during his early and middle childhood a double loss.

Fortunately Giovanni was there to hold him. In his oldest son, Giovanni had found a fellow voyeur, someone as visual as he was.[22] Alberto responded to his father's rapturous delight in having found a soul mate by turning to him more readily and frequently than he turned to his preoccupied, distant mother. His sister's birth had been an additional catalyst for a movement already underway. Thus, at the age when children are avidly exploring new horizons, Alberto, frightened and possibly traumatized by witnessing a birth and a death, turned decisively to his father's entrancing world to escape the terrible visions now associated with women's bodies.

On September 2, 1904, while Giovanni was away on one of his travels, Annetta wrote a remarkably revealing letter to Anna Amiet. The letter tells of the great pleasure she takes in nursing Ottilia, who acts like a wild puppy when she gets the breast. She writes of how much she enjoys watching her daughter play and of how "spoiled the little Fraulein is" when she wants to be carried; one can't do anything but "love" her. Then follows a telling anecdote about "the two bad boys": "Alberto also pays more attention now to her [Ottilia] than in the beginning. Diego is very sweet to her but naturally in his own way. Poor Ottilia, if she were in his care. Luckily our young servant is a great lover of children and she must have much patience with the two bad boys, yet she's still always in a good mood. In general the Lombardin have much more love for children than the Bergellerin."[23]

The letter portrays Annetta's conflicting feelings as a mother, but subtly. Annetta is herself a "Bergellerin"—a woman of the Bergell valley—and she

FIGURE 1.2 *Giovanni Giacometti, Annetta and Alberto, 1902. Oil on canvas, 50 x 64 cm. Bündner Kunstmuseum, Chur.*

has less love and patience for her two "bad boys" than does the servant from Lombardy—"Lombardin." Four years later, in her 1908 annual Christmas letter to Anna Amiet, Annetta writes that when Alberto was fifteen months old he was "crazy about his father. Every time Giovanni leaves the room there [was] screaming and yelling." Recognizing her children's attachment to their father, Annetta often commented about a famous family photograph: "You see, when he is around they all go to him, not to me."[24]

In keeping with both the sentimental aspects of contemporary artistic currents as well as his personality, most of Giovanni's many portraits of his wife and children have a sunny, optimistic aura; his subjects are smiling or in repose. But in the spring 1902 painting *Annetta and Alberto*, a sad-looking Annetta is shown awkwardly holding her infant Alberto, a restless baby who seems mostly unconnected to her (fig. 1.2). Could this reflect the burdens of being a young mother without a mother of her own to guide and support her? A remarkable *Sketch* on a postcard to Amiet by Giovanni of his wife, himself, and his two sons offers striking evidence of the Giacometti family dynamics in 1903 (fig. 1.3). Annetta is on the right in profile, staring expressionlessly ahead, above and past her family. Giovanni embraces a smiling Alberto and inclines affectionately to kiss the infant Diego, who, turning his back to his mother, reaches up toward his father. They are all up in a tree—undoubtedly a reference to Segantini's celebrated images of women in trees, which invariably referred to motherhood—either as cold and neglectful *bad* mothers or as idealized, loving, *good* mothers.[25]

The Mother (1905) shows Annetta holding Ottilia with stiff awkwardness (fig. 1.4). In this, as in other similar paintings, she neither leans toward the children she holds or feeds, nor does she usually look at them. Her hands rarely seem relaxed or able to caress; their purpose is to contain a child, not to provide emotional warmth or comfort. Her sons and daughter respond by remaining aloof. They do not nestle in her arms and settle themselves against her body. Not until she holds Bruno, her last child, born in 1907, do we see

FIGURE 1.3
Giovanni
Giacometti,
Sketch, 1903.
Ink on paper,
dimensions
unknown.

easy intimacy. The large painting *Maternity* (1908) shows Annetta nursing Bruno under a blossoming tree, with Diego and Alberto in sailor suits at her feet.[26]

Bruno Giacometti has claimed that there were never any arguments in the household. When I asked him how it could have been that his parents never disagreed, he responded: "My parents respected each other, if my father saw that mother said or wanted something, another person would have said 'no,' but he let her [have her way]."[27] "Respect" sounds like a code word for the known futility of confronting or disagreeing with Annetta Giacometti. The characteristic family relationships are implied in a famous photograph taken in 1909, with mother and eldest son staring at each other from across a distance, seemingly oblivious to the four other family members. The photograph is often cited as evidence of the intense and loving connection between Alberto and his mother, yet a closer look reveals fear and questioning on the eight-year-old's face—an ambivalent bond to Annetta, who looks confident of her power to control her son. Both the profile and frontal views, visible in another photograph (fig. 1.5), capture the tight-lipped, withholding quality of her expression and the woodenness of her smile. Her clasped hands reach toward neither husband nor children, yet Giovanni manages to embrace or be embraced by all the children. Giovanni never lost his place as the parent most able to be close to his children. In his role as the affectionate parent, he left the less-pleasant disciplinary efforts to his wife. As Bruno explained: "At home he was

FIGURE 1.4
Giovanni Giacometti,
The Mother, *1905.*
Oil on canvas,
50 x 55 cm. Bündner
Kunstmuseum, Chur.

an ideal father . . . he gave advice but he was not a father who said, 'Do this, do that' . . . it was the Mama who ruled the entire home; it was always the Mama who made the structure."[28] Though Giovanni saw himself as liberal and open to the most current trends, Annetta anchored him to a profoundly bourgeois culture, grounded in religion, patriotism, and a conventional lifestyle. And for the most part he let her dominate. As we will see, only when her husband's passion and talent spurred him to break with the highly moral Protestantism of the valley culture would her influence be overruled.

One anecdote about Alberto and two about Diego disclose much regarding Annetta's tough-mindedness and its effects. First, Alberto's story: "When I was a child, my father went on a journey. Two days later, I burst out in tears, screaming: I don't remember my father's head."[29] It took his brother Diego's concrete description of their colorful father to calm Alberto. "You know, he's that man with the red beard."[30] The incident became a family "joke," which Annetta told often. Of all the children, Alberto suffered most intensely when

FIGURE 1.5 *Giacometti family, 1909. Alberto is at left, Bruno is behind Diego, and Ottilia is between Giovanni and Annetta.*

his father was away. That it seemed amusing to her, evidently unable to tolerate or empathize with its deeper meaning about her son's difficulty with separation, suggests that her own difficulties with loss interfered with her ability to calm him when he was frightened.[31]

The two stories about Diego involve his "first memory" and his "accident." First or earliest memories are usually symbolic nuggets containing condensed truths about a person and his experience in childhood. The story about Diego was often retold by Annetta, who must not have realized how revealing it was about their respective characters.[32] Diego's memory is of an event occurring on the day of the move to the Piz Duan from the family's first home in Borgonuovo in 1904. "In the confusion, two-year-old Diego wandered outside unnoticed. The street was full of milling sheep, and he became lost among them. . . . Alone, helpless, terrified, Diego began to scream and sob. A girl came to the rescue, lifting him up from the flock of sheep, and he saw his mother at the window, laughing."[33] Rather than sympathetic alarm for his fright, Diego saw amusement on his mother's face. At such a young age he could not have understood that anxiety rather than indifference could have prompted his mother's laughter.

Two years later, Diego would prove to his mother that he could suffer enough for her to take pity and that he could bear pain without complaint— even better than she. One spring day, when he was four and a half, an "accident" occurred while he was helping with farm work like all the boys and able-bodied men of the valley. Diego's right hand was caught between the gears of a feed thresher, slicing off half of one finger and crushing the ends of two others. Decades later he told the story to Lord, Alberto Giacometti's biographer, after Lord had questioned him many times about his maimed fingers.

Diego said that he had always disliked the physical appearance of his fingers and so he deliberately placed them on the machine, waiting for the interlocking metal teeth to crush them. He made no sound, so the boy operating the machine wouldn't stop cranking before all his fingers had been mashed.[34] It is impossible to determine the accuracy of this version because Diego misremembered the date of the event, placing it in summer 1908. A letter from Giovanni Giacometti to Cuno Amiet, written on March 24, 1907, confirms that the accident occurred on March 2, 1907. Diego's father was astonished not only that his young son could bravely bear the pain of the surgery without anesthesia, but that he could even recall the appearance of the scissors used to cut off the mostly severed finger as well as the type of needle used in the operation. Both parents became nauseated watching the procedure.[35]

Such extraordinary behavior in a young child calls for explanation. The relationship between a mother and her young child can establish enduring patterns of behavior. A little more than a year before the accident, Annetta Giacometti's sister, Cornelia, who had recently returned to Stampa, died at age 37. The sisters had been very close, and Annetta, who had lost so many female relatives, was bereft. She described her loss to Anna Amiet in a letter dated June 28, 1906. "Tomorrow my cousin from Davos comes for a visit to Borgonuovo. I'm very pleased and I'll go there often *for in Stampa I have no intimate company.* Luckily, the dear children give me much to do and think about and keep homesickness for my dear sister, Cornelia, from coming so painfully to the fore."[36] A few sentences earlier, Annetta had referred to the pleasure the family was taking in their new apartment and garden. "The three big ones play around in shirts or also naked for many hours. Diego now wears pants and is the worst of them all."

What this "worst" could have meant we can only guess. When Diego was born, he did not accept his mother's milk and consequently was bottle-fed. Her description of the intense pleasure she and her third child took in breastfeeding suggests how much she may have minded Diego's refusal. We cannot know what caused the feeding difficulty between mother and son, but it probably created an emotional distance that would shape their relationship. By 1904 Diego had already been displaced by a new sibling and must have keenly felt his mother's emotional and physical withdrawal. The family moved again in 1905, finally resolving their prolonged discomfort of two years without a stable home base. Annetta contracted mumps and had a difficult recovery in early 1906. She was still mourning her sister's death in mid 1906, as expressed in her letter to Anna Amiet. Now, in spring 1907, she was pregnant again and had new cause to pull away from her "worst" son. Perhaps his response was to imitate her toughness and express his longing for her through ever more frantic activity and play. Her new pregnancy could have exacerbated both her impatience with her exceptionally active toddler as well as her unavailability.[37]

In time, Diego's role in the family became more sharply delineated. His nonchalance about dangerous or life-threatening activities continued well beyond the episode with the threshing machine. For many years he remained the "worst" bad boy, and by adolescence he had become the family's black sheep—drinking, whoring, and engaging in semicriminal activities. He never married and avoided intimate relationships with women who were his equal; he was taciturn, an alcoholic, willing to tolerate extraordinary amounts of pain without complaint, and he was practically allergic to expressions of sympathetic concern.[38] When Diego was living alone in Paris during World War

II, Alberto was terrified for his safety, as he had been when they were adolescents and Diego would scale the highest and most dangerous peaks in the Bergell. His daring became proverbial, as did his stoic patience and reliable responses to the outrageous demands of the family members to whom he was devoted—Alberto and his mother.

Alberto's reaction to the stressful events of 1904 and 1905 was radically different from his younger brother's. Using his agile intelligence and imaginative powers he turned emotional anguish into fantasies and rituals—a lifelong pattern. The almost simultaneous birth and death of the two Ottilias occurred when Alberto was in the developmental phase during which children are especially imaginative, creative, and perceptive. Their daily lives seem touched by magic, as they believe that their own thoughts and wishes can cause events. Although the magical excitement is generally a source of pleasure, three-year-olds can find murderous wishes and thoughts particularly worrisome, and for Alberto such wishes laid the foundation for his inclination to believe, albeit secretly, in the efficacy of rituals.[39] Unconscious magical fantasies underlying rituals are common in childhood. The belief that stepping on a crack will break one's mother's back is one such example. Many of these fantasies are given up in adulthood. Wishes to destroy or create life are fundamental to all human beings, yet they are usually forbidden. As a result they go underground and become unconscious.

The first known of Giacometti's lifelong obsessional rituals developed during this time of family turmoil and confusion. Every night before going to sleep, he would line up his shoes and socks in a precise order by his bed. If one of his brothers disarranged them, he would become furious and sleepless.[40] Psychologically motivated rituals are usually designed to ward off or counteract painful, dangerous thoughts and imaginings. The more dangerous the fantasy, the more powerful the ritual. In 1933, Alberto Giacometti wrote about a falling-asleep fantasy he had between ages four and seven. He claimed that, in order to go to sleep, every night he imagined himself murdering two men and ravishing and subsequently killing two women—a mother and daughter.[41] Abundant evidence in Giacometti's later behavior sustains the hypothesis that he had intense hostile feelings toward his parents dating back to his childhood, and he needed to suppress those feelings most of his life. As in many families of that era, "negative" emotions like anger or disappointment were discouraged and were certainly not to be directed toward the parents of a "happy family." Alberto Giacometti learned very early to keep his secret wishes to himself. He could believe in magical fantasies with one part of his mind and vigilantly hide them from the world at the same time.

FIGURE 1.6
Giovanni Giacometti,
Bathing, 1908. *Oil on*
canvas, 110 x 76 cm.

In October 1907 Giovanni went to Paris with Amiet to visit a Cézanne exhibit at the Salon d'Automne. He saw many large canvases of nude figures in nature—such as Cézanne's series of bathers as well as Matisse's huge paintings of nude figures celebrating life, love, and art, *Le Luxe I* and *La Musique*. The trip had a spectacular catalyzing effect. Giovanni's output increased in size and quality and his style ripened, as though he had been waiting for one final factor to give him permission to become himself. The landscapes and still lifes he had been painting before 1908 expressed his need for sensual pleasure and joyous use of color, but something was missing.

Stimulated by the Paris trip, two visits to his liberated friend Amiet (in 1907 and 1908), and familiarity with the spreading European trend toward joyous arcadian scenes, Giovanni poured forth twelve oil sketches of nude figures in landscapes. Painted quickly and freely, these sketches lack the specificity of works done from models and were probably completed at Amiet's home, where the atmosphere was conducive to spontaneity. That same year (1908) Giovanni painted one study of a nude woman, *Bathing* (fig. 1.6), using his wife as a model. She stands, Degas-like, in a wash basin, bending and drying herself with a towel, her dark, flowing hair a dramatic backdrop for her distinctive profile. The model's awkwardness in the pose is palpable.

Amiet produced many images of his wife in the nude throughout their long marriage. Not so Giovanni Giacometti. With the exception of *Maternity*

(1908), which shows Annetta breast-feeding, Bathing is the only nude painting of her on record. Plainly, she did not enjoy the experience but acceded to her husband's entreaty once, during the year of his "breakthrough."Annetta apparently resisted further modeling, a refusal that left him stranded. In the tiny, prudish community of Stampa it would have been inappropriate to ask a neighbor to pose nude, thus Giovanni turned to his children, evidently with his wife's consent.

Giovanni's success and fame (and his local reputation as a man of integrity) was such that he could ignore any gossip or censure, and a wall of silence settled around his practice of drawing and painting his pubescent children without clothes. He was used to being seen as a "Sonderling," and if his extremely correct wife permitted it, what was there for neighbors to say? His four children posed for their father dutifully, if not always willingly. It was his one rule, his one demand on his family—that they cooperate with his work. "With father there was a special thing, we were all models for him . . . from when we were very small we worked together," Bruno recalled. "He was very kind, to pose is very tiring; [we did it] during vacations and when we did not go to school, we posed 40–50 minutes, a little pause and then, [more posing]."[42]

The human body, with its complex and appealing shapes and colors, had fascinated Giovanni for years.[43] In the painting Boys on the Beach at Torre del Greco, which he carried back to Switzerland in 1893, he had already displayed his fascination with the possible positions of the body and the way skin colors are transformed by the sun. Sixteen years later, he returned to the subject for which he was so ideally suited—beautiful young bodies set in landscape backgrounds.

Drawing and painting children in the nude was part of a well-rationalized artistic tradition at the turn of the century, as was depicting man in his natural environment. Oneness with nature's grandeur was understood as spiritually uplifting—an idea common to Symbolist painting, German Romanticism, and the Christian mystical views of the Rosicrucians popular at the end of the nineteenth century. Ferdinand Hodler, a painter from Geneva, was known for his mural-sized canvases of nude youths in semierotic poses cloaked in mystical, pantheistic philosophical garb. Hodler was the most important revolutionary Swiss artist at the turn of the century, and Giovanni Giacometti knew him well and was acutely aware of his work.[44] He also knew that the nude boy depicted so often in Hodler's paintings was his son, Hector. By the time he began to paint his own children as uninhibited nude nature-lovers basking in the pleasurable feelings of sun and water on flesh, he had plenty of encouragement to do so.[45]

Between 1909 and 1920 Giovanni Giacometti exulted in his talent for sensuous painting with a splendid series of canvases, drawings, and woodcuts portraying his children outdoors. He transformed the glories of the flesh into an elegiac hymn of color and lyrical line, praising youth and nature. In 1909 he produced the magnificent canvas of his strawberry blond daughter, *Ottilia* (Stiftung für Kunst, Kultur und Geschichte, Küsnacht), in which the delectable curves of her nubile body are accentuated by the profile position. He plays color off against form, and his daughter's red-gold hair and pink- and yellow-tinted flesh are set against the blue flowers and cool green grass of the meadow. We cannot see her face, but, unlike her mother the year before, her body language suggests that she is comfortable in the pose.

The next summer Giovanni began a large canvas (130 x 200 cm) of his three eldest children in the open air, *Children in the Woods*, completing it in 1909.[46] Ottilia appears twice—standing on the left, as in the previous painting, and sitting in the middle of the canvas, facing us but looking down. Alberto also appears twice, flanking his sister but seated; with his back to us he watches both her and the other version of himself. Two years later Giovanni painted a third version, calling it *Children in the Sun*. Slight changes of the children's positions confirm that he had them pose again.[47]

Obviously pleased with the results of his work so far, Giovanni planned the largest and most ambitious painting of the series, *Children of the Sun* (1913), in which the earlier group compositions are expanded into three connected canvases (fig. 1.7). We see twelve-year-old Alberto twice on the two side panels of the triptych and Ottilia in two different positions on the central panel. Diego is no longer included. In each position, the children look down or cover their

FIGURE 1.7 *Giovanni Giacometti,* Children of the Sun, *1913. Oil on canvas, 141 x 315 cm. Bündner Kunstmuseum, Chur.*

eyes. Are they now embarrassed about having their maturing bodies exposed to each other and to the world? If so, Giovanni is oblivious to their unhappiness. He writes breezily to Amiet that the painting is his main summer project and that his challenge is making all the parts interesting and vital, since there is such a large surface to fill.[48]

By selecting the title *Children of the Sun* for his major work, Giovanni was making a complex statement. The Bregaglia valley is lined on both sides by mountains so high that, five months out of the year, the sun does not shine directly into it. Indeed, each March the inhabitants celebrate the return of the sun with feasting and ceremonies. As a painter who relished light and color-filled canvases, Giovanni profited from every opportunity to paint in Maloja and the surrounding mountains. He had, after all, begun his career at the side of Giovanni Segantini in the magnificent upper Alpine mountains of the Engadine. By 1905 most families in the valley had pastureland and summer dwellings in Maloja.[49] Typically, the Giacometti family spent the three summer months there enjoying the brilliant sunshine on the lake and the towering mountains. It was a valuable location for them because the sophisticated neighboring towns of St. Moritz and Sils provided stimulating cultural activities. At the same time these communities attracted wealthy vacationers who might buy Giovanni's paintings.

Between 1912 and 1915 Giovanni made a series of works—a sketch, a painting, and two woodcuts—showing two boys wrestling, a theme used previously by Gauguin and Courbet. Variously titled *The Battle* or *Boys Wrestling*, the scene depicts Alberto and Diego bent over, locked in an embrace.[50] The largest version is a dramatic painting showing the wrestlers in golden tones against a fiery red background, their forms echoed by an ominous shadow almost equaling them in size.

In the painting, contrasts of color and light are the striking elements, while the prints emphasize the interplay of complex positive and negative forms against the ripple of silhouetted muscles. In the woodcut *Two Boys Wrestling*, flowing curves are punctuated by bony angles as knees, elbows, and heels jut out and interrupt the linear stream (fig. 1.8). In all three versions the two figures read as one syncopated form. To achieve this effect, the father had his sons pose at length in arduous and physically intimate positions. In actuality, Diego usually won the wrestling matches with his older brother, and it is likely that holding the pose reminded both boys of Diego's superior physical strength.

In 1916, shortly after the wrestling series, Giovanni again persuaded his two eldest sons to model nude—in an arduous, even humiliating, position for

FIGURE 1.8 *Giovanni Giacometti, Two Boys Wrestling, c. 1912. Woodcut, 30 x 24.6 cm.*

an unforgettable image of bare human flesh in an open landscape. The definitive version, *Boys in the Lake* (1917), is a tour de force; the bodies of the two teenage boys dominate the canvas, their large, bent forms standing out against the sky and blue water. Shimmering water reflects the variegated flesh tones of their pasty white backs and buttocks as well as their healthy, tanned arms.[51] The work began as a sizable painting and inspired the color lithograph of the same subject, which Giovanni used as a poster to publicize his 1920 exhibition at the Kunsthalle in Bern (fig. 1.9).

FIGURE 1.9 *Giovanni Giacometti, Boys in the Lake (exhibition poster), 1919.*
Color lithograph, 109 x 71 cm.

Did Giovanni ever consider how Diego and Alberto might feel having their bent-over bodies with bare buttocks plastered across the Swiss capital? Could he not imagine what it must have felt like for them to be watched, drawn, and painted naked or in direct physical contact with each other for forty- to fifty-minute sessions, hour after hour, while he sang and talked with them to keep them cheerful? Could he deny that the boys would have to exercise unnatural control over the sexual feelings stirred up by the intimate poses? Could he ignore that this enforced submission to paternal authority was occurring in the very period of life when most boys are rising to the challenges of adolescence and taking steps toward independent life away from their parents? Either he was oblivious to the psychological effects the posing could have on his children, or he could not stop from placing his self-interest above his children's well-being.

I speculate that Alberto's eventual impotence stemmed in part from the rage and shame stimulated by this prolonged experience of helplessness. He rarely experienced genuine sexual satisfaction combined with affection, and he was able to feel "free" sexually only with prostitutes, over whom he had total control. Not surprisingly, some of his most gratifying adult sexual experiences were voyeuristic. Passivity became a cornerstone of Alberto Giacometti's character. As an adult, he frequently presented himself to the world as a man *forced* into situations, behavior, and relationships as though he had no choice or control of his own. It marked his personality and thus also his sexuality. To love and be loved, either he or his lover must submit. An intimate relationship—usually with prostitutes or much younger women—would almost always be a contest of unequals, usually involving humiliation and pain, at least in fantasy.

FIGURE 1.10
Giacometti apartment and studio in Stampa (author photograph).

To be sure, other factors in the Giacometti household could also have contributed to the sexual difficulties Alberto later experienced. The houses in Stampa, like most of the communities in the Bregaglia valley, are relatively compact. The Giacometti apartment consisted of two floors and an adjacent studio (fig. 1.10). On the ground floor was a spare room, which was used after 1919 as a bedroom for children and sometimes for storage.[52] On the second floor was the kitchen and the "stua"—the living/dining room (fig. 1.11). Off the stua were two bedrooms, one for Giovanni and Annetta, and another very small one shared by the four children. Only the stua and Giovanni's studio next door—which served as a second living room, where the children played and Alberto drew and sculpted—were heated. In such close quarters the parents' sexual life could not have been completely private, and abundant opportunities for sexual overstimulation existed for all the children. At the same time, sharing a small bedroom and a bed with siblings close in age obliges children to learn rigorous self-restraint, or to devise some means of turning natural sexual curiosity and excitement into other channels—for example, physical activity or fantasy. When those outlets were blocked by other burden-

FIGURE 1.11 Stua (living/dining room) of Giacometti apartment in Stampa (Ernst Scheidegger photograph).

some demands, such as observing nude siblings while naked themselves during compulsory posing sessions for their father, the children's sexual feelings are likely to have been expressed in voyeuristic, masochistic, or sadistic ways.

Had Alberto Giacometti only to deal with a dominating mother—in other words, a prototypical "phallic" woman—he might still have found a way to feel and be his own master, combining his fear with love and respect for her genuine strengths.[53] Unfortunately, his father—the man to whom he should have been able to turn as a model during the crucial years of his middle childhood and adolescence—had let him down, and loving Giovanni was even more complicated than loving his mother. He had to integrate his positive feelings with inexpressible rage.

Giovanni's description of his life as an artist was consistently elegiac: "The brush and my colors are my only familiar means of expressing myself. They are the things which faithfully interpret my thoughts, dreams, my life. My life is my art and my art is my life. This little tract of land closed off in the narrow circle of mountains is my universe. . . . Every day the mysterious spectacle of life and its infinite beauty of nature is renewed before my eyes."[54] Giovanni had found his subject matter in the brilliantly lit local landscapes and his family. "A good star guided me. . . . I have lived a happy life surrounded by my children who . . . live in my canvases."[55] But the most gifted of Giovanni's talented children paid a price for his father's passion.

Experiencing firsthand his father's blindness and failure of paternal empathy taught Alberto that the claims of art, and especially the press of talent, can transmute loving gestures into tyrannical acts. At the end of his life Giacometti recalled his earliest feelings about drawing: "I drew in order to communicate and dominate. My pencil was my weapon. I had the feeling I was able to reproduce and therefore appropriate whatever I wished."[56] As a boy his pencil gave him power that he did not otherwise have. His younger brother Diego was physically stronger. His father, he felt, was more skilled. His mother was indomitable in the household. Only in fantasy and, eventually, through his art, could Alberto prevail.

CHAPTER 2

1914-1919

COMING OF AGE

In spring 1911, an epidemic of typhoid fever struck the Bregaglia valley, and Alberto's mother was one of the most gravely ill victims.[1] Lying alternately comatose or delirious for several months, she was not expected to live. Diego and Bruno were also sick, but less severely. None of the children was allowed to see their mother in her haggard state, because it was feared that Annetta's alarm about their illness would interfere with her chances for recovery. At first Giovanni nursed his wife and two children. When he, too, fell ill, outside help was brought in. Alberto and Ottilia were the only unafflicted family members.

Death was very close in the tiny community. A nearby neighbor, Clemente Faschiata, mother of five children, succumbed at the end of October. Her funeral cortege passed directly beneath the windows of the Giacometti home. Straw placed on the ground muffled the sound of the wheels so that Annetta wouldn't find out about the death.[2] In another month she recovered, emerging from the sickroom white-haired, skeletally thin, and toothless at age forty.

The virulence of the epidemic and his mother's near-fatal illness were never a part of Alberto Giacometti's public biography, but they must have profoundly touched the highly impressionable ten-year-old. I believe that the drawing he described as "the oldest I remember"—an image of Snow White lying in her crystal coffin surrounded by grieving dwarfs—is a veiled reference to it.[3] Lord has proposed that the image of Snow White in her crystal coffin makes the tantalizing female figure safely neutral, thereby giving the image an underlying Oedipal meaning.[4] But it is not the Oedipal rival, the prince, who is presented as chief mourner, but rather the artist's siblings from the devout and hard-working valley community of Stampa. I suggest that the troop of dwarfs mournfully watching their beloved but apparently dead Snow

White probably represent the Giacometti children watching and worrying about their stricken mother during her bout with typhoid.

All the associations condensed in Giacometti's "first" drawing signal his method for warding off fearful events. He makes an image of the very thing he fears or hopes. At the same time, the unmoving, untouchable female figure could stand for Giacometti's sense of his mother as cold and distant— emotionally dead. Normally children have fantasies about hurting or even killing the parents who frustrate, subjugate, and discipline them. When a fantasized victim falls ill and nearly dies, they experience the shame of seeing their secret wishes realized, imagining themselves to be responsible. It is easy to imagine the remorse a fearful, guilt-prone child like Giacometti might have felt about hostile wishes directed toward the mother who was the magnet for his disappointment and anger as well as his love. We shall see that this unmentionable experience of seeing his mother almost turn into a skeleton before his eyes reappeared with extraordinary force decades later as one of the catalysts for Giacometti's bold postwar style.

Though he had been drawing in his father's studio from earliest childhood, Giacometti placed the beginning of his sense of mastery as an artist in his tenth year, after his drawing of Snow White. "I was so pretentious when I was ten years old," he said. "I admired myself, I had the feeling I could do anything with this powerful medium: drawing. . . . That I could see more clearly than anybody else. . . . I dominated my vision, it was paradise."[5]

With his powerful artistic skills, the young boy tried to counteract his helplessness in the face of his mother's illness. Two years later, in May 1913, during his twelfth year, the boy had another intimate encounter with death when his maternal grandfather, Giovanni Stampa, died. Annetta's father was a familiar figure in the Giacometti home, stopping in every morning for coffee. Very fond of his talented eldest grandson, Stampa, a teacher, had spent much time with Alberto, carrying him on his shoulders and taking him on nature walks throughout the valley. Giovanni Stampa's death profoundly affected the boy in several ways, recalling memories of his mother's recent illness as well as the earlier death of his grandmother, Ottilia Santi.

The repetition of a profoundly disturbing event often has a far more traumatic effect on a child than the original painful experience.[6] And it often leads to unexpected disorders and temporal confusion of the sort that Alberto Giacometti experienced throughout his life. In his correspondence with family and friends, for example, there are many striking allusions to his confusion about time, especially in reference to his twelfth year.[7] "I feel very close to that which I was at twelve and that in all spheres, I feel myself to be at nearly the same point and I no longer know what the time means."[8] There are at least ten statements, similar to the one just cited, scattered throughout the artist's published and unpublished conversations and writings, all containing references to age twelve.

Several months before his death in 1966, Giacometti wrote the text for a book of his drawings (all of which were copies of past art), *Giacometti: A Sketchbook of Interpretive Drawings.*[9] Having procrastinated for months, he wrote three versions of the text during ocean voyages to and from New York on the occasion of his exhibition at the Museum of Modern Art. The text he finally produced is his most poignant: "Somewhere I am still twelve years old, . . . that may even be essentially my age. But I don't know, I just don't know! I don't know why it is so difficult to talk about [these copies]. I can't unless perhaps I tell about my whole life, about everything I remember. And what can I say here, in the midst of this endless, nameless ocean, in the midst of these black waters where I might drown at any moment, where I might be swallowed, devoured by blind and nameless fish."[10]

Giacometti's preoccupation with his twelfth year may have been further exacerbated by his mother's emotional withdrawal after losing the one parent who had been with her all her life. There are no letters or published recollections that tell us how she reacted to this death, but her response to later losses gives ample evidence of her pattern of proud, silent turning inward in the face of personal sorrow. Though she would surely not complain to her children about her sadness, they would feel her emotional absence. Thus, at twelve, Giacometti lost both his doting grandfather and, to some extent, his grief-stricken mother.

COPIES

It is natural that Giovanni should have been Alberto's first art teacher and even predictable that, as a loving son, Alberto would admire and imitate his father's painting style. No other model was so readily available. For centuries, artists have learned to draw by copying the work of other artists, but the intensity and persistence of this practice for Giacometti is unusual. Most of his childhood drawings were copies and at least half of his entire output in drawings were copies. As a young child he was surrounded by his father's images and invited to look at the history of art as his playground. He recalled "no greater [childhood] pleasure" than running to his father's studio after school to draw and read.[11]

The complex, multifaceted motives behind Giacometti's copy-making begin with his natural desire to grow and learn as an artist. Other motives are more subtle and conflicted. For example, imitation works as a complex psychological defense—it expresses love and protects from disaster. Rather than taking responsibility for feelings, thoughts, or actions, a person who imitates can hide from consequences and even avoid being seen as a separate—and competitive—person. Thus, if one's father is also an artist, imitation is the perfect disguise for someone fearful of revealing himself.

Giacometti needed to break away from his father without openly opposing him. Copying may have seemed a perfect route to independence, which coalesced into an ingrained habit, or even a compulsion, sometime around his twelfth year. Many twelve-year-olds ferociously imitate their peers rather than seem weird or different. Alberto's imitation was less noticeable because his peers at that time were actually his father and his father's friends. Imitation allowed Alberto to deny that he might be on the verge of surpassing his father in skill and invention.[12] Giovanni Giacometti was a generous man and wanted his son to succeed. Nevertheless, Alberto was aware at an early age of the envy his talent and precocity could provoke. Beginning in adolescence and continuing to the end of his life, he energetically denied his superior abilities (most of the time).

It is difficult to tease apart the influences on Alberto Giacometti during his rapid artistic development as an adolescent, but the lifelong continuity of his preferences and the heights to which he was inspired by them help locate the most significant influences. In addition to his father's style, two artistic directions captivated the youthful Giacometti, each in its own way helping him gain the tools he would need to tell his own story. One—Albrecht Dürer—came from a culture close to home and the other—ancient Egypt—from an exotic realm distant in time and place but touching the young artist so deeply that it would eventually supplant most other influences. Serious beyond his years, Alberto was looking for answers to life's mysteries. Dürer and Egyptian culture provided the aesthetic and spiritual lessons he was seeking.

Dürer

In Dürer, Giacometti found an artist whose wide-ranging curiosity and erudition were a good match for his own ambitions and enthusiasms. The German master was a precocious and brilliant draftsman who straddled northern and southern European artistic styles, bringing line and color together. A man of natural science and modern philosophy, he was also familiar with alchemy and the occult arts. In the years just before and during World War I, examples of Dürer's work appeared often in the German language art journals to which Giovanni subscribed. They were usually found in conjunction with commentaries on the war, such as the 1914 winter issue of *Kunstwart*, which included reproductions of Dürer's renowned prints *Knight, Death and the Devil* and *Riders of the Apocalypse*.

Giacometti chose Dürer's famous etching for his first "serious" copy. By "serious" he meant that he intended to make "his own exact reproduction" of *Knight, Death and the Devil*.[13] The subject of Dürer's great etching was a memento mori—a reminder of life's cruel brevity. Only a determined Christian knight defending the truth and serving the Lord from morning till night could triumph over death and the devil. Such ideas and imagery would have appealed to the phobic boy who had just survived one death and another near-death. The 1513 date of the engraving, almost exactly four hundred years earlier than the boy's copy, added to its appeal.

Alberto copied Dürer's painted *Self-Portrait* (1500) in pen and ink, and, around the same time of his grandfather's death in 1913, Alberto made a copy of his father's 1911 painting of his grandfather, *Giovanni Stampa*. Done in the same style as his copy of Dürer's engraving, it is signed with a monogram conflating the signatures of Dürer, Amiet, and his father. Giacometti's copy of his father's painting hung on the wall of his parent's bedroom—an honor and a memorial to loss.[14]

When Giacometti combined his father's image of his grandfather with the style of a master so adept at dealing with death he was setting in motion a pattern for a lifelong practice. He turned to Dürer for inspiration again in 1934 just after Giovanni Giacometti's death, when he made a copy of the engraving *Melancholia* and used some of Dürer's themes from the print in his sculpture. The pattern of making copies of works by artists he deeply admired at times of sorrow suggests that the very act of copying was one of the young artist's ways of managing the feelings and thoughts death stirred in him.[15]

Egypt

By the end of his life Alberto Giacometti had made more copies of Egyptian sculpture and painting than any other. Of these, the greatest number are from the 18th Dynasty and the circle of works produced for Akhenaten, the rebellious and brilliantly original sun king. Not discounting the sheer formal appeal of Amarna art to the young Giacometti, I believe that a far richer explanation for his fascination exists.

Readers of German language art journals could follow the astounding sculptural discoveries emerging from German excavations at el-Amarna in Egypt between 1910 and 1913, and one of the most spectacular finds was the workshop of Thutmose, the major sculptor of Akhenaten's last years. Hedwig Fechheimer reported the discoveries in a series of four articles in spring 1913 in *Kunst und Kunstler,* one of the best illustrated journals regularly arriving at the Giacometti home in Stampa.[16] Fechheimer's articles contained details of the ruler's sun worship and revolutionary reforms and included beautiful photographs of sculpture showing Akhenaten, his consort Nefertiti, and their daughters. Unlike the art of previous Egyptian dynasties, Amarna art depicted Akhenaten's family in relaxed intimacy, the daughters being touched by their parents or touching one another with tender familiarity (fig. 2.1). The vibrant carved and modeled portraits of the royal family were lavishly praised by the author, who repeatedly emphasized the artist's goal of making the persons portrayed look alive and creating an illusion of living flesh.[17] Initially some of the newly discovered works were thought to be death masks but were soon understood as momentary impressions of living persons in the form of sculpture—a counterpart to Egyptian mummies whose purpose was to preserve the body for its active role after death. The arrival of these articles in the very month of Giovanni Stampa's death made a lasting impression on Alberto Giacometti.

The historical Akhenaten, as he was inaccurately represented by Egyptian scholarship in the early part of the century, offered the young Giacometti a mixture of facts and idealizing fantasies: his reign began at age twelve under the regency of his dominating but astute mother, Queen Tiy. At a young age he married the beautiful Nefertiti, whom scholars mistakenly believed to be his nine-year-old sister.[18]

Many aspects of Akhenaten's story would have struck Giacometti as re-

FIGURE 2.1
Akhenaten, Royal
Family, c. 1345 B.C.E.
(Egyptian, 18th
Dynasty). Plaster,
32.5 x 39 cm.
Staatliche Museum,
Berlin.

markable parallels to his own life. The ancient ruler had a forceful, domi-neering mother, a close relationship to a beautiful younger sister, the pros-pect of eventually overturning his father's way of seeing, and a fervent devo-tion to truth. Photographs of Giacometti's profile show a striking similarity to the young sun king, and we can imagine Giacometti's ready identification with the fascinating ancient ruler, who, like himself, had bushy hair, a pro-nounced chin, and rebellious ideas. Further reinforcing this identification was the remarkable fact that artists during Akhenaten's reign regularly de-picted the royal children in the nude, playfully enjoying everyday activities or assuming royal roles. This may have seemed a particularly compelling paral-lel given that the four articles on the Amarna finds were published the same year (1913) that Giovanni Giacometti portrayed his children nude in the dap-pled sunshine for the large triptych *Children of the Sun*. The idea of kingship beginning at age twelve would also strongly appeal to a twelve-year-old boy who would say later about himself, "I thought I was great, I thought noth-ing was impossible for me with that wonderful technique, drawing, and I thought I could copy absolutely anything and that I understood it better than anybody else."[19]

But above all, Egyptian art fascinated Giacometti because of its association with death and its aftermath. The word *sculptor* in ancient Egyptian means "one who keeps alive," and the idea of aliveness or lifelikeness runs like a red thread throughout the forty-five years of Giacometti's documented com-ments on Egyptian art.[20] The artist may have first discovered that idea in his twelfth year through Fechheimer's articles, but, whenever and however he first learned it, the association of Egyptian art and sculpture with lifelikeness was evident throughout his life, especially at times of loss.

In October 1917, four years after the publications about el-Amarna, Giaco-metti professed his enthusiasm for Egyptian art and culture in his initiation speech at Amicitia, the club he had joined at his boarding school, the Evan-gelical secondary school in Schiers. He was unequivocal in his affirmative an-swer to the question he raised with the title of his talk: "Which culture is more sublime: ours or the Egyptians'?" "Egyptian [culture] stands higher than ours. . . . Sculpture and painting reached a high level with the people on the Nile. Today's art relies in part on Egyptian art. . . . Life at that time was more ideal and beautiful than now . . . In all respects I find Egyptian culture more ideal and sublime than ours."[21] Giacometti's fascination with Egyptian art and culture lasted throughout his life, and, as we will see in a later chapter, it had a profound intellectual, aesthetic, and spiritual effect on his work.

The year 1913 marks the beginning—so far as we know—of Alberto Giacometti's first serious, successful portraits. He dated two drawings of his mother, and one of his brother Diego, to that year.[22] In one of the 1913 drawings Giacometti portrayed his mother in a characteristic activity: sewing.[23] On a chain around her neck she wears a locket, with a woman's head just visible inside. It is a photograph of Domenica Baldini Stampa, Annetta's mother, who died when Annetta was four and a half.[24] Worn only on Sundays and holidays, the locket held an important place in the young artist's imagination. Annetta's father, his grandfather, Giovanni Stampa, died in 1913, the year of this drawing, and the locket was a constant reminder to mother and son of death and absence.

When Giacometti drew his mother several years later, again sewing and wearing the locket, in The Artist's Mother (Sewing) (1913–14), his effort was more ambitious, and her moving fingers and air of concentration are convincingly lifelike (fig. 2.2).[25] On the back of his portrait is a drawing of Diego (1913–14), whose insouciance in the complex pose is well conveyed. The combination of mother and brother on the same paper prefigures their future willingness to pose for Giacometti. It has other import: the maternal, or at least protective, role that Diego later played for his elder brother almost his entire life invites us to see the conjunction of these drawings as prophetic.

World War I changed everything in the Engadine and Bregaglia valleys. Soldiers filled the elegant hotels in the upper valley, camping even in the Palace Hotel across the road from the Giacomettis' house in Maloja. The border at the lower end of the Bregaglia valley at Castasegna was closed, shutting off contact with Italy. In the summer of 1915 Alberto left for boarding school, and later that year soldiers were quartered in the Giacometti apartment.

We know little about the period that preceded his departure. One event must have marked this time for Alberto, because throughout his adult life he referred to the sculpted head he made of Diego in 1914—he declared it to be his first and best portrait sculpture, and it remained in his possession all his life.[26] Diego is a poignant piece, tenderly modeled and full of expression. The personality differences between Diego and Alberto were great; they led separate lives with diverse friends and interests, but each supplied the other's missing traits, and they did not thrive when they were too far apart. Alberto understood his brother's needs and frailties better than anyone. He knew that Diego was the unhappy, unfavored son who needed special consideration.

FIGURE 2.2
*Alberto Giacometti, The Artist's Mother (Sewing),
1913–14. Pencil on paper,
36.5 x 25 cm. Kunsthaus
Zurich.*

Likewise, Diego knew and respected Alberto's fears, fragility, and rituals. He tended to chores Alberto disdained and always treated his brother's objects with keen regard.

The two boys were separated for the first time when Alberto left the valley to go to secondary school. The school at which Alberto studied from 1915 to 1919—the Evangelical Secondary School in Schiers—a Lutheran establishment in a mountainous valley near Davos, provided a superior education for sons of Switzerland's elite families. He found companionship at his intellectual level and classmates and teachers who appreciated his intelligence and artistic talents. The iron-willed Protestant moralism of his native Bregaglia valley was carried to new heights at the strict school, but its structure and rituals suited him remarkably well. One of his first school assignments, aimed at teaching him proficiency in German, obliged him to write over and over the aphorisms *Work makes life sweet,* and *Lies have short legs.*[27] Until the end of his life Giacometti filled notebooks with similar messages to himself. Though Bargiot was the local dialect in the Bregaglia valley, Italian was the Giacometti family's mother tongue, and Alberto took half a year to learn to write German well enough to join his classmates in regular classes. Then he skipped from first to third.[28]

The pleasure Giacometti took in finding comrades with whom to share curiosity, taste, and mental agility is evident from his correspondence. Returning after a vacation at home, he writes of a delightful journey back to the school: "I will never leave, never! its green meadows, blue sky, the gaiety of the students is so beautiful."[29] His letters are filled with enthusiastic detailed observations about his experience—from skiing jaunts and school trips to nearby villages to character descriptions of the school director's wife and Giacometti's classmates. At Schiers horizons had opened up and Giacometti stretched and grew beyond the confines of the narrow Bregaglia valley walls. Surrounded by respectful and admiring classmates and teachers, and ignoring for the moment his mother's many criticisms, he rebelled on various fronts. He organized his fellow students into an association designed to reject some of the rigid religious rules, and he started to smoke in secret. He had, in effect, a normal adolescent flowering.

During his second year at Schiers, Giacometti was invited to join Amicitia, a student association with a clubhouse in the sunny hills above the school. By then he was part of a triumvirate with two boys who would be his lifelong friends: Christof Bernoulli, a future art historian, and Lucas Lichtenhahn, another future art historian and the eventual curator of the Basel Kunsthalle. Bernoulli had been assigned as mentor to Giacometti when he arrived at Schiers, but Bernoulli was somewhat intimidated by the younger boy's brilliance and maturity.[30] Lichtenhahn (Lux), on the other hand, became Alberto's best friend.

Giacometti's letters to "Liebster Lux," which began in 1918 when the older boy graduated and continued for several years, eloquently reveal the younger boy's interests, passions, and turns of mind, showing him to be a somewhat teasing companion, an earnest complimenter, and an occasional complainer. The picture he paints of himself is richly nuanced with discordant emotions and intense ambivalence, veering far to either side of a conflict before flinging himself into action. From one letter to another he seems to forget that he had taken the opposite point of view in his previous communication. A voracious reader, he confided his preferences to Lichtenhahn. (His favorite authors at the time were Gottfried Keller and C. F. Meyer, Swiss authors and splendid storytellers.) He made frequent references to his artwork—mostly the drawn, painted, or modeled portraits of his fellow classmates.

Giacometti's early drawings are appealing but not compelling. His models mostly avert their eyes, thus freeing themselves from the grasp of their portrayer. Some of Giacometti's subjects objected, and others merely squirmed. Two portraits of Lucas Lichtenhahn—one a linocut (1917), the other a drawing (1918) (Alberto Giacometti-Stiftung)—reveal little of the sitter's personality. In both he looks down, at a book or something else that is out of the picture. Extremely bright and obviously visual, he must have noticed Giacometti's unpleasant practice of staring at and through people. The future curator protected himself, keeping his inner life from posterity's prying eyes. When Alberto persuades his subjects to look directly into his eyes, he captures them in frontal portraits like those by Hodler which he so admired. It is as though their souls are revealed and brought from the deepest depths to the surface of the page.

The year 1918 was a year of outstanding portraits by Alberto Giacometti. In the spring his cousin Renato Stampa sat for a drawn portrait when he visited the Giacomettis. Stampa was a close relative, intimate with family and deeply loyal to the Bregaglia valley and to Alberto's family. His frank description foretells all the future experiences of Alberto's models. "Having seated me in a chair in just the right light, Alberto . . . began to capture me as if he wanted to devour me. His way of observing a person created a strong tension, almost hostile, between the subject and object."[31]

The extraordinarily powerful *Self-Portrait* (1918), modeled after Dürer and Hodler, shows a mature young man soberly facing us with a questioning look in his eyes (fig. 2.3). His mouth, generous and sensitive, is set in an expression that hovers between sadness and determination. Behind the expression we feel the force of his personality; we even can surmise his anger and controlled agitation. Using a frontal format, he hearkens back to some of his father's self-portraits. In the portrait *Mother* (1918), a companion to his self-portrait, Annetta Giacometti looks resigned but resolute, a serious woman with unsmiling lips whose critical eyes stare challengingly at the artist (fig. 2.4). The two Giacomettis are presented with striking similarities, which the artist must have recognized—from their bushy hair to their sad demeanor. Judging from the known early drawings and paintings of Annetta by Alberto, as well as from his correspondence with her, the young artist was often confronted with a frowning face—literally or figuratively. In the forty-eight letters and cards he sent to Lichtenhahn from Schiers he mentions his mother only two times: once to report her complaint that his letters were too long; the other time to relay her willingness to have Lucas as a guest in Stampa. To his godfather, he states: "My mother says I should be ashamed of myself for not

FIGURE 2.3 *Alberto Giacometti, Self-Portrait, 1918. Ink on paper, 36.5 x 25.3 cm. Kunsthaus Zurich.*

writing sooner."³² Only when he made portraits of her was Alberto able to make Annetta do his bidding. Still, he stood his ground and showed his mother as he saw her, deeply and starkly.

A comparison of portraits made by father and son of Annetta Giacometti during Alberto's youth reveals subtle differences in emotional tone. Gio-

FIGURE 2.4 *Alberto Giacometti, Portrait of Mother, 1918. Ink on paper, 25.4 × 19.9 cm. Kunsthaus Zurich.*

vanni, who most frequently portrayed her in profile or three-quarter view, evidently accepted his wife's depressive personality and presented her sadness sympathetically. He loved her and "went along," smiling, singing, and never arguing. Besides, he could usually lift her mood. He seemed to understand her sadness—he knew how many people she had lost in her childhood, how much suffering she had endured, and how important his loving attention was for her, especially as he could make it visible with his many portraits. He understood that her sense of herself as strong, stable, and beautiful—the way he depicted her—was her bulwark against the painful sense of herself as a vulnerable, even damaged person—like the child who so often felt at risk of losing a loved one and who had to hold so tightly to those close to her. He seemed to realize that through his gaze, she found her better self. In the 1950s, when Alberto became famous, his mother complained that his portraits made her look like a witch. Too often he painted what he saw—a sad, frightened person. Furthermore, his later portraits of her, unlike his father's, would eloquently express his own shifting sense of reality, and that would add fuel to his mother's fears. This suggests several reasons for her lifelong dissatisfaction with her son's art, which she claimed was "fit for a dung heap."

In his years at Schiers, Giacometti frequently wrote to his father expressing his love and asking him to visit. In January 1918, in letters to Lichtenhahn, Amiet, and his family, he admits that he is torn between taking the difficult Matura exam at Schiers or dropping out and heading home to work on his art at Giovanni's side. Two events could have precipitated his conflict about remaining at the school he had so enjoyed: the graduation of Bernoulli and Lichtenhahn, and the mumps, followed by orchitis, that Giacometti contracted sometime after spring 1917. The latter is an extremely painful swelling of the testicles and usually results in lessened fertility and smaller testicles.[33] Alberto may not have known at the time that he had become sterile, but he certainly would have known that the potentially serious consequences of mumps/orchitis included compromised chances of becoming a father.

The absence of his two close friends certainly seems to have thrown Giacometti off stride. The letters to Lichtenhahn read like a lifeline to a soul mate—sharing enthusiasm for the landscape and for his favorite new writers. This leads him to a discussion of homesickness, which Giacometti had not expressed before, as his longing for Lux is transmuted into longing to be with his father in Stampa and Maloja. A poignant letter from June 1918 illustrates his state of mind. Though at first he describes his "strong desire and longing for the beautiful hours of the last quarter" (when Lichtenhahn was still at school), he admits "in general I'm fine, actually it's up to you how you feel."[34] He needs to see his friend or be assured that their relationship was, as ever, close and mutual. Giacometti commented on how distant Lux could seem at times, searching for explanations that would not leave him feeling abandoned.

Simon Berard, a handsome younger boy at Schiers, provided companionship after Lucas left and became a pawn in the relationship between Lichtenhahn and Giacometti. Giacometti tells Lichtenhahn about his walks with

Simon but it is clear that Simon's major appeal for him was as much his willingness to pose patiently as it was his physical attractiveness.[35] While the younger boy could not satisfy Giacometti's more complex needs for close companionship, it would not be the last time that he chose a friend, and hence a model, because of that person's willingness to sit or stand still for hours and days on end while Giacometti painted or sculpted.

Giovanni was always the paradigm for the richly complex, mutually affectionate friendship Giacometti enjoyed with men. Lucas Lichtenhahn was his successor. Michel Leiris, André Breton, Jean-Paul Sartre, and Isaku Yanaihara were later variants. Each of these men not only appreciated Alberto's talent and wide-ranging intelligence, they were also exquisitely visually sensitive and intent on plumbing the depths of life's profundities. It cannot be coincidental that each would eventually contribute to Giacometti's career by writing about him.

Finally, at the end of the spring term in April 1919—seventeen months after the beginning of his painful period of inner conflict, Giacometti received permission to take a three-month leave and went to stay in the Bergel at his father's side. He never returned to the school, but in his letters to Lichtenhahn over the next year he continually went back there in his imagination, commenting on how the weather must be at a given moment and what this or that teacher might be feeling or doing.[36] In other words, he divided himself mentally so that he could not really be separated from the place and people he had so enjoyed, just as he would soon divide his mental energies for the next forty years between Paris and Stampa.

CHAPTER 3

1920-1925

TRAVEL IS BROADENING: GENEVA, VENICE, AND ROME

Giacometti's original plan of studying art in Munich was vetoed in the uncertain aftermath of World War I. Dutifully following his father's recommen-
dation to pursue formal art training, Giacometti had left Maloja for Geneva
expecting to like neither the city nor the school there. Despite his initial unhappiness on arriving in September 1919, he stayed in Geneva six months,
changing schools, exploring the city's artistic treasures, and eventually discovering much to enjoy.

Giacometti's decision to study sculpture in Geneva has not been sufficiently explored. At Schiers he had been painting *and* sculpting. His drawings
were masterful and often original, but his paintings were mostly pale imitations of his father's vibrant landscapes. To find his way as a mature artist Giacometti would have to turn to sculpture, where he could find a unique place
for himself without having to compete with his father.

The war had slowed Giovanni's career, forcing the cancellation of his first
major solo exhibit in Jena in 1914. The Giacometti home in Stampa, though
only a few miles from the Italian border and close to centers of culture and
commerce, was sometimes inaccessible, because the steepness of the valley
often made winter travel impossible. That insularity mattered less before the
war, because the Engadine valley, one thousand meters above Stampa, had
long been popular with intellectuals and artists, such as Nietzsche, Rilke, and
Segantini, as well as with the wealthy and powerful throughout Europe. The
latter had been Giovanni's usual customers, but during wartime they disappeared. Eventually they returned, as did the momentum of his career, but his
remote location kept it circumscribed.

Giovanni's search for recognition had always been tempered by love for his family, especially for his wife. Annetta Giacometti could help her husband financially, but her discomfort with strangers, combined with her aversion to living away from familiar surroundings, placed a subtle but effective limit on her husband's success. Between her personality and her four young children, she was reluctant to travel with him when he visited exhibitions and served on art juries, and she rarely opened her home to the wide variety of artists and possible patrons who could keep him in direct touch with rapidly changing currents of modern art. Giovanni closely followed art-world events through journals and newspapers, but his participation was often indirect. It was a point Alberto Giacometti did not miss. Throughout adolescence he inquired about his father's sales and exhibits in letters home, and however much he loved the magnificent landscape of the Bregaglia valley, it would be in gray, grimy Paris that he chose to live and make his career.

In his first letter from Geneva to his friend Lichtenhahn, Giacometti tells of having been depressed and reports with some chagrin on how badly he gets along with his teachers.[1] One teacher claimed that he was "not advanced enough to draw from nature," making him draw from plaster casts instead. Recognizing that he and the teacher "couldn't stand each other from the first session," Giacometti quit the class. Four months later Giacometti reports his undistinguished grades to Lichtenhahn. Though his carving teacher gave him a passing grade, he described Giacometti as "untalented." Bored by having to "just chisel leaves into stone the whole afternoon," the young student must have made his contempt evident. His instructor for modeling also gave him passing marks but wrote that "he does not listen to the advice he is given."[2]

During his first days in Geneva he met Kurt Seligmann, a well-educated fellow art student with whom he became instant comrades, visiting museums and taking country walks. As his first Jewish friend, Seligmann seemed alien to Giacometti, and his comments about him veered from hostile to enthusiastic. Yet, the friendship lasted. Two portraits of Giacometti by Seligmann, one from Geneva, the other executed in Paris in the early 1930s, attest to its endurance.[3] Among other interests, Seligmann and Giacometti shared a fascination with the occult.[4] In the museums of Geneva the two friends saw numerous Egyptian artifacts made for magic rituals, including sculpted hands, which would find their way into Giacometti's work decades later.

Giacometti's arrival in Geneva, the city of Ferdinand Hodler, occurred at a crucial juncture in his artistic development and had deep significance for the young artist. Giacometti had been attracted to Hodler's style, especially his searching frontal portraits, and a year earlier had called Hodler the best of all artists and said that he wanted to steal one of his drawings.[5] With Hodler's death in 1918, Giovanni Giacometti along with Cuno Amiet had become Switzerland's foremost painters. Despite their stylistic differences, Giovanni had been strongly influenced by Hodler's vision of nature, and he in turn influenced his son. For all three men, art reflected the truth about nature. On a hiking trip into the mountains above Maloja, Giovanni pointed to the oval-shaped clouds floating overhead and said to Alberto: "Look at those clouds, they are the same clouds painted by friend Hodler, and as you can see, the art critic who suspected the master of having invented such clouds was wrong."[6] Feeling might color perception, but for Giovanni, art was always grounded in what could be seen by the artist's eye. Alberto Giacometti was beginning to disagree.

Near the end of his life, Giacometti recalled that his father had critiqued the tiny pears he kept drawing as an adolescent on the grounds that there were right and wrong ways to see things, that objects had right and wrong sizes. It was the young man's first reported sign of conflict with his father's way of seeing things. "My father . . . made life-size portraits quite instinctively, even if I was sitting for him ten feet away. . . . Once when I was about eighteen or nineteen . . . drawing some pears that were on a table, at the normal distance for a still life. And the pears kept getting tiny. I'd begin again, and they'd always go back to exactly the same size. My father got irritated and said: 'But just do them as they are, as you see them!' And he corrected them. I tried to do it as he wanted but I couldn't stop myself rubbing them out . . . half an hour later they were exactly the same size . . . as the first ones."[7]

While this text is often quoted as evidence in the implied debate about the nature of reality, the clues it provides about the sources and meaning of the younger artist's later perceptual "distortions" have usually been overlooked. By age "eighteen or nineteen" Alberto had been the subject of dozens, if not hundreds, of portraits by his father, sitting immobile for long hours while his father captured him on canvas and paper from various distances. It must have puzzled the son to discover that each of his father's images of him appeared to be the same size, no matter the distance between them.

I speculated in chapter one about Giacometti's feelings while posing for his father, especially in the nude, and how that experience played a significant role in shaping his character, making passivity his habitual mode of being in the world and influencing his sexuality, which was essentially voyeuristic. Later, whenever Giacometti discussed one of his stylistic innovations or inhibitions, he effectively denied responsibility, claiming that he could do it no other way. "I was amazed that everything became so small . . . I can no longer get a figure back to life-size."[8] Thus, the tininess of the pears, the disappearing women of the late 1930s and early 1940s, the attenuated thinness of the postwar figures, the distortions he wrought in the human form and the deliberate destruction of half his postwar work—even his inability to stop while working on portraits of that era—all are linked to his experience in his father's studio. By seeing and presenting himself as the hapless victim of perceptual tyranny he could free himself from the considerable guilt he felt because his artistic vision, his way of seeing the world, was different from his father's. His passivity released him from an intolerable bind. If *he* were not the cause of the perceptual differences between him and his father, then he was a "good son."

The story of the diminishing pears may also be an unconscious reference to Giacometti's orchitis. Once the swelling in one or both testicles had passed, he was changed forever—a diminished man, his sensitivity to the size of his testicles became an enduring factor in his life and almost certainly in his art.[9] By the time he told the story of the pears in 1964, Giacometti knew of the link between his adolescent illness and its consequences—a fateful punishment for competing with a fertile father.

Changing the size of objects had other meanings for Giacometti. It would become his preferred means for dealing with difficult realities. By making something larger or smaller, he could control images that were too exciting or too frightening, or both. For example, during a drawing class in Geneva, a fellow student, Pierre Courthion, recalled an occasion in which Giacometti would not draw an overripe nude in her entirety, the customary assignment in the class. Instead, he drew one of her feet in gigantic proportions, enraging his professor.[10]

Both Courthion and Lord have explained this event as an instance of Giacometti's obsessive interest with feet—by implication his disinterest in a woman's body—but I think it has another, more obvious and deeply significant meaning. At the time of the incident, Giacometti had not yet had a full sexual experience with a woman. Nor had he many, if any, opportunities to stare at the nude bodies of adult women. Now he was obliged to do just that for hours. The experience must have made him intensely uncomfortable (and probably sexually excited). So he found an excellent rationalization for averting his eyes.

In March 1920, near the end of his studies in Geneva and less than a month before his first trip outside Switzerland, Giacometti visited the Amiet family in Oschwand for eleven days.[11] Soon afterward he left for a brief visit to Venice and Padua with his father, who was inspecting the Swiss section of the Venice Biennale as a member of the Swiss Art Commission. He returned to

Maloja and Stampa for the summer and then to Geneva for several months. By November 1920 he was back in Italy on his own for an extended nine-month trip. He was headed for Rome where he would stay with an Italian branch of his family he had met in Maloja. On his second Italian trip he was going to see the major artistic sights of central Italy, just as his father had done twenty-eight years earlier. Each of Giacometti's trips, first Oschwand, then Venice, and finally central and southern Italy, was momentous and would have lifelong reverberations.

Though the Amiet and Giacometti families met regularly in Maloja during the summer, Alberto Giacometti had not traveled to Oschwand for a decade. Once there, he posed for a sculpted bust by his godfather. In 1918–19 Amiet had begun to work in marble and bronze, and he may have spoken to his godson about the dilemma of being gifted at both painting and sculpture—a feature which differentiated both of them from Giovanni Giacometti, who was solely a painter and printmaker. While in Oschwand, Giacometti also visited a rich young student of Amiet's, Josef Müller, who had amassed an impressive collection of African sculpture and modern paintings in the neighboring town of Solothurn. The two young men would soon be fellow sculpture students in Paris.

In Oschwand, Giacometti did several drawings of Greti Amiet, the second oldest of the three Amiet daughters, and his tender portraits of her are probably an early example of a secret infatuation, though Giacometti never writes about his feelings for her, anymore than he writes of his feelings about his mother's near-fatal illness discussed earlier.[12] In a polite note to the Amiets he thanks them for their hospitality and for teaching him how to dance, an activity he would later claim he could not do.[13]

To keep his secrets hidden, Giacometti devised many disguises. His deepest emotions were expressed through art, either his own or his appropriation of other artists' art. He had haltingly used Dürer to reveal the sadness of his twelfth year. A more dramatic example is found in his essay "May 1920," in which he describes his visit to Venice with his father.[14] The chief characteristic of his eloquent prose is the violent alternation in the young man's aesthetic preferences between the Renaissance masters, Giotto, Tintoretto, and Cimabue.

"May 1920" was published in the luxurious art magazine *Verve* in December 1952, a month after the death of Paul Eluard, the surrealist writer and friend who had helped edit most of Giacometti's surrealist texts. The essay contains the artist's distorted recollection of his first visit to Venice, a pivotal moment in his artistic development. It was written more than three decades after the fact, in the year of a large joint exhibit in Basel of works by Giovanni Giacometti and Antoine Bourdelle, Alberto's sculpture teacher in Paris. Included among his father's paintings in the exhibit were nude portraits of the Giacometti children. Even more significant, it was the year in which Alberto Giacometti exhibited his own paintings in Switzerland for the first time in many years.

After recalling the transparent gray color and shimmering light of Venice, Giacometti launches into his infatuation with Tintoretto: "Tintoretto was for me a marvelous discovery. My love for him was exclusive and biased. I felt only hostility and antipathy for the other Venetian painters. Tintoretto was right and the others were wrong."[15] In the text he reports that on his last day in Venice he ran to Tintoretto's major mural cycles to say goodbye, as if bidding adieu to his greatest friend. Later that afternoon he visited the Arena Chapel in Padua, about which he wrote: "Standing in front of Giotto felt like a violent punch in the chest. I was disoriented and lost. I immediately felt an immense pain and great grief. The blow hit Tintoretto too. The strength of Giotto overcame me irresistibly. I was crushed by those immovable figures, solid as basalt, with their precise and accurate gestures, their expression heavy and often infinitely tender, for example, when Mary's hand touches the cheek of the dead Christ. It seemed to me that no hand could ever make a different gesture under similar circumstances."[16]

A critical misremembering is contained in this portion of the text. The gestures of Giotto's figures are justly famous for their tender expressiveness, but Mary's hand does not touch her son's cheek in Padua. There is only one scene in the chapel, one of the most celebrated, where a woman's hand affectionately touches a cheek. It is Meeting at the Golden Gate, where Joachim and Anna meet after learning that Anna will finally bear a long-awaited child (fig. 3.1). A black-draped woman sets off the tender couple and can easily be interpreted as a mourning figure.[17] For Giacometti the conjunction of birth and death as well as a longing for a child would always be associated with Cuno and Anna Amiet, whose home he had just visited. As their godchild born only a few days after their loss, Giacometti could easily have associated the openly expressive Amiets with the "touching" couple—Anna and Joachim.

The young Giacometti's recollection of his Venetian trip continues: "The Tintorettos were now vague and indecisive, the figures seemed to be making great empty superfluous gestures. . . . But I rebelled against the idea of giving him up. I felt guilty, the estrangement I felt growing already seemed like a betrayal. I had a sense of losing something irreplaceable, like a gleam or a breath far more precious than all Giotto's qualities, even though I was convinced that he was more powerful."[18]

These words and all the preceding ones make sense at several levels if we understand that, in 1920, Giacometti's major conflict was whether to be a sculptor or a painter. Giotto, whose "strength overcame [him] irresistibly," stood for sculpture—his own or Amiet's.[19] Cimabue was a painter influenced by sculpture, and Alberto's sculpture was beginning to influence his father's painting. Tintoretto, whom the elder Giacometti described as having an "overflowing and unlimited, fantastic genius," was a symbol for painting and his father. Alberto knew that Amiet was not much impressed with the Venetian artist.[20] To side openly with Amiet against Giovanni on this matter could have felt like a "betrayal." But no betrayal fits the text as well as the one Giacometti must have felt as he contemplated becoming a sculptor. The battle between the titans shifts suddenly when young women appear:

> The same evening [that he saw the Tintorettos] all these contradictory feelings were thrown into confusion by the sight of two or three young girls who were walking in front of me. They appeared immense to me, all out of proportion to normal size, and their whole presence and their movements affected me with terrible violence. I stared at them hallucinated, invaded by a sensation of terror. It was like a fissure in reality. Everything meant something else, the connections between things had changed. The works of Tintoretto and Giotto seemed small, meaningless, weak and insipid. . . . But precisely what seemed to me so important [before] about Tintoretto was a faint image of this apparition, and I understood why I didn't want to lose him at any cost.[21]

As living human beings enter the picture, the young man is knocked off his feet. When he can focus on art, he can be passionate, but when he faces

FIGURE 3.1
Giotto, Meeting at the Golden Gate. Fresco, dimensions unknown. Arena Chapel, Padua, Alinari.

women and their "fissures," he becomes shy and awkward: The three girls in Padua are most likely a coded reference to Amiet's three adopted daughters. It is he who feels "weak" and "insipid" in their presence. Staying at the Amiets' shortly before the trip, he had seen their three young daughters, one of whom had been the object of Alberto's affection. He had also seen them nude in paintings by their father.

When Giacometti imagines being apart from his father and having to confront women directly, he stares and is "terrified" and seems to hallucinate: "I recognized that same gleam far more intensely that autumn in Florence, in an Egyptian bust, the first head that struck me as lifelike, then in the Cimabues at Assisi which filled me with tremendous joy. . . . All those works appeared a little like recreated doubles of the three young girls from Padua the same quality which cast a spell on me since Cézanne [Amiet's favorite artist]; it is that which gives to him for me a unique position in all the painting of recent centuries. All this was subjected to the time lag of recent days . . . I don't know exactly where I am."[22]

Whenever he was frightened or overwhelmed by a visual image—external or internal—Giacometti seemed to lose his orientation in time and place. He usually refound himself with the help of his father and his father's art. The entire text of "May 1920," which Giacometti had begun by describing his strange state of mind as "like a time lag," is framed by confusion as he gains, loses, and regains his link to Giovanni. "I no longer have the same relationship to what I had wanted to say," he writes, "the facts no longer have the same importance, or rather they have slipped to another level, to another place and I am no longer the same at all."[23]

Giacometti later made several statements suggesting that he was aware of a subtle pressure from his father to be a painter even though he had begun moving toward sculpture in Geneva. Perhaps it was no more than Giovanni's wish that the son would love the same things he loved. He recollected talking to Giovanni about leaving Schiers before graduation: "After I finished my first exam I asked my father for some time off—to get clearer about what I wanted to do. . . . 'You want to be a painter?' my father asked. 'A painter or a sculptor,' I said."[24] The blind zeal which permeates Giovanni's love of painting could have made his son reluctant to openly reject his father's invitation to follow in his painterly footsteps. Until he left for Paris Giacometti continued to paint, especially when he was near his father. He complained loudly about his sculpture classes in Geneva and would soon bitterly lament a failed sculpture in Rome. But once he was in Paris he turned his full attention to sculpture and avoided painting except on trips home. Giacometti was probably not conscious of the contest raging inside him. His love for his father was genuine and his desire to please him long-standing.

In 1920, at age nineteen, Giacometti needed to find a path that diverged from his father's. He resorted to many protective devices before stepping out on his own and seemed to need to hide any sense of his superiority or true difference. How could he honor his father yet turn away from painting? How was he to deal with the fact that he was beginning to influence his father? His letters home were redolent with anxious desire to both reveal and conceal his growing independence. In a poignant letter he enthusiastically describes the landscape in and around Rome, then catches himself, claiming that the landscape is "so much more beautiful at our place than Italy."[25] Soon, he returns to an elegiac description of the beauties of his present locale. Giacometti's attempts to disguise his roving eye seem to be aimed at his father, the landscape painter of the Bregaglia valley. But he also knew of his mother's belief that all the beauty an artist could ever want in life was right at home.

In Rome Giacometti was like a whirling dervish, running through the Eternal City in search of pleasure and beauty. He was discovering delights at every turn: music, architecture, antiquity, and urban life. He joined an art club to make friends and attended concerts of Mozart, Wagner, and Strauss. He waxed rhapsodic about Egyptian painting and sculpture, buying art books on the subject; he even purchased a small Greek sculpted head, declaring it to be "the most beautiful."[26] His brief bout of hedonism included haberdashery, when he bought an elegant new outfit and sketched himself dapperly dressed, *Self-Portrait*, in a letter (fig. 3.2). Accompanying the sketch were his lighthearted words: "Here I am. . . . A nice, new fashionable suit, a walking stick, and of course, a scarf and gloves. . . . At first I felt as though I were dressed up like a doll under a bell jar. . . . But one feels better when one is well dressed, and one enjoys oneself more, providing the money lasts."[27]

Giacometti also made a more careful drawing of *Seated Man*, a jaunty young man with a top hat, seated at a café table, an elegant cigarette holder in one hand and a cane in the other—a caricature of an urban sophisticate. Oscar Wilde's words at the top of the page foretell a lifelong habit: "The cigarette is the truest pleasure." There is a marked difference in his two sketches of debonair modernity. For his parents, he omits the cigarette and gives himself wild bushy hair, a feature he shared with his mother. All in all, he seemed relaxed and able to enjoy himself and to take pleasure in possessing beautiful objects. It was a lamentably short episode, and an overtone of apology gradually began to seep through his exuberant missives home. He presented his activities as "useful not wasteful," as though expanding horizons and enjoying oneself were neither proper nor correct enough for his readers in Stampa.

Giacometti's artwork in Italy ranged from copies of older art to studies of architecture in his father's style, but his most notable works were portraits of friends and relatives whom he depicted with exceptional sensitivity. From a text published twenty-seven years after the event we learn that Giacometti had a major perceptual crisis during his stay in Rome while sculpting the head of his fifteen-year-old cousin, Bianca Giacometti Galante. Giacometti was infatuated with Bianca, oldest daughter of his Roman hosts and a friend of his sister, but she scorned his attentions.[28] The girls were classmates at boarding school, and they even shared a name, as Ottilia's childhood nickname was "Bianca Neve"—Snow White. The relationship between Alberto and Bianca, however, was one of alternating unequals—one the master, the other a slave. She was a flirt, allowing him to give her gifts and to escort her, then pushing him away. In turn, he became her tormentor, imposing on her a straitjacket of prolonged posing. Months of fruitless work exceeded the limits of Bianca's patience, and she knocked the unfinished sculpture off its stand, smashing it to pieces.[29] Giacometti recalled the painful experience: "For the first time I could not find my way out, I was lost, everything escaped me. The head of the model before me became like a cloud, vague, unlimited."[30] Similar experi-

FIGURE 3.2
Alberto
Giacometti, Self-
Portrait, 1921.
Ink on paper.

ences later suggest that Giacometti's rage at being unable to master his subject led to his first artistic breakdown.

Giacometti received Bianca's loving attention a few years later, when they met during the summers in Maloja. The young couple walked "hand in hand like children," but he did not pursue a sexual relationship. Instead, he continued the companionable master/slave relationship, shimmying back and forth on a seesaw of control. One evening when they were alone in her room he persuaded her to let him carve his initial into her arm. Cutting into Bianca's flesh with his knife and "claiming" her as his "very own little cow," he exacted a sadistic revenge for her earlier rejections.[31]

In 1947, Giacometti described the Roman episode in a now famous "letter" to his new dealer, Pierre Matisse, summing up his artistic development beginning in 1914. "In 1920 to 1922 I lived in Italy. . . . I stayed nine months in Rome where I never had enough time to do all I wanted. I wanted to see everything, and at the same time I painted figures and landscapes in a somewhat pointillist way . . . and compositions inspired by Sophocles and Aeschylus that I was reading at this time (*The Sacrifice of Iphigenia*, *The Death of Cassandra*, *The Sack of Troy*, etc.). I had also begun two heads, a small one . . . and I ended by destroying them before I left."[32]

The memory distortions begin with the extra year (1922) Giacometti gives himself in Italy and culminates with the destruction of both sculpted portrait heads, when in fact one survived, and it was Bianca, not he, who destroyed the other. He also misremembered the titles of plays by Sophocles and Aeschylus, thus revealing the parts of the stories he found most compelling. One royal daughter was sacrificed and another forced to be the concubine of a conquering hero—two female victims cruelly exploited by powerful men in their family. Several painted compositions that survived the trip show women being attacked or sacrificed. The predominant feeling emerging from Giacometti's garbled story is his ambivalence—indeed aggression—toward women.

Miserable in Rome, without power to work at his art, Giacometti felt "like an expulsion from Paradise . . . before that I believed I saw things very clearly, I had a sort of intimacy with the whole, with the universe. Then suddenly it became alien. You are yourself and the universe is beyond."[33] As a boy, Giacometti, like all children, had sought his mother's smiling approval. Instead he was often criticized. Now, far from home, he encountered the frowning face of another woman who would not do his bidding. Bianca's mistreatment could have stirred painful and angry memories of that earlier rejection at home in Stampa. He was penalized for his hostile feelings by losing his vision—the cruelest punishment for an artist.

Art had been Giacometti's refuge since childhood. When he felt himself master of his craft, he was at one with his artist father and all the previous artists he admired. When he was unable to work, he felt desolate and alone, just as he felt as a child when his father would travel and the boy couldn't remember his father's face. His unconscious hostile feelings for the father who left him were punished by blind forgetfulness. "Suddenly . . . you are yourself and the universe is beyond." In Rome Giacometti's feeling of abandonment made the image disappear, and for a time he could master neither his feelings nor his craft.

VENICE REVISITED

In April 1921 Giacometti left Rome for the south. Aware of his father's earlier pilgrimage, he wrote him from Naples that he had seen Torre del Greco from a distance, "your old home at the foot of Mt. Vesuvius."[34] Paestum and Pompeii held great attraction for Alberto. Pompeii's paintings reminded him of Gauguin—"modern in form and lighting"—who was often discussed in the Giacometti household. At Paestum Giacometti was entranced with the temples. They were "majestic . . . extraordinarily severe and solemn conveying more religious spirit than all the Christian churches in Italy."[35] A month later, near the end of his Italian stay, Giacometti wrote of painting compositions "based on imagination and memory," using the landscape of Naples and Paestum combined with classical figures. He summed up the results of his visual education and preferred masters. "Considering all I have seen so far, I have enough material to keep me going for a while. But there is still one thing I must see before I come home—that is Venice and the paintings of Tintoretto."[36]

Giacometti's second visit to Venice took place in September 1921 following the death of the elderly Dutch scholar with whom he was traveling. The trip to Venice and the events surrounding the Dutchman's death are often presented as the turning points in Giacometti's life. I will examine Giacometti's various accounts of what happened there, because his multiple versions lead to vastly different insights. During his spring trip to the south in 1921, Giacometti had taken the train from Naples to Paestum. On the ride back from Paestum to Pompeii (only a few kilometers from Torre del Greco, his father's "old home") Giacometti had met Peter van Meurs, a Dutch archivist who was traveling alone, and the two men passed the time in entertaining conversation. Several months later, when Alberto was back at home in Stampa, van Meurs advertised in Italian newspapers to find the Swiss-Italian art student he had met on the train. By chance, Giacometti learned that he was being sought and responded, thinking the older man had lost something. He was then invited to be the sixty-one-year-old man's traveling companion on an all-expenses-paid trip to Italy. Venice was to be their goal, and Giacometti agreed.

Before embarking on the journey with van Meurs, Giacometti had "stolen 1000 Swiss Francs out of his father's drawer thinking that if it ended badly [he] could get home on his own."[37] They departed in early September 1921, and after a few days traveling through the Tyrolean mountains, Giacometti found himself in a hotel room in Madonna di Campiglio with a very sick man. At first he read and drew van Meurs's portrait. Then he realized his companion was dying, and he was terrified.

> He was old and alone. I really wanted to go to Venice. I was poor. He paid. . . . In the Tyrol he caught cold. The next morning the pain was so bad. . . . They gave him shots. I spent the day by his bed reading. . . . It was raining. From time to time he would say: 'Tomorrow I'll be better.' By the end of the afternoon I had the impression his nose was getting longer. He had difficulty breathing. His cheeks were sinking in. I was very frightened and thought 'he's going to die.' The doctor came: the end; his heart is giving out; tonight he will be dead. It became for me an abominable trap the negation of everything I had believed about death. . . . Within a matter of hours, the old Dutchman became a mere thing, nothing. But from that moment on death became a constant possibility, for myself and for others. . . . It was like a warning. There had been so many accidents, the meeting, the train, the announcement as if everything had been arranged so that I would be present at that miserable end. My life changed on that day. Children are so confident. . . . One believes in permanence. Everything became fragile for me at twenty. Since then I have never been able to sleep without a lamp, nor go to bed without the thought crossing my mind that I might never wake up. . . . At that moment I just wanted to get out of there fast.[38]

A suspicious red spot had appeared on the dead man's chest, so Giacometti had to remain for another day in Madonna di Campiglio under police watch. The sudden, unexpected death of the fatherlike stranger plunged Giacometti into a panic. Desperate for advice and the calming effect of his father's voice, he telephoned Giovanni in Switzerland. Sensibly, his father told him to entrust the matter to local authorities.[39] Once it was clear that van Meurs had died of natural causes, Giacometti was allowed to leave. He went straight to Venice. "Two days of drinking coffee and running after girls. I ran through my 1000 Francs and went home."[40] After his return to Switzerland, Giacometti received a gift of van Meurs's gold cufflinks from the dead man's brother. Immediately Giacometti began to embroider the event with inaccurate details. He told his family that he had gone to Venice to wait for van Meurs's brother, who then gave him the cufflinks, which he threw into a Venetian canal.[41]

The first firm, factual record is a postcard from Venice dated September 7, 1921, and written to his parents. "I am in Venice. I like it more than ever. It is an enchantment and for the most part one feels like whistling and humming. . . . Little by little the ugly memories . . . fade away."[42] The second, more explicit piece of evidence is in a letter written during December 1921 to Lucas Lichtenhahn about his entire Italian adventure, "ending [with] a journey through the Tyrol with a very fine, intelligent and good Dutchman who there, where I was alone with him, died; and I went on to Venice and then came home sick and half disturbed."[43]

The first published account by Giacometti of the death of van Meurs appeared in 1946. It was embedded in the text of "The Dream, the Sphinx, and the Death of T.," in which he wrote about another death at which he was present and about a vivid dream concerning the venereal disease that he had recently contracted after intercourse with a prostitute. The postwar text is extremely rich and filled with significance for the period during which it was written. I discuss it fully in Chapter 10. Here, I take up only the portion dealing with the death of the Dutchman:

> I had recounted my dream to R. M., but when I reached the moment when I bury the remains, I saw myself in another meadow, surrounded by bushes at the edge of a forest. Brushing the snow off my feet, digging a hole in the hardened soil, I buried a piece of barely-touched bread (a theft of bread in my childhood) and I saw myself again running in Venice clenching tightly in my hand a piece of bread I wanted to get rid of. I crossed all of Venice looking for remote and solitary areas and there, after numerous failed attempts on the most obscure, small bridges, at the side of the darkest canals, nervously trembling, I threw the bread into the rotting water of the last arm of the canal closed in by black walls and I ran away in a panic, scarcely aware of myself. This led me to describe the state in which I found myself at that moment. By dint of recounting the voyage to Tyrol and the death of van M., see note, (that long rainy day when I sat alone by a bed in a hotel room, a book by Maupassant on Flaubert in my hand) I saw the head of Van M. transform (the nose became more and

more pronounced, the cheeks hollowed out, the nearly immobile, open mouth barely breathed and toward evening while trying to sketch this profile I was taken by a sudden fear that he was going to die), the stay in Rome the preceding summer (the newspaper that fell into my hands by chance and which carried an ad seeking my whereabouts), the train at Pompeii, the temple at Paestum.[44]

The dream, occurring in midlife, helped the artist to face his deepest fears about death, homoeroticism, and his father. It also reflects upon issues troubling him since adolescence. A significant change was the mutation of the object he had discarded. The cufflinks became bread. In actuality, the only item we can be certain that he threw away was his father's money, since he did not receive van Meurs's cufflinks until after his return to Stampa. The elision of bread, jewels, and money, which he used on "coffee and girls," was woven and rewoven in his mind. The result increasingly resembled Thomas Mann's *Death in Venice*.[45] In Mann's novel, which connected death, Venice, intense gazing, and repressed homoeroticism, Tadziu, a beautiful young Polish boy, is the love of von Ashenbach, a creative older man who dies of the plague in Venice. Tadziu, by seeming to respond to the aging swain, causes his death.[46]

Giacometti believed himself to be loved by the older, repressed van Meurs, who gave him jewels. In his recollection (we can never know the truth) he was compelled to discard a tightly clenched end of bread "after several failed attempts." "Trembling nervously," he threw the bread into the rotting water of the canal and ran away into distraction, hardly conscious of himself.

In Giacometti's native Italian, *pane* (bread) and *pene* (penis) are so close linguistically and morphologically as to be symbolically equivalent. By using this connection as the key to unlock the story's meaning, a comprehensible subtext emerges. Giacometti had to somehow discard the use of his penis—his heterosexuality—which he was anxiously "clenching." Running all over the city looking for obscure rotting trenches—cavities to receive his *pane*—echoes his feelings about the vaginas of prostitutes, whose "rotting breaches" had caused his venereal disease in 1946. In the postwar version of this complex tale, he refers to a feminine opening: "The trip I made in 1921 (the death of Van M. and all the related events) was for me like a gap in [my] life. Everything became other (changed) and that trip obsessed me continually for an entire year. I told the story constantly and often wished to write about it, that was always impossible for me. Only today, in relation to the dream, in relation to the bread in the canal, has it become possible for me to mention it for the first time."[47] An earlier vision of a female hole—his experience of watching his mother give birth to his sister—had transfigured his life at age two and a half. Now, an encounter with another "gap" catapults him backwards to that earlier nodal moment.

The fatherly van Meurs and Giacometti's father were fused in the young man's mind before and after van Meurs died, and it was that conflation that gave the incident its fateful flavor. The psychological parallels between van Meurs and Giovanni help explain the usually fearful young man's remarkable decision to travel with a stranger. On the one hand, he associated the region "south of Naples," where he had met van Meurs, with his father. Giovanni's *Boys on the Beach at Torre del Greco*, which epitomized the elder Giacometti's fondness for painting nude young boys, was constantly visible in Giovanni's studio. At the same time an appeal to travel to Venice with a "fine, intelligent, good" older man who would pay for the trip could also have reminded the young man of his recent voyage there with his father.[48] The attraction to an older man had led Giacometti to make the trip in the first place but overwhelming feelings of repulsion impelled him to escape as soon as possible. He fled to an activity that seemed certain proof of his heterosexuality—"running after prostitutes." Their cold, mechanical comfort was safe—emotionally uninvolved. The sexual pleasure he received was not attached to unbearable feelings; it was guilt-free.

Homosexual panic is a psychological phenomenon frequent in men when they are drawn to other men and fear that their heterosexual orientation is at risk. Adolescent boys are particularly prone to these feelings. But it was not only guilt about unconscious homosexual feelings that threw Giacometti into a panic. The sudden death of the benevolent Dutchman kindled a more formidable self-reproach—that he may have somehow been responsible. Several clues point toward this conclusion. The first is the severe deprivation Giacometti began to inflict on himself immediately after the event—and for the rest of his life—punishment severe enough for a horrible crime. "It's because of the Dutchman that I have lived life in a 'provisional' way," he told an interviewer. "That I never recovered from my horror of all possessions. To settle in, to buy a house, to arrange a nice existence for oneself with such a threat always hanging over it. No I'd rather live in hotels cafés, places where people come and go."[49]

Another signal was Giacometti's intense reaction to this event when compared to his silence about the death, in 1913, of the grandfather he had seen every day or the near-death of his mother in 1911. About van Meurs's death he wrote: "Before that I had never been face to face with death. . . . I had never seen a dead person close up. . . . I felt so threatened that I didn't dare go to sleep. But I fell asleep anyway and felt in my sleep how my mouth was open—just like the dying man's! I woke up and did everything I could to keep from going back to sleep, for fear that I would start to roll my head from side to side like he had done."[50]

The death of the Dutchman occurred as Giacometti was trying to resolve his rivalry with his father. The prize of the contest was not a woman, but fame and fortune as an artist. Because he could not permit himself to know that he was competing with and distancing himself from his artist father, Giacometti could also not know that he was afraid of winning and defeating him. A related fear, and perhaps an even more formidable one, was the fear of losing his closeness to his father as he became increasingly more independent of him. Giacometti's desperate need to hear Giovanni's voice after the Dutchman's death supports my hypothesis that he may have harbored a superstitious fear and unconscious fantasy that he had killed van Meurs, his father substitute. His father's voice would reassure him that at least Giovanni was still alive.

September 1921 was not the first time Giacometti had been fearful about his father's possible death or injury; as a child he was prone to panic and paralysis whenever Giovanni stayed longer than expected while painting in the mountains.[51] He experienced similar fears when Diego went mountain climbing. Phobic individuals characteristically live with unconscious hostile wishes toward the people they love, and these wishes are in direct conflict with their powerful loving feelings. When aggressive feelings toward someone cannot be expressed or even recognized, they are frequently transformed into their opposite—excessive fears for that person's safety. The fear then leads to a compelling need for close contact with the threatened victim in order to be reassured that nothing bad has really happened. The death of the Dutchman was like a lightning bolt opening a cleft in Giacometti's personality and drawing him backward to the panicky moments of the first death he had experienced—that of his grandmother Ottilia. That never-mentioned seminal trauma in 1904 occurred simultaneously with a move to an inn, "a place where people come and go."[52]

One dramatic change in Giacometti's behavior after Venice was his need to sleep with a light, a new ritual added to the growing number of Giacometti's phobic devices. (The first, placing his shoes and socks in a particular order on the floor before going to bed, had begun around the time of the simultaneous birth and death of the two Ottilias.) Why did van Meurs's death make Giacometti fearful of sleeping without a light? To be certain he knew with whom he was sleeping? To be certain he was not alone in the world, as one is in the dark? Or to be certain that the recumbent sleeper was still alive?

At the end of his life Giacometti recalled his time in Rome: "I had the mentality of a rich young idler."[53] As we have seen, his decision to turn away from worldly goods and luxuries was a direct consequence of the incident with van Meurs, a self-inflicted punishment for guilty thoughts and feelings that could be neither fully known nor expressed. Giacometti had felt safe enough to acquire worldly goods while in Rome, and the description of his life there sounded normal, like that of any young man on his own for the first time in a big city.

What began as a temporary reaction to trauma became a fixed trait. The immoderately modest life that Giacometti pursued from that time on, even when he could afford better, represented the opposite of his father's preferences. Giovanni enjoyed himself, sang, ate, drank, painted, and sired a large family, all with gusto. It was Annetta who watched the pennies and kept her pleasure-loving husband in check. The abruptness of Giacometti's shift into asceticism suggests an unconscious guilt so powerful that it needed urgent and immediate atonement. His elegant Roman outfit had not prevented the horror of van Meurs's death; if anything, it may have attracted it and therefore must be shunned.[54]

The other enduring habits beginning after van Meurs's death grew out of Giacometti's need to avoid sleep—the equivalent of death in the unconscious. His headlong trip to Venice contains the first report of both his caffeine addiction and his new nightly ritual—wandering the streets and cafés searching for company. Both activities reveal his fear of dying and of facing frightening dreams each time he let himself fall into the arms of Morpheus.

Soon after van Meurs's death, Giacometti moved to Paris. For the next decade his principal task was to find his own artistic path. The sculpture classes in Geneva could be seen as a step in that direction. Fretting in Geneva, under the thumb of teachers who neither understood nor appreciated him, Giacometti must have been pleased to move on with his career and begin his travels abroad. The life plan he was following more or less mirrored his father's. They both left secondary school before taking final exams. Both were considered not quite qualified at the first art schools they attended. Finally, they both were to be inspired by their initial Italian itineraries.

Giovanni had communicated in subtle ways his wish for his eldest son to become a painter, despite outward efforts to stand by his son's decision.[55] A remarkable double portrait of Alberto sculpting and Annetta posing, *The*

FIGURE 3.3 *Giovanni Giacometti,* The Sculptor, *1923. Oil on canvas, 73.5 x 65.5 cm. Kunsthaus Zurich.*

Sculptor (1923), can be seen as a metaphor for Giovanni's acceptance of his son's choice (fig. 3.3). Alberto's devouring eyes are fixed on his mother's face, while the green plastilene head on which he works sits serenely behind and above the colorfully painted head of the actual subject. Her white hair and reddish flesh contrast sharply with the sculpted green head. Alberto's work lives and breathes in this painting. Neither of the human subjects, however intensely alive they seem, can hold a candle to it. Whether he was consciously aware of the difference in the way he painted the three heads, Giovanni seems to have guessed by then that his son could surpass him. Of the

57

two men, Alberto would have the greater difficulty accepting this fact, and Giovanni had to give his son permission many times before Alberto could comfortably accept his desire to be a sculptor.

The younger Giacometti experienced much guilt about turning from his father's painterly vocation, and I believe he experienced his growing desire to be independent of the father as a kind of murder. The love he felt for the elder artist who continually encouraged him, even as Giovanni saw himself being surpassed, prevented Alberto from openly expressing either the hostile component in the natural rivalry between the two men or the son's eventual triumph.

CHAPTER 4

1925-1929

PARIS, PREHISTORY, AND SEXUALITY

Giacometti arrived in Paris on January 9, 1922, to study sculpture at the Academie de la Grande-Chaumière with Antoine Bourdelle, a disciple of Rodin, and he remained to live in that city more or less continuously for the next forty years.

With the death of the Dutchman in the Tyrol, the magical fantasy that his wish could be responsible for someone's death became a permanent feature of Giacometti's inner life. As much as he needed to get away from his family and the insular valley culture, he never again let his parents know how eager he was to separate from them and no longer ignored his mother's pleas to stay close to her. Indeed, Giacometti developed a persistent need to keep in close contact with his family and to see them often, and his life in Paris was frequently interrupted by trips back to Switzerland.[1] On the eve of his first trip to Paris he wrote to his mother from Basel: "Six months go by quickly, I'll be back to enlarge the family again before you know it."[2] Though dutiful children commonly make such a comment at the point of their departure as adults from home, it also suggests his wish to remain eternally a child who would not have to make choices.

Giacometti's periodic return visits to Switzerland had significance beyond family contact. Until the development of his postwar style he maintained several aesthetic approaches simultaneously, seemingly unable to give any of them up. In Switzerland, however, he did mostly conventional work, making landscapes, portraits, and family sketches as his father had always done. This phenomenon was especially true during his first fifteen years in Paris while he was exploring the avant-garde currents swirling around him. There are two possible explanations: he might have been responding to his mother's desire for continuity, or he may have been trying to protect his father—and himself—from an awareness of their growing differences. Living in Paris, tasting the possibilities of urban life and dreaming of international success, Giacometti could see the limitations of his father's career, just as he could see himself growing beyond the confines of Giovanni's beloved "little tract of land."

During his first Parisian years Giacometti stayed in hotels and spent half the year in Switzerland. In his rooms he surrounded himself with images of home, placing family photographs and his father's prints of domestic life in Stampa on the walls. Swiss friends visiting Giacometti's Paris studio noted that it felt exactly like being in the Bergell—small, sparsely furnished rooms with no hint of Parisian luxury.[3] With the notable exception of making his space an unmitigated mess—the opposite of his mother's meticulous house-keeping—Giacometti re-created his childhood environment in the midst of the most cosmopolitan city in the world. Until Diego moved to Paris in 1925 and Alberto's stays in Paris became longer and his Swiss vacations briefer, Giacometti did not, perhaps could not, have a permanent studio or home away from the Bregaglia valley.

Unlike his father, who had arrived in Paris with a close friend, Giacometti initially spent his time with the "foreign students"—non-Parisians, European and American, who gathered at Bourdelle's academy. For his first three years he felt isolated from the native Parisians. He quickly set out to differentiate himself from his neat Swiss heritage and became famous among his fellow students for epitomizing Bohemian life. "He wore durable utilitarian clothes that looked slept in, never brushed his strong teeth, or combed his woolly hair and kept clay embedded under his ruined fingernails. His studio . . . was an unbelievable litter of plaster chips up to the ankles. . . . The place may have been a shambles but the force of Giacometti's character and vision altered it in our minds to the exact blueprint of what an artist's studio should be."[4]

Bourdelle taught his students to take care of the "machine"—the body—which would be used to produce art, but Giacometti's fellow students noticed that he did not comply. At Schiers he had grumbled about the lack of hot water for bathing and in Rome he had enjoyed stylish clothing and pleasures of the flesh. By the time he was in Paris, the insomnia exacerbated by the Dutchman's death had evolved into a pernicious behavioral pattern—an inability to stop working no matter the bodily needs or external pressures he felt.[5] He seemed unable to organize his routine daily tasks, which until then had almost always been managed by others.

Giacometti's insistent self-denigration as an artist began at this time. He roundly praised his fellow students at the Grande-Chaumière and constantly belittled his own efforts, all the while quietly demonstrating his exceptional talent and skill. Despite praise from Bourdelle, Giacometti frequently destroyed his work, beginning again at a point at which his fellow students would have been satisfied.[6] He had learned about the envy of academic instructors in Geneva and had been punished for the hubris of his Italian interlude in Madonna di Campiglio. At the same time, he was prone to magical thinking and apparently felt that fate would punish him for competitive strivings, so he hid them for the rest of his life by donning a cloak of "failure."

At the beginning of his life in Paris Giacometti was known as a papa's boy because he spoke of his father so often. His emphatic devotion to his mother did not appear until after his father died in 1933. Only then did he begin to present his mother to the world as a sainted woman from whom he could barely stand to be parted. And the more negatively he felt about her, the higher her pedestal. Giacometti's idealization of her served to protect them both from the painful knowledge of his ambivalence.[7] Deeply sensing his mother's need for control (as well as her need for having loving children), he was careful not to cross her openly and presented himself as the obedient son of a devoted mother.[8]

Unlike Schiers, in Paris he did not have like-minded classmates to cushion the discomfort of being a stranger in a country hostile to "barbarians"— people who do not speak the native language. But he found familiar comfort in the art of museums—his habitual means for orienting himself—and he usually went to the Louvre on Sunday, the traditional family day in Europe. There, he was drawn to images that connected him to his early life. In Le Nain's *Cart*, one of his favorite paintings, the solemn, unsmiling faces of the children clustered on and around the cart recall the dismayed expressions notable in all known photographs of the Giacometti children (figs. 4.1, 4.2).[9] To Giacometti, the most "marvelous figure" in Le Nain's painting was the young boy seated at the left edge of the canvas, staring solemnly at a stern-faced mother who inattentively holds her infant while she sourly looks out at the viewer from her prominent position at the far right of the painting.

Little remains of Giacometti's Parisian work from 1922–24. He was gradually moving away from his father's style, and his few paintings from the period are markedly influenced by Cézanne, especially his modulated hues. Color always had complex psychological meaning for Giacometti, and a shift away from Giovanni's strong color almost invariably meant he was distancing himself from his father. His classmates jeered when he painted his sculpture in Bourdelle's class, and he retreated to a more fashionable monochrome.

FIGURE 4.1 Le Nain, *The Hay Cart, seventeenth century. Oil on canvas, 56 x 72 cm. Louvre, Paris.*

His principal motive for painting sculpture then and throughout his life was to attempt to bring these works to life—to finish them—the way he had once needed to "finish" a sculpted portrait of his father while the older Giacometti was away.[10]

One of the few surviving paintings of the period, *Skull* (1923) is a harbinger of his postwar work and future preoccupations.[11] The subject naturally appealed to the young man already obsessed with death and fresh from his recent experience with van Meurs. Additional motivation for his concern with a skull during the winter of 1922–23 was provided by his military service that fall and the sensational discovery in November of the tomb of King Tutankhamen. An avid newspaper reader, Giacometti would have followed the dramatic events and fabulous discoveries.

At the Grande-Chaumière Giacometti's drawings done from models were influenced by his teacher, who insisted that drawing was the foundation on which sculpture must stand.[12] But they are much more than illustrations of Bourdelle's didactic program. Like the portraits done in Rome, they reflect the artist's ability to capture the sensation of touching his subject with his pencil. In their tactile elegance these figure drawings also reveal the fruits of his efforts to copy Egyptian sculpture from el-Amarna.[13] His close attention to naturalistic details and his representation of the contours and volumes of his models also indicate that he was leaning away from his father's expressionism and toward visual precision.

Some of Bourdelle's injunctions about truth and nature fit with Giacometti's ideas, but a letter to his parents in December 1923 makes it clear that the young man saw the limits of Bourdelle's teaching and style, and he often found his master to be a blowhard. "A few times I got him to contradict himself completely. Why does he think he is talking to children? Perhaps he will notice that we are not like American girls who gullibly swallow everything."[14] Given such comments it is somewhat surprising that Giacometti continued to

FIGURE 4.2 The
Giacometti children,
c. 1912. From left:
Ottilia, Bruno,
Alberto, and Diego.

attend sessions at the academy for several more years. Nevertheless, it was a stable sanctuary where he could retain student status while searching for himself in the swirl of rapidly shifting styles around him in Paris. Behind the scrim of obedient imitations of avant-garde artists like Brancuși, Lipschitz, Laurens, Archipenko, and Duchamp-Villon, as well as the primitive and archaic sources that inspired them, Giacometti was preparing to leap to the center stage of the Parisian art world.

MAN AND WOMAN, WHO ARE THEY?

Giacometti arrived in Paris in 1922 with burning questions for which he had no acceptable answers: What is Man? What is Woman? His father was gentle, bending, feminine, and generous; but he had penetrated his son with his eye and brush. His mother was hard, upright, masculine, phallic, fragile, and withholding; but she had fed him, housed him, and kept him clean. Man and Woman, as he knew them, did not fit traditional roles or act in traditional ways. To understand the sculpture Giacometti made at the outset of his career in Paris, we must first address his pressing questions.

Growing up in his family Giacometti seems to have developed unconscious fantasies with contradictory content—that both men and women have a phallus and that both men and women can be castrated, damaged, and dangerous. These fantasies defended him against many forbidden wishes and fears. (Evidence that the artist had such fantasies will appear during his surrealist years, which I discuss in Chapters 5 and 6.) Forbidden and contradictory fantasies are characteristic of all children, but for Giacometti their intensity created unremitting conflicts in which his talent and capacity to master anxiety through his art were constantly counterpoised against fear and inhibition.

The artist's early memories about an entrancing boulder with an inviting small cave at its base (to which his father had introduced him), and an enormous, frightening dark rock rising out of the brambles can be seen as a symbolic screen for confused and conflated images of male and female genitals. A photograph of the cave with its sawtooth mouth suggests how an imaginative boy might have had such associations (fig. 4.3).

> I considered this [huge golden-colored] rock a friend, a creature animated by the best intentions toward us, calling us, smiling to us. . . . Every morning when I awoke I sought the rock. From the house I saw it in its most minute details; everything else was vague and inconsistent, air attached to

FIGURE 4.3

Cave at Stampa

(author photograph).

nothing. . . . I was overcome with joy when I could crouch in the little rear cave; . . . all my desires were realized. . . . One time I got further away than usual . . . before me, a little below in the midst of the brambles, reared an enormous black rock in the form of a narrow and pointed pyramid. . . . I cannot express the feelings of spite and defeat I experienced at that moment. It . . . struck me immediately as a living creature, hostile, threatening. . . . Its existence was intolerable to me and I suddenly felt . . . that it must be ignored, forgotten, and never mentioned to anyone. Nevertheless I did approach it, but with the feeling of delivering myself to something reprehensible, secret, suspicious. One hand barely touched it, with repulsion and fright. I walked around it . . . no trace of a cave which made the rock still more intolerable . . . an opening would have complicated everything and I already felt our cave's desolation if one were to be occupied with another at the same time . . . I fled from this black rock, I did not mention it to the other children, I ignored it and never returned to see it.[15]

Giacometti recalled these memories during the 1930s, when surrealist fascination with psychoanalysis made public revelation of early memories fashionable, especially if they were erotic. They are significantly related to both the form and content of the sculpture he was working on during that decade and are particularly revealing of his shifting mental images of his parents: his father receptive, embracing, and at the same time solid; his mother upright, narrow, and threatening. In all likelihood the yellow rock with its beckoning cave represents Giovanni, in whose substantial presence and warm studio Alberto had found refuge. The enormous, narrow, pointed black rock, which inspired feelings of defeat and spite, probably symbolizes Annetta. This image connects with Giacometti's earliest memory of her. In 1933 he described her "long black dress that touched the ground [and] disturbed me with its mystery; it seemed to be part of her body and this caused in me a feeling of fear and confusion."[16]

Giacometti wanted to be original, yet he was compelled to stay with the subjects driving him: tough and masculine women, gentle and yielding men. As a result, his first surviving Parisian sculptures were strongly marked by androgynous features. He would have to define his own sexuality as he worked out his intimate relationships—physically with women and mentally with men.

As we have seen, in addition to his conscious and unconscious memories of his parents, Giacometti's views of man- and womanhood were also marked by the experience of mumps/orchitis in his sixteenth or seventeenth year. To some degree, his art and his view of himself would reflect the effects of that illness throughout his life. Referring to his adolescence, Giacometti said: "As a young man I thought nothing was impossible for me. That feeling lasted until I was seventeen or eighteen years old. Then I suddenly realized that I could do absolutely nothing, and I asked myself the reason. I decided to work to find out why."[17] Years later he added: "I do not know whether I work in order to make something or in order to know why I cannot make what I would like to make. It may be that all this is nothing but an obsession, the causes of which I do not know, or compensation for a deficiency somewhere."[18]

These two statements, together with the observation that the first sign of Giacometti's sense of punctured grand ambitions and failure coincided with the timing of his orchitis, alert us to a way of understanding the artist's choice of art making as a means of solving, or at least partly compensating for, his lost physiological intactness.[19] It also suggests why he felt he needed to insist that he had failed, would always fail, but must nevertheless go on.

Giacometti's relationship with women was colored by his impotence, and his reluctance to penetrate women seems to come from conclusions he drew in earliest childhood about the dangers of sexuality. The child who had been the single visible result of the Amiets' sex life was born dead. In his own family, Ottilia, the first baby born when he was old enough to understand, seemed magically to cause the death of her grandmother.

In the crowded space of the small Giacometti apartment, the children, especially the highly imaginative and visually precocious Alberto, could have overheard or perhaps seen his parents' lovemaking. For most children, the sounds and sights accompanying lovemaking are associated with conflict and pain, because they can be interpreted as cruel mistreatment of one partner by the other. Psychoanalysts refer to this as a "primal scene" fantasy.[20] Giacometti later asserted: "I thought that between a man and a woman there could only be incompatibility, war, violence. The woman would not submit till bodily resistance was exhausted; the man raped her."[21] This statement, made in the late 1950s, is part of a continuous line of thought, first publicly expressed in Giacometti's surrealist text "Yesterday, Quicksand" (1933), in which he claimed to recall a chilling fantasy that he experienced when falling asleep between the ages of four and seven involving the rape and murder of a mother and daughter.

> For months, I could not sleep at night without first imagining myself . . . to have arrived at a grey castle. . . . There I killed, without their being able to defend themselves, two men, one of whom, around seventeen years old always seemed pale and terrified, and the other of whom wore armor on the left side of which something shone like gold. I raped after having torn off their dresses, two women, one thirty-two years old, all in black, with a face like alabaster, then her daughter, dressed in flowing white veils. The whole forest resounded with their cries and whimpers. I killed them too, but very slowly. . . . Each time with slight variations. Next I burned the castle and, content, fell asleep.[22]

This text, rich with preconscious and unconscious meaning, is a caricature of an Oedipal fantasy, in which a young man murders his father and has intercourse with his mother. Since the artist was aware of his conscious role in its construction, the unconscious content is more likely to be found in insignificant details.

The players in this Freudian fantasy seem to be Giacometti family members: Alberto as the pale and terrified seventeen-year-old, the age at which orchitis compromised his adult sexual life; Giovanni as the armored man with "something which shone like gold," referring probably to his bright red-gold hair; Annetta, all in black, is stone-faced and thirty-two years old, her exact age at the birth of her daughter. Finally, the daughter appears in floating white veils, presumably a reference to virginal purity. But the white veils could also refer to the swaddling clothes Ottilia was wrapped in as a newborn. That Alberto dated the beginning of his need for a falling asleep fantasy to his fourth year again underscores the likelihood that he was traumatized by ob-serving his sister's birth.

Giacometti's fantasies were probably reinforced later during adolescence in the stimulating proximity of his sister. Like most boys with sisters close in age, Giacometti had to suppress his erotic feelings for Ottilia to maintain emotional equilibrium. They were nevertheless present and are part of the mixture of conflicting feeling underlying all his relations with women. As dis-cussed earlier, the awkward balance of allure and repulsion experienced by most adolescent siblings was compounded by Alberto and Ottilia's sharing space as nudes in their father's canvases. That complicated mix of emotions he felt for his mother and sister spilled over to young women in his age group, for example, his cousin Bianca in Rome. The young man's fear and fantasies were further complicated by his adolescent illness. By taking away (or reducing) the possibility of becoming a father like his father and grand-father, orchitis removed a motivation that might have helped the young man overcome the psychologically based inhibitions of his impotence.

Throughout his life women found Giacometti attractive—his witty con-versations, sensitivity, mordant humor, attractive physique, and expressive face gave him a compelling charm. After the failure of Giacometti's much-publicized attempt to develop a mutually satisfying loving relationship with a woman his own age and status (probably the culmination of many previous attempts), he split all womankind into two.[23] Women could either be ideal-ized, untouchable figures with whom he could have intellectual exchanges on the model of his mother; or they could be subordinates whom he could dom-inate like the prostitutes he began to frequent in Rome at the start of his adult sexual life. But he kept his distance from the women who might be his equal but who were known for their libidinal appetites.

The Madonna-whore dichotomy is not an uncommon pattern and is found frequently in Mediterranean and Latin cultures. Mothers can attain and keep their saintly status when their sons are small and weak. In the presence of such Madonna-goddesses, men can only adore from a distance and be obedi-ent acolytes—well behaved and nonsexual. With whores, such men can relax, show their imperfect selves with both sexual and aggressive feelings. By di-viding women into two distinct types they avoid the inevitable challenge of adulthood—loving and disliking the same person and learning to tolerate the ebb and flow of shifting feelings. In Giacometti's case, seeing women as either Madonna or whore allowed him to avoid confronting his aggres-sion toward his ambivalently loved mother. Though Giacometti loved her for her many strengths and what she could give him, he also feared her toughness and was dismayed by her toughmindedness. The divided mixture of love, fear, and dismay bound him more tightly to her than anything else could have, and, after 1933, he maintained such close contact with her that his Parisian friends saw him as having a serious "mother problem."[24]

Because he held hard to his idealized view of her, Giacometti was mostly unaware of how much anger he could feel toward his mother—anger going back at least to his earliest years when she had been the family disciplinarian, the tough parent who frustrated and limited. To master his negative feelings toward her and to protect her from his criticism or rage, he idealized her. When that failed, his anger and disappointment would emerge in disguise. Consider how, in relationship with Bianca, Giacometti held her captive as his model, as he was unable to hold her physically close to him.

His anger toward women was at the heart of his problems with intimacy and impotence. If he got close to an available lovable woman with whom he could communicate he would feel trapped. The trap consisted largely of confronting his hostile feelings toward women in general. He must have felt that he would irreparably damage or be damaged by any woman with whom he had intimate contact for too long. Women who could be "touched," whom he could dominate without guilt, were not familiar, they were at the opposite end of the social spectrum—prostitutes. Even with them he was not free to fully enjoy himself emotionally but he could dominate them without guilt or shame.

In an interview with Pierre Schneider, Giacometti described his first experience with a prostitute, revealing the necessary limits for intimacy. "Prostitutes are goddesses; the ultimate in womanhood. I took one home, in Rome, when I was adolescent, to draw her. Then I slept with her. I literally exploded with enthusiasm. I shouted, It's cold! It's mechanical."[25] Prostitutes and goddesses are not mere women, they are the "ultimate"—the end—anonymous and far away from ordinary mortals. With them, a man cannot be close. Coldly and mechanically he could get a prostitute to service him and bring him physical release without having to touch her at all and barely having to be touched by her.[26] There was no risk of messy merging; no danger of entangled feelings or bodies blurring together. They would challenge him neither to perform beyond his capacities nor to reach toward intimacy and tenderness. "Whores are the most honest girls; they present the bill right away. The others hang on and never let you go. When one lives with problems of impotence, the prostitute is ideal. You pay, and whether or not you fail is of no importance. She doesn't care."[27]

Many features of Giacometti's emotional makeup are consonant with a homosexual orientation—his impotence and difficulties sustaining sexual intimacy or closeness with women, his sadistic fantasies and treatment of women, and especially his ready emotional intimacy with men. Yet Giacometti seems not to have acted upon whatever homosexual feelings he felt. Despite considerable efforts to paint a portrait of the artist as a would-be homosexual—an exercise which offended some of the artist's friends—Lord came up short. The artist could tell his biographer of only one near-event when he had felt tempted to respond to the advances of a young male prostitute late at night in Paris, but retreated into a taxi at the last moment.[28] As much as Giacometti's complicated closeness and identification with his father drew him toward homosexuality, it also kept him away from it.

One of Giacometti's core conflicts was between the lure of the visual and the tactile senses. Sometimes when he turned toward one and away from the other he felt safe. At other times he felt deprived. The conflict necessarily affected his relationships with women as well as his art. The artist's early experiences consigned him primarily to an asexual life or perverse sexuality in which he remained true to the most positively colored sensual experience of his childhood—posing for his father and being penetrated by his gaze. For Giacometti, looking was exciting and frightening. During adolescence his family teased him about his odd form of sexual expression. Whenever he was infatuated with a girl he would sit and stare at her, causing inevitable embarrassment.[29] The displacement of erotic excitement to voyeuristic behavior continued, and gazing became his profoundest way of knowing women, frequently replacing genital sexuality. In the early 1920s, Giacometti became known in Paris for standing immobile, arms held stiffly at his sides and fists clenched, staring with hallucinatory intensity at women. In his late twenties he had an affair with a prostitute whom he shared with another one of her regular customers. In his fifties he encouraged his wife to make sketches of her experiences during her extramarital affairs, which he condoned and even fostered.[30] Even into his sixties during his prolonged liaison with Caroline, a Parisian prostitute, it was widely known that he enjoyed hearing detailed descriptions of her work as well as occasionally watching her at it.[31]

Giacometti's relationship to the sense of touch was equally ambivalent. That he was sensitive in the minutest degree to the tips of his fingers is evident from early drawings and sculpture, where the exquisite tactility of line invites us to experience the pleasures of the surface. That he fought against the sweetness of touch is clearly visible in his postwar work, the surfaces of which he constantly violated, leaving them pocked and shattered so that we cannot imagine touching them with pleasure.

Giacometti's preference for the visual mode is central to his perceptual difficulties. In part, looking and seeing became erotized, because of his childhood experience modeling for his father. This was not balanced by a reservoir of experiences with a loving, touching mother, a woman comfortable with caressing. Indeed, as we have seen, Giacometti's legacy from his mother was a general unease about emotional closeness and physical intimacy. We recall his memory of the "hostile, threatening" black rock, which "one hand barely touched with repulsion and fright."

Touch that pleased and was pleasing was evidently very difficult for both mother and son. Remarkably absent from almost all the known photographs of Giacometti is any instance showing him touching—warmly grasping another human being. He is shown touching himself, holding his head in his hands or his hand on his knee, or clasping his hands together. Other people—the women in his life—might touch him, but we rarely see him reaching out to them. However tightly Annetta held on mentally and emotionally, the physical distance she maintained between herself and her children was repeated in the life and art of her son Alberto. We can surmise that his mother's discomfort with touch, combined with the ambivalence he felt toward his father's readiness to touch, severely limited Giacometti's ability to take pleasure in the pleasures of his own body (sex, swimming, dancing, etc).

Giacometti's uneasiness with touching could also help explain his artistic preferences—Byzantine, Chaldean, Egyptian, even Cimabue. Rarely do pre-Renaissance mothers hold or touch their children with affectionate caresses. They are too spiritual or regal for such humble tasks. Giacometti had not been well held as an infant or young boy, and it might have been too painful to see hands holding children with loving gestures.

Diego had been at loose ends since he left Schiers in 1919. He had tried various vocations, none of which fit—office work, factory work, sales, and daring and dangerous illicit activities, such as smuggling. His parents urged him to go to Paris, perhaps recognizing that the two brothers needed each other. In 1925 the Giacometti brothers moved to rue Froixdevaux and took a studio so small that Diego had to use the closet as his bedroom. Alberto's role was to protect his slightly delinquent younger brother.

But shortly after the move the relationship gradually began to shift, and by the 1930s it was Diego who served as caretaker, watchdog, and helpmeet, a mothering role that henceforth remained unchanged. Lacking his brother's wide-roving imagination, Diego learned to use his hands and did for Alberto what most artists have to do for themselves or hire out. Giacometti's relationship to his younger brother Diego has been the subject of speculation, their closeness often idealized or partially understood. Essential to their bond was Diego's unswerving loyalty and a total ban on criticism of Alberto's work.

The three years preceding Diego's move to Paris generally represent the only time that the two brothers voluntarily lived apart. Lost on their own, they were synergistically brilliant together. Once the brothers were reunited in Paris, Giacometti began drawing and sculpting Diego—an experience that had emotional meaning far beyond the success or failure of the resulting artwork. At first it could have transported them both back to the years of posing for their father, which bound them together for life. Diego knew how easily Alberto could panic when he lost sight of someone he needed and loved. He had calmed his brother before by describing his father in concrete terms when Alberto lost the memory image he needed for equanimity. Diego could and did take the punishment involved in prolonged posing, as he knew intuitively what it meant when his brother said he couldn't really see him unless he did more work on a portrait. He could also tolerate his brother's volatile emotional outbursts. Perhaps Diego's presence was enough to ground Alberto and free him to do original work, as none is evident before his brother's arrival.

Giacometti's first Parisian love affair also did not, perhaps could not, begin until Diego was present to anchor him. Paris was a hotbed of sexual freedom during the wild 1920s, but Giacometti's inhibitions kept him largely on the sidelines. He used his impotence, which he declared to all and sundry in Paris to rationalize his disinterest in romantic attachments.[32] When the talk at the cafés turned to amatory conquests, he could escape the rivalry by claiming an exemption. Diego's arrival and Flora Mayo changed that. Flora, an attractive young American heiress, joined the other students in Bourdelle's studio in April 1925. Their initial affectionate encounter, as later reported by Flora, is instructive: "When I didn't show up [in class] . . . Alberto came to see me. I was sick in bed. He sat at the foot of the bed and looked at me with such compassion and love, that I held out my arms and he fell into them. There was nothing wrong or lustful about that embrace. We just held each other as if we never wanted to let each other go—ever."[33]

The young couple held hands, went to the Louvre and strolled through the parks of Paris. Their affair lasted several years and was Giacometti's first sustained, intimate liaison with a woman. Retrospectively, Flora acknowledged that her predominant feeling at the time was the "horror of being alone."[34] Though she probably never spoke about her dependent feelings to Giacometti, he would have sensed them and was simultaneously attracted and repulsed. Far back in his emotional history was the template for such a relationship: when he loved he wanted to be very close to—and even merged with—the person he loved, and when that closeness became too overwhelming he had to make a rapid retreat.

Frequent impotence plagued the young artist, and he would not spend the night with his lover. Eventually, his difficulties with the intimate aspects of the relationship led him to begin to avoid Flora. She, in turn, exacerbated his fear of suffocation with her increasingly frantic attempts to hold onto him.[35] She moved into the same ramshackle complex of studios at Hipolyte-Maindron where he had moved, and she posed for a portrait. Finally, when she turned to another man as a means of reigniting the flame with Alberto, Giacometti—who regularly frequented prostitutes—became enraged at her infidelity and ended the relationship. During Giacometti's relationship with Flora, his fantasies about the sexual nature of men and women and the ways they could or should relate to each other took the form of Cubist and primitive sculpture.

SCULPTURE—1925–1929

Woman eats son, son sucks woman, man penetrates woman,
woman swallows man, on the same level. (c. 1932)—A. Giacometti[36]

In summer 1925, while painting a portrait of his mother, Giacometti allegedly experienced a crisis and gave up representational painting. He later wrote that he "became convinced of the total impossibility of conveying even an approximation of the impression I had of a head, and I gave up the effort, I thought, forever."[37] Many factors could have made him want to turn from the realistic style of his father's art at that moment. His mother's frowning face was one, and the death of his uncle Otto on October 11, 1925, the day after Giacometti's birthday, may have been an additional spur. If Giovanni's youngest brother could die, so could Giovanni. Giacometti had to move forward, and he threw himself into modernity.

In the 1910s and early 1920s European artists were looking for new ways to portray fundamental truths about men and women. Following the lead of innovative sculptors like Brancuși, Laurens, and Lipschitz, Giacometti studied artifacts from archaic Greece, the Cyclades, Africa, Pre-Columbian Mexico, and Polynesia, which gave him access to the themes that would fascinate him for the rest of his life—the female body and genitalia.[38]

By the mid 1920s Giacometti was friendly with a group of Italian and Swiss-Italian artists who exhibited together. His closest friend among these young men was Massimo Campigli, whose studio was around the corner from the Giacometti brothers.[39] Campigli was a painter from Rome with a taste for Etruscan and prehistoric art. Fascinated by Cro-Magnon skulls, dolmens, and the prehistoric cult of the sun and wheel, Campigli enjoyed imagining himself as the artist-magician of prehistory: "I constantly have the illusion of an atavistic memory. I sense the caveman in myself, the horse thief, the slave, the magician."[40]

By allying with Italians—and the Mediterranean cultures worshipping the female goddesses Isis, Ishtar, Astarte, Cybele—Giacometti took another subtle step away from his father, who had made his career with the German-speaking Expressionists and whose friendship with Kirchner was in full swing. Since 1913 Giacometti had found answers to insoluble riddles in non-Western cultures, and his impulse in a crisis was to pull away from home ground for inspiration. He wanted to understand the first fertility figures and the first upright men in history. Egypt could not supply those answers; he needed an earlier antecedent.

While Giacometti's first works of 1926–27, *The Couple*, *Little Man*, *Spoon Woman*, *Figure*, and *Dancers*, seem blatantly derivative of African and Mexican styles, they actually stem from prehistoric art, which was much closer to him both culturally and emotionally.[41] Prehistoric art was the most fundamental source in the mix out of which Giacometti's first figurative sculptures evolved. Its frontality, its essential focus on sex and gender, its connection with death and immortality, and its mysterious and magical purposes are unmistakable influences on Giacometti in his most formative moment as a sculptor.

The Bregaglia valley has many prehistoric remains—mostly cupules, concave shapes carved in stone—familiar to every child of the region. Proud of their ancient heritage, natives cite the origins of civilized activity dating back to the Stone Age.[42] Fairly soon after his arrival in Paris, Giacometti began to explore the artifacts of prehistory that were easily available in nearby museums, such as the Musée des antiquités nationales in Saint-Germain-en-Laye just outside Paris.[43] Salomon Reinach, an expert in prehistory and a prolific writer, was director of the museum, and with each new discovery in the field he had a cast made for the museum, enabling Parisian artists to be as current about recent archaeological finds as any scholar. By 1922, Reinach had put on display the originals or plaster casts of all the major known prehistoric engravings and sculpture in Europe, numbering nearly one hundred fifty objects.

The frank, emphatic treatment of male and female sexual attributes in prehistoric art fascinated scholars beginning in the late 1900s. Some argued that the huge breasts, buttocks, and thighs were symbols of pleasing physiological characteristics. An alternate theory held that these prehistoric Venuses served magical purposes as fertility figures. The tireless Reinach made the case constantly, and ultimately persuasively, on the side of magic. "This art is not like art for civilized people, a luxury or a game, it is the expression of a very crude but intense religion made of magical practices."[44]

It took several generations of prehistorians to conclude that many of the marks painted on cave walls and etched into sculptures were schemata for male and female genitalia and were related to rites or beliefs about fertility (fig. 4.4).[45] Males were frequently symbolized by three or four parallel lines or arrows, often oriented diagonally, while triangular or slightly rounded rectangular shapes with a midline crevice symbolized females. As we shall see, Giacometti's sculptures of the mid 1920s, especially his flat plaques of 1927 and 1928, show that he was familiar with the ancient schemata and had deciphered their meaning. Eight drawings titled *Woman*, provisionally dated 1926 (probably studies for a sculpture of the period), reveal how obsessed the young artist was with female genitalia, as each progressively emphasized the woman's sexual parts until they were reduced to coded schemata.

Giacometti launched himself as a sculptor in Paris depicting three genders —male, female, and androgynous. *Torso* (1925) (Alberto Giacometti-Stiftung) combines the Cubist idiom with a touch of prehistory. The cross-hatched triangular crotch comes from the Badarian culture of 4000 B.C. and has been impressed onto a revision of Brancuşi's *Torso of a Young Man* (1922). The young sculptor turned Brancuşi's remarkably condensed masculine symbol into a subtly curvaceous female who still retains an upthrusting phallic character.[46] In a drawn version, Giacometti eliminated the arm—itself a phallic object—

Male

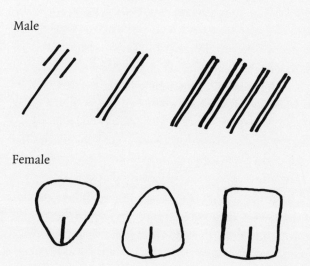

Female

FIGURE 4.4
Schemata for prehistoric depictions of gender.

FIGURE 4.5 *Anonymous,*
Menhir, Neolithic.
Limestone. Musée des
antiquités nationales,
Saint-Germain-en-Laye.

and added a mysterious projection near the top of the torso's torso. Where there was a breast, now only a suggestive rectangular projection with a concave surface remains. In one cast of the sculpture, the shape is split by a horizontal indentation that makes it look like a mouth. *Torso* is the first of Giacometti's masculine women.

Little Crouching Figure of 1926 (Alberto Giacometti-Stiftung) pays homage to both Brancuşi and prehistoric art. Its rough-hewn blockiness echoes Brancuşi's *Wisdom* (1908) and *The Kiss* (1908). The upright neolithic stone slabs, called *menhirs* in France, have mysterious markings, and their gender is often unclear. In the 1920s they were understood to be receptacles for disembodied souls. Giacometti saw many examples like the *Female Menhir* (fig. 4.5) at the Musée des antiquités nationales, and their rounded rectangular or ovoid shapes resemble the overall outline of *Little Crouching Figure.* Giacometti's innovation was to make his Ur-figure sexually ambiguous, containing in itself both male and female, too young and small to have decided what it will become. A breast is visible on the sculpture's right. The ears are not quite human, and its necklessness also suggests a prehumanoid state closer to the neolithic works from which it derives. With its parts merged, it has been flattened and pockmarked, yet the subtle interplay of diagonals, verticals, and horizontals, along with the lively surface, produce a dynamic effect. Around the same time, the artist sketched an androgynous figure resembling the *Female Menhir* in preparation for a sculpture (fig. 4.6).

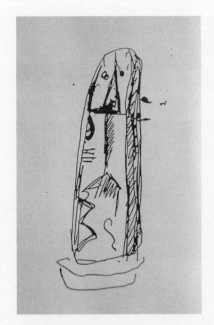

FIGURE 4.6 *Alberto Giacometti, Androgynous Figure, n.d. Ink on paper (lost), dimensions unknown.*

Giacometti turned next toward Africa. Three works, all from 1926, should be considered together as answers to his questions about masculinity and femininity—*Little Man, Woman* (fig. 4.7), and *The Couple. Little Man* is no longer extant, but drawings of it appear in Giacometti's studio drawings from 1932 (Öffentliche Kunstsammlung Basel, Kupferstickabinett) and in the lists of his early work he made for Pierre Matisse in 1947. Both the title and the figure's squat stance suggest juvenilia, especially when it is placed alongside the taller, more imposing *Woman*. Its fundamental maleness is symbolized by the jutting, penis-like nose, which dominates the rectangular plaque on legs. Another visible influence on *The Little Man* is a Bakota figure lent or sold to Giacometti by his artist friend Serge Brignoni, in which the open lozenge was the figure's body.[47]

Woman (1926), also not extant, is more complex and mysterious. She holds a vagina-shaped shield that could be either her actual body, her means of protection, or a threat to the man. She is faceless and breastless, unfamiliar and unnurturing. Instead of eyes and breasts she has hollow spaces that pierce the upper reaches of her shield. What does the lozenge at her center mean? Is it a baby within her womb or a phallus within her body? Is it the fantasy of a wide-eyed boy staring at a large woman with frightening genitals? The sculpture's shape and central position recall the neolithic *Venus of Laussel*, which Giacometti copied a few years later.

FIGURE 4.7
Alberto Giacometti, Woman,
1926. Plaster (destroyed),
dimensions unknown.

In *The Couple* Giacometti evokes the puzzled perplexity and astonishment of a man discovering the anatomical differences between man and woman (fig. 4.8). Though relatively small—the man is less than two feet tall—the figures are monumental in their static statuesqueness. He rises up, growing wider as he reaches his full height from which he can gaze upon the world with a single staring eye. The roughness of the surface and the slight crudeness of the features on both figures convey their archaic and primitive nature. The sexual ambiguity of this work is evident in the vagina-shaped lozenge that serves the woman as her entire being and the man as his eye—that receptive organ both father and son used to absorb the world.

Unlike *Little Man*, the big man of *The Couple* extends himself into the world through his arm, his ear, *and* his penis. His right hand, made up of three or four phallic fingers on a diagonal, is actually Giacometti's secret code symbolizing the essence of masculinity. As we observed earlier, the code derives from prehistoric art where the schemata invariably indicated maleness. Here, the hand precisely targets the woman's vagina. It is not the last instance in which a male lance is aimed toward a female opening in Giacometti's art. That symbolic combination suggests that, for Giacometti, hands might have to do the work of the penis, especially when the vagina has a large and formidable shape. In *The Couple* the female partner is self-contained and stands on her own small feet, an attribute lost to the man. She is mostly a mouth, her

FIGURE 4.8 *Marc Vaux photograph of* The Couple, *1926, plaster (destroyed).*

face and body merged. Giacometti's subtle asymmetries—the right breast and hand a little higher than left—add to her dynamism. *The Couple* is a brilliant synthesis of contemporary sculptural currents and a metaphor for the artist's confusion about the sexual beings surrounding him.

In *Dancers* of 1926–27 (Musée national d'art moderne), the sculpted man and woman are locked apart on a small platform, leaning away from each other, neither embracing nor dancing together. The male is a cone that pulls away from the female, projecting his sexual parts at too high a level for penetration. The female is concave, a partial cylinder, her arms reaching out but not enfolding. She is now the small one, vulnerable and squat in her proportions. Like her male partner, she leans away from direct contact, and both are immobilized in fixed positions.

Dancing was an inherently sexual activity for Giacometti, and in adolescence he would select a girl for an evening and then send his younger brother Bruno to the dance floor as her partner while he stared at her from the sidelines, fuming with wrathful jealousy if someone attempted to cut in.[48] Given Giacometti's discomfort with dancing, it is doubly striking that he revealed his view of coupling so openly through that theme.

SPOON WOMAN

Spoon Woman of 1927 is Giacometti's first acknowledged masterpiece (fig. 4.9). Made soon after The Dancers, it was originally called Large Woman, 1926–27.[49] The figure, including its simple columnar base, is only fifty-seven inches high, yet it appears larger, its monumentality enhanced by the transfixing concavity of the bowl. With an admirable economy of means Giacometti produced an almost abstract figure that is legible as human, female, and ambiguously hovering between large-headedness and tiny-headedness—an entrancing work of apparent simplicity that can be understood in a bewildering variety of ways.

The calmly hieratic Spoon Woman confronts the viewer directly with her oval emptiness. Seen head on, the sculpture is a carefully balanced play between curvilinear and angular shapes. At the top a lunar crescent shape echoes the enormous spoon bowl, much worked and alive with traces of the sculptor's tools, and is separated from the bowl by a subtle sequence of wedges and horizontal accents. In profile, the figure is unstable in her seat, threatening to slip off at any moment.

The original plaster contains two features absent from the final version: knobs on either side of the wedge shape above the large concavity and a small ridge crowning the figure's "topknot." The removal of these details drastically changes the way the work can be read. In the original, the medium-sized wedge represents a torso, and the knobs read as arms. Likewise the topknot becomes the figure's small head and the ridge becomes a topknot. Without these features, the figure is reduced to an armless torso with a larger head, and

FIGURE 4.9 *Marc Vaux photograph of* Spoon Woman, *c. 1926–27, plaster (destroyed).*

the viewer's eye is led directly to the bowl of the spoon, beginning just below the horizontally ringed neck. In a misdated sketch of 1947 Giacometti gave eyes to the topknot and thereby privileged the former reading of a small-headed, big-busted, wasp-waisted woman with a waiting womb—an empty vessel.[50]

Like many of his works of this period, *Spoon Woman* is usually placed in the context of the enthusiasm for tribal art in the Parisian art world of the 1920s. Grain spoons from the Dan tribe on the Ivory Coast, prehistoric Venuses, and Cycladic fertility idols are cited as formal and iconographic models for the young, ambitious sculptor from the Swiss provinces. These sources give weight to the interpretation of *Spoon Woman* as a modern fertility goddess, imperiously near yet inaccessible.[51] Other exotic sources have unaccountably not been mentioned—for example, the charming Egyptian spoon women on permanent display at the Louvre and the anthropomorphically shaped spoons from Giacometti's native canton in Switzerland, displayed in the local and regional Swiss museums, as well as in the Musée de l'homme. But despite an extensive search for this work's formal sources in tribal and archaic art, a central question remains unanswered: Why did the twenty-five-year-old artist conflate the forms of a woman and a spoon?

Students of the human mind from Freud to Proust have observed the stimulating power of early memories—those composites of present and past experiences containing cogent truths.[52] Less has been said about the multiple revisions and creative reconstructions that such memories undergo in an artist's hands. I hypothesize that *Spoon Woman* is Giacometti's creative reconstruction of an intimately personal memory. To celebrate Alberto's birth, Cuno Amiet sent his godson a silver spoon with a letter for the baby. "To my dearest godchild, Alberto, I send you something so that whatever you eat with it may do you good . . . you should use this daily and when you do, you should remember that your godfather will loyally stand by you in case of need. Take a real good swallow and know that nothing would make me happier than to be with you."[53]

During every childhood Christmas holiday season, another spoon arrived for Alberto, thus loading this everyday object with emotional significance. Amiet and the young Giacometti were inextricably linked, not only by their godparent relationship but also by personal similarities.[54] Like Amiet, Giacometti was both a painter and sculptor. Another point of kinship was more emotionally laden—because of his inability to father a child Giacometti was like the Amiets. Though he later claimed that he never wanted children, Giacometti nevertheless made many works between the late 1920s and mid 1930s with woman as a filled or empty vessel. The relation of this subject matter to Giacometti's personal life seems inescapable.[55]

GAZING AT THE GAZER

Giacometti's fascination with female sexuality became more explicit in the series of plaques he made during 1927–28. But before he could carry the theme further he had to tackle his feelings toward both his father and the subject of gazing. In summer 1927 Giacometti returned to his family at Maloja, making six heads of his father and one of his mother. Though he had drawn his mother many times, there are few known earlier portraits of his father. The first head, *Portrait of the Artist's Father*, with its expressive and faithful rendering, showed the mastery Giacometti achieved during five years of study at Bourdelle's. This was followed by a portrait carved in red granite, a native Alpine stone matching Giovanni's colorful hair and combining the African and Oceanic influences popular when Giovanni was part of the avant-garde twenty years earlier.[56]

The two bronzes that came next (both in the Albert Giacometti-Stiftung) are more original. The more conventional of the two has a jaunty air, combining the surface touch of Rodin with Cézannesque attention to planes and composition. Its subtle surface, recalling *Spoon Woman*, and the wedge-shaped nose and triangular face from several recent portraits (such as that of Joseph Mueller) are brought together here, better integrated with dynamic asymmetries and diagonal axes. Giacometti's formal inventiveness is most visible from the side and three-quarter views, where the indented mouth and beard are unexpected.

The second bronze portrait has a flat face, the features incised rather than modeled. It is close to caricature, with eye sockets, round like glasses, containing crudely carved shapes—the left eye merely a hole and the right a deeply cut line. The artist's aggressive elimination is compelling. Giacometti has flattened his father artistically, and the result is a masterpiece of portraiture. It is gentle Giovanni to a tee, unrecognizable from a distance or in profile but, up close, the man himself. (With its tantalizing combination of presence and absence it is prophetic of Giacometti's late dark portraits of his brother Diego.)

Last of the series of paternal portraits is an almost undecipherable marble abstraction. Brancuşi-like in its pared-down simplicity, it retains the triangular face, a bare hint of features, and the collarlike base of the two previous works. Some scholars believe it to be an unfinished work, abandoned because Giacometti's debt to Brancuşi was too obvious. Giacometti's father probably did not understand the deeper meanings of his son's portraits, but by the end of the series he might have guessed that Alberto was going beyond the confines of the valley. Perhaps he also knew that his willingness to pose for a series of portraits by his son could be profoundly helpful, but Giovanni couldn't have known that this would lead to a quantum leap in the quality of Alberto's work.

If the 1927 portraits were the son's first artistic response to decades of posing for his father and receiving his "gaze," *Gazing Head* of 1927–28, which immediately follows Giacometti's portraits of his father, is the second—a stylistically remarkable work that established the young sculptor as an artist of note and gained him entrée into the surrealist circle (fig. 4.10, back-left).[57] A simple rectangle with slightly curving sides sits on a neck facing us frontally. A large, oblong vertical crevice marks the juncture of neck and head, and a shorter horizontal indentation placed higher on the plaque is an unmistakable ocular cavity. The crevices make *Gazing Head* unique and separate it from its archaic sources. The indentations evoke the artist's passive longings and could be read as signs of Giacometti's feminine self. In his works of the mid twenties Giacometti equated eye with breast and often used the eye as a symbolic equivalent for the vagina.[58] Making an eye into a "feminine" cavity symbolically expressed some of Giacometti's fantasies. He had been penetrated and was penetrable. Nothing else need be added to the sculpture.

The plaques that followed *Gazing Head* were almost all female, and their subdued elegance has inspired most viewers to see them as cool echoes of Cycladic marble idols and neolithic Egyptian cosmetic palettes.[59] What has been missed is their origin in the bulging vulvae and schematic scratching of the prehistoric and archaic fertility figures Giacometti had seen at the Musée de l'homme and Musée des antiquités nationales.[60] *Woman* of 1927–28 is similar in overall shape to *Gazing Head*; it sits on stubby columnar legs but lacks the careful modulation of the earlier work (fig. 4.11). On the upper left is a conflation of three body parts in the form of a convex eye-head-breast. Below and on the left, four parallel diagonal lines approach a bulging, partially split rectangular shape that resembles the prehistoric schemata representing female genitals (see fig. 4.4).

Another version of this theme is represented in *Woman* of 1928, which was photographed in the artist's studio in 1929 (see fig. 4.10, front-right). The vulva is now pressed into what will become Giacometti's standard symbol for the woman's belly or womb—a large, shallow, rounded concavity at about the position of the stomach. A third *Woman* (1928–29) is the artist's most sophisticated version of the theme (fig. 4.12). It has a predominantly triangular shape apart from the base, and its internal indentations proceed logically from the squat two-legged *Woman* of 1927–28, in which the vulva appears in its crudest form. Here, both head and belly are gentle concavities, and the vulva, now elongated and almost leglike, is less-easily identified as prehis-

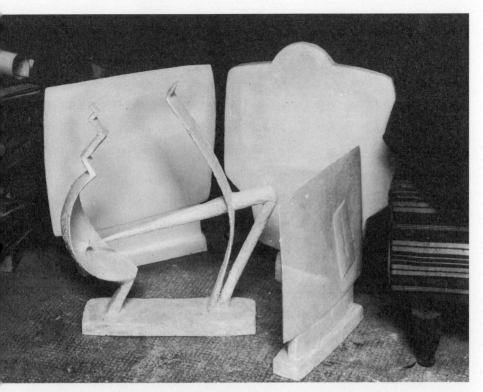

FIGURE 4.10 *Marc Vaux photograph of* Gazing Head *(back-left) (1927–28), plaster (destroyed). Also shown are* Man *(back-right),* Man and Woman *(front-left), and* Woman *(front-right).*

torically based genitalia. By the time he arrived at the triangular format, Giacometti had developed formal and iconographic subtlety and a canny way of disguising his intentions.

Evidence that he saw the triangular *Woman* as representing the essence of femaleness can be seen in his sketch of the work that accompanies his puzzling prose poem "Man and Woman," dated about 1932. "Woman 32 years old, two children, long black hair, a lock of hair on the forehead, tender blue eyes, infinitely arched forehead and gaping lips, white skin, full and soft belly, the enormous bloody thigh, and the *man shining* with gold suddenly appearing there, not two, but all an eye, and blind, mother, woman, belly."[61]

The poem, so suggestive of a repressed early memory, invites interpretation. It was written in Italian, the language of Giacometti's childhood and the language of the group of Italian artists with whom he was affiliated in 1927–29. In spring 1904, Annetta Giacometti, who had long, dark hair, was

FIGURE 4.11 *Marc Vaux photograph of* Woman, *1927–28, plaster (destroyed).*

thirty-two years old and pregnant, and she had two children. She could easily have had a lock on her forehead that was high and swelling. If Giacometti saw her give birth to his sister, Ottilia, he would have seen "gaping lips," white skin, a huge belly, sweet and full, "an enormous and bloody thigh."[62] His father would have been present with his fiery red hair glittering like gold—an image that reappears in Giacometti's early falling asleep fantasy as does a thirty-two-year-old mother.[63]

An eye is drawn. It is less and more than normal—"not two"—and, finally, it is blind—too much must be absorbed through it. Giacometti's need as a

FIGURE 4.12 *Marc Vaux photograph of* Woman, *1928–29, plaster (destroyed).*

young child to protect himself from a shocking experience must have been intense. Closing his eyes was not sufficient, because the image stays in the mind's eye forever, especially if the seer is a visually sensitive child.[64] The poem ends: "mother, woman, belly." Giacometti's poetic statement eloquently evokes the traumatic and visually arresting experience of watching his sister's birth—an event he would artistically rework countless times in an effort to make it less terrifying.

In the first article written on Giacometti, Michel Leiris presciently referred to the works of this period as seeming like the petrification of an inner crisis, moments when outer and inner worlds conjoin, the most important moments of one's life.[65] Giacometti later insisted that he was the passive victim of an inner compulsion when he made the plaques. He had begun them after he stopped working from models at Bourdelle's atelier: "I started with a fully articulated figure. . . . To make it true I had to gradually reduce [it]. . . . (What I actually felt was reduced to a plaque standing in a certain way in space and having only two hollows which were . . . the vertical and horizontal aspects found in every figure). . . . I started two or three different pieces and they always got to the same point. [The plaque] seemed to resemble things and myself . . . a mixture from which one never escapes."[66]

Such vivid recollections occurring more than twenty years later suggest the emotional force fueling the creation of the plaques, whose subject matter was both the seer and the seen object—the "mixture" from which Giacometti never escaped. The intimate formal and iconographic relationship of *Gazing Head* to the plaque women shows how close the seer and the seen had moved in the evolution of Giacometti's art.[67]

The artist's rage toward women, which would soon erupt in works of consummate cruelty during his surrealist period, was still under wraps. But we can better understand these later images by seeing the experiments of 1927–29 as foundational. Searching for magical essences before he joined the surrealists, Giacometti found himself face to face with several insoluble problems. He could neither enter the door that women held open to him nor fill their concavities. Nor could he conceive of union between man and woman as anything but dangerous and painful. Women must therefore serve some other purpose—but what was it? In the course of the next five years he found some answers as he moved forward toward the myths and images which were to inspire him until his death.

CHAPTER 5

1929-1933

ONE OF THE BOYS: SURREALIST SPLENDOR

By June 1929, when he exhibited his work at an important gallery in Paris, Giacometti had "arrived"; the avant-garde now recognized him as an exceptional sculptor. Many of his friends and, later, scholars of his work believed that the desires, conflicts, and crises of his early years were "petrified" in the sculpture of this period, even though specific connections between biographical events and later sculptural transformations are difficult to construct.

Not so with a work from 1932, *Caught Hand*, a sculpture of a wooden mannequin's hand set in a metal cage with mechanical gears and pulleys. As a result of James Lord's persistent research, we can now connect the genesis of this sculpture to the childhood incident in which the cogs of a threshing machine crushed Diego's hand.[1] During his lifetime Alberto Giacometti never revealed the key biographical sources of his work, nor did he acknowledge to anyone except his closest fellow seekers his secret belief in alchemy and magic, which underlay many of his important surrealist works. Giacometti had been superstitious and susceptible to tales of the occult throughout his youth. He had heard the family stories about his grandmother Ottilia's "magnetic powers" to perform feats such as lifting a heavy walnut table using only her fingers, and about an aunt who could move tables without touching them.[2] At the same time, he was no fool and knew that people whose opinions he valued and whose support he needed might discredit him as a serious artist if they thought he believed in magic or mystical philosophical doctrines.[3] Then as now, surrealist interest in the occult usually engenders suspicion, scorn, and skepticism.[4]

With Giacometti's genius for synthesizing disparate elements, scholars understandably have largely missed his alchemical inclinations. There is so much else to find in his surrealist "objects," and it is easy to be distracted by juicy sexual references or hints about dreams and childhood memories. Not surprisingly, the artist's successful efforts to hide his interest in the occult have been perpetuated by the critical and scholarly distaste for far-out approaches and literature often linked to it.[5] Only vague, occasional references to cosmic meanings have been made to Giacometti's surrealist works. But close study suggests that his interest in the occult was both more specific and pervasive.[6]

WHY SURREALISM

Surrealism had multiple attractions for Giacometti: by the late 1920s it had become the most exciting game in town, and the major participants had considerable personal magnetism. But more important, the movement's ideas and goals perfectly suited his personal needs when he joined the group in the spring of 1929. Like his father, Giacometti was always alert to contemporary currents in the art world. By the time the surrealists and their antics surfaced in 1924, his French was good enough to enable him to grasp the movement's elliptical messages, and his curiosity led him both to read the periodicals and manifestoes of its leading proponents and visit its exhibitions.

The principles espoused in the *First Manifesto of Surrealism* (1924) by André Breton, the founder of the surrealist movement as well as its leading theorist, poet, and publicist, resonated with Giacometti's own beliefs and inclinations. Among these were freedom; imagination; the profound messages of dreams and memories; appeal of the unusual; chance; access to the inner life and the unconscious through a passive, receptive state of mind; the conjunction of opposites to arrive at new truths; the acknowledgment that childhood "comes closest to one's 'real life'"; risk-free possession of oneself; and the joy of non-conformism.

World War I had brought unimaginable horrors to Europe. The subsequent rebellion against the establishment was mixed with despair about the futility of the values that had led western civilization to massacre the flower of its youth. Like the Dadaists before them, the surrealists turned against all agents of organized society: family, country, religion.[7] Breton, in particular, wanted a clean sweep of all previous means of understanding how the mind apprehended reality, and he defined surrealism as a philosophy "based on the belief in the superior reality of certain forms of previously neglected associations, in the omnipotence of dream, in the disinterested play of thought. It tends to ruin once and for all other psychic mechanisms and to substitute itself for them in solving all the principal problems of life."[8]

Breton had learned about Freud in 1916 when he was an intern in neurology.[9] Immediately enthusiastic, he tried some psychoanalytic techniques, namely free association and dream analysis, while working with shell-shocked veterans. He studied Freud's works as they were published in French during the twenties; he also met and corresponded with Freud.[10] Respecting Freud's discoveries, especially those about the unconscious and sexuality, Breton attempted to go beyond the medicalization of psychoanalysis and turned those discoveries to his own complex purposes—the revitalization of society and art—a mission he shared with Max Ernst as early as 1923.

Since the 1880s, Freud had been writing about the importance of sexuality, not only as an erotic act but as a driving force in human experience. Breton transmuted Freud's observations about sexuality into a passion for love—free love, mad love. Moreover, fascinated with the idea of the unconscious, he invented the term *psychic automatism*, his version of Freudian free association, and proclaimed it to be the first and best-known method of arriving at "surreality." "Psychic automatism in its pure state, by which one proposes to express—verbally, by means of the written word, or in any other manner—the actual functioning of thought. Dictated by thought, in the absence of any control exercised by reason, exempt from any aesthetic or moral concern."[11] The goal was always to outwit the conscious and logical and to find the place and means to connect conscious and unconscious, inner world and external reality. For surrealists, psychic automatism was but one route to the nonrational; dream analysis, love, and alchemy were others.

Alchemy was part of a long-respectable cultural tradition which included Dürer, Rembrandt, and Mozart. It had been fashionable intermittently among artists and writers in France since 1873, when Arthur Rimbaud wrote his celebrated verse, "Alchemy of the Word," a shorthand reference for artistic transformation. With its focus on the cycle of death and rebirth, alchemy was a way for disillusioned young artists and intellectuals to make sense of the horror of World War I. Giacometti would also have liked alchemy's use of Egyptian imagery for many of its concepts and figures, such as Isis and Osiris as symbols of birth and resurrection. Moreover, Hermes Trismegistus and other important alchemist authors were thought to have been Egyptian.

The main aim of surrealism, as Breton conceived it, was to enrich human life by creating links between the separate realms of macrocosm and microcosm, dream life and waking life, and the inner world of the unconscious and the external world of matter and spirit. In his two manifestoes and his book

Communicating Vessels, Breton emphasized alchemy's power to move man through the passage between the two realms. "I hope [surrealism] will be considered as having tried nothing better than to cast a *conduction wire* between the far too distant worlds of waking and sleep, exterior and interior reality, reason and madness, the assurance of knowledge and of love, of life for life and the revolution, and so on."[12]

"Love, dreams, madness and art" were keys for Breton as they were for Freudians, who found the mysteries of the unconscious closest to the surface in dreams, madness, and art.[13] When Breton proclaimed, "It is incumbent on us . . . to try to see more and more clearly what is transpiring unbeknownst to man in the depths of his mind," he was addressing a matter of interest to both fields—creativity.[14] Freud lay down his arms on the subject; Breton did not.[15] He saw it as precisely the arena in which surrealist poets and artists could give something back to psychoanalysis. He felt that the paramount clinical concerns of psychoanalysts held them back from sufficiently exploring the roots and nature of creativity and sublimation.[16]

For alchemically inclined surrealists, the goal was the spiritual perfection that resulted from engaging in "the work." They were not "puffers," who were foolish alchemists trying to turn base metal into silver and gold with secret chemical formulae. They were "philosophical" alchemists, the alternative tradition aiming at the transformation of man's soul, and through it, the world. "After so many interpretations of the world it is high time to proceed to its transformation."[17] As artists and poets, they knew the power of their art to change themselves, to change their desires and fears, to sublimate or transmute them, as art always has, into something less crude and undigestible. By freeing the unconscious raw material—the base matter lying hidden and detested inside the human heart—surreal acts and art could invigorate life, allowing people to live creatively at the boundary of their own inner and outer worlds.

Alchemy seemed to offer an ideal solution for Breton and his fellow adepts, because, like psychoanalysis, it contained both sex and aggression. The stages of the alchemical process were metaphors of transformation and included dismemberment, sublimation, revivification, putrefaction, purification, amorous coupling, the massacre of children, androgynous unions, and miraculous resurrections. Puffers might see the allegorical metaphors as guides to chemical transformation, but philosophical alchemists would understand them as steps in a maturational process. Because so many rational belief systems were being overturned in the 1920s, the occult did not seem so far-out to the avant-garde, and for many it was like a game.

Alchemy spoke of the many false paths and courage needed to persist in the process of creation. And, as always when men play at godlike games, it had to be secret. Adepts at alchemy had always kept themselves apart from the uninitiated. There had to be hurdles and serious challenges to test the mettle of true seekers. The Bureau de Récherches Surréalistes, familiarly known as the "Centrale," opened in October 1924 as a laboratory for surrealist "research." Having attracted too many sensation seekers, it closed its doors to the public four months later. The work would continue in private.[18]

Breton's *The Second Manifesto of Surrealism*, published in 1929, was the product of a similar exclusionary impulse. "The public must absolutely be kept from entering if we wish to avoid confusion. . . . I demand the profound true occultation of Surrealism," he wrote.[19] Breton was aiming to protect the deeper purpose of the movement—the search for the philosopher's stone. For the puffers, the philosopher's stone was the catalyst which, when added to the alchemical vessel, would permit the transmutation of metal into gold. For the philosophical alchemists, it symbolized the elixir of life, sometimes called the quintessence, and was understood to be the essence of creativity.[20] The metaphor of the alchemical vessel was understood to represent the womb, or the egg, which would bring forth new life.

In 1914, Herbert Silberer, a respected early psychoanalyst from the Vienna circle, wrote *Hidden Symbolism of Alchemy and the Occult Arts* to show that psychoanalysis and alchemy were two parallel ways of symbolically interpreting human behavior and spirit. An expert in symbolism, Silberer explained at length how all psychic and aesthetic experiences can be viewed from a variety of perspectives, none of them mutually exclusive. "The problem of multiple interpretation is quite universal, in the sense that one encounters it everywhere where the imagination is creatively active. So our study opens wide fields, and art and mythology especially appear to invite us."[21] He described three types of interpretation but focused on the first two: "the psychoanalytic, which leads us to the depths of the impulsive life; then the vividly contrasting hermetic religious one," which he called the anagogic.[22] Observing that "the two interpretations externally contradict each other, although each exhibits a faultless finality," Silberer developed a complex theory to explain how two such "antithetic meanings as the psychoanalytic and the anagogic [alchemical] exist side by side."[23] Further, he wrote, "One symbol continually appears as the representative of several ideas and is therefore interpretable in several ways. . . . A product of the imagination harmonizes with several expositions (multiple interpretations) because this variety of sense had already operated in the selection of the symbol."[24] Silberer succeeded in harmonizing the psychoanalytic and anagogic [alchemical] through the concept of sublimation.

> "sublimation"—This Freudian concept is found in an exactly similar signi-
> ficance in the hermetic writers. In the receptacle where the mystical work
> of education is performed, i.e., in man, substances are sublimated; in psy-
> chological terms this means that impulses are to be refined and brought
> from their baseness to a higher level. Freud makes it clear that the libido,
> particularly the unsocial sexual libido, is in favorable circumstances subli-
> mated, i.e., changed into a socially available impelling power. This hap-
> pens in the evolution of the human race and is recapitulated in the educa-
> tion of the individual.[25]

Silberer took "primal tendencies," by which he meant the fundamental human desires described by psychoanalysis (such as the wish to kill the father,
have intercourse with the mother, and the death instinct), and found their
precise parallels in alchemy (killing the old Adam, spiritual regeneration, and
attainment of the ideal). He concluded that all primal tendencies "take place
in each and every one of us, otherwise we should be mere beasts. Only they do
not in every one of us rise to the intensity of the mystical life."[26]

It is likely that Breton and Ernst, along with other alchemically inclined
surrealists that included Yves Tanguy, Juan Miró, Michel Leiris, André Masson, and René Crevel had studied Silberer's book and learned from him how
alchemy and psychoanalysis could be compatible.[27] His book also taught
the surrealists that each individual selects symbols that are most personally
meaningful. "The choice of a symbol is strongly influenced by what im-
presses the mind, what moves the soul, whether joyful or painful . . . whatever touches us nearly, whether consciously or unconsciously."[28] If Giacometti did not actually read Silberer, he learned from his surrealist friends how
to comprehend his own work and life through the types of the intertwined
multiple interpretations Silberer had postulated.

GIACOMETTI AND THE DISSIDENT SURREALISTS 1929–1930

The surrealists were only periodically a cohesive group. Original member-
ship had evolved out of the Dada movement in the early twenties. Breton periodically purged the movement of individuals who had slipped from the standards he set, no matter that the standards were in constant evolution. In
March 1929, yet another schism occurred during a famous meeting at which
Breton attacked some politically incorrect former followers. In December he

denounced an even larger group in *The Second Manifesto of Surrealism*. Prominent in that coterie was Georges Bataille, a librarian and writer who had begun to gather around himself some of the discontented former allies of Breton—Leiris, Masson, and Antonin Artaud.[29] It was this group of dissidents that first recognized the talents of the young Swiss sculptor, who until then had been largely ignored by the Parisian art world.

Leiris and Bataille were rebellious middle-class intellectuals, and in April 1929 they had founded their own journal, *Documents*. The difference between the dissidents and Breton's group soon became evident through the editorial guidance and writings of Bataille, who contributed to most of its issues. Like Breton, he was revolting against mediocrity and western European values, but his emphasis lay on a celebration of baseness and perversion. His articles, illustrated with unappealing ugliness, celebrated chaos and sadism, and, along with Leiris and Masson, he expressed sadistic and aggressive desires through provocative words and images.[30]

In June 1929, Giacometti exhibited two sculptures at the Jeanne Bucher gallery: *Gazing Head* and, probably, *Man*. *Gazing Head* was bought by Charles de Noailles, a principal patron of the surrealists. Masson noticed Giacometti's work, and the two quickly entered into what would become a lifelong friendship. Once Giacometti had been "discovered" by Masson, he was immediately made part of the group of like-minded artists and writers—including Leiris, Jacques Prévert, Tanguy, Bataille, and, peripherally, Ernst—who met at the rue Blomet in Montparnasse, where Miró and Masson had adjoining studios. All but Ernst, who lived around the corner on the rue de Plantes, were distancing themselves from Breton. They saw each other daily and participated jointly in surrealist activities of all kinds, social and intellectual. After years of relative isolation in Paris, Giacometti was delighted to have become part of a circle of such talented individuals.

That summer, not long after they met, Leiris wrote the first article ever devoted to Giacometti and his work. Leiris placed the unknown artist squarely in the middle of his thinking about art, spirituality, and primitivism. He honored the young artist by claiming that he had made "true" fetishes. "One finds some objects (paintings or sculptures) capable of responding more or less to the exigencies of true fetishism," Leiris wrote, "to the love of ourselves, projected from the inside out and clothed in a solid carapace which imprisons it within the limits of a precise thing and situates it, like a piece of furniture of which we can make use in the vast strange chamber we call space . . . like the true fetishes which one can idolize (those which resemble us and are the objective form of our desire), prodigiously alive. . . . the beautiful expression of that emotional ambivalence, the tender sphinx that one always nourishes more or less secretly, at the center of oneself."[31]

A poet, ethnographer, and art critic, Leiris was a wealthy man who had begun his own psychoanalysis that year, allegedly for help with impotence. Despite sharp disparities in their lifestyles and personalities, Leiris and Giacometti recognized in each other a kindred soul. They were both extremely observant and sensitive, their lives had been shaped by wounding experiences from their early years, and both were "dominated," as Leiris wrote, by childhood fears and superstitions."[32] For Leiris, the first of these crises was an unanesthetized throat operation at age five or six (he had been told that he was going to see the circus). As he explains in his autobiography, Manhood, his "whole image of life was scarred by the incident," leaving him with the feeling that life was "a trap, a terrible perfidy on the part of the adults who had been kind to me only to be able to make a fierce assault upon my person." Leiris describes this trauma in a chapter he titled "Throat Cut," a striking forerunner of Giacometti's 1932 sculpture Woman with Her Throat Cut.[33] Later in the book, Leiris reports a childhood illness which caused his penis to be inflamed and swollen, an experience which subsequently led him to confuse his erections with illness and to feel that they were "bad and abnormal."[34]

In the prologue, Leiris announced his impotence, immediately followed by an expression of his "disgust for pregnant women, fear of childbirth, and frank repugnance for newborn babies," feelings dating back to his "earliest childhood" when he observed the birth of his sister's daughter and was nauseated by the sights and smells of the event.[35] A favorite childhood game was "Eye Put Out," and, like Giacometti, he had a preference for sadistic fantasies and for passivity as a mode of relating to the world.[36]

From his autobiographical tale we understand how Leiris came to respect the power of primitive magic. First, it opposed the rationalistic culture into which he was born and opened up another world, brilliant, secret, and eternally alive. Second, it allowed him to deal with the unremitting fears and guilt he felt about his aggressive and erotic fantasies. Like his new friend Giacometti, he was obsessed with female genitalia and turned to magic as a way of placing his obsessions within a less personal context.

In May 1929, one month before Giacometti was welcomed into the group of dissident surrealists, Leiris had written:

It is important to note the pivotal role of the genitals in occultism, . . . this primordial importance of the sexual element is verified by the capital role of the snake—another phallic symbol in a large number of religions. . . .

[T]hese mythological themes are fully confirmed by Freud's theory of sexuality. Besides showing the extent to which man's psychology is tied to his sexuality, psychoanalysis provides the key to the idea of God.

If this great truth about sexuality has been so long disdained since the ancients clearly presented it, the fault is to be found in rigid rationalism which has predominated in recent centuries.

Now, against that intellectualism which cut man off from half of himself, occult science rises up with its formidable armature of symbols, like a great involuntary force of protest. . . . [I]ts symbols are invaluable from the point of view of poetry, therefore from the point of view of human significance.[37]

The young Giacometti, who had been poring over prehistoric and archaic genitals in the museum at Saint-Germain-en-Laye for years, would naturally have been drawn to Leiris's remarkable statement linking the genitalia to occult science. In his autobiography, Leiris made fairly frequent references to his taste for hermeticism and clairvoyants as well as brothels, another combination that would find resonance in Giacometti. Sexuality and the occult were in the air during the 1920s.[38] Putting the two together was nothing new. Symbolists had done it in the late nineteenth century, but without the benefit of psychoanalysis to explain why they fit together so well. Fascination with forbidden knowledge was at the heart of psychoanalysis, as the French understood it, and the occult was, by definition, about secrets.

GIACOMETTI'S SCULPTURE

When he saw Giacometti's sculpture for the first time, Leiris immediately caught on to its erotic nature, recognizing that much of it was about the body as a source of sexual experience. In the photographs illustrating his 1929 article about Giacometti, Leiris carefully positioned the pieces to suggest their hidden meanings.[39]

At least three of the sculptures Leiris included are known to predate Giacometti's contact with the surrealists.[40] Several made in 1929 clearly come after it. In one of the photographs (see fig. 4.10), Leiris suggestively placed *Gazing Head* (1927–28) and *Man* (1927–28) next to each other at the back of a group of sculptures. *Gazing Head*, discussed in chapter four, conflates a horizontal ocular cavity with an upright, phallic one. In *Man*, body parts are all concavities—phallus and face are both indented, denying them their masculine protrusiveness—echoing the concavities of *Gazing Head*.

Man (1929), another sculpture illustrated in Leiris's article, has an open grillwork style and presents a perplexing psychological story (fig. 5.1). Here is a man caged within or behind bars; his cage has legs while he has none.[41] They are missing, like his penis, unless we consider the vertical emerging in his mouth as its displacement upwards—an artistic conflation, which has overtones of a Freudian defensive maneuver, in frequent use among the surrealists.[42] To prevent our experiencing the rigid position as intolerable, the artist placed the figure slightly off-center within the grid, a device he used regularly to create tension. *Man* probably represents Giacometti himself, stuck in a pose he cannot change. Lifted off his stable base, *Man* has spread his legs and lost his manhood. The sculpture coincided with the end of his troubled affair with Flora Mayo in 1929 and may refer to his feelings about the impotence he frequently experienced with her and her suffocating demands for more commitment.[43]

FIGURE 5.1 Personnages: *Marc Vaux photograph of* Man *(left-front), 1929, plaster (destroyed). Also shown are* Three Figures Outdoors *(right-front),* Man and Woman *(back-left), and* Reclining Woman Who Dreams *(back-right).*

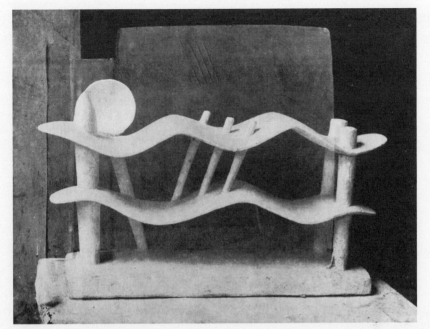

FIGURE 5.2 *Superimposed photograph by Marc Vaux of* Reclining Woman Who Dreams *and* Woman, *1929, plaster (both destroyed).*

The third of the photographs Leiris included is actually a superimposition of separate photographs of two sculptures (fig. 5.2). Prominently displayed, *Reclining Woman Who Dreams (Femme Couchée qui Rêve)* is set in front of the 1929 plaque *Woman*, which has been placed on its side, resulting in a startling juxtaposition. It appears that Leiris and Giacometti wanted to make a point about the four parallel diagonal lines on the plaque, which, as discussed earlier, symbolize the male in prehistory. In the photograph, the lines are precisely placed so that they are aligned with the three parallel diagonal rods piercing the middle of the reclining woman's body.

Leiris's inclusion of *Reclining Woman Who Dreams*, which is similar to *Reclining Woman (Femme Couchée)* of 1929 (Alberto Giacometti-Stiftung)—Giacometti's two sculpted spoon images from 1928–29—suggests that he understood Giacometti's ambivalent feelings about women's bodies. In French, the titles of these two works can connote fertility and childbirth.[44] *Accoucher* means to deliver or to give birth, and *Femme Couchée* can be literally translated as woman in bed, though its customary translation is "reclining woman." The very evident spoon shape in *Femme Couchée* was probably inspired by an allusion to pregnancy and its opposite, an empty womb.[45] Giacometti's focus on a woman's genitals and the possible outcome of a sexual encounter had not really changed since 1926–27, when he made his first *Spoon Woman*, only now the artist was willing to let his associations emerge more openly.

Leiris's photographic composition *Personnages* (fig. 5.1) includes four works, all from 1929, and makes a similar play on forms. *Man* and *Three Figures Outdoors* stand in the foreground, and behind them are *Man and Woman* and *Reclining Woman Who Dreams*. The three parallel lines of *Reclining Woman Who Dreams* are aligned exactly at the crotch of the zigzagging lady in the center of *Three Figures Outdoors*. The parallel lines practically intersect with the stabbing, lancelike "arms" of the man on the right in *Three Figures Outdoors*. The sexual meaning of the zigzagging and the lancelike stabbing, which is reinforced by the presence of *Man and Woman*—an explicitly sexual and aggressive work—is unmistakable.

The inclusion of the four works in the same photograph suggests two things: first, that Giacometti was already on his way to surrealist psychodramas when he met Masson and company in summer 1929 (*Reclining Woman Who Dreams* and *Man* probably date from the first half of the year); and second, his immediate inclusion in the heady group released an inner spring, freeing him to depict his erotic and sadistic fantasies more openly. *Three Figures Outdoors* and *Man and Woman* almost certainly date from the second half of the year. The fantasies were already nearing the surface or he could not have so readily produced such a sizable oeuvre of wickedly wanton sculptures.

Man and Woman (visible in the left foreground of fig. 4.10 and in the left background of fig. 5.1) is the first in a series of sculptures done between 1929 and 1932 centering on the theme of sadistic penetration. Its importance for Giacometti is suggested by a drawing of works intended as outdoor monuments, indicating that he hoped to have it reproduced as a life-size work. Although the two figures lean away from each other just as they did in *Dancers* of 1927, their contact is at once tantalizing and terrifying, since the man's phallus has become a diagonally pointed weapon. The woman's labia rise up, puckered and poised in the vast expanse of her spoon-shaped torso. Will he or will he not pierce and penetrate his serpent-necked partner with his swordlike penis?

The same question is raised in *Three Figures Outdoors*, in which the woman is again serpentine. She is grasped but not penetrated by the phallic rods of the second figure. The artist inscribed a variant title on a photograph he had painted of the original plaster: "Man, Woman, and Ghosts."[46] In the painted photograph the man seems to ogle her with popping eyes, and his red-hot hands hold her, but nothing more. The outdoor setting and plural phantoms

FIGURE 5.3

Photograph of Wall Relief,
1929–30, plaster
(destroyed). Illustration in
Art et industrie.

of the alternative title suggest a sexual encounter observed by several gently undulating treelike onlookers, an experience Giacometti might have had or been encouraged to imagine in the milieu of his new surrealist friends.[47]

Only when the serpentine woman is asleep, as in *Reclining Woman Who Dreams*, do male verticals actually penetrate her. The little spoon-headed man leans away from the parallel phalluses, standing uneasily by the woman's head, perhaps waiting for her to awaken and discover what has been done to her. Even the bedposts plunge through her undulating outline.

Before 1930 Giacometti did not depict consummated acts of hostile eroticism. *Man and Woman* portrayed a threat, not an action. The first sculpture suggesting murder and rape was tentatively accomplished as a flat *Wall Relief*, a "decoration" (fig. 5.3).[48] Dating from late 1929 or early 1930, the work depicts an embracing couple in a clear and linear manner. Both figures seem subhuman, very much in the Bataillian tradition. Their feet and hands intersect, and the male's large stabbing phallus penetrates the upper part of the woman's torso, presumably killing her. She has a long open-mouthed beak and the bulbous eyes of a praying mantis.

The 1929 wall relief *Woman in the Shape of a Spider* is another work resembling a praying mantis, one of several insects fascinating to the surrealists because of its metamorphic fluidity and its conflation of sex and violence.[49] In captivity, the female praying mantis devours her mate during or immediately after copulation. According to the surrealists, orgiastic ecstasy blinded and stimulated the female to release her voracious inner nature. Before his induction into the surrealists, Giacometti had confined himself to prehistoric, Cubist, primitive, and archaic sources. Once part of the group, he began to use insectoidal metaphors, incorporating their segmented bodies, angular thin limbs, and bulbous eyes in his work.[50]

From 1929 on, Giacometti's art was characterized by metamorphic transformations merging man and animal, male and female, insect and infantile fantasy. *Woman in the Shape of a Spider* has insectoidal limbs, spider-belly bulges, and a segmented lance approaching a tender spot. The lower "limbs" seem pulled apart in a painful position. There is no clear head, mind, or cognition to watch over the swirling fantasies. Hung by the artist from a cord over his bed, this work evokes the sword of Damocles, ready to crush anyone who dares rest beneath it.

ENTER BRETON:
GIACOMETTI AND THE SURREALISTS 1930–1935

The year 1930 was a time of decision for Giacometti. Under pressure to choose between the dissident surrealists, led by Bataille, and the orthodox followers, led by Breton, he sided with Breton. But burdened by his ambivalence, Giacometti would always be torn by conflict, rocketing back and forth, unable to make a clear, constant, sustainable choice. Both Breton and Bataille were interested in the same sources: sexuality, aggression, alchemy, and psychoanalysis. Breton's clear tilt toward the pleasures of heterosexual love and nonperverse relationships made him seem like an idealist to Bataille. Serving in the First World War as a doctor, Breton had seen bestial human aggression up close. He understood its power and knew that without acknowledging its presence, we are hollow, desiccated idealists. However, he had no desire to wallow in it. He wanted it transformed. Bataille just wanted it and despised Breton's "higher aims."[51]

Breton, in turn, attacked Bataille for his fascination with the base and perverse. "It is to be noted that M. Bataille misuses adjectives with a passion: befouled, senile, rank, sordid, lewd, doddering, and that these words, far from serving him to disparage an unbearable state of affairs, are those through which his delight is most lyrically expressed."[52] In December 1929 in *The Second Manifesto of Surrealism* Breton announced that only initiates should be allowed to be members of the orthodox inner circle.[53] By this he meant spiritually and morally evolved individuals.

In response to Breton's call to purity, Giacometti produced a work that was recognizable to initiates as double-edged, as *sexually perverse and occult.* "I wanted my sculptures to have interest and meaning for other people," he later wrote, "and I was worried whether or not I could make contact with them."[54] In *The Second Manifesto,* Breton's call for "occultation" included a cry for exclusivity and moral integrity among the true believers. No more sensations-seekers. Alchemical adepts had to be pure or they would not succeed at the "great work" of transformation.

The *Suspended Ball / Hour of Traces* was made in the winter of 1929–30 for both Bataille and Breton, a switch-piece facing two directions simultaneously (fig. 5.4). Hence there are two ways of reading it, Bataillian or Bretonian: on the one hand sadistic, on the other occult and libidinal.[55] Perversion and sadism were tempting and deeply felt elements of Giacometti's personality. But loyalty, kindness, and generosity were also part of his character. The dissidents Bataille, Leiris, and Masson pulled him toward perversion and sadomasochistic fantasies and behavior. The orthodox surrealists Breton, Ernst, Eluard, and Miró drew him toward the sublimated planes of alchemy.

Giacometti's original title for the work was *Hour of Traces.* Later it came to be known as *Suspended Ball,* an empirical description.[56] In a metal cage, a plaster ball with a crescent-shaped notch hangs directly over a sharply edged wedge that is sitting on a plaster base. The elements look as though they are about to connect, but they don't. With a single work Giacometti had captured the essence of surrealist conjunctions and proved that he grasped the movement's arcane spirit.

Pairing incongruous objects is at the core of surrealist theory and practice. The poetic source was Lautréamont's famous line from *Les chants de Maldoror,* "beautiful as the chance meeting of a sewing machine and an umbrella on an operating table."[57] The metaphor, an emphatically sadistic evocation of intercourse, appealed to both the dissident surrealists gathered around Bataille and the orthodox Bretonians, for whom it also could be understood as an alchemical symbol pairing the opposites of love and aggression. The *Suspended Ball* is a seminal work, for both Giacometti and other surrealist artists; it will be the focus of the rest of this chapter.

Breton saw *The Suspended Ball* in spring 1930, bought it, and invited Giacometti into the inner circle of the group at precisely the time it was closing in on its occult mission. Unquestionably Breton recognized in the newcomer's work a sculptural representation of sun and moon, alchemical symbolism denoting the conjunction of male and female principles.[58] In *Second Manifesto* Breton had written:

FIGURE 5.4 *Marc Vaux photograph of* Suspended Ball, *1930, original plaster (destroyed).*

I would appreciate your noting the remarkable analogy . . . between the surrealist efforts and those of the alchemists: the philosopher's stone is nothing more or less than that which was to enable man's imagination to take a stunning revenge on all things . . . to the attempt to liberate once and for all the imagination by the "long, immense reasoned derangement of the senses. . . . "Perhaps we have thus far only managed to decorate modestly the walls of our abode with figures which, at first glance seem beautiful to us, again in imitation of Flamel [a French alchemist]. . . . He liked to portray thus "a king with a great cutlass, who was having a multitude of infants killed before his eyes . . . whilst the blood of said children was then gathered by the other soldiers and put into a large vessel, in which the Sun and the Moon of heaven came to bathe" . . . doesn't this sound like the surrealist painting?[59]

Giacometti had been primed for at least a decade to accept magical systems as foundational—by Seligmann in Geneva and by Campigli in Saint-Germain-en-Laye. The occult was not new to him when he arrived in Paris, but it had taken him until 1930 to find mentors worthy of his penchant for hero-worship.[60] As the outspoken, self-appointed spokesman for surrealism, Breton was both endearing and intimidating. For all his dogmatism and periodic excommunications, he was a kinder man than Bataille. Neither perverse nor naturally inclined to sadism, Breton was loved by his friends, disciples, and former friends, despite his infuriating expulsions and shifting enthusiasms. Moreover, Breton was a healer—a trained physician who took his Hippocratic oath seriously. Giacometti must have known that he needed healing.

Given Giacometti's history and character, his outburst of aggressive sculptures was probably followed by intense guilt. Since childhood Giacometti had used fantasy as both comfort and escape. Breton's *Second Manifesto* offered the young man an ideal solution, "revenge through imagination" and the metaphors of alchemy, which could be a way to be true to himself, all of himself. The writings of both Bataille and Breton contained sex and aggression. In 1930 only Breton's alchemy added love and rebirth to the mixture. Breton claimed, "Surrealism aims quite simply at the total recovery of our psychic force by a means which is nothing other than the dizzying descent into ourselves, the systematic illumination of hidden places and the progressive darkening of other places, the perpetual excursion into the midst of forbidden territory."[61]

In the winter of 1929–30, the likely link between Giacometti and the orthodox surrealists was Ernst. He was closest to Breton but maintained good terms with most of the dissidents. A natural intimacy between Giacometti and Ernst was grounded on common experiences, including artist fathers who had inspired hostile daydreams, younger sisters who were the subject of disturbing memories, and the omnipotent fantasies common in highly gifted children.[62] Ernst's interest in magic grew out of the coincidence of his sister's birth occurring simultaneously with the death of his pet cockatoo. In a brief autobiographical résumé, Ernst described the event making him susceptible to magic:

> (1906) First contact with occult, magic and witchcraft powers. One of his best friends, a most intelligent and affectionate pink cockatoo, died in the night of January the 5th. It was an awful shock to Max when he found the corpse in the morning and when, at the same moment, his father announced to him the birth of his sister, Loni . . . he fainted. In his imagination he connected both events and charged the baby with extinction of the bird's life. A series of mystical crises, fits of hysteria, exaltations and depressions followed. A dangerous confusion between birds and humans became encrusted in his mind and asserted itself in his drawings and paintings.[63]

With wit, keen insight, and emotional balance, Ernst described how he had overcome a "dangerous confusion" and "haunting obsession" through artistic effort and thereby made peace with both sides of his nature—male and female. Giacometti had a comparable trauma in the nearly simultaneous birth and death of the two Ottilias, but he was either not aware of the profound effect of those experiences or chose not to make them public.

Compared with Giacometti, Ernst was astonishingly liberated. He had painted his way into and out of his rivalry with his father by addressing the subject directly in the early 1920s. Ten years older than Giacometti, Ernst was one of the least dogmatic and most persistently fruitful of all surrealist artists. A voracious reader like Giacometti and characteristically candid, Ernst made no effort to disguise his lifelong interest in magic. He concluded the story of his youth by stating: "(1914) Max Ernst died the 1st of August 1914. He resuscitated the 11th of November 1918 as a young man aspiring to become a magician and to find the myth of his time."[64] The artist is telling us how he survived the First World War without descending into the abyss of many fellow survivors and Dada colleagues: despair, drink, mental illness, or suicide. He had turned magical thinking into creative purposes.

Profiting from his close reading of Freud and his familiarity with Silberer, Ernst transmuted some fundamental ideas of psychoanalysis into aesthetic principles. The notion that early experiences and memories remain alive and recuperable propelled Ernst to seek symbolic ways to integrate his painful early memories. For example, once he understood that in his unconscious the death of his pet bird and his sister's birth were condensed into one event, he decided to use this technique consciously. The mind spontaneously uses condensation to disguise hidden content—but, like Ernst, Giacometti learned to use it masterfully and consciously.[65] They both shared the ability to use alchemical and psychoanalytic concepts for aesthetic aims. The constancy of their artistic judgment kept them anchored to the visual impact in a work of art, while many other surrealist artists, in their eagerness to shock, lost sight of that focus.

Ernst also knew how to combine the uncombinable and arrive at the new, earning Breton's staunch support as early as 1919. Seeing himself as the spiritual descendent of two prominent alchemists/magicians who were earlier residents of Cologne near his birthplace, he was knowledgeable about alchemy and the occult and explained his collages as "something like the alchemy of the visual image."[66] Ernst's report of the effect of collage in direct alchemical terms shows that he understood the parallel of sexual and alchemical union and how metaphorical transformation could free someone from a fixed memory: "The mechanism of collage . . . is the complete transmutation, followed by a pure act . . . the coupling of two realities, irreconcilable in appearance."[67] Ernst also wrote that "the more arbitrarily elements were brought together, the greater was the certainty that a new interpretation had to occur through the transcending spark."[68]

In 1923 Ernst dedicated a remarkable painting, *Of This Men Shall Know Nothing*, to Breton (fig. 5.5). Ernst's painting is a visual representation of the alchemical process, and the title refers to arcane knowledge beyond the ken of ordinary men.[69] In descending order a sun, an inverted lunar crescent, a pair of male and female legs widespread and joined at the genitals, and a hand and whistle suspended by wires or threads occupy the center of the mysterious painting. Giacometti probably saw this painting sometime between meeting Ernst in summer 1929 and creating *Suspended Ball/Hour of Traces* in spring 1930. The conjunction of crescent moon barely touching spherical sun at the top of Ernst's canvas is one striking parallel between the two works. Another is the suspension of an object by strings or wires. In Ernst's painting, "the little whistle is kept from falling to the earth by the wires hanging from the crescent moon."[70] For Giacometti, it was the ball. Both works have potential for erotic action. The titles are equally enigmatic, meant simultaneously to keep the ignorant at a distance and to inform adepts.

Sun and moon, the astrological and alchemical symbols for gold and silver, respectively, are joined. Representing fire and water, two of the four primal elements, they also symbolize man and woman. Alchemically speaking, these overlapping conjunctions are often represented by a copulating

FIGURE 5.5 *Max Ernst, Of* This Men Shall Know Nothing, *1923. Oil on canvas,* *83 x 63.8 cm. Tate Gallery, London.*

couple.[71] In fact, the sexualization of all matter is a fundamental tenet of alchemy and one reason it meshed so well with Freudian psychoanalysis. Ernst and other alchemically inclined surrealists could use coded images for marriage and the cycle of birth and death without having to reveal openly occult meanings.

Ernst's belief in alchemy supplied him with the principles of analogy and metaphor which became the foundational tenets for surrealism. Analogies are drawn between the various levels of creation—for example, human, animal, and vegetable—the spiritual essence of all things showing the true nature of life. By uniting opposites—man and woman in the androgyne, heaven and earth, birth and death, spirit and matter—one can obtain the philosopher's stone. "Analogy is the quintessence of the Philosopher's Stone. . . . Harmony consists of equilibrium by the analogy of contraries."[72]

When the surrealists found Giacometti in mid 1929, they recognized how perfectly he fit into their "researches."[73] He was Swiss like the founder of modern alchemy, Paracelsus. He believed in the unity of man and nature, and he was extremely sensitive and superstitious. They may even have learned from him that he had an aunt who was a medium.[74] As a new recruit, he could give sculptural form to their fantasies the way Ernst and Miró had been doing for a decade with paintings and collages.

With its original title, *Hour of Traces*, *The Suspended Ball* is a surrealist timepiece, its mobile mechanism made by a Swiss clock maker and its alchemical pendulum tolls the hours of man's life.[75] Breton's view of surrealism and alchemy involved a notion of timelessness. Choosing the enigmatic phrase *l'hors du temps* for his tombstone, Breton was making a profound pun that could be simultaneously translated either as "the gold of time" or "outside of time."[76] Always seeking to join contradictory elements, Breton wrote about the intersection of time and motion, the solidification of time, the transformation of time into space, and time as the site where perception and memory meet. Giacometti's sculpture *Suspended Ball/Hour of Traces* was the perfect embodiment of these contradictions.

The Suspended Ball/Hour of Traces at its most metaphoric level represents the two principal alchemical elements and their symbolic equivalents—sun and moon, gold and silver, man and woman. Both alchemy and surrealism were, above all, about relationships. The version in wood which Breton commissioned from Giacometti has a different feel from the original plaster version. It is warmer, gentler, less sadistic, and much more playful. It evokes the possible pleasures of sliding and gliding in and out of a partnership—the lusciousness of sexuality as well as its sadistic potential. Breton kept the sculpture as a treasured object in his collection to the end of his life.

The sculpture owes its origin to several sources. It was partly inspired by the sensational sadism of Luis Buñuel and Salvador Dali's shocking movie *The Andalusian Dog*. In the film's graphic opening scene the viewer is confronted with a huge eye sliced by a razor, vitreous humor oozing out. The scene was famous even before the movie's official opening in October 1929.[77]

Buñuel, the famous surrealist filmmaker, always touched the chord of

Giacometti's sadism, and Dali was crazy, albeit high functioning. They were wooed at first by Bataille, who made sure their works were discussed and included in Documents during 1929. By 1930, Breton had co-opted Dali, and by 1933 he had also drawn Buñuel into his orbit. Initially Dali appeared like an ideal recruit to surrealism, a shy, artistically talented madman. As Dali's behavior became more bizarre and his cupidity more prominent, orthodox surrealists distanced themselves, but not before he brought lasting obfuscation to Giacometti's Suspended Ball/Hour of Traces.

The Suspended Ball is a phenomenological title assigned to the sculpture by Dali at least a year after Giacometti made it.[78] As a title, it reveals nothing of the work's secret meaning. In his influential article on surrealist objects, Dali established a powerful interpretive trend in describing Giacometti's "suspended ball": "A ball of wood marked by a feminine cavity is suspended, by a fine violin cord above a crescent of which the ridge grazes the cavity. The spectator finds himself instinctively forced to make the ball glide on the ridge, the length of the cord only permitting him partial fulfillment." He sees the work as an example of "the incarnation of desires, their manner of being objectified by substitution and metaphor, their symbolic realization constituting the process—sexually perverse type."[79]

The Spanish painter's eagerness to find sexual perversion in Suspended Ball/Hour of Traces has infected most later commentators.[80] It is not difficult to see frustrated sexual desire in the relationship of the parts. The ball has a crescent-shaped slice taken out, and the crescent is the sliced-off portion of a ball. Frustrated desire is undeniably present but not the only meaning inherent in the work.[81]

Giacometti scholars have been mesmerized by the perverse elements in the artist's work and life, often ignoring a more complex picture. Both the perverse/aggressive and the pure/loving were present in Giacometti as undigested trends at the beginning of his surrealist adventure. With Suspended Ball/Hour of Traces Giacometti began his move away from perversion and toward love and spirituality. By 1930–31 he had pretty well sided with Breton's semisecret alchemical program.

Giacometti's later claim that he didn't understand the meaning of his surrealist works is characteristic.[82] He may not have grasped their full meaning (who can?), but he must have been aware of the alchemical references in Suspended Ball. Breton, who bought it, certainly knew that the sun and moon were not only man and woman but principal players in the alchemical drama. According to Balakian, the alchemical significance of Suspended Ball was so widely accepted at the time that it needed no explanation.[83] Only now do we have to refind the occult reference for this famous work, because Dali's words set the interpretive ball rolling decisively in a perverse direction.

In 1931, another alchemical surrealist delighting in sexuality, Miró, made a sculptural collage that is informed by Giacometti's *Suspended Ball/Hour of Traces* and that supports my nonperverse reading.[84] Miró's *Man and Woman* (1931) was also owned by Breton and was included in his book *Surrealism and Painting*.[85] Two images are painted on a wood plank, which is the largest element of the work. The images are semiabstract representations, a man and a woman. The man's shape is an alchemical vessel, bulbous and white at the bottom with a long, dark, serpentine neck and a mouthlike opening spewing out liquid substance, ejaculate perhaps, or a newly created (al)chemical formula. Next to him is a scythe-shaped lunar lady whose black body is topped by a white mask, like an archaic eye goddess. The shapes and colors of the two images inform us that, in addition to representing male and female, they are also sun and moon.[86] A clunky chain attached to two sides of Miró's "plaque" wittily connects the work to Giacometti's suspending cord and ball.

In *Communicating Vessels*, a book Giacometti studied closely, Breton made an eloquent case for the conjunction of diverse elements. His argument sounds remarkably like a description of Giacometti's talents and working methods: "Desire arranges multiple ways to express itself . . . the least object to which no particular symbolic role is assigned, is able to represent anything. The mind is wonderfully prompt at grasping the most tenuous relation that can exist between two objects taken at random, and poets know that they can always, without fear of being mistaken, say of one thing that it is *like* the other. . . . Whether in reality or in the dream [desire] is constrained to make the elements pass through the same network: condensation, displacement, substitutions, alterations."[87]

Giacometti commented on this passage in a notebook: "Dream activity— same functioning, *condensation—displacement—the only viable things*."[88] Breton expanded his ideas: "To compare two objects as far distant as possible one from the other . . . to confront them in a brusque and striking manner remains the highest task to which poetry can ever aspire. . . . The stronger the element of immediate unlikeness appears, the more strongly it should be surmounted and denied. . . . So two different bodies, rubbed one against the other, attain through that spark their supreme unity in fire."[89]

The wish to unite opposites fits with Giacometti's ambivalent nature. Not able to bring his own conflicting desires into a harmonious whole, he might have hoped that alchemical surrealism would give him a tool to quiet his inner discord. In this quest the principles of "dream activity" may have seemed useful. They had first been described by Freud; Breton raised them to aesthetic and philosophical principles.

Giacometti's surrealist sculptures meet the criteria set out by Breton and Ernst. They are conjunctions of dissimilar elements, brilliantly brought together and lighting a spark that spawned a multitude of imitations, becoming the prototype for subsequent surrealist objects. The *Suspended Ball/Hour of Traces*, with its different bodies rubbing against one another, was an unachievable meeting of parts, full of potential pain and poignant opportunities. Because, for Giacometti, connection was always accompanied by the prospect of imminent loss.

CHAPTER 6

1930-1932

SURREALIST SCULPTURE: THEMES AND VARIATIONS

Certain universal themes appear in startling relief during Giacometti's surrealist period: the family, sexuality (its dangers and delights), androgyny, aggression, and the kinship of birth, death, and rebirth. In this chapter, I turn to some of Giacometti's most famous surrealist sculptures as well as to little known works to comprehend those themes and track the principal sources for the sculpture—fantasies and concepts established in childhood, and their alchemical equivalents.

First, some biographical context: 1931 and 1932 were years of endings as well as beginnings for Giacometti. The deepening economic depression adversely affected the survival of all artists dependent on wealthy patrons. And the rise of Hitler was particularly alarming to his leftist circle of friends. His godfather, Amiet, lost fifty of his most important paintings in a 1931 fire. In late winter Diego, whose health was uncertain because of a newly discovered irregular heartbeat, moved into his own studio around the corner from Alberto in Paris.[1] For the first time in seven years, the two brothers had separate living and studio space. Throughout 1932 Giovanni Giacometti seemed exhausted, showing symptoms of the illness that would kill him in less than a year. In April 1932, Alberto took part in a group drug experience, during which an acquaintance died beside him. In May 1932, Giacometti had his first one-man exhibition at the prestigious Pierre Colle Gallery, an event that marked the end of his long apprenticeship and financial dependence on his father. In the summer of 1932, both Bianca, Giacometti's cousin and first love, and his sister, Ottilia, became engaged, ending their easy availability to him on his visits home. Francis Berthoud, Ottilia's fiancé, an avid mountaineer, often tempted Diego to scale dangerous peaks, throwing Alberto into paroxysms of fear for his brother's life. In 1932, during his most intense political involvement, Giacometti produced a series of virulent political cartoons for Louis Aragon's radical but short-lived journal, La Lutte.[2] Finally, in May 1933, Giacometti published his fantasies of the rape and murder of a mother, a father, and their daughter for Le Surréalisme au service de la révolution, a journal edited by Breton.

These events had profound psychological effects on the artist, ranging from guilt to terror, feelings that became evident after the death of Giacometti's father at the end of June 1933. At the very least, the events reinforced his susceptibility to superstition and magical thinking that had begun with his phobic bedtime rituals in childhood.

THE FAMILY: TIGHT KNIT OR A STRANGLEHOLD?

Sculpture centering on family themes begins to appear in 1930, a year in which Diego was often away from Paris. Giacometti had just been taken up by Breton and his friends. After a severe bout of appendicitis, which he ignored for three weeks, Giacometti traveled to Switzerland in June for an emergency appendectomy. His brush with death seemed to sharpen his sensitivity to relationships. Convalescing in the midst of his family, and with Diego's help, Giacometti made the large outdoor work Three Figures in a Field, consisting of a man, woman, and child, as preparation for a commission by the Count de Noailles for his sculpture garden in southern France; later that year he also made Portrait of a Family (Carlsberg Glyptotek), a small wood sculpture also depicting a mother, father, and child whose postural positions echo those of the three outdoor pieces.[3]

Giacometti's surrealist images of family groups seem stuck together, perhaps because most members of the Giacometti family were so emotionally attached to one another. Portrait of a Family is a telling metaphor for the relationship between Giacometti and his parents. Three pointed vertical objects are locked into position by a tilting horizontal plane that holds them at waist level. There is no chance of individual movement for any of them; they must move in tandem or not at all. The largest object, a fatherly shape at the uppermost corner, leans toward both other elements, his lower body bending underneath the tilted surface. The medium-size object is upright, rigidly vertical, and open-mouthed, and it seems to face away from the others. Its size and concavity suggest motherness. The smallest shape faces the father directly and leans toward him but is at the greatest distance possible from both him and the mother. The horizontal plank that supports the trio tilts sharply toward the youngest member, causing him to lean backward. As in the famous 1909 family photograph, mother keeps her distance—facing her own direction and going against the tilt of the group—leaving father to be intimate with his children.

The father's complex posture—he seems to lean in two directions simultaneously, toward both wife and son—raises questions. Is he bowing? Is he trying to reach toward someone with his upper body? Is he expressing his complex attachment to both wife and son? Is he trying to keep his balance as the slab is pulled away from him by the other figures? Is the sculpture an unconscious statement of the son's awareness of character differences between a flexible father and a mother whose rigidity he mirrored? Could all these things be true? Perhaps so, given Giacometti's ability to synthesize kinesthetic observations and unspoken emotions and transform them into seamless artistic statements.

The horizontal surface acts to separate above from below, and we sense the nakedness of the underlying parts as each expresses the fundamental character of its metaphoric equivalent. That there should be a sharp separation between surface and underneath is characteristically Swiss, a nation where privacy is treasured and the inner life is locked away in the safe deposit box of the mind. But it also speaks to Giacometti's confusion about the mysterious differences between the sexes.

Giacometti made *Portrait of a Family* shortly after he became friendly with Breton. We cannot know how much the younger man's longings for his father were stimulated by his new closeness with the charismatic Breton, but the sculpture certainly suggests that the warm embrace of the orthodox surrealists touched him. Five years older and authoritarian, Breton was a paternal figure for the remarkably compliant Giacometti. From 1930 to 1934, Breton inspired him to record his dreams, produce automatic writings and drawings, work from imagination rather than external reality, and seek inspiration for his sculpture in early memories and dreams. During this sustained self-reflection, Giacometti reexamined old conflicts and long-standing fixations while practicing the free-association method Breton prescribed. His participation in these surrealist activities led toward a freer fantasy life and probably toward a freer sexual life than he had ever had before.

Giacometti continued to turn away from his father's artistic style at this time, perhaps because Breton and his surrealist compatriots provided Giacometti with a family that enabled him to be himself shamelessly, and it was the only period of his life in which he defied his family's rules, showing his deepest feelings with heretofore unimagined freedom. To tell the truth about the Giacometti family through sculpture and written texts was no mean feat. But it was Alberto's only way. As he wrote at the time: "I can only be true to myself in the objects, in the sculpture, in the drawings (perhaps in painting) much less well in poetry. Not in anything else."[4]

Another work from 1930 that I propose as a family portrait is *The Cage*, visible as the first image in the etching *Moving and Mute Objects* (fig. 6.1). Among the barely distinguishable figures is a tall, bent column that recalls the father figures of *Portrait of a Family* and *Three Figures in a Field*. Another interior figure, made up of two concave leaf shapes, has a feminine quality and leans away from the columnar figure.

In the maelstrom of relationships crowded together in the slatted wooden container, masculine and feminine are conflated in a perverse mixture. Phallic ovoids nearly collide with clasping concavities, and a rakish hand threatens to rip the smooth surface of the plumply phallic object in the center of the sculpture. Bulbous spheres appear suspended like body parts. In the plaster original, the mix is even messier, giving a sensation of claustrophobic

Toutes choses... près, loin, toutes celles qui sont passées et les autres, par devant,

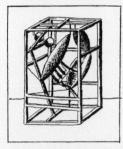 

trois personnes, de quelle gare? Les locomotives qui sifflent, il n'y a pas de gar

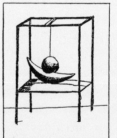 

qui bougent et mes amies — elles changent (on passe tout près, elles sont loin), d'autres approchent, montent, descendent, des canards sur l'eau, là et là, dans l'espace, montent,

on jetait des pelures d'orange du haut de la terrasse, dans la rue très étroite et profo nuit, les mulets braillaient désespérément, vers le matin, on les abattait — demain

descendent — je dors ici, les fleurs de la tapisserie, l'eau du robinet mal fermé, les dessins du rideau, mon pantalon sur une chaise, on parle dans une chambre plus loin ; deux ou

elle approche sa tête de mon oreille — sa jambe, la grande — ils parlent, ils bouge là, mais tout est passé.

ALBERTO GIACOMET

FIGURE 6.1 *Alberto Giacometti, Moving and Mute Objects, 1931. Illustration in Le surréalisme au service de la révolution.*

panic—like four children sleeping in the same bed, locked together with their parents in a small apartment, always threatening to merge with or impinge upon each other. In addition to being a family portrait, *The Cage* could be read as a metaphor for the artist's character. Constrained by inhibitions, Giacometti lived in a transparent box with enough bars to provide a sense of safety. His terrifying feelings and fantasies could be admitted only if kept within the limits of his rule-bound personality. The work can also refer to the artist's complicated feelings about his own body.

Man, Woman and Child, also called *Three Mobile Figures on a Plane* (ca. 1931–32; Kunstmuseum Basel), continues the family theme.[5] Here, the figures move, but barely; their respective roles are set, but only relatively. An upright metal wedge–shaped father can spin in place and point in any direction. An open-armed metal mother on the other side of the platform can sway from side to side, dodging or trying to receive the father's pointed attention. Behind her, the baby ball rolls from one end of his narrow rut to the other, never out of his parents' reach. The flat, rounded rectangular base on which the figures are set emphasizes the isolation of the family unit. A viewer's empathic response to this work is frustration with the limits the artist has imposed on the players in this familial game. Why let the figures move at all if they cannot move more freely?

How can we understand the symbolic meaning of this work? Was Annetta unable or unwilling to protect her children from their father's pointed gaze while they posed nude hour after hour? Did Alberto feel small and stuck, torn alternately by desire and repulsion? Was Giovanni equally trapped, unable to escape the orbit of his wife, whose widespread arms both blocked and embraced him? By their silence and denial both parents forced their children to constantly reenact the subtle cruelties of a closed family system. Yet, by comparison with the earlier family portraits, these three figures seem comfortable in their separate positions. At least they have limited independence and are clearly differentiated as man, woman, and child. But not for long.

ANDROGYNY

Giacometti's first explicitly androgynous work is the small, undated *Drawing*, probably intended as a study for sculpture. Clearly phallic in shape, it has a large vaginal opening and labia. Another early example of sexual ambiguity is the *Large Figure*, done for the Noailles' garden at Hyeres in 1930–31.[6] Giacometti's decision to transform the original group of three family members into a single androgynous figure solved his dilemma about a masculine mother and feminine father, and it reflected his own bisexuality. That androgyny was a prime alchemical principle made the blend of personal and philosophical/spiritual an easier solution. So too did the heady intellectual/artistic atmosphere in which Giacometti now found himself. Even though homosexuality was frowned on by Breton, bisexuality was accepted as natural in the community of artists, who knew how important it was to remain connected to their "feminine," that is, passive/receptive, nature. Given Giacometti's particular complex identifications with both parents, occasional glimpses of bisexual imagery emerge throughout his career. By making occasional androgynous images he could also unconsciously express his need to connect so closely to another human being that the images seemed fused together.

COUPLING

From 1925–29 Giacometti explored female cavities. Once he joined Breton and Ernst at the heart of the surrealist project he seemed to shift his attention to phallic pleasures. With the money he was beginning to earn from his work, he could afford to visit prostitutes, and he was part of a crowd in which men and women coupled casually. Giacometti might have been emboldened by Breton, Miró, and Ernst, all of whom celebrated love's pleasures in their work. Like alchemy, this facet of Giacometti's life had to be kept secret from his parents, who would not approve.[7]

Giacometti's troubled experiences with heterosexual relationships is well reflected in his surrealist work. *Moving and Mute Objects*, composed of seven scenes reproduced as a single print depicting the artist's finished or intended surrealist sculptures, might be considered his guide to coupling at that time. The drawings were accompanied by an enigmatic but suggestive prose poem.[8]

> All things . . . close, far
> . . . and my girlfriends—
> they change . . .
> others approach, ascend, descend, . . .
> here I sleep:
> the flowers in the tapestry
> the water from the poorly turned-off faucet
> my trousers on a chair, . . .
> in the night the mules brayed desperately,
> toward morning one slaughtered them—

tomorrow I leave—
she moves her head toward my ear—
her leg, the big one—
they talk, they move, here and there—
but all is past.[9]

We can read the story of Giacometti's disagreeable intimate relations in the mute, moving objects of his imagination and memory. He is the quintessential witness in this text, sleeping or departing—the passive perceiver of the world's minutiae while others act in ways that could lead to union. He notes subtle perceptual events while keeping everything and everyone at a distance, in place or time.

The first drawing is *The Cage*, already discussed as a metaphor for the crowded Giacometti household. The second is *Dancing Serpent with Partner and Chaperone*, which reflects Giacometti's adolescent initiation into intimacy, stabbing women with his gaze. A young serpent stands on tiptoe, menaced by her skinny partner, while a mature lady snake in the role of chaperone or procurer observes the scene from the side. The young snake looks boldly at her partner, not allowing his glance to penetrate. In this image, women are pincerlike containers of ovoid eyes. Whether the elder snake is there to protect her species or to urge the younger female to enter the fray is difficult to determine, but the tension between the three participants is palpable. The conflation of testicles and eyes on the dance floor with a young female is probably another reference to Giacometti's orchitis and the sexual inhibitions that impelled him toward voyeurism. Like the earlier *Dancers* of 1926, the two figures lean away from each other, but with the passage of time their concourse has become more hostile.

Giacometti made the third work, *Disagreeable Object to Be Discarded*, into a sculpture. It is an alleged family portrait. From one angle it is a smiling face resting on sharply pointed supports, from others a confusing mix of female concavities and masculine projections. *Project for a Square*, the fourth work, could represent the family fractured into component parts, a hieroglyph of possibilities. Next in the sequence, *Suspended Ball/Hour of Traces* is the consummate consummation: sun and moon as well as a man and woman whose parts echo each other for a perfect fit, as long as no messy merging is required. The sixth image is another coupling witnessed by an outsider. The open-armed, straw-clothed woman is paired with a skeletal mate on a tipsy surface. She is crowned with the lunar crescent identifying her as Ishtar-Astarte.

The culminating image is larger than all the others. It is an "object" titled "disagreeable" by the artist—an erect penis—vital and alert to a touch but dangerous at its point of detachment from the owner's body, where sharp thorns warn us to keep our distance. Giacometti lavished formal attention on three different versions of Disagreeable Object in a single year (1931). In marble it evokes erotic pleasure, smooth to the touch and fully engorged like a tumescent phallus or an ever-available dildo. In wood or plaster, with thorns or spines attached to its pointed end much like its illustration in Moving and Mute Objects, it becomes a large pain-provoking weapon. As the seventh image in Giacometti's alchemical journey, Disagreeable Object speaks not only about the artist's bodily self but also about surrealism's enduringly modern goal—love and desire.

Along with its other meanings, the entire sequence of Moving and Mute Objects was probably an alchemical allegory. It consists of seven frames, mostly mysterious and undecipherable scenes, culminating with the artist's most conflict-laden "object." This would seem a desirable end point, for surely an erect penis would be a goal for an impotent man; yet it is simultaneously disagreeable because it frustrates the man who cannot control his own body. It is also possible to relate this image to Giacometti's sadistic thoughts (almost certainly unconscious) of mutilation and murder via phallic penetration—fantasies that likely contributed to his impotence. Phallic lances aimed toward feminine cavities were a major preoccupation for Giacometti at this time and the impetus for some of his greatest surrealist sculptures.

Pointed images, which can wound, excite, blind, stab, stand up straight, collapse, and occasionally attract a tender touch, are so pervasive during Giacometti's surrealist period as to suggest that this was one of the few brief episodes of relative freedom from oppressive sexual inhibitions. It is equally possible that his intense desire for phallic freedom was frustrated by his inability to overcome the inhibitions he had carried for so long.

"WOMAN WITH HER THROAT CUT"

One of alchemy's most frequent metaphors is the joining of male and female. Giacometti was rarely able to approach the subject without anxious hostility. The work that most powerfully expresses Giacometti's frightening feelings and fantasies about sexual intercourse is Woman with Her Throat Cut (1932), as seen on the floor of Brassai's photograph of the original plaster (fig. 6.2).[10] Even without the title, we would experience the jagged edges of the creature and its broken parts as mutilating and mutilated. An intense travail stretches the creature's energies beyond her agonized resources: legs and

FIGURE 6.2 *Brassaï photograph of Giacometti's studio, 1932–33. In foreground is a plaster version (destroyed) of* Woman with Her Throat Cut.

back arch off the floor, the rounded belly and breasts hover over a rib cage splayed open like a cracked crab shell.

The original plaster revealed that even the neck, with its knobby, open-mouthed head, is arched upward away from the floor in a spasm of pain. Looking directly down on the work, we are not so aware of the cut throat. The body rises from its earthly mooring, but its leg is shackled to a menacingly monstrous carapace. Sawtoothed spines dominate the view from above—a probable recollection from the cave of Giacometti's childhood (fig. 6.3; see also fig 4.3). The spines distract our eye from the detachable, podlike right hand resting in the large, petal-shaped left hand. When we wrench our eyes from the arresting jagged shapes we begin to feel the oddness of the creature's twisted right arm crossing her body as if to shield it from attack, only to end in a heavy stanchion.

The belly and podlike hand are visually akin—oblong, swollen containers. Likewise, the left hand and rib cage resemble each other as open containers or backdrops for the pod forms, especially when the podlike right hand is placed in the petal-shaped left hand as the artist intended. The petal hand is spoonlike, calm and full, an unexpectedly peaceful harbor contrasting with the spiky shape of its nearest neighbor, the rib cage.[11] The neck, spine, and pod are all phallic equivalents. So too is the arching belly-body when seen from above. The only clearly feminine shape is the petal hand—like a spoon it is ready to receive. Giacometti places the detachable phallic pod in this spoon—suggesting perhaps a fantasy that the seemingly safe petal shape can contain a flimsily connected body part that could be broken off at a moment's notice.

The phallic pod also resembles a swaddled child—its podness suggests new life waiting to emerge, or a newborn recently separated from its mother. That meaning is underlined by the neck's umbilical nature. But the pod does

FIGURE 6.3 *View from interior of cave at Stampa, showing the cave's sawtooth-shaped mouth* *(author photograph).*

not rest comfortably in the petal hand. Perhaps the oversized hand does not really hold the vulnerable structure but seductively invites trust, making this feature as ominous as the other parts of the sculpture.

From a lower viewpoint or in profile, the gash in the "woman's" throat is notably similar in shape to her mouth a few notches away. It is an open V repeated four times in the rib cage and culminating in her spread-leg crotch position. The head is small and far away from the menacing parts.[12] For the viewer, the spiky rib cage is the greater visual menace; it evokes pain. The message seems to be: she will retaliate for the damage done to her.

Certain interpretations are obvious. The woman has been raped and murdered—her throat cut, an explicit depiction of Giacometti's violent childhood falling-asleep fantasy, as well as his feelings of revenge for the female's phallic allure. By cutting her throat, the artist symbolically eliminates her capacity to make any sound, either of anguish or of ecstasy. The perpetrator has come and gone. This separates it from Giacometti's earlier works, which had shown woman as either an anguished figure or a dangerous spider. Here she is both violated and killed. Since the work is meant to be seen from above, we now stand in his place looking down at the helpless victim. Though we may be horrified, we can still see that she is both enticing and dangerous. She reminds us that bodies can be dismembered or castrated, and that life-sustaining skeletal structures like the rib cage can become forbidding and ferocious.[13] We find her humanoid features familiar, but we also know that she is not of our species: she is alien, insectoid—an appalling composite of animal, crawling creature, and woman.

Fueled by unconscious fantasies about bisexuality, *Woman with Her Throat Cut* is a masterpiece of ambiguity. The conflation of genders is a complex point/counterpoint of male and female parts, a statement of the multiple dangers men and women represent for each other. The phallic torso is arched upward and surmounted by breasts, which can be easily read as testicles or even as ovaries. Giacometti uses her androgynous nature to taunt the viewer standing above the figure. The spread legs, which most observers have linked to rape and violation, have other likely connotations. In primitive art that position was favored for depicting childbirth, as Giacometti would have known from New Guinean examples. Thus the work may be a veiled allusion to one of the crystallizing events of Giacometti's childhood: the birth and death of the two Ottilias.

The formal story of the *Woman with Her Throat Cut* begins in 1929 with a group of sculptures and sketches about women and the relationship between man and woman, among them *Anguished Woman in Her Room at Night* and a pair of drawings now in the Musée nationale d'art moderne.[14] The preliminary drawings clarify some of the artist's intentions and fantasies. The absent perpetrator, or at least his weapon, appears in the drawings, which were probably done shortly before the sculpture, each revealing a different aspect of the fantasies contributing to the final form. Both drawings show a reclining creature with spread-eagle legs and twisted arms. The drawing on the lower part of the page is presumably the earlier one because it is more distant from the final composition. The later one shows the cut throat most clearly, more clearly than can be seen in most views of the sculpture. Her head is raised from the floor, held in tense arrest at the end of her broken neck. The weapon used to cut her throat is nowhere evident, but another weapon is disturbingly present. A stake has been thrust into and through her pelvic area. This phallic weapon already appeared in three earlier works by Giacometti: *Man and Woman* (1929), *Wall-Relief* (1929–30), and *Project for a Passageway* (1930–31) (Alberto Giacometti-Stiftung).

Though the aim of the stake in the upper drawing is clear, its origin is ambiguous. Was it broken off from the female's foot? The jagged edges suggest that the two parts could fit together. This hints at a combination of fantasies, one concerning castration and the other based on the idea that the foot is so dangerous that she could hurt herself with it if she is not careful. The idea of self-inflicted pain or stimulation is a direct part of the lower drawing, where a pointed hand grazes the creature's genitals. Confusingly, it appears to be an extra limb in addition to the two armlike appendages attached to the upper part of her spine. The convoluted angles and twists of all the limbs in the lower drawing presage the convolution of the right shoulder of *Woman with Her Throat Cut.* They also provide a preview of an imminent mutilation—a sense that some part will be severed, bitten off perhaps, like a mantis at a meal. So twisted and tortured are these limbs it is hard to imagine them whole and wholesome.

The phallic lance hidden behind (or inside) *Woman with Her Throat Cut* soon becomes an overt part of Giacometti's sculptures. Its next appearance in a sculpted work is probably in *Point to the Eye* (1932). The original title was *Disintegrating Relations*, illustrated by a Man Ray photograph in Zervos's article.[15] In *Point to the Eye* an exaggeratedly long masculine member is aimed at the orbital cavity of a plaster skull that sits atop a metal post with three abbreviated ribs. The two parts are firmly fixed on a flat wooden platform marked by shallow grooves and cavities very like the ones in *Man, Woman, and Child.* The pointed phallic lance is attached to a vertical metal rod topped by a ball about the same size as the baby ball in *Man, Woman, and Child*. In Man Ray's photograph, the point seems to be aimed at the empty eye sockets. The work has been interpreted in many ways, but all have focused on the importance for the artist of the gaze.[16] For Giacometti, union between people began with a glance or a gaze. The sockets' concavity is here associated with death and the simultaneity of seeing and being seen. Gender confusion is also present, along with the fantasy that a glance can be fatal.

With this sculpture, made during his his most artistically rebellious year, Giacometti might have been announcing his disintegrating relationship with Giovanni as well as his appropriation of his father's function as an aggressive gazer. The previous year he had already hinted at the pointed nature of the father's gaze and the helplessness of the ball baby in *Man, Woman, and Child*. Now, in *Disintegrating Relations*, the track for the little ball is present but empty, and the skull directly faces the point that has a ball for a head. The schematically marked rectangular platform also bears a striking resemblance to representations of female genitals as well as to the schema Giacometti had used for vaginas in his series of drawings from 1927–28.[17]

"NO MORE PLAY"

Created in late 1932, *No More Play* was photographed by Man Ray for an important article on Giacometti by Christian Zervos in *Cahiers d'art*, the leading contemporary art periodical in Paris (fig. 6.4).[18] That photograph is the only document showing the work with its original parts intact and placed as Giacometti preferred. Made first in plaster, it was reproduced in white marble for an exhibition in New York at the Julien Levy Gallery in winter 1934.[19]

No More Play is a rectangular slab 58 x 46 x 4 cm high.[20] On its surface, a field of hemispherical and egg-shaped craters is divided by a central panel, with a shallow rectangular depression at one end and three deeply carved burial vaults at regular intervals along the panel. Using the Man Ray photograph as a reference point, the right side of the sculpture is larger but has fewer craters, since a rectangular panel at the bottom right—which displays the words *On ne joue plus* (no more play) as a mirror-image inscription—takes up some of the space. The largest crater in each side panel contains a standing figurine. The figurine on the right is farther from the viewer than is the crescent-crowned figure on the left.[21]

In the foremost grave we see the tip of what looks like a rib cage. In the second grave there is a snake. The third grave is covered. Coffin lids have been

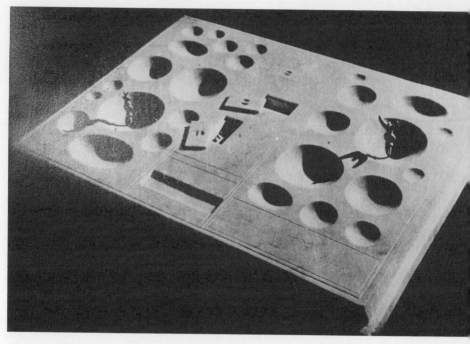

FIGURE 6.4 *Man Ray photograph of* No More Play, *1932, plaster and wood (original destroyed).*

pulled back so the dead can arise. But who or what are they? By writing the title in reverse the artist implies the opposite of finality: resurrection rather than death.

What, then, is the magical or ritual intent of *No More Play*? The answers lie in the work's antecedents. Giacometti had used his innovative tabletop format several times in the previous two years but never so often as in 1932 when he produced five sculptures built on a horizontal platform (like a tabletop). I propose that a significant inspiration for all these works was a celebrated Elamite sculpture at the Louvre: the *Sit-Shamshi* (Ceremony of the Sunrise) (fig. 6.5). The ancient bronze work, the only three-dimensional depiction of a ritual in Middle Eastern art, depicts a ceremonial ablution. On a flat rectangular base two nude bald men, probably priests, are surrounded by cultic paraphernalia: ziggurats, an offering table, a sacred grove, cone-shaped columns, basins, and a large water jar.[22] Giacometti's tabletop pieces resemble the Mesopotamian sculpture in size, format, and general configuration of the parts on the platform. A magical ritual centered on sun worship would also have appealed to the artist. An ideal magnet for childhood recollections, the

FIGURE 6.5 Sit-Shamsi (*Ceremony of the Sunrise*), *twelfth-century* B.C.E.. *Bronze. Louvre, Paris.*

Sit-Shamshi could have reminded him of his father's paintings, especially *Children of the Sun* or *Boys in the Lake.*

The shallow rectangular depression at the base of the central panel of *No More Play* closely resembles the indentations of Egyptian offering tables (flat rectangular slabs usually decorated with images of bread and wine), where relatives or mortuary priests could leave food and drink as symbolic sustenance for the *ka*, or double, of the deceased. Giacometti's indented shapes also resemble the numerous false doors (shallow, rectangular door-shaped indentations) of Egyptian tombs on exhibit at the Louvre.[23] Typically the mummified body was placed in the burial shaft behind the false door so the *ka* could come and go in order to see the sun god and be replenished by his rays and the offerings. Among the Louvre's impressive collection of offering tables are several, such as *Nakht*, that are generally the same size and shape as those in *No More Play* (fig. 6.6).[24] The idea of an obligatory funerary rite related to feeding the *ka* would appeal to the ritual-minded Giacometti, who was fascinated with death as well as with Egyptian culture.

According to Egyptian belief, the *ka* was only one of the three parts of a person to survive after death. In a widely available handbook on Egyptian religion an Egyptologist states:

The difference between the living and the non-living was that the former were imbued by a special active force, which they called the *ka*. Every mor-

FIGURE 6.6
Offering table—
Nakht (Egyptian,
Middle Kingdom).
Calcite. Louvre,
Paris.

FIGURE 6.7
Tomb of Roman
soldier, Stampa
(author
photograph).

tal received this *ka* at birth, and as long as he possessed it he is one of the living. The *ka* is seen by no one, but was assumed to be the exact counterpart of the man in appearance. When the man died his *ka* left him, but it was hoped that it would still concern itself with the body in which it had dwelt so long, and that it would occasionally reanimate it . . . it was probably for the *ka* that the grave was so carefully attended and provided with food.[25]

The graves in the central panel of No More Play can be traced to at least three other sources; the graves in Fra Angelico's Last Judgment in Florence are one such proposal.[26] I suggest two others: the *Tomb of the Roman Soldier* (fig.

FIGURE 6.8 *Statuette of a woman holding her breasts, second millennium* B.C.E. *Terracotta. Louvre, Paris.*

6.7) in Stampa, an elongated ovoid trough only a few kilometers from Giacometti's home, and an engraving illustrated in Silberer's *Hidden Symbolism of Alchemy and the Occult Arts,* which includes a skeleton and a grave, both of which were frequent images in alchemical manuscripts.

With their large, round pelvises, the two figurative game pieces in Man Ray's photograph are identifiable as archaic Mediterranean mother goddesses, similar to the many neolithic Egyptian and Middle Eastern fertility figures at the Louvre, such as a statuette from Elam dating to the second or third millennium B.C.E. (fig. 6.8).[27] They also resemble the figurine in *Palace at 4* A.M., made the same year as *No More Play,* which the artist identified as his mother.[28] The iconic stance and upraised arms of the figurine on the right—typical *orant* (worshipping) fashion—supports my hypothesis that the sculpture refers to some ritual worship or act. The Egyptian hieroglyph for *ka* is simply upraised arms, and the hieroglyphic figure with upraised arms signifies worship and veneration. The upraised arms of the *ka* also signify the transmittability of the *ka* or life force through the embrace of father to son, god to god, god to man, king to man, and so forth.[29]

A lunar crescent–crowned goddess stands on the left side of *No More Play.* Tantalizing and dangerous, the armless figure evokes Ishtar-Astarte, formidable goddess of the underworld, the frightening, fickle female who can abandon former lovers and bring death to all living things. As the dark goddess of war and love, she can make the dead rise from their graves.[30] Again, many examples of horn-crowned goddesses were available at the Louvre. The two representations of the Mediterranean mother goddess in No More Play are Giacometti's conscious or unconscious portrayal of his split view of women—idealized or debased, Madonna or whore. While the figurine on the right is celebratory and welcoming, shining with all the reflected warmth of the sun—the artist's idealized woman—the figurine on the left is sinister and dangerously seductive.

In the burial vaults of No More Play, two familiar symbols from ancient Egypt appear, the djed pillar and the serpent. The djed pillar was a popular Egyptian amulet thought to represent the vitality, stability, and uprightness of the tree from which it was originally drawn.[31] Because of its vertebral, ladder-like form, the djed pillar was associated with the backbone of the god Osiris, who survived death and dismemberment at the hands of his evil, envious younger brother, and symbolized the triumph of the soul over the forces of darkness.[32] According to legend, Isis, his sister-wife, found his scattered body parts (except his penis) and reassembled them, resurrecting him and hiding him in a tree. The raising of the djed column was a formal funerary rite corresponding to rebirth and verticality after the horizontality of death.[33] For Giacometti, sexually impotent and a self-declared coward, lack of backbone and vertical rigidity had personal meaning. Placing the djed pillar in the half-covered grave between two goddesses, Giacometti may have been pointing to a source of his sexual difficulties.

It is impossible to make a single exact interpretation of the snake in No More Play. Its association with fertility, sexuality, and danger indicates something of its place in this sculpture. Because it sheds its skin, it stands for resurrection, but, poised in the open burial vault at the feet of two mother goddesses, the serpent could also represent the male who fertilizes, the female who sinuously entices, or the alchemical androgyne who combines both.

BIRTH—DEATH—REBIRTH

Pregnancy and birth were important surrealist subjects, though often presented in guarded ways now largely ignored by scholars. Breton and Eluard devoted an entire volume to The Immaculate Conception, Miró painted Maternity in 1924, and major works by Ernst depicted brides and pregnant women.[34] The combination of birth, death, and rebirth was a common theme in medieval and Renaissance art, and many nativity scenes contained references to Christ's resurrection. The Symbolists had reworked the topic several decades before the surrealists.

Pregnancy and birth were the enigmas behind the curtain that men were forbidden to raise in many ancient mystery religions. Surrealists experienced the natural dilemma of creative individuals—how to understand the genesis of new ideas and images. Breton developed a theory about the birth of the new from the union of existing entities by carrying forward Freud's concepts about creativity and sublimation. Creation was the universe's deepest and most precious secret, and the entire operation had to be conveyed by metaphor, as alchemists had discovered centuries earlier.

In 1917 Silberer had explained that the goal of the alchemist's quest was the production of the philosopher's stone, which resulted from the alchemical marriage of male and female, their embrace leading to the birth of new life. "Now begins the main work—marriage, prison, embrace, conception, birth, transfiguration."[35] A woman's pregnant belly symbolized the culminating step in alchemy—the production of the philosopher's stone. Grillot de Givry, the Parisian alchemist whose recently published book had inspired Leiris, was eloquent on the subject: "The chapter of Genesis is the greatest page of alchemy . . . whoever understands the mystery of creation knows the secret of the Philosopher's Stone."[36] Silberer observed that the "alchemists like to dwell on the process of procreation" and on infantile sexual theories. They studied nature in an attempt to improve on it, through the artificial creation of man.[37]

Throughout his career Giacometti wanted to create life. At times, his hubris frightened him and he kept it secret, aware of the superstitious nature of his wish and the ridicule it would generate. By 1932 he probably knew that he could not have children and that his only progeny would be his artwork. His surrealist sculpture already seemed to have procreative power: *Suspended Ball/Hour of Traces* had spawned a new genre—surrealist objects—and his table-top works moved mature artists in new directions.

Secretly present since Giacometti began sculpting women's bodies, pregnancy and birth became overt themes in two large surrealist sculptures of 1932: *Despite the Hands/Caress* and *Fall of a Body on a Diagram/Life Continues*, both at the Musée nationale d'art moderne.[38] Earlier works such as *Spoon Woman* showed a woman's empty womb, as did *Reclining Woman* (1928–29). The crescent moon, a common ancient symbol for fertility, crowns the headdresses of *Spoon Woman*, as well as some of the figurines in *Mute and Mobile Objects* (1931), *No More Play* (1932), and the androgynous *Large Figure* (1930–31), appearing again in *Suspended Ball/Hour of Traces* (1930).

Despite the Hands/Caress is a medium-sized marble plaque that is shaped like a snub-nosed head cut by two ladderlike indentations that can be read as either a sharply profiled mouth and nose or vertebrae. The whole work can be understood as both a head and a bulging pregnant belly. A youthful hand is incised on each side of the head/belly. Usually interpreted as a vague reference to life and death or the relationship between men and women, the work has more specific intentions. The pregnancy is both real and alchemical, since Giacometti symbolizes generation itself—the alchemist's ultimate goal. The artist has conflated a gently swelling head with a pregnant woman's belly. By making them equivalent, he has made a philosopher's stone. The alchemical philosopher's stone, or egg, has the double meaning of being both "the philosophical egg [vessel] in which the great masterpiece is produced" and/or the Great Work itself.[39] In *Caress*, the miracle of birth is discovered by the delicately profiled man's or boy's hands as he tenderly touches her stomach. When the work is construed as a head, the hands cover its eyes, forcing it to look inward, where new life is discovered through imagination—the quintessential surrealist theme.

The second work, originally titled *Fall of a Body on a Diagram/Life Continues*, is a horizontal platform piece on which has been placed the snub-nosed pregnant head of *Caress* with its ladderlike profile. The steps of the ladder lead to a grave/mouth, and two small pyramidal shapes along with one familiar concavity stand for eyes, mouth, and nose when the work is seen from above. The mysterious words "but the bridges are rotten—life continues" are incised on the platform.[40] According to Breton, bridges were "the clearest sexual symbols," an idea analogous to the bridging of incongruous elements at the heart of the surrealist enterprise.[41] Giacometti's inscription linking life's apparent opposites, birth and death, can be taken as an alchemical motto, a personal statement, or both. Alchemical thinking embraces and overrides oppositions.[42] A bed represents the alchemical vessel where both birth and death take place. Putrefaction is followed by parturition, an essential step toward alchemical rebirth and new life. On the biographical level: as an impotent man, Giacometti's sexual life was compromised (rotten), but as an artist, he could make life continue.

Befitting Silberer's concept of multiple interpretations, Giacometti's two sculptures relate the combination of the artist's unconscious fantasies *and* his grasp of the occult: the personal meaning of pregnancy and birth for Giacometti, especially when coupled with death *and* universal generativity. As a child Giacometti had experienced powerful events linking birth to death. Alchemy insisted upon the same linkage. Images of death stalk the occult manuscripts studied by Giacometti and his fellow surrealists. But they are always followed by symbols of rebirth, like the serpent devouring itself or the egg that had to be broken for the chick to emerge.

Giacometti's one recorded image of an infant from the 1930s, *The Newborn* (Musée nationale d'art moderne), supports this same linkage.[43] In the drawing, which was part of the cartoon series attacking rightist oppressors in *La Lutte*, an infant lies helplessly in a cradle ringed with spikes. Though guarded by a crocodile-dog wearing a policeman's cap with a truncheon for a tail, the baby has been gored through the stomach with a flagpole, and a huge cross impales its head. Each part is straightforwardly presented as if to make the message transparently clear. Among other meanings, the infant symbolizes the powerless proletariat being savaged by church, state, and police—a fit topic for the leftist journal.[44] But the savagery of the image suggests a source deep within the artist's psyche. The crocodile-dog is probably Giacometti's alter ego, his tail synonymous with the pseudonym *Ferrache* (iron rod or whip), which Giacometti used for these cartoons.[45] Alertly watching the cradle but not preventing the brutal attack, the animal assumes a position that hints at the sort of hostile wishes common in older siblings as they look upon their helpless newborn rivals.[46]

"PALACE AT 4 A.M.", OR "PALACE OF FOUR HOURS"

Like other major works from the surrealist period, *Palace at 4 A.M.* of 1932 has multiple meanings. The original French title, *Palais de Quatres Heures*, can be translated as either *Palace at 4 A.M.* or *Palace of Four Hours*, though the first version is invariably used. Triggered originally by contemporary personal events, the sculpture also recalled childhood memories and expressed Giacometti's metaphysical and magical beliefs.

As can be seen in an early plaster version, the sculpture is a fragile architectural construction of wood and wire elements containing four distinct images on a tabletop base (fig. 6.9).[47] On the right, a spinal column hangs from a thread in a transparent cage. Above and slightly behind it, a prehistoric birdlike creature is suspended in a frame. On the left, a hieratic female figure stands before three panels. At the center, a concave columnar shape with a ball suspended and nestled in its lower end sits on a small platform leaning against a plank.

Giacometti wrote two texts about the sculpture. The first, a prose poem titled "Charred Grass," was written in late 1932 or early 1933, close to the time the work was completed and was published in the last issue of *Surréalisme au service de la révolution*. The second text, a direct discussion of the work, was titled "I can only talk indirectly about my sculpture." It was published in *Minotaure* in December 1933.[48] The first text was closer to the artist's alchemical

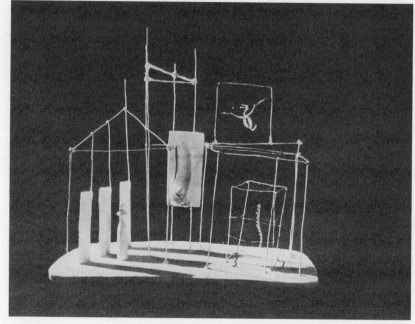

FIGURE 6.9 *Man Ray photograph of* Palace at 4 A.M., *1932–33, plaster version (destroyed).*

ideas, but the second text provided the data for the psychological interpretations Giacometti invited. Early in 1932, along with Aragon, Giacometti had briefly left the Breton circle for political reasons. For his return to the fold, he may have felt a need to produce a typically surrealist text—autobiographical, allusive, and Freudian.

I can only talk *indirectly* about my sculpture. . . .

This object took shape little by little in the late summer of 1932; . . . By autumn it had attained such reality that its actual execution in space took no more than one day. It is related . . . to a period in my life . . . passed in the company of a woman who . . . magically transformed my every moment. We used to construct a fantastic palace at night, days and nights had the same color as if everything happened just before daybreak; a very fragile palace of matchsticks. At the slightest false move a whole section of this tiny construction would collapse. We would always begin it over again. I don't know why it came to be inhabited by a spinal column in a cage—the spinal column this woman sold me one of the very first nights I met her on the street—and by one of the skeleton birds that she saw the very night before the morning in which our life together collapsed—the skeleton birds that flutter with cries of joy at 4 o'clock in the morning very high above the pool of clear, green water. [In] the statue of the woman on the left I recognize my mother, just as she appears in my earliest memories. The mystery of her long black dress touching the floor troubled me; it seemed to me like a part of her body, and aroused in me a feeling of fear and confusion. . . . I cannot say anything about the object in the center, leaning on a small board, it is red; I identify myself with it.[49]

By 1936, when the sculpture was purchased by the Museum of Modern Art in New York, the translation of the title was firmly established as *Palace at 4 A.M.*, which fit with Giacometti's endorsement of an autobiographical/psychoanalytic reading of the work. Such a reading was a natural outgrowth of the artist's need for secrecy about any hermetic symbolism embedded in the sculpture. I propose that the use of this second title was inspired by Yves Tanguy's 1929 painting *A Quatres Heures d'Été, l'Espoir* (*At 4 o'clock in the Summer, Hope*) (Musée nationale d'art moderne), which was also a source for some features of Giacometti's work (fig. 6.10).

Early in 1930, Tanguy moved into the same studio complex as Giacometti, and they became friends. Tanguy's canvas presents his usual mysterious dreamlike scene and includes suggestively palatial columns, a bird similar in shape and position to Giacometti's, and a shadowy female form in the upper

FIGURE 6.10 *Yves Tanguy, At 4 o'clock, in the Summer, Hope, 1929. Oil on canvas, 129.5 x 97 cm. Musée national d'art moderne, Paris.*

right that anticipates Giacometti's hieratic female figure. Most compelling are the similar titles. The word *Hope* in Tanguy's title echoes the title of Amiet's 1901 triptych *Hope/Transitoriness*, a work inspired by the tragic death of the Amiets' baby, which had coincided with Giacometti's birth.

Many factors are at play in Giacometti's choice to title the work *Palace*. In summer 1931, Breton had visited the bizarre "ideal palace" of Ferdinand Cheval in southern France, returning with photographs and much to say about the obscure postman who had created a huge, fantastical structure. In 1932, Giacometti had recently spent time at the palatial Noailles family chateau in Hyeres and was designing furniture for the large, luxurious apartments of the haut monde in Paris. These dwellings were palaces compared with Giacometti's dingy studio, just as the Piz Duan, the paternal family home and inn where Ottilia was born, was a palace compared with the Giacometti apartments in Borgonuovo or Stampa. Furthermore, Freud and Silberer had explained that, in the unconscious, palaces and royal figures could stand for the family home and parents.[50] By mentioning his earliest memories of his mother in his text about *Palace at 4 A.M.*, Giacometti firmly locates his psychodrama in the Bregaglia valley. We know that the long, black dress that he recalled was associated with her prolonged mourning. Because of the many similarities of the rigid mother figure to Annetta Giacometti, we can also link it to the autobiographical falling-asleep fantasy, discussed in Chapter 4, which he reported in the same issue of *Le Surréalisme au service de la révolution*. Shaped like a chess piece, the mother figure could also symbolize the artist's wish to control the mother, who treated her children's lives like a game in which only she knew the correct moves.

The woman in Giacometti's second text about the sculpture—"I can only talk indirectly about my sculpture"—was probably Denise, a drug-using streetwalker likely to sell him a spinal column, especially since that part of the body was metaphorically linked to erections and resurrections, and giving backbone to an impotent man is a streetwalker's role. In taking up with Denise, Giacometti had gone from an infatuation with Flora Mayo, an immature alcoholic heiress, to a ménage-à-trois with a worldly addict and her lover, Dédé le Raisin.[51] Giacometti's text is replete with other erotic metaphors like "Birds who flutter with cries of astonishment," which surely refers to orgiastic women.

For Giacometti *Palace at 4 A.M.* probably was a genuine source of perturbation. His earlier text about the sculpture, the prose poem "Charbon d'herbe," contains clues as to why:

I return to the constructions that amuse me
and which are alive in their surreality; a beautiful palace . . .
the shafts of the columns, the ceiling in the air which laughs . . .
I try gropingly to catch in the void
the invisible white thread of the marvelous
which vibrates, and from which facts and dreams escape . . .
It imparts life to living
and the shining games of the needles and the turning dice
develop and succeed each other alternately
and the drop of blood on the milky skin,
but a piercing scream rises suddenly
that causes the air to shiver and the white ground to tremble
. . . I seek out the women of the light gait,
. . . the same who existed within the little boy
. . . who looked within and without so many marvels.
Oh! Palace palace! [52]

Like *Palace at* 4 A.M., Giacometti's poem has multiple meanings, both personal and alchemical. The title can be alternately translated as charred grass and charcoal plant life. The inherent incompatibility of charcoal and grass lights the spark of surreality and "imparts life to the living"—the essence of surrealism's secret contribution. There are also references to life in the Giacometti family in the poem. "The shining games of the needles and the turning dice [which] develop and succeed each other alternately" could refer to the ever-present sewing needles of the Giacometti women and the games played frequently by the Giacometti boys. And most certainly "the women of the light gait, / . . . the same who existed within the little boy / . . . who looked within and without so many marvels" refers to the very visual young Giacometti, who carried mental images of his mother and sister inside his head for life.

Giacometti's first published reference to a drop of blood on skin appears in "Charred Grass." The phrase "a drop of blood" also stands by itself in the upper right corner in *Poem in Seven Spaces*, a picture poem published on the same page. Twenty-six years later, Giacometti walked out of the dress rehearsal of *Krapp's Last Tape*, a play by his close friend Samuel Beckett, at the moment where a character describes a drop of blood on a woman's thigh. He apologized for his abrupt departure without being able to explain it.[53] Giacometti's intense reaction to "a drop of blood" suggests a powerful unconscious fantasy, calling to mind either the idea of intercourse as a violent and bloody act or the trauma of observing some or all of the birth of his sister. "A piercing scream rises suddenly / that causes the air to shiver and the white ground to tremble" may be another reference to the predawn delivery of Ottilia.

In the same 1933 issue of *Le Surréalisme au service de la révolution* in which the poem appeared, Giacometti wrote again of that piercing scream and pool of green water. Both images occur in his report of the violent fantasy that he claimed was necessary for falling asleep between the ages of four and seven.

As discussed earlier, the alternative reading of the sculpture as alchemical relates to the translation of the title as *Palace of Four Hours* rather than *Palace at 4 A.M.* In alchemy, the fourth hour, or stage, is the last cycle of death and rebirth, and the most difficult. With this in mind I will interpret Giacometti's four sculptural elements one by one. The caged spinal column symbolizes Osiris's backbone, a frequent alchemical analogy that shows up in Giacometti's work from the period. The cage around the spinal column evokes the box used to kill Osiris as well as the coffin in which he was revived, making the unit a symbol of death and resurrection.

The unearthly skeletal bird suspended above the caged column also refers to eternal renewal, as it does in countless cultures.[54] Giacometti's winged creature has a strangely unbirdlike segmented tail, suggesting a phoenix rising from the flames that destroy it—another symbol of rebirth. The phoenix symbolizes the destruction and recomposition of the elements leading to the philosopher's stone and is one of the immortal winged creatures found in alchemical manuscripts. The glass pane hovering over the spinal column in front of the concavity and ball suggests yet another bridge between death and birth. It can refer to an ability to face death, to look inside an enclosure (a coffin or an alchemical vessel) and to see the potential for rebirth.[55] The female figure on the left is a hieratic mother goddess, an Isis matching the Osirian symbol on the right. Rigid like the Louvre's predynastic Egyptian figurines labeled concubines of death, she stands in the part of the construction most associated with death. The scaffolding above her is crumbling, and the three panels behind her echo Bocklin's *Island of the Dead* and Lurçat's surrealist landscapes.[56]

In the center of the composition are the vaginally shaped concavity and the emerging ball. That the concavity and the ball can be read as both female and male fits with the frequent alchemical use of an androgyne accompanying the birth of the philosopher's stone.[57] The plank on which the concave object leans is tilted forward, augmenting the instability of the ball and cylinder. At any moment the ball could drop, re-creating the suspense of a closely watched childbirth. The central position of the ball and cylinder, their abstraction, and their essential instability are keys to their significance. They represent the fundamental goal of any artist or alchemist: new life or creativ-

FIGURE 6.11 *Ernst Scheidegger photograph of* 1+1=3, *c. 1935, plaster version (destroyed).*

ity itself. Thus the entire work can be understood as representing the culmination of the alchemical process in the fourth hour—primary creativity within the cycle of birth, death, and rebirth.

Giacometti's final work in the series of surrealist sculptures related to procreation was never exhibited and probably no longer exists. Photographs by Ernst Scheidegger in the Maloja studio where it was made show that 1+1=3 was a tall, white, cone-shaped plaster sculpture with a rounded cavity where a belly would be (fig. 6.11). Eyes and mouth are summarily indicated at the rounded top of the cone, and two small breasts have been attached to the upper part. The title clearly indicates the work's symbolic meaning, and the figure's hands are incised just above the indented concavity. A likely antique source underscores its significance. White, conical monuments inside the temples of Astarte-Aphrodite at Paphos in Cyprus and at Byblus and Golgi were worshipped as representations of the great nature goddess of motherhood and fertility.[58]

By his own account, the artist found the sculpture troubling. 1+1=3 was the last work Giacometti listed in the sequence of surrealist sculptures in his famous 1947 letter to Matisse. His laconic comment is striking: "One last figure, a woman called 1+1=3, from whom I have not escaped."[59] At a personal level, it could symbolize Giacometti's mother, who remained rooted in Stampa and Maloja, with her combination of masculine and feminine features and from whom he never "escaped." Furthermore, the sculpture's androgynous character—a fertility symbol in the shape of a phallus—was too close to Giacometti's own gender confusion. Trying to make peace between the internalized masculine mother and feminine father with whom he had identified was an impossible challenge. Though the alchemical androgyne could be a code for Giacometti's ambivalence and gender confusion, it did not help him overcome his conflicts. By the time he arrived at 1+1=3, his father was dead and his artistic generativity was in question.

CHAPTER 7

1933-1935

A DOUBLE LOSS: DEATH AND DEPARTURE

The unexpected death of Giacometti's father in June 1933 dramatically affected his son's trajectory through the surrealist style, which the elder Giacometti had tolerated but never liked. In early 1933, Giovanni, looking old for his age, was advised to go to a sanatorium for a rest. While there he suffered a stroke. Giacometti received an urgent summons to return to Switzerland from Paris; he arrived the next day to discover that his father had already died. Giovanni was sixty-five, the same age that his own father was when he expired. Instead of taking charge of funeral arrangements, a duty expected from the eldest son, Alberto took to bed in a nearby room of the hospital, lying rigidly stiff like his dead father. Though he had a fever, no illness could be diagnosed. Giacometti recovered only after his father's funeral, which he did not attend.[1] He joined the family in Maloja shortly after the service and within a week was on his way back to Paris.[2]

Until Giovanni's death, Giacometti had plumbed the depths of his psyche with Freudian tools—dream analysis and free association—seeking to express his past or present sexual and aggressive urges. He had built his career and surrealist style on a subtle but certain opposition to his father's way of working—expressive naturalism. It was the way he had differentiated himself from the man who meant so much to him as both a nurturing and intrusive parent. Now he was left without the mooring against which he had launched himself. His new family, the surrealists, was supportive, but as he came to terms with the depth of his loss, they could not help him ward off his guilt and depression.

In August 1933, not long after Giovanni's death, Giacometti wrote a poem titled "Sonno," a play on words in Italian meaning both "sleep" and "I am."

I am no longer afraid . . .
before I trembled . . .
death always
haunted me . . .
now
nothing, it's worse,
it's dreadful, this calm.[3]

The father he had imagined killing in his falling-asleep fantasies, published only a few months earlier, was dead, leaving only a dreadful calm.

Giacometti must have written this poem in Maloja, where he had gone to prepare a memorial exhibit for his father. Writing frequent letters to Breton, Giacometti tried unsuccessfully to persuade his friend to visit him in Switzerland, explaining that he felt lonely, unable to work, and completely disoriented—lost in a void.[4]

From 1933 until at least 1935 Giacometti mourned his father's death. In the same period, two of Giacometti's paternal uncles died, leaving him as the oldest man in the family.[5] The deaths affected every aspect of his life and art and were a loud but unspoken factor in the works he produced in these years. Indeed, they go far to explain the major upheaval of his subsequent years. During this desolate time Giacometti tossed and turned on his characteristic bed of nails—ambivalence and unacknowledged guilt.

His notebook jottings reveal his struggle. One day he argues vehemently against work from nature: "The impossibility of doing a naturalistic painting in three dimensions, a complete aversion" (c. 1933–34).[6] But soon we read the opposite. He claims he *loves* his father's work—from nature. "But Papa knew how much I loved his paintings. . . . Papa was happy with my success and he knew that I loved his paintings and he knew, how much, how very much admiration I had for him" (c. 1934).[7] The vehemence of the protest belies his ambivalence. He repeatedly commands himself to do his work—new work:

I, I will work on *my new* sculptures!
I will make drawings, prints.
I will write new things, they will take shape.
Against religion, country and capitalism, of course, politics of course,
but I want something else, new revelations, I will have them. And
then I will exhibit new sculptures, soon, completely new. (c. 1934)[8]

The commands are in part the internalized voice of his father as Giacometti worked through the despair and dissociation that overtook him.[9]

Everything happens as if in a dream.
I am a nebula, yesterday I was a plant, a leaf, a large green leaf
in slow motion . . .
Everything happens as if in a dream, time, space,
I no longer understand . . . (c. 1933)[10]

His mood of almost unbearable loneliness was eloquently evoked in his self-portraits. *Self-Portrait* of 1935 (Sainsbury Collection) shows a sad man with a searching look in his eyes—the same feeling Giacometti expressed in his poetry that year.[11]

MALOJA, 1934

By 1934, Giacometti had practically stopped working. Recalling the pain of his previous summer in Maloja, Giacometti persuaded Ernst to join him in August 1934 when he made his next extended visit to Switzerland.[12] Ernst was the most generous and even-tempered of his surrealist friends, and he had already mourned his own father's death with a series of paintings done in the early 1920s. The biggest event of the summer was the stone fever infecting the two friends, especially Ernst, who described the experience in a letter: "Alberto and I have been seized with a fever to sculpt. We are working on large and small granite blocks on the moraines of the Forno glacier. These have been strangely carved by time, ice and the weather, and look fantastically beautiful."[13]

Giacometti helped Ernst by providing tools, demonstrating techniques, foraging for perfect stones among glacial remains, and arranging for having the stones carted back to the studio, while he himself did almost no work except the design for his father's *Tombstone*.[14] The design was probably modeled after the egg-shaped sculptures Ernst had carved from the glacial stones, which were in turn inspired by an Egyptian "eye-stone" of magical-spiritual interest that Ernst had been given by a friend.[15] These works have recently been discussed as examples of Ernst's continuing interest in alchemy.[16] That Ernst was also interested in the occult was apparent to Giacometti's family, as during his visit he told them about his communications with the spirit world.[17]

For his father's *Tombstone* in the small cemetery at Borgonuovo, Giacometti selected a traditional rectangular slab like those used for most of the neighboring graves.[18] He had Diego carve it into a rounded-off organic shape that, from the rear, resembled a torso, with a spinal furrow and buttock-shaped bottom. The front, though apparently more conventional, is like an Egyptian hieroglyph or rebus (picture-puzzle) disguised as a collection of Christian symbols. In low relief, Giacometti depicted a cup, bird, star, and sun. Each element would have been recognizable to local inhabitants: the cup as a chalice; the bird as the Holy Ghost or Spirit; and star and sun—symbols so unexceptional they would not appear foreign to Giovanni's friends and family who would be visiting the cemetery.

Giacometti and Ernst must have known that these symbols, grouped together like a hieroglyph, were a common honorific in ancient Egypt, found at the base of many commemorative columns (fig. 7.1).[19] Their meaning was, "All people worship the sun," a statement of unusually complex significance for Giacometti. The sun, and sun worship, had many meanings for him. First, the local custom in the entire Bregaglia valley was to celebrate the return of the sun in mid March with festivities after each long, dark winter. Next, Giovanni had painted his very large 1913 triptych, *Children of the Sun* (see fig. 1.7), which gloriously portrayed the Giacometti children, their nude bodies bathed in brilliant summer sunlight. Almost certainly "children of the sun" referred as well to the sun-worshipping religion of the heretical Egyptian pharaoh, Akhenaten, whom Giacometti so admired and who was featured in Fechheimer's articles on Amarna art appearing the same year. Did the Egyptian images remind Giacometti of his father's paintings of the Giacometti family? It certainly seems feasible. Finally, it is a psychological truism, confirmed by most cultural myths, that the sun symbolizes the father.

FIGURE 7.1

All People Worship the Sun: *Egyptian hieroglyph on column from Temple of Luxor, New Kingdom, 18th–19th dynasties. Sandstone/granite.*

For the rest of his life Giacometti was fascinated by Akhenaten and his brief reign, and by sun worship. In a conversation with his friend Isaku Yanaihara in 1956, he averred that the sun worship of ancient Egyptians was "the natural shining real religion," which he contrasted with Christianity—"the cruel, dismal and anti-humanistic religion."[20] Sun worship was at the core of Giacometti's profoundest spiritual beliefs. It was the critical juncture yoking his experience of longing for the sun in the dark Bregaglia valley to philosophical alchemy and its celebration of the sun's supreme power. The use of a personal hieroglyph for his father's tombstone was a disguised way to convey his thoughts, and Giacometti would soon employ it again, especially in his abstract works of the next few years.

On their return to Paris in the fall of 1934 the close friendship between Giacometti and Ernst endured. Ernst moved into a studio around the corner from Giacometti, and they continued to see each other daily.[21] They also met frequently at Stanley William Hayter's graphic workshop, where Giacometti had been working since 1933, his first foray into graphics since his school days. Giacometti had avoided painting since 1925, probably because it was his father's province, and the internal prohibition would have applied equally to printmaking. But now that his father was dead, Giacometti sought avenues to reconnect emotionally or identify with Giovanni as part of his mourning; becoming a printmaker was a natural step in that direction.

The crystalline forms Giacometti included in the graphic works he produced between 1933 and 1935—when he comes as close to abstraction as he ever would—suggest, among other things, his continuing interest in alchemy.[22] The occult meaning of crystals is complex. Known throughout the ancient world, the five platonic regular polyhedra, or solids, were associated with the five essential elements of the physical universe—air, earth, fire, water, and ether. They signified spiritual perfection, transcendency, and the meeting point of macrocosm and microcosm. As forms, they had the power to act as an interface between physical and spiritual realms and were understood to have magical powers, used for divination by moonlight.

Giacometti's first image of a crystal or geometric solid was the now-lost sculpture *Figure in a Polyhedron*, visible in the 1932 drawing of his studio.[23] Breton had used the idea of a man inside a crystal in a 1934 article in *Minotaure*, "Beauty Must Be Convulsive," to refer to "the transparency of his life for all to see."[24] But the Swiss artist found the personal transparency of self-exposure less comfortable than did the Parisian poet, who loved dramatic gestures. That could explain why the little figure in Giacometti's sculpture seems trapped, rather than comfortably on display.[25]

The next appearance of a geometric solid is the polyhedron on The Surrealist Table (1933) (Musée nationale d'art moderne), the last sculpture Giacometti made before his father's death.[26] On a small tabletop perched upon tall legs, four objects are placed like sacral offerings—a polyhedron, a woman's veiled head, a mortar and pestle, and a mannequin's hand. The work is an excellent example of Giacometti's overt and sometimes ironic use of occult imagery, as each element is a shorthand familiar to those who could understand these symbols. An enduring aspect of Giacometti's sculptural genius was his ability to transform formal and iconographic ideas derived from multiple sources into seamless visual statements. It is only in his discarded or less-successful surrealist works, such as The Surrealist Table, that the seams widen enough to follow the tracks of his wide-ranging visual and iconographic net.

The largest object on the table, the partially veiled head, is recognizable as an archetypal clairvoyant, much like the photograph of the veiled medium Mme. Sacco, which Breton included in his book Nadja of 1928.[27] Giacometti's sightless medium who can see "the great beyond" has one very large eye linking her also to the Chaldean sculpture he admired. With her open mouth she can pass judgment, uttering the ancient magical words of power that accompany rituals or amulets.[28]

The hand has numerous sources and keeps company with the many severed hands in the works of Man Ray and Ernst, who had placed one prominently in his hermetic painting Of This Men Shall Know Nothing (1923) (see fig. 5.5). As a young man, Giacometti had seen and admired several examples of ritual hand sculptures, including an Egyptian bone hand at the Musée de l'histoire in Geneva in 1919 and Etruscan bronze hands at the Vatican Museum in 1920–21. By 1932–33 he knew that the hand had been used in the ancient Egyptian funerary rites to help the newly deceased survive into afterlife and that its magical purposes ranged from healing to the "opening of the mouth" ceremony.

The adjacent mortar and pestle on the table most likely alludes to "puffers," those materialistic alchemists who try to turn base metal into gold through a variety of chemical mixtures. Mortar and pestle are also obvious sexual symbols, equally recognizable by Freudians, alchemists, and surrealists.[29]

The enigmatic "cube," which is actually a crystalline polyhedron, has direct links to the artist himself, not only because of the carved initial A in one of the drawn versions of The Surrealist Table, but also because Giacometti carved a self-portrait in a freestanding variant of Cube (1933–34) (Alberto Giacometti-Stiftung). Both the small crystalline form on the table and the larger version evoke the polyhedron in Dürer's famous print Melancholia (1514), which had been exhibited in Paris from May to the end of summer 1933.[30] Since Dürer was one of Giacometti's favorite artists from childhood, he probably knew that the polyhedron in his print symbolized geometry, the technical arts, and the material world—all fitting interests for a sculptor. He may also have known that Dürer produced *Melancholia* not long after the death of his mother, a fact usually included in commentary on the print's mysterious symbolism.[31]

Man Ray satirized the occult objects on Giacometti's *The Surrealist Table* with his own photographic sculptural collage in the frontispiece of *Minotaure*, December 1933. One mannequin's hand holds a light bulb (crystal ball), while another emerges from a multicolored soccer ball (crystalline polyhedron). A cup-and-ball toy game (mortar and pestle) flank a plaster self-portrait, and Man Ray's famous photograph of a woman crying crystal tears serves as background. The only serious note is the somber look on the plaster self-portrait. After working in the Dada-surrealist circuit for twenty years, Man Ray could afford to make fun of occult juxtapositions.[32] As if to guard against being perceived as a naive occultist, Giacometti turned frequently to both Man Ray, one of the most irreverent and sophisticated figures on the scene, as well as the more serious Ernst, for collage elements and iconographic bits.

However ironic his intentions had been about the polyhedron he made for *The Surrealist Table*, by the summer of 1933 Giacometti knew that the polyhedron was a Saturnian symbol associated with death and a type of hopeless abolition. In a letter to Breton from Maloja he noted that Saturn was also a god of the golden age—an ancient agricultural divinity associated with prosperity and abundance.[33] The double-sidedness of the Saturnian symbol fit with Giacometti's unstable mood as well as with the complex contradictions of alchemical and psychoanalytic interpretations.

The most abstract of Giacometti's crystalline works is the large sculpture *Cube*, 1933–34 (fig. 7.2). The sculpture resembles the polyhedrons in *Lunaire* and *The Surrealist Table* and was first known as *Pavillon nocturne* (its title in *Minotaure*, 1934). Described in 1934 as "an impressive plaster crystal," *Cube* struck early observers as mysterious.[34] The self-portrait of Giacometti in the uppermost facet of one of the two plaster versions and the formal similarity of the *Cube* to a work he made the following year, *Head-Skull* (1934) (Alberto Giacometti-Stiftung) have led scholars, myself included, to interpret the work as an abstract self-portrait.[35] The crystalline polyhedron represents a person who feels the weight of death, the hardness of loss, and the pain of longing, but it also stands for hope (creativity itself). Like Saturn, and the artist himself, Giacometti's polyhedron had many faces.

FIGURE 7.2
Man Ray
photograph of
Cube (Pavillon
nocturne), 1934,
plaster version
(destroyed).

In *Lunaire* (1933), an ink drawing nearly contemporaneous with *The Surrealist Table* and *Cube*, an open-mouthed androgynous head with sightless eyes suspended at the upper left in an unlit sky stares down at a partial polyhedron, a disembodied crystalline form on the lower right with one facet reflecting white light back toward the head.[36] The artist seems to be exploring the dark side of his grief. The extraordinary power of this image expresses Giacometti's feelings for the father who had reigned so brightly and colorfully in his life. The reflected light of that sunny countenance shining down on him for so long was gone forever. The moon's reflection could never equal its warmth or brightness. The obsessive cross-hatching of the sky suggests his sadness, anger, and fright, and the repetitive marks and patterns of the bleak background can simultaneously convey and deny the vast new emptiness in his life. The sad expression and open mouth on the face of Giacometti's drawing embodies longing for the now lost person. Giacometti synthesized centuries of symbolism about moons and crystals into a powerful statement about all of life's lost loves and the void they leave behind.[37]

The small head, so high in the dark sky, is isolated. Though it could seek contact with the crystalline object below it, the two images do not face each other. The physical distance between them accentuates the yearning and symbolizes achingly empty psychic space, effectively communicating Giacometti's unutterable sadness.

But Lunaire's imagery is ambiguous, so we also can interpret the two objects as the two Giacometti survivors who most felt the loss of Giovanni and who must now face each other directly without his mediating influence— Alberto and Annetta. The androgynous or female head could stand for Annetta. She must now serve as both mother and father to the family, yet she looks as needy as her son seemed to feel. And the lower figure could represent Alberto, whose stonelike stiffness in the hospital after his father's death was a short step to an identification with the crystal on The Surrealist Table and with Cube. With his body, he persuasively symbolized the congealed brittleness of depression.[38]

In these and later surrealist works Giacometti transformed traditional occult principles into personal symbols—crystals, serpents, and suns. The merge-and-mix approach to imagery that Giacometti so effortlessly used in his surrealist period explains the multivalence of so many of his images. Free to look in the crystal ball of his own imagination, Giacometti plucked whatever surfaced and suited his formal aims, confident that the synthetic artistry of his unconscious would forge the necessary unity.

Ernst, Breton, and Masson were preoccupied with images of the death and destruction coming to Europe earlier than most artists in the surrealist milieu. They had seen too much of it in 1914–18 not to recognize a renewed peril. As Giacometti's coterie of friends and colleagues began to shiver in the panic caused by the unchecked rise of Nazism and Fascism in Germany, Spain, and Italy, he no longer had the circle of psychic safety that had allowed him to dream his fantastic dreams and depict them with impunity. Perhaps adding to Giacometti's distress was the fact that he had sold no works from his exhibit in New York at the Julien Levy Gallery in December 1934. Feeling psychologically cornered, he did what individuals often do: he retreated. Returning to the figurative studies of the early 1920s, now without the competing presence of his father, Giacometti moved on by moving backward.

"INVISIBLE OBJECT"

Invisible Object, which dates from 1933–34, was Giacometti's first life-sized sculpture of a full-length nude woman, and his largest figure since *Large Figure* (1932).[39] It marks the end of his semiabstract surrealist works and the start of the ten-year path that would eventually lead to his postwar figures. It is likely that he created *Invisible Object* partly in reaction to his father's death, using the sculpture to defer the effects of earlier traumatic memories and experiences. The sculpture is an example of how long-forgotten memories and occult ideas can be intricately interwoven. While Giacometti apparently sensed that *Invisible Object* would radically change his life and art, his attitude toward this work characterized the contradictoriness that was to become his trademark during the postwar years.[40] On the one hand he could say: "I made this statue . . . to renew myself. Perhaps that is what makes it worthwhile."[41] And on the other he could wish to destroy the figure because "he found her too sentimental."[42]

The elegantly formed figure sits precariously on a tilted, shallow bench that is an element of a thronelike, cagelike frame. Next to her right hip the artist originally placed an enigmatic shape, usually identified as a bird, which he later removed. An oblong plank rests incongruously on her feet, leaning against her lower legs as if to prevent escape from her awkward position. Her thin upper arms and the long, even vertical spaces between arms and torso make the woman a partial echo of the scaffolding to which she is joined. The merging of furniture and figure is more evident in *Hands Holding a Void*, the engraving made after the sculpture.[43] The legs appear to grow directly out of the bench, with no demarcation of the torso's end or the bench's beginning.

The head, originally that of a sad-faced woman, was replaced by a more abstract, less emotionally revealing face that was inspired by a gas mask from World War I.[44] Frustrated hope has always been understood as the emotional subject of *Invisible Object*; indeed, frustration was the artist's lifelong preoccupation. The entire figure, restrained from below and reaching out above, epitomizes his conflict.

Enormous schematic eyes dominate the simple, open-mouthed face, which has retained its look of poignant longing. The figure's elongated torso provides space for three important anatomical features—delicate, firm young breasts; a suggestive oval protrusion of the belly; and the much-discussed long-fingered hands, expectantly outstretched. The hands and lower arms have exceptional vitality, springing upward from the tubular upper arms. The subtle arrangement of spread fingers and palms facing each other off-angle enlivens and mystifies by the ambiguity of the gesture. Seen in profile from a distance, the splayed fingers resemble a bouquet or sunburst. Seen frontally, they are in dialogue—the right hand pulls away, and the left inclines toward. Such hands inquire, bless, or speak to us in the eloquent gestures of a Mediterranean tradition. They are tantalizing, like Giacometti's *Suspended Ball*. Each part of each digit has been considered. The index finger of the figure's left hand is delicately raised instead of being poised to grasp.

The most celebrated story about *Invisible Object* was told by Breton. Wandering with his friend one spring morning through a Paris flea market, Giacometti chanced upon a metal mask, which he felt compelled to purchase. Using it as the model for the figure's new head, Breton maintained, Giacometti found a way to overcome the paralysis that had kept him from finishing the sculpture, so different from his other, more easily realized, surrealist works. In his glowing critical assessment of the work, Breton explained Giacometti's obstacle as his inability to resolve the conflicting sentiments he had depicted on the figure's naturalistic face—venom, astonishment, sadness, and tenderness.[45] By covering the face with a mask and therefore avoiding the sentimentality of a naturalistic visage, Giacometti had succeeded in creating distance from the specific narrative of his own life and past, raising the sculpture's meaning to universal significance. He also avoided confronting a difficulty that would grow in the coming years—his inability to find a satisfying image of women and a face that integrated ambivalent feelings.

Breton's interpretation quickly became the principal way of seeing and understanding the work. It focused attention away from puzzling details, such as the oval protrusion in the belly and the bird beside the woman's hip. Eventually, alternative hypotheses for *Invisible Object* were proposed; most were vaguely philosophical or broadly general and tied to finding specific sources in tribal or ancient art.[46]

Over the years, Giacometti added a number of alternative "explanations" of his own and remembered sources for the hands as well as for the whole figure. Soon after making the work, for example, he told Marcel Jean that he had always known what the figure had in her hands, without saying what that was.[47] To Masson, Giacometti said that the inspiration came from a girl holding a vase; to Leiris, the artist claimed it was a Swiss girl holding a ball.[48] In an earlier published account, Leiris reported that the source for the position of the figure's hands was "a girl with knees half bent as though offering herself to anyone who looks at her (a pose suggested to the sculptor by a little girl he once saw in his native land)."[49] Giacometti wrote to Pierre Matisse in 1956: "I don't know where the idea for this sculpture comes from. I had the wish to make two hands and the rest was solely to support that."[50]

Giacometti's contradictory stories sound more like associated memories than conscious fabrications. They engender confusion but lead us toward a fundamental insight about an artist's memories and sources. Whatever the precipitating factors setting the chain of associations in motion, the artist's work consisted of weaving and reweaving those various threads, synthesizing their essence with his own aesthetic and personal concerns.

I propose that one of the key strands for *Invisible Object* is Cuno Amiet's painting *Hope*, the central panel of his triptych eventually retitled *Hope-Transitoriness* (1900–4). In Amiet's *Hope*, Anna Amiet is depicted holding out her hands while joyously awaiting the birth of their firstborn child, the baby boy in the horizontal panel above the hopeful mother (fig. 7.3).[51] After the tragic stillbirth of their only biological child, Amiet added the two side panels of himself and his wife as skeletal figures and changed the title to *Hope—Transitoriness*.[52] The triptych was a statement to the world of the Amiets' deepest feelings, exhibited in public like a shrine many times and painted in four versions. It remained in the Amiets' bedroom as a poignant reminder of their dead child.[53] Anna Amiet's hopeful hands are awaiting the child who never arrived.

FIGURE 7.3 *Cuno Amiet, Hope-Transitoriness, 1900–4. Tempera on canvas. Overall dimensions: 79.5 x 86 cm. Kunstmuseum Olten.*

Though he knew of his godparents' tragedy from childhood, Giacometti might not have fully understood it until years after the event when he saw Amiet's memorializing triptych. In *Hope*, both the mother and baby have outstretched hands, and each of Amiet's four versions of the central panel focuses on his wife's waiting hands, which are startlingly similar to those of the woman in *Invisible Object*.[54] The powerful images represented in Amiet's painting, especially the empty hands, remained lodged in Giacometti's memory. Now, in the midst of mourning his father, the young artist transformed them in his own memorializing work.[55]

The motif of the Swiss girl, mentioned in the story Giacometti told Leiris, can also be connected to Amiet, whose three adopted daughters were a part of Giacometti's childhood. The connection of the Amiet family to the *Invisible Object* becomes more certain in light of *La Toilette* of 1908, Amiet's portrait of his second-eldest daughter, Greti Flury Amiet, shown in profile with her knees bent (just like the woman in *Invisible Object*) and her hands outstretched, waiting to be towel-dried after her bath (fig. 7.4). As one of Amiet's favorite paintings—he made five versions of it—Giacometti would have seen *La Toilette* during an early visit to the Amiet home and again on his eleven-day visit of 1920—the visit marked by Giacometti's infatuation with Greti.

An intriguing confirmation of the link between Amiet and Giacometti is Breton's poetic response in 1934 to the question, What is surrealism? He

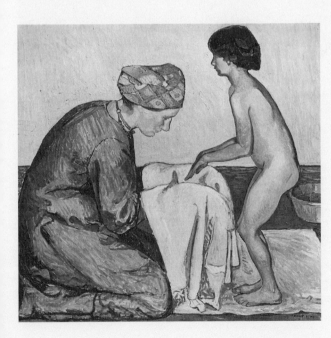

FIGURE 7.4
*Cuno Amiet, La
Toilette, 1908.
Oil on canvas,
dimensions
unknown.*

replied, "It is the battle of Alberto Giacometti against the angel of the Invisible who meets him among the flowering apple trees."[56] Did Breton know about Giacometti's close connection to Amiet, who was famous for his depictions of apple trees? Had Breton accompanied Giacometti to Amiet's 1932 exhibition at the Galeries Georges Petit and seen Amiet's portrait bust of his godson?[57]

In *Invisible Object*, the strange object at the side of the figure's pelvic area, which Giacometti removed from later bronze casts, has been identified as the head of a bird, symbolizing death.[58] I, however, interpret it as a densely packed, emotionally charged symbol of sexuality. It appears phallic in overall form, with a protuberant eye and what can be perceived as a vaginal slit. The conic shape is a condensation—part male, part female, merging the symbolism of both. Its overt phallicism, familiar from Giacometti's earlier surrealist sculpture, makes sense next to the woman's pelvis.[59] Perhaps, because it roused conflicts for the artist, he eventually eliminated it.

The precise placement of the hands of *Invisible Object* caused Giacometti great distress, and Lord reported this as the beginning of the artist's increasingly pronounced compulsion to discover the "perfect" placement for various objects.[60] Giacometti later described an example of his difficulty: "In my room I found myself unable to do anything for days on end because I could not discover the exact and satisfying arrangement of the objects on my table. . . . The search for this order, either by reflection or by trial and error, was a veritable torment for me. So long as I had not found it, I was as if paralyzed, unable even to leave my room, to keep an appointment."[61]

The doing and undoing connected with *Invisible Object* and the obsessional placing and replacing of objects in his room were probably related, both expressing Giacometti's anxiety. His father had just died at age sixty-five; Alberto was thirty-two, precisely his father's age at the time of his own birth. Remarkably, Giacometti's grandfather, also named Alberto, died at age sixty-five, at which time his son Giovanni was thirty-two. That coincidence could have served as one more reminder of the dangerously fateful link between birth and death.

Invisible Object, like Amiet's *Hope*, has a double title, *Hands Holding the Void*, a pun in its original French—*mains tenant le vide* (now emptiness)—its alternate meaning having a typically surrealist twist. Giacometti began work on *Invisible Object* in spring 1934, on or near the first anniversary of his father's death. With Giacometti's father gone, there was no longer an affectionate parent to hold him. His mother's hands had never been good at touching her children. As he confronted a world without Giovanni Giacometti, Alberto felt only emptiness: a mother's *hands* are able only to *hold a void*—not a live child. An-netta Giacometti had grown up with too many voids and losses. With the death of her husband, she returned to a life of emotional absence, with no nearby love object to hold on to or to reflect her strength back to her through his loving glance.

The engraving of *Invisible Object* mentioned earlier reveals Giacometti's pre-occupation with the oval shape in the figure's belly. In the sculpture this form can be rationalized as abdominal muscle, but in the etching a separate or-ganic being, such as a fetus, is implied—perhaps the child that Giacometti could never father. The highest goal of alchemy was creation, symbolized by the philosopher's stone. In *Invisible Object*, the missing product of a creative gesture, the invisible object, is transmuted into creativity itself.

With *Invisible Object* and the related work 1+1=3, Giacometti arrived at an end point. Participating in surrealist activities allowed him, like many other artists, the opportunity to explore fears and desires and to give form to his fantasy life, thereby providing a kind of psychological treatment—psycho-analysis without a psychoanalyst. Soon after his father's death, Giacometti terminated his "treatment."[62] Though surrealism as a movement was still vi-tal, it no longer offered him enough safety to stem his anxieties. He spoke of his surrealist phase as a "detour" and "masturbation" and of his work during this time as "grotesque" and "fit for the junk heap."[63] Old inhibitions re-asserted themselves. Most likely he had come too near unbearable inner truths—hostile wishes and unloving perceptions of both parents. Without his father's presence he did not have the resources to forgive himself or to inte-grate these truths harmoniously into his personality. Some of his fears and wishes continued to obsess him, and he spent the next thirty years depicting immobilized women with empty hands at their sides and gaunt men striding away from them.

As for alchemy, Giacometti's subsequent relationship with its principles is unclear. Overt references completely disappeared, but hints of his continuing belief in the power of art to bring new life into being—alchemy's greatest goal—suggest that he never gave up the hopes fanned into existence during his surrealist sojourn.

1935-1941

TRANSITION AND TIMELESSNESS

In the winter of 1934–35 Giacometti was at the end of a ten-year episode during which he had been catapulted to the center of the most sophisticated art milieu of the era. Now he had to surmount several emotional hurdles before he could move forward in his work. First he had to recover from the sadness, anger, and guilt he felt after his father's death in 1933. The sense of loss was almost unendurable and stirred recollections of childhood distress when his father had been away. Artistically, he had to either abandon his interest in magic and the occult or find a new way of expressing it. Finally, he needed to sort out his feelings toward the female members of his family and women in general. All three tasks involved him in a major change of style.

THE FATHER IS DEAD—LONG LIVE THE FATHER

During his surrealist years Giacometti had explored the inner world of memory and imagination partly as a way to escape the rivalry with his father and other artistic forefathers. Not having to compete with his father for ten years had given Giacometti some psychological independence, and his greatest freedom had been freedom from external perception—his or anyone else's.

It was a calamitous coincidence that Giovanni Giacometti died only five weeks after the publication of "Yesterday, Moving Sands" in 1933, in which his son expressed murderous fantasies in his transparently symbolic "falling asleep fantasy." His first reported outbreak of obsessional behavior as an adult, occurring as it did in the year after his father's death, suggests that Giacometti believed that his wishes had precipitated actual events. Making and unmaking his work, or rearranging objects on a surface many times in an effort to find the "right" combination, were rituals to magically "protect" him from the harm he had wished on someone else. When Alberto was a child his mother had meted out the punishments for occasional misbehavior. As an adult he made himself suffer through his ascetic lifestyle. After 1933, the punishment was never sufficient to assuage the remorse that tormented him for the rest of his life. After his father's death his unconscious magical fantasies were sometimes too near the surface of his mind, and no matter how rational he could be, they seemed believable. He had, for a moment, wished his father dead. And now he was dead.

Unconsciously, he may have expected retaliation for his crime—the imagined murder of his father. After his father's death, and particularly after Giacometti's departure from the surrealist brotherhood, he moved away from making art based on imagination and returned to working from nature.[1] (Work from imagination usually requires an easy conscience, especially when the artist is depicting or writing about rape and murder.) Having spent the summer of 1934 with his family in Maloja, and in the company of Ernst, Giacometti returned to Paris that fall and soon turned to working on life-size heads of Diego and of Rita Gueffier, a professional model.

By working from reality and by artistically identifying with the person whom he had imagined murdering, Giacometti attempted to find relief from his inner torment, binding himself, like Ulysses, to the mast of representation to protect himself from surrealist temptations. He had done very few representational works in Paris and even fewer surrealist works in Switzerland, where the studios in Stampa and Maloja no longer felt like safe zones. Now they reminded him of sadness, not rebellion, and he began to out-Giovanni Giovanni.

Painting or drawing heads from models made him feel close to his father, as if he were seeing things Giovanni's way. As a child Giacometti had sometimes not been able to hold on to the memory of his father's face when he was absent. The grieving adult returned to figuration partly to refind him, or at least to find a comforting mental image of him. By imitating the man who had spent years making portraits of his children, Alberto could feel less alone in the world. But turning to Giovanni meant turning away from Breton—the man who had served as a father-substitute for four important years.

Like Giovanni, Breton had always shown respect and sympathy for Giacometti and seemed to understand the emotional consequences of his bereavement.[2] In spring 1934 Breton wrote a long text celebrating their close friendship and mutual concerns, and eloquently praising Giacometti's sculpture

Invisible Object. Later that year he also invited Giacometti to illustrate one of his most romantic and occult texts, *L'air de l'eau*.[3] Yet that winter Giacometti felt pressed to decide between continued concurrence with Breton's strictures or exile from the group. He knew the sorts of small acts of disobedience that would upset the notoriously exigent surrealist leader, and he probably provoked the break by a series of small infractions.[4]

The tale of a bitter aesthetic falling out between the two men makes a good story but is probably a distortion of the facts. Their correspondence reveals that, immediately after the break, they reestablished an amicable relationship. In addition, Giacometti remained close to other important surrealists such as Ernst and Eluard, both of whom he continued to meet frequently. Giacometti's dramatic departure from Breton was as much an emotional step as it was an aesthetic/philosophical one.

Over the years Giacometti often cited a particular anecdote when describing his break with surrealism—Breton's response to Giacometti's work from models: "Every one knows what a head is!" It is easy to imagine the young artist feeling hurt and angered by his mentor's ridicule. In response to Breton's remark he claimed repeatedly that "[n]o one had ever succeeded in modeling or portraying a valid representation of the human countenance; the whole thing had to be started again from scratch."[5]

Superficially the rupture appeared to have several causes. Giacometti may have felt excluded by Breton's involvement with Jacqueline Lamba, whom he married in August 1934 after only three months of "mad love"; Giacometti was a witness at their wedding. It was the first time in Giacometti's friendship with Breton that the surrealist leader was in a relationship with a woman who returned his passion in equal measure. Breton's romantic passion would have presented no particular obstacle for his other friends, but for Giacometti, who was trying to overcome a serious depression after his father's death, the new preoccupation and distancing of the surrealist leader may have been devastating. Rather than face abandonment by another father figure, Giacometti took a preemptive step, turning his back on Breton by forsaking the leader's fundamental principle—imagination.[6]

After Breton's marriage Giacometti needed a new father figure on whom he could depend. He soon found a replacement—André Derain, whose confident air and large physical presence suggested Olympian majesty and tranquil certitude along with a touch of pugnacity. Derain enjoyed life and gathered beautiful women around him, including Isabel Delmer and Sonia Mossée, two women who would have a major impact on Giacometti's later work and life. The transition from one idealized hero to another would have been eased by Giacometti's awareness that Breton had always admired Derain; he owned some of his work and wrote about him on several occasions.[7] In less than a year after his departure from surrealism, Giacometti had become one of Derain's loyal visitors.

Derain's art and taste had been celebrated as revolutionary during an earlier era, but now many observers considered it *retardataire*. For some young artists in Paris, however, Derain represented a spirit of independence, combining modernism with the best of traditional art. The fact that Derain had developed a bold, vanguardist style before turning back to figuration made him an even more suitable role model for the uneasy Swiss artist.

Derain's departure from Paris in the mid 1930s to work in relative solitude in the countryside was indicative of his taste for meditation and philosophy, including his inclination toward the occult.[8] Known for a famous phrase— "the supreme power underneath things"—he was fascinated by the "correspondences" between man and the spiritual world, which he saw as a transmutation of a lower material nature into one of higher value. Derain's work appeared in the surrealist journal *Minotaure*, and he wrote a brief article on the interpretation of tarot cards for its first issue.[9] Interested in the animism and totemism of primitive and prehistoric cultures, Derain was one of the first European artists to collect African art. Like Sir James Frazer in *The Golden Bough*, which he admired, he believed that archaic, folk, and primitive art all were motivated by magical intentions. And, like the surrealists, he consulted the works of medieval alchemists, particularly Paracelsus.[10]

By 1936 Derain was surrounded by a coterie of enthusiastic, younger figurative painters who were seeking the values of past art. They became Giacometti's new artistic family: Francis Gruber, Balthus, and Tal Coat. Of them, Giacometti was the most fanatical proselytizer for a return to nature.[11] Intense devotion to a cause is often fueled by equally intense conflicts, and fervent proclamations can be the mind's attempt to keep doubts at bay. A closer look at Giacometti's transition from surrealism will clarify what those doubts were.

The earliest published explanation of Giacometti's radical departure from his surrealist style is contained in his 1947 letter to Pierre Matisse:

And then the desire to make compositions with figures, for this, I had to make (quickly I thought) one or two studies from nature, just enough to understand the construction of a head, of a whole figure, and in 1935 I took a model.

This study should take me (I thought) two weeks, and then I could realize my compositions. I worked with the model all day from 1935 to 1940. Nothing turned out as I had imagined. A head (I quickly left aside figures, it was too much) became for me a completely unknown object, one with no dimensions. Twice a year I began two heads, always the same without ever ending, I put my studies aside.[12]

His statement is not persuasive nor entirely trustworthy. Giacometti had fully completed some sculpted heads, such as Head of Isabel (1936), and a figure, Walking Woman, in fall 1936. Why claim he had used only one head or that he has used "always the same [model] without ever ending"?

When Giacometti stopped seeing reality through his father's eyes during the 1920s, he cut himself off from an important anchor. Much of his perceptual difficulty after 1933 had to do with no longer having his father before him. Initially, his father's death interrupted his ability to keep the fantasy objects of his surrealist period in his memory. Later, the nature of his perceptual problem changed.

Humans are not born with the capacity to form a secure mental image of another person. Initially, for example, an infant can remember only parts of the mother—her face, her smell, the sound of her voice. When a child is flooded with powerful negative feelings—such as rage, fear, or sadness—as well as positive ones, remembering the absent mother becomes more difficult. Not before the age of three or four can a child hold in its mind an integrated image of its mother or another important caretaker when that person is out of sight.[13] Even older children still can become anxious if the duration of the absence is long enough.

As we have seen, when frightened or angry Giacometti could become unable to remember a person's face—an extreme response that can usually be traced to early childhood. During his father's frequent absences, Giacometti felt abandoned—giving rise to an inability to remember his face. Experiencing anger directly toward this beloved parent was too dangerous and could have terrible results—in Giacometti's mind harboring or expressing such negative feelings actually could cause his father never to return—so his father's face gets erased from memory instead. Without the ability to recollect the familiar visage, Giacometti was left with the feeling that the world was peopled by strangers.

After 1933, without his father's physical presence to be close to or rebel against, Giacometti occasionally couldn't recognize a person directly in front of him or a very familiar model he had been in the process of drawing or sculpting. Nor could he trust his memory. He knew that it simplified and reduced: "Memory is short, very short. When you look at reality, it is so much more complex, and when you try to do the same thing again from memory, you realize how little you remember. So the work becomes simpler because there's less of it."[14]

Giacometti seemed to be trying to remove the mental static that interfered between his memory and his visual perceptions. But he knew that such a task was impossible—not because of the perceptual challenge, but because it would mean emptying his mind of the complications of memory: the thoughts, feelings, and fantasies that entwine themselves around and through any remembered image. When he lost his ability to recognize a model he had known for years, he was left alone with a stranger. In his words: "The more I looked at the model the more the screen between his reality and mine grew thicker. One starts by seeing the person who poses, but little by little all the possible sculptures of him intervene. The more a real vision of him disappears, the stranger his head becomes."[15] "All the possible sculptures" and all the possible ways of seeing reality thickened the screen between the reality of the model and Giacometti's visual perception of that model, which "intervened" between the actual comfort of an external object and a stable memory of a lost person. All his conflicted feelings and different ways of thinking about a person caused the interference between "reality" and his perception of it.

Having Diego as a model in 1935 helped to ground Giacometti, making life feel more like the old days at home when posing for a portrait or making a portrait was a way to establish emotional closeness. It wasn't a perfect solution, but it was better than working from imagination. In a letter to his mother in fall 1936 Giacometti recounted how the daily events of his life never changed and how he saw himself as an echo of the "old master" who reared him: "I almost never go out. I always work from morning till night . . . I see few people . . . I started working again on my heads which are going well. I shall also start a figure . . . Diego often poses for me . . . *I've really become an old master* . . . and I'm looking forward to starting that figure like when we were children waiting anxiously for the Christmas tree . . . the same feeling and the same pleasure. . . . At 1 PM sharp we [Diego and Alberto] go to eat, always at the same table, each of us seated at his own place . . . I've never enjoyed it so much."[16]

The entire letter is designed to appeal to his mother's wish for unchanging routine and stability in the presence of separation or loss. By recalling to her the "happy childhood" memories of past Christmases, of the way things used to be, he too could return to earlier times, times when his father was still alive. Whenever he had felt lost and alone, Giacometti turned toward the sustaining source of his father's representational style. In the mid 1930s, because representational portraiture, like surrealism, was not working well enough to calm him, he turned to ancient Egypt.

EGYPT

Giacometti's involvement with Egyptian art and culture was lifelong, and his thoughts and observations about it were complex, affecting his beliefs about life and death as well as his conception of art. He was drawn to the ancient art for several compelling reasons, only one of which is usually emphasized by scholars: his admiration for its timeless beauty. Another factor, though somewhat speculative, is more emotionally important: the ritualistic and magical purposes of Egyptian art were a natural resting place for Giacometti's long-standing superstitiousness and interest in magic, which also fit well with his fearful and obsessional personality.

Giacometti's interest in the occult had always been an object of ridicule in the family. Bruno, Francis Berthoud (Ottilia's new husband), and even Diego teased him about his superstitiousness. In the early 1930s they joked about a green witch coming to Maloja; Alberto took it so seriously he could not sleep, and his father had to intervene.[17] After his father's death, Egyptian magic took on a new relevance, designed as it was to assuage the pain caused by death and to reduce the anxiety and guilt associated with hostile feelings. More direct and primitive than the philosophical alchemy of surrealists, it was the strong medicine Giacometti needed to calm his augmented anxiety. For thousands of years Egyptian culture had been synonymous with a belief in magic, especially its efficacy in relation to death.[18] Giacometti's fascination with ancient Egypt was a perfect cover among his Parisian friends for his superstitiousness and magical ideas.

Giacometti's enduring interest in Egyptian art was also related to his belief that the ancient artists of the Nile valley had mastered the artistic dilemmas confronting him now: the relative roles of perception and memory in representational art, and the relationship between ideal and real. Visual son of a visual father, Giacometti had dedicated his life to questions about perception, memory, and mental images and how they related to one another. In the Giacometti household these were common topics for discussion. Egyptologists, especially those like Borchardt and Schaefer, who were concerned with aesthetic and philosophical aspects of their subject, wrote about perception and mental imagery in Egyptian art, thereby returning Giacometti to home base.

Egypt and Alberto

As noted earlier, Giacometti's first serious encounter with Egyptian art was probably his discovery, at age twelve, of the sculptures from the workshop of Thutmose (one of Akhenaten's principal court sculptors) around the time of his grandfather's death. In the periodicals in his father's studio, Alberto could peruse Hedwig Fechheimer's articles about the astounding archaeological finds at el-Amarna. A few years later, in 1917, Giacometti announced his admiration of Egyptian art and culture to his classmates at Schiers. From then on his interest in Egypt was continuous. In letters home from Rome in 1920–21 he enthused about the many Egyptian works he saw at the Vatican. "I don't think my view of the most beautiful statue I've seen will change. . . . It is neither Greek, nor Roman and even less Renaissance, but Egyptian . . . Egyptian sculpture has a greatness, a rhythm of line and form, a perfect technique never equalled. Everything is carefully considered down to the last detail . . . and *those heads are alive . . . they seem to look and speak.*"[19] In 1952 he referred to an Egyptian portrait bust he had seen in Florence in fall 1920 as "the first head which seemed lifelike to me."[20] I propose that the Egyptian bust Giacometti so admired in Florence was the limestone *Bust of a Woman* from the Amarna period of the 18th Dynasty (fig. 8.1). A highly prized work in the National Archeological Museum at the time of his visit, it was called the *Dame of Florence* and was pictured in one of Fechheimer's two lavishly illustrated books on Egyptian sculpture, *Kleinplastik der Aegypter* and *Plastik der Aegypter.* Giacometti bought both books in the early 1920s and repeatedly studied the illustrations over the next forty years.[21] Furthermore, the sculpture itself bears a remarkable resemblance to Giacometti's mother, particularly as she had been depicted by him two years earlier (see fig. 2.4).

Giacometti immediately began to make copies from both books.[22] In the 1940s he pored over books on Egyptian art with his young nephew, telling the history of Akhenaten in such stirring terms that the boy remembered the story forty years later.[23] In the 1950s he spoke passionately about Egyptian art and culture to Yanaihara, his model and close friend. And in the 1960s, only a few months before he died, Giacometti spent hours in the British Museum in London looking at a small ivory carving of an ancient king from Abydos and some Egyptian paintings that he found "marvelously real and life-like."[24]

Throughout his life Giacometti made drawings of Egyptian sources. In fact, they outnumber his copies of all other sources. He made the first group of such copies in 1921–23, probably stimulated by the death of the Dutchman; the second group date from the mid 1930s when he was mourning his father.

FIGURE 8.1
Bust of a Woman,
Egyptian, 18th
Dynasty. Limestone,
h 50 cm.
Archeological
Museum of Florence.

He apparently worked on a third group during the war while he was in Geneva.[25]

Though the copies range across all Egyptian periods, Giacometti favored the 18th Dynasty, especially its revered and reviled ruler, the heretic pharaoh Akhenaten, also known as Amenophis IV (fig. 8.2). The young ruler turned away from the religion and customs of his powerful father, Amenophis III, as he set up a new monotheistic religion dedicated to the sun god Aten, moved to a newly created city, and changed his name to Akhenaten.

W. Flinders Petrie, an influential early Egyptologist, set the course of scholarship with his book on Akhenaten in 1894. Petrie's ideas were popularized by James Breasted, perhaps the most influential historian of the early twentieth century. Both prolific writers, they established the received wisdom on Akhenaten for nearly half a century.[26] Petrie described the object of the young king's life as attaining and spreading religious "truth" by replacing

FIGURE 8.2
Photograph of Bust
of Akhenaten
included in 1922
Fechheimer article
published in Die
Plastik der
Aegypter.

polytheism with monotheistic worship of the sun.[27] The young ruler's motto was "Ankh-em-Maat" (living-in-truth), and the solar disc appearing in so many reliefs of the royal family shows rays of the sun placing the hieroglyph of truth at the mouths of family members.

Physically Giacometti bore certain similarities to the legendary ruler—both had a long chin, thick lips, spindly legs, and long arms. The resemblance is suggested in a Man Ray photograph of Giacometti (fig. 8.3). Furthermore, many aspects of the Akhenaten story (as it was known then) could have struck him as parallels to his own life. Both men had formidable, dominating mothers, close relationships to beautiful younger sisters, and prospects of over-turning a father's way of seeing. In his single-minded search for truth and his devotion to a single deity, Akhenaten was a revolutionary figure with whom the artist could identify.

Giacometti was well aware that Akhenaten eventually lost the battle

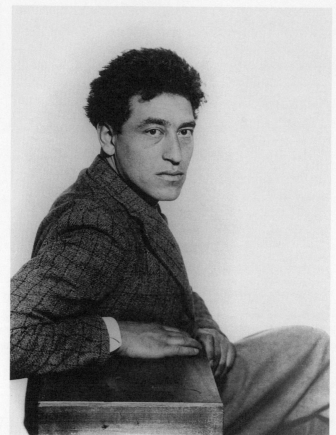

FIGURE 8.3

*Man Ray
photograph
of Giacometti,
c. 1932.*

against the old order, and that magic with its arcane rituals triumphed after the pharaoh's death. Though appalled by the ferocious and largely effective efforts by Akhenaten's son-in-law, Tutankhamen, to obliterate his predecessor's images and return to the old religion, Giacometti with his contradictory nature took comfort in the return of magical rules and formulae.[28]

Tutmania

A significant event that overlapped Giacometti's interest in Egyptian culture was the discovery in 1922 of the tomb of Tutankhamen, with its glittering contents and aura of mystery. The story of Howard Carter's discovery of Tutankhamen's tomb was masterfully managed by the media and set off an international craze called Tutmania.[29] Before 1922, Egyptology had been a scholarly discipline with a limited public. Afterward, the popular thirst for knowledge about ancient Egypt seemed insatiable.[30]

The archaeological work lasted for more than ten years, as Carter carefully proceeded toward the inner chamber where the pharaoh's body was encased in a magnificent golden coffin. The popular press broadcast the news of each astonishing find, from mummified fetuses to exquisite jewelry and cosmetic jars. The "Nile Style" became popular in France in the world of decorative arts, as seen in the large Exposition des arts decoratifs in 1925. A few years later, Alberto and Diego Giacometti designed Egyptianate objects for Jean-Michel Frank, such as their plaster *Lamp* (1936), which was almost an exact replica of an alabaster lamp from the anteroom of Tutankhamen's tomb.[31]

Basic information about Egyptian religion—especially its emphasis on death—and the discovery of an intact tomb set off a fad for magical thinking of all kinds. When a few people who had been present at the opening of the tomb died soon after, the "mummy's curse" became a heated topic, feeding into the long-standing European conviction that powerful secrets with occult meaning lay hidden in Egypt's past.

EGYPTIAN ART THEORY: WHAT DID GIACOMETTI KNOW AND HOW DID HE LEARN IT?

The foremost authority on the theoretical foundation of Egyptian art was Heinrich Schaefer, director of the Egyptian Museum in Berlin, where half of the finds from el-Amarna, including the famous Nefertiti bust, were housed.[32] His masterwork, *Principles of Egyptian Art*, published in 1919 with many subsequent editions, was considered the most comprehensive attempt to explain the theories underlying the artwork.[33] Whether Giacometti had actually read Schaefer's book or merely had learned of its principal ideas through Fechheimer and other writers, he certainly understood and absorbed its main messages. First, Egyptian artists were the intermediaries of immortality: their aim was to create life through art, especially through sculpture.[34] In his many statements describing Egyptian art, beginning as early as 1921, Giacometti frequently used the words "alive" and "lifelike." Second, Egyptian artists evolved a system of representation based on mental images and frontality, which summarize the essential physical character of the person depicted.[35] Initially some works from Thutmose's workshop were thought to be death masks but soon were seen as anomalous achievements—momentary impressions of a living person and the illusion of living flesh.[36] Fechheimer described them as counterparts to Egyptian mummies, whose purpose was to preserve the body for its active role after death. In *Die Plastik der Ägypter*, she wrote: "[T]o create an image is called in Egyptian to bring to life."[37]

Schaefer and other Egyptologists who dominated the field during Giacometti's youth were unequivocal about the magical intentions of Egyptian artists. In *Principles of Egyptian Art* Schaefer wrote: "Works of art which represent living beings or things do not have the same meaning for us as they do for the Egyptians. . . . For them figures could have not only aesthetic qualities but also those of *living beings*. Only if we take such attitudes to representations seriously shall we understand quite why figures were so often worshipped in Egypt . . . a secret power in every image. This belief in the independent life of images was one of the reasons why ancient Egypt left behind it such an unbelievably rich legacy of sculpture and two-dimensional representations."[38]

Egyptologists were particularly interested in having their readers understand the difference between modern and ancient magic. "We ought not to attach to the word, magic, the degrading idea which it almost inevitably calls up in the mind of a modern. Ancient magic was the very foundation of religion."

THE DOUBLE

The idea that most Egyptian sculpted images of figures were "doubles," or *ka* figures, was well established and accepted by scholars in the nineteenth century. The idea of the double would stay with Giacometti all his life, and its formulation by the French Egyptologist Gaston Maspero was probably the foundation of Giacometti's understanding of the term, which he later adopted to describe his own work. As director-general of the Antiquities Service in Egypt, Maspero wrote numerous books on Egyptian art and life, and these reached a large popular audience, especially French speakers.[39] One example of his concept of the double comes from *The Manual of Egyptian Archaeology*: "The Egyptians regarded man as constituted of various entities, each of which possessed its own functions and life. There was the visible form, the body to which the *ka* or *double* was attached during life. The *ka* was a replica of the body, of a substance less dense, a colored but ethereal projection of the individual. . . . The existence of the *ka* depended on the body. . . . By the process of drying and embalming the body they could prolong its existence, while by means of prayers and offerings they saved the *double*, the *soul* . . . from the second death."[40]

Egyptian artists, especially sculptors, had to follow the rules of Egyptian religion. "As soon as the *ka* statue was regarded as the posthumous support of the *double* it became absolutely necessary that the new body of stone or other materials should be a copy—even if only a summary—in order that the *double* might adapt itself with ease to its new support. The head is therefore a faithful portrait, while the body on the contrary is that of a person in the highest state of development in order that he may fully enjoy his physical powers in the company of the gods. The men are always in the prime of life, and the women have *the slender proportions of girlhood.*"[41]

Is this the unconscious purpose of Giacometti's post-surrealist figures? Were they contemporary ka statues whose function was either to bring people back to life or to keep them alive? Unconscious fantasies can propel an individual to action, even becoming the nucleus of a life goal without his ever realizing the source.[42] For Giacometti, wishes to both destroy and create life were compelling forces. His aggression was more obviously visible in the way he treated himself and his artwork—by taking many destructive steps. It seems likely that his wish to create life took the form of an unconscious fantasy of magical transformation—that as an artist he could bring his work to life. Though he knew consciously that this was both impossible and absurd, he nevertheless continued to believe it in a part of his mind. This belief emerged even more forcefully after World War II.

If a person believes that an image has magical power, then that person will likely also believe that the power will be lost when the image is damaged or destroyed. The destruction of so many images of Akhenaten by the enraged priests he had overthrown was meant to eliminate the power of those images, just as Akhenaten had eliminated his father's power by erasing his name from monuments. By the time Giacometti began to make and then destroy his figurative work in the 1930s, he would have understood that the power to destroy images was a direct counterpart to the magical power of images themselves.

MENTAL IMAGE, TRUTH, PERCEPTION

The search for truth in Egyptian art involved two conflicting dilemmas, both discussed by Schaefer: how to balance between ideal and real, and how to balance between perception and memory. Before and after Akhenaten, Egyptian artists' portrayals were idealized. "Only youthful, firm, and well-formed bodies are to be seen."[43] At the beginning of Akhenaten's brief reign, Petrie believed, artists were encouraged to make portraits that were truthful representations, and the gifted court sculptor Bek claimed to have been instructed by the pharaoh to do so.[44] The images of the sun king's odd physiognomy (especially his long neck and drooping chin in the early years of his reign) make him appear distorted or diseased, and Petrie saw these as expressions of the new style of art, that is, as exemplifying living-in-truth and

Akhenaten's revolutionary ideas.[45] Though never completely departing from the fundamentals of Egyptian religion, Amarna period art shifted from exaggerated realism toward subdued naturalism. By the end of Akhenaten's reign a moderated version had emerged, represented by the sculpture from Thutmose's workshop.

Schaefer discussed how the essential character of Egyptian art resided in the idealization of the human figure and face, but it was not a simple strategy: "However capable the Egyptians were of producing true portraits, the tendency to the typical and idealizing is dominant. Both occur together at all periods."[46] Rather than reduce the Amarna controversy to a simple dichotomy between free, naturalistic representation and rigid adherence to ideal rules, Schaefer saw the situation in a more complex and probably accurate light. Giacometti's aesthetic goals from the mid 1930s on—to make a head seem alive and to find a path combining the specific and individual—resonate remarkably well with Schaefer's statements, and they are part of the artist's continuing fascination with Egyptian art.

The other idea emphasized by Schaefer and incorporated in Giacometti's future aesthetics was that Egyptian artists depicted a person according to mental images summarizing his physical essence rather than his actual appearance.[47] Schaefer's argument was based on a belief that perspective, introduced by the Greeks, distorted reality. He discussed the role of memory and argued that it was necessary "to correct the appearance of perspective or to remove it because it was an illusion that distorted things."[48] Though the artist might perceive a foreshortened object, to reproduce one would be to go against truth. The remembered image—via a frontal or profile view not distorted by perspective—provides the most characteristic and complete impression of an object. Schaefer observed: "The great majority of the non-foreshortened views which dominate Egyptian drawings go back to the data which the eye at some time provided," or what he calls "mental image," by which he meant the frontal view of an object being depicted.[49] Schaefer clarified his theory with a "rule of straight directions."[50] With one plane as a starting point, "the other principal planes of the torso and limbs . . . form an intersection of planes at right angles."[51] Using illustrations and line drawings of Egyptian art, Schaefer demonstrated how the artists represented perceptual reality when it diverged from their attachment to mental images. Schaefer's certainty that the ancient system accounted for the long-lasting success of Egyptian art is most likely reflected in Giacometti's increasingly insistent thoughts about an aesthetic "system." In the mid 1950s he told Yanaihara: "I have to find a system. If I follow the system faithfully it will lead me closest to reality. There has to be one. The Egyptians must have possessed such a system. Otherwise it would have been impossible to produce such fantastic works for such a long period of time . . . no other sculptures as closely resemble real people as Egyptian sculpture."[52]

Giacometti used Egyptian imagery and symbolism at various times throughout his surrealist period, but he did not return to making a large number of drawn copies of Egyptian art until after his father died. Between 1932 and 1936 he made two Egyptianate sculptures, Walking Woman and Head of Isabel (The Egyptian).[53] In its earliest state Walking Woman (1932–36), with its mysterious triangular indentation just below the figure's breasts, was suffused with surrealist symbolism. For an exhibition the next year Giacometti temporarily added delicate long and outstretched arms, whimsical hands made of feathers, and the scrolled top of a cello for a neck and head (fig. 8.4). With its "slender proportions of girlhood" described by Maspero, that version of the work bears a striking likeness to statuettes of the two Egyptian goddesses who protect the canopic coffers in Tutankhamen's tomb, Isis and Nephthys (fig. 8.5). The elegant young bodies and long, outstretched arms of the ancient and modern sculptures are notably similar. That Walking Woman walks might be the principal reason for her existence, since she illustrates what Giacometti found most magical about Egyptian art. She was like a "double" on the verge of coming to life.

Isabel the Egyptian (1936) (Hirshhorn Museum) is a terra-cotta head with a Nefertiti-shaped face, and hair that resembles a pharaonic headdress. The sculpture relates to "Isabelle of Egypt," an obscure story by Achim von Arnim, one of surrealism's heroes, and was republished by Breton in 1933 in a small volume of von Arnim's works titled Bizarre Tales, which Giacometti read with enthusiasm.[54] It was an eerie tale of a female golem (double) produced from clay by the gypsy daughter of a magician of Egyptian descent. By definition an exact and magical replica, the golem was indistinguishable from the real Isabelle.

The model for the Head of Isabel was Isabel Delmer, a young English woman who had posed in London for Jacob Epstein, the English sculptor, and for Derain after she moved to Paris in 1934. Giacometti met her in the mid 1930s, probably through Derain.[55] Fascinated by the vivacious beauty, Giacometti observed her from a distance for some time. Capricious and flirtatious like von Arnim's Isabelle, the actual Isabel had three husbands, numerous lovers, and a reputation as a femme fatale.[56]

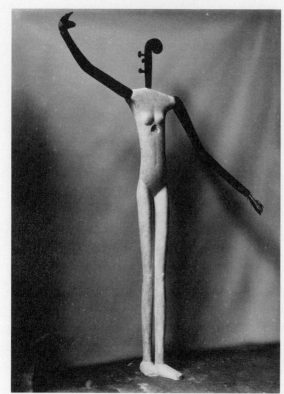

FIGURE 8.4
Marc Vaux
photograph of
Walking Woman
(surrealist version),
1932–36, plaster
and wood
(destroyed).

PORTRAITS: THE REAL AND THE IDEAL

For Giacometti the portraits from Thutmose's workshop, and the Amarna style in general, conveyed the pervasive Egyptian overtones of magical intent but through a prism of naturalistic representation. The portraits could have inspired the artist to return to representation in the mid 1930s without having to abandon magical intentions. Like Thutmose, he could struggle to achieve masterly portraits of real people while simultaneously serving the deeper and more secret purpose of keeping the dead alive.

Identifying with Akhenaten's wish to serve and even deify "truth," Giacometti may have begun at this time to merge his search for truth in portraiture with aliveness. Late in life he said: "Egyptians . . . translated their vision of reality as closely as possible . . . it was a religious necessity . . . a matter of creating doubles as near as possible to human beings. An ancient text . . . talks about sculptures so true that they seem living and that they are able to frighten those who see them. . . . I have never yet succeeded but there is something in my sculpture that comes rather close."[57]

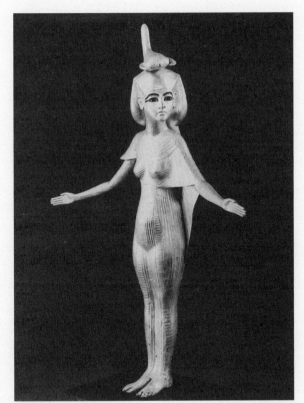

FIGURE 8.5

Isis, c. 1347–1337
B.C.E. (Egyptian, 18th
Dynasty). Gilded
wood, dimensions
unknown. Egyptian
Museum, Cairo.

TRANSITION AND TIMELESSNESS

The hallmark of Giacometti's work in the 1930s and early 1940s was his search for the perfect universal models of man and woman through individualized portraits. It was his personal attempt to solve the Egyptian dilemma, as posed by the books he read on Egyptian art and culture and the images he found in the Louvre. With the brief exception of Akhenaten's reign, Egyptian art had provided an excellent model of how to turn specific individuals into idealized universal symbols, each practically interchangeable with others.

Giacometti's struggle with the issue of individual versus universal is eloquently stated in an interview with Drôt, in which he claimed that he always turns familiar models into strangers—everyman and everywoman. "You are no longer the person I thought I knew. You no longer have any particular characteristic. As for individuality, you become a generalized head, the head of everyone."[58]

Why would Giacometti wish to deny individual characteristics? Why would he want or need to interchange one person with another? In Egypt such exchangeability had served the political goal of maintaining the appearance of an unbroken line in the royal house, providing stability for the culture. For Giacometti it had a similar psychological goal: it could help him avoid the traumatic impact of individual loss or separation. As we have seen, "forgetting" his father's face threw him into a panic as a child. As an adult, a similar panic occurred when he lost contact with Diego, especially in moments of danger.

With his brother Diego willing to pose endlessly and be represented in a variety of guises, including a bald Egyptian priest or scribe, Giacometti found the prototype of a safe and familiar man. Over the next thirty years, he would make portraits of other men friends, but only onto Diego could he project his views of mankind, including his sense of himself.[59]

If a particular individual he was portraying became everyman or everywoman, Giacometti would not feel bereft when the work was completed. There would always be someone else. Generalizing and idealizing heads and bodies could also protect Giacometti from too much intimacy—the opposite danger but one closely connected to loss and separation. It was better and safer to create generalized figures toward whom he could not attach any unmanageable feelings such as love or hate.

Giacometti's search for the perfect model of a woman was more difficult. For most people, the internal visual female template is the mother, as perceived in childhood. Giacometti's mother lived to age ninety-three, dying less than two years before he did. His conflicting feelings for her were more complicated than those he had felt toward his father. For public consumption, she was the nurturing mother who fed him, fussed over him, and washed his hair when he went home. Privately, he also knew her as the critical parent who lashed him with her acrid remarks when he did not comply with her wishes or when he wavered in his conformity to her view of the world. As observed earlier, only by isolating his loving feelings from the bitter anger he also felt could he hold on to his idealized view of her and keep her on a pedestal. If he had been able to tolerate his anger and disappointment with her he would not have had to idealize her; the idealization was necessary to ward off knowledge of her faults.

The emotional and geographic distance Giacometti kept from his mother had been obscured by his closeness to his father. But with Giovanni's death that distance no longer was possible. Giovanni's unexpected early death had reawakened the traumas of Annetta's childhood, exacerbating her sensitivity to separation and her emotional brittleness. She assumed that Alberto would act as the senior man in the family, making up in some way for the loss of her husband. The parental bedroom was passed on to him, and she moved into what had been the children's room. For the next thirty-one years she maintained her home almost completely unchanged and sent daily letters to her children, expecting a response from one of them every three days. To some degree Giacometti complied, writing relatively often and visiting regularly. For his compliance, he expected her support in return—moral and, at times, financial. She gave strictly limited quantities of each, thereby intensifying his longing for the nearly unqualified support he had received from his father. She had the same craving for Giovanni's loving support—an impossible situation, leaving mother and son bound to disappoint each other. Neither could provide a steady loving gaze for the other since both suffered from similar fears and doubts about themselves. While she presented a mask of absolute certainty to the world, her son was perfecting his presentation as the quintessentially anxious man, forever filled with doubt. As his Parisian life diverged increasingly from his mother's expectations of him, Giacometti kept more of that life secret from her, knowing that her disapproval would create a breach between them.

WOMEN

I have already discussed how Giacometti's ambivalence toward women was expressed by dividing them into ideal or debased creatures. But because he also loved women and enjoyed their company, Giacometti kept trying to find a solution to his dilemma. On some occasions he would select women, like Isabel Delmer, who were already attached to other men and therefore were unlikely to bind him so tightly that his hostility would be aroused. The essence of the tough woman's toughness would be her contempt for him, which would allow him to feel that his hostile and cruel feelings were deserved, thus easing his guilt over having them.

An essentially gregarious man who enjoyed companionship, Giacometti spent time with several women simultaneously in the mid 1930s. In addition to Isabel Delmer, he saw the tempestuous Denise and other prostitutes, and he was friendly with Sonia Mossée, a beautiful bisexual. But to none of these women was he as tightly bound as he was to the women in his family. Giacometti could no more integrate his divided views of the women he loved—bad and cruel on the one hand, loving on the other—than he could integrate divided views of himself.[60]

One of the few women to whom Giacometti could be close was his sister, Ottilia, who had moved to Geneva when she married in 1933 (fig. 8.6). By 1937 Ottilia had taken center stage in the family, first as a figure of hope and

FIGURE 8.6 *Alberto and Ottilia Giacometti, c. 1923–24.*

regeneration, and then as a figure of tragedy. Ottilia was closest in appearance and personality to her father: gentle, warmhearted, light-haired, and uncomplaining. After Ottilia was married, her energetic efforts to bear a child were discussed in the Giacometti family.[61] Her mother and siblings probably hoped that her pregnancy would fill the gap created by Giovanni's death. When she died, hours after giving birth to Silvio Berthoud, the family's only grandchild, on October 10, 1937—Giacometti's birthday—Alberto was thrust again into profound mourning.[62]

Giovanni's death had paralyzed his son but led to one of his greatest masterpieces, *The Invisible Object*. Ottilia's death, four years later, intensified his superstitious fantasy that birth and death were inevitably yoked. His own birth had coincided with the death of Amiet's baby, his grandmother Ottilia's death coincided with his sister Ottilia's birth, and now Silvio's birth and Alberto's birthday elided with his sister's death. It was shortly afterward that Giacometti began to diminish his figure sculptures and to destroy most of what he made.

In summer 1937 Alberto had eagerly placed his hands on his pregnant sister's abdomen and listened for the baby's heartbeat. At the time he was working on two paintings, *Apple on a Sideboard* and *Portrait of the Artist's Mother*. Ottilia's pregnancy had offered Giacometti a second chance to come to terms with an early childhood trauma—her birth, which he had witnessed up close, and the subject of childbirth in general. When the joy of her impending motherhood was shattered by her death he was retraumatized to the extent that, for the next eight years, he was obliged to create, destroy, and re-create tiny images symbolizing her.

In *Artist's Mother* Annetta Giacometti is shown as a solid, white-haired figure dressed in her habitual black, facing front and slightly off the central axis of the canvas, staring at the viewer.[63] The dense intensity of her face, which is barely covered with flesh, is achieved by myriad small brushstrokes that build up a vitally faceted surface. She is seated before a background of loosely brushed ocher and faded rust, roughly divided into verticals on the left and horizontals on the right, suggesting the wood panels and windows of the Maloja apartment where it was painted. His mother's face, which he probably painted over after Ottilia's death, embodied her sadness, her terror about death, and her vulnerability. It also conveyed his pain and guilt at surviving the deaths of both his father and sister.

There are several singular aspects in this painting. Annetta Giacometti, a thin sixty-eight-year-old woman, is shown with a large stomach, suggesting pregnancy or obesity. When bodily distortions appear in Giacometti's figures, they usually arise because a hidden, even unconscious, mental image conflicts with his perception. Was Annetta portrayed as large-bellied because Ottilia's pregnancy revived Giacometti's memories of when his mother was pregnant with Ottilia? Or because it covertly restored Ottilia to life? Annetta's bulky body can also be read as a covert masculine presence—the missed and missing father.

The second remarkable feature is the combination of Annetta's skull-like face and strangely styled white hair. The paint on the background and the rest of the figure is laid on thinly, while that of the face has been thickly applied. Annetta's sunken eye sockets and gaunt cheeks make her look as though she were either severely ill, near death, or under extreme tension. When Giacometti looked at his mother, did he see a woman who had survived her husband and her daughter, a woman once again abandoned by a close family member as she had been so many times in her childhood? Did Ottilia's death also recall the traumatic period of 1911–13, during which his beloved grandfather died and his mother was beset by a bout of nearly fatal typhoid fever? As a result of that illness Annetta had lost her teeth, and her hair had so whitened that she probably resembled the ghostly face of the portrait painted over a quarter of a century later.

Giacometti's first painted portrait after so many years presents the striking combination of imagery referring to both pregnancy and death and suggests the power and traumatic valence of his unconscious fantasies as well as the role they played in stimulating his new style and greatest work that would follow.

TINY FIGURES

Giacometti often claimed he couldn't account for his obsession with the tiny figures he made and unmade for almost a decade. It is impossible to know how many he produced during this time, but only about two dozen are still in existence, most less than three inches in height. Many years after the fact, the artist claimed that the heads and bodies simply got smaller while he was working on them. At other times he asserted that he was compelled to keep reducing them by forces beyond his control.[64]

"One is no longer secure of the real aspect nor the dimensions, one isn't secure about anything," Giacometti later wrote. "That is how the heads became tiny and tended to disappear. I couldn't distinguish the numerous details. To see all of them together I had to move the model as far away as possible. By distancing oneself the head became small and this terrorized me. The fear of things which disappear."[65] If we understand these ex post facto explanations as rationalizations, Giacometti's real reasons emerge. Giacometti's loving feelings drew him toward women, but his fears and aggression forced him to maintain a distance. His extreme ambivalence was expressed in perceptual terms. He would not see (that is, love) a woman if she were too close. For several years, after complaining that his models were becoming harder to see, he increased the physical distance between him and them. Another way of creating distance was to reduce the size of a figure.

In 1963, in two published interviews, Giacometti explained that Isabel Delmer—"an English girlfriend"—was his inspiration.[66] In one report he states: "In 1940 to my great terror my statues began to diminish. It was a horrible catastrophe: I remember for example that I wanted to reproduce from memory a girl that I loved as I had seen her one night on the boulevard Saint Michel. I wanted to make her (about 80 centimeters from the ground). It became so small I could no longer put on any details. I didn't understand anything about it. All my sculpture ended up inexorably, no larger than one centimeter. A touch of the thumb and whoops. No more statue."[67]

More recently, a book by David Sylvester, an English writer on art who was friendly with Giacometti in the 1950s and 1960s, cites an unpublished letter to Isabel from 1945 in which the artist tells her she was the model for his tiny figurines.[68] I suspect Giacometti's claim was a piece of his ingratiating politesse, similar to his telling his mother that she and Diego were the subjects of all his heads and figures at this time. In 1941 Giacometti experienced his first unsuccessful attempt at making love to Isabel the night before she was leaving Paris to return to England. Four years later the artist was on the verge of returning to Paris from Switzerland and resuming the relationship with Isabel. He had good reason to tell her that she was the object of his fascination, that he could not get her out of his mind, and that he wanted to return to Paris to be with her. Still, he said he couldn't leave Switzerland until he made larger, better figurines. Giacometti's style of dissembling is consistent. He told stories designed either to make the listener feel good or to hide a deeply disturbing truth.[69] Isabel was always another man's wife or lover, and Giacometti's relationship with her was invariably about distance.

In the late 1930s Giacometti reportedly told Picasso that the model for the tiny figurines was a tall, beautiful Jewish Parisian, Sonia Mossée, who used to join them at the Café Flore. They discussed perfect measurements and what her silhouette looked like from afar. In 1944 Picasso told his lover Françoise Gilot about Sonia's importance to Giacometti and that it was her body and characteristic stance that served as Giacometti's inspiration for the small images seen at a distance. "[Even though] she was dead, when Giacometti or Pablo were speaking of recognizing somebody from a distance they would always cite her. She was like the archetype of what was necessary for Alberto."[70] There is no record of a romantic relationship between Sonia Mossée and Giacometti; indeed, she had a female lover and only occasionally had affairs with men. The only written record of Giacometti's attitude toward her was a comment in a letter to Isabel that Sonia was boring.[71]

Who was Sonia Mossée? Like Isabel Delmer, Sonia had posed for Derain, had been photographed by Man Ray, and was one of the lively café regulars in St. Germain and Montparnasse. Simone de Beauvoir described her as "An extremely attractive girl frequenting the Café de Flore in the 30s, superb features and body, though perhaps a little overblown for a girl of twenty, she had inspired many painters and sculptors, Derain among them. She had gorgeous blond hair, which she brushed back over the nape of her neck in artfully arranged coils, the quiet originality of her clothes and jewels."[72]

Sonia's long blond hair and perfect measurements might have been enough to make her stand out in the discriminating Parisian café crowd, but for Giacometti it would have been her bearing and stride that was discernible from afar and made her "necessary." Sonia believed that standing and walking with her arms held unmoving at her sides was both elegant and appeal-

FIGURE 8.7 *Marc Vaux photograph of* Three Miniature Figurines, *c. 1945, plaster versions (destroyed).*

ing, and she tried to convince her friends to take up this unnatural posture.[73] From a distance the stance would resemble the idealized Egyptian girls depicted as concubines of the dead in so many of the Egyptian sculptures that Giacometti admired at the Louvre. It became Giacometti's prototypical pose for female figures for the next twenty-five years.

During the years in which Giacometti actually began to make his tiny figurines he told his friends, "If I made them larger you could recognize who it is."[74] The figurines were certainly not large enough to identify their model yet Giacometti felt compelled to eliminate most of them. I believe that he was making images of his sister but didn't want this fact known or didn't fully realize what he was doing. If Sonia had indeed been the physical model, reducing her to minuscule size made it possible for Giacometti to reduce both her physical power and her character flaws while avoiding any potential resemblance to Ottilia.

Most of the small figurines from the late 1930s to the mid 1940s were female, with large pelvises and rounded bellies, traits they shared with the prehistoric fertility figures Giacometti knew from the Musée nationale de l'antiquité at Saint-Germain-en-Laye. A particularly evocative photograph by Marc Vaux presents them as the artist wanted them seen (fig. 8.7).[75] The few male figures he made either resemble Silvio or are actual portraits of Giacometti's nephew. The time period in which the figurines were created and their link to both fecundity and Silvio suggest that Ottilia, especially the pregnant Ottilia, was often present in Giacometti's mind as he worked. Like Sonia, Ottilia was beautiful, fair-haired, statuesque, and artistically inclined.[76] And one woman had disappeared from his life at approximately the same time that the other was appearing.

Interchangeability of idealized figures was a concept familiar to Giacometti from his knowledge of Egyptian art. Egyptian sculptors (at least from Thutmose's workshop) established an ideal model and used it for various individuals. The sculpted heads of Akhenaten and his mother (Tiy) and wife (Nefertiti) are sometimes difficult to differentiate. Interchangeability gave the Egyptians the same comfort it gave Giacometti. It obliterated loss and hid any break in the flow of continuous ancestry.

Giacometti's tiny figurines resembled Egyptian sculpture, either the small female figurines representing concubines for the dead (as those he had first seen in Florence) or the amulets whose role as described in the Book of the Dead was to protect the souls of the departed from evil and help them on their way toward eternal life (fig. 8.8).[77]

Repeatedly making and demolishing the tiny figures might have been Gia-

FIGURE 8.8

Concubines for the
Dead, 2040–1780 B.C.E.
(Egyptian, Middle
Kingdom). Wood,
dimensions unknown.
Archeological Museum,
Florence.

cometti's way of trying to combat the helplessness he felt at having lost his sister. He could not bring her back to life, but he could make both amulets honoring her fertility and images of her son. The magical power of the amulets set on their steep pedestals synthesized the artist's attempt to find a new form of image magic to combat his old, dreaded enemies—death and his own aggression. The power of those adversaries ascended throughout the 1930s as did Giacometti's frantic but futile attempts to gain some emotional power over them. Alchemy, magic from ancient Egypt—nothing availed, and little of Giacometti's work survived the long, dark period in which his mourning was soon to be matched by that of the world.

CHAPTER 9

1940-1946

THE WAR YEARS: GENEVA AND PARIS

In the years before the war, many French intellectuals were drawn to the themes of aggression and death. Chief among them was Georges Bataille, whose lifelong preoccupation with death had attuned him better than most to the coming conflagration. His writing and editing focused on mankind's darkest sadomasochistic behavior, transgressions, and taboos, as well as life at the edge of death and the unspeakable and disgusting. "Nothing is more important for us," he wrote, "than that we recognize that we are bound and sworn to that which horrifies us most, that which provokes our most intense disgust."[1]

Bataille grew up in a household touched by illness and despair, and by repeatedly challenging himself to face horrors with equanimity, he spent most of his life trying to overcome it. When he was born in 1897, his father was already blinded by syphilis, and when he reached age three his father was paralyzed. His mother was suicidally depressed, and both Bataille and his elder brother recalled witnessing sights that left them "permanently damaged."[2]

In 1914 the adolescent Bataille rebelled against his parents' atheism by converting to Catholicism. When the First World War began, Bataille and his mother were evacuated from their home in Rheims, leaving his father behind to die two years later. Plagued by guilt about abandoning his father (and also about hostile fantasies regarding both parents) while attempting to be a model young man, Bataille enrolled in a seminary in 1917 with the intention of becoming a monk or a priest. But he gave up the religious life several years later, allegedly after experiencing his first sexual relationship. A somewhat priestly quality, reflected in his high seriousness and asceticism, always flavored his personality.[3] Rejected by his first girlfriend because her family feared hereditary syphilis, Bataille turned to a life of dissolution masked by elegance and erudition. Ever after, sexuality was tainted for Bataille.

Bataille began his career in Paris as a librarian at the Bibliothèque Nationale. A scholar and intellectual firebrand, he joined the surrealists, and Masson, Leiris, and Theodore Fraenkel became his closest friends. He proved to be a gifted editor with a flair for attracting talented writers, scholars, and artists, but was ambivalent about his own work, and most of his early monographs were published in very small editions under pseudonyms. They have since become famous, and at least one, The Story of the Eye (1928), fits closely with Giacometti's preoccupation with seeing and being seen.

Giacometti had been drawn to Bataille and his ideas in 1929 but had turned away for a few years, pursuing instead the orthodox surrealists around Breton. When his official connection with surrealism ended, Giacometti reconnected with Bataille and socialized with him in Paris throughout the 1930s. The artist was drawn by Bataille's intensity, sadism, disregard for convention, passion about death, and sense of guilt. Both men scorned organized religion yet believed in some form of spirituality. Both were dedicated to a liberated, unconventional lifestyle yet were rule bound and enwrapped in inhibitions. Both were obsessional and masochistic. Calling that last characteristic "a damnable meanness toward himself," Bataille was more aware of his inner conflicts, possibly because of his brief brush with psychoanalysis in the late 1920s.[4] Giacometti, on the other hand, seemed puzzled and irritated when friends observed his self-punitive behavior.

Masochism and its paired opposite, sadism, made Bataille and Giacometti exquisitely sensitive to wounds and wounding. They could detect in others what they felt in themselves—a deep sense of pain and vulnerability—qualities which also drew them to prostitutes, whom they tended to glorify. Both sought to free themselves from their psychological fetters by throwing themselves into ecstatic experiences—sexual, artistic, or mystical—but Bataille succeeded more frequently than Giacometti.

Psychoanalysts believe that the major roots of obsessionalism and sadomasochism are often painful experiences that occur during early childhood, when children begin to say no to the pressures of caretakers, particularly those relating to toilet training. As children discover how to master their own bodies and feel the exquisite pleasures of being in charge of what goes in and out of them, their physical selves can become a battleground for control between them and their parents.[5] The fantasies and wishes children typically experience around these issues involve the torture of and total power over helpless victims as well as a desire for revenge. When they are obliged to accede to the demands of adults, children often turn to their imaginative fantasies to satisfy their wishes for control. In the course of so-called normal development those fantasies and wishes are usually moderated or given up; when they are retained, the frequent result is sadistic or masochistic character problems later on. Like Giacometti and Bataille, adults who remain caught in childlike battles for power with their parents or intimates perpetually long for a freedom they don't know how to achieve. This lack may not prevent them from achieving success in life, but it almost always inhibits them from forming mutually supportive relationships with intimates and taking whole-hearted pleasure in their accomplishments.

Though both Giacometti and Bataille disdained ambition and material success, they were considered leaders by their peers. Still, both men were beset by corrosive self-doubt and repetitive, self-lacerating thoughts that destroyed their inner peace. Only by doing and undoing—or by destroying and creating—their artistic work did they come close to transmuting their uncertainties and resolving their conflicts.

Both also danced on the razor-thin boundary between the possible and the impossible, between life and death. Like Bataille, who saw completeness as exclusively God's prerogative, Giacometti rarely believed after 1933 that any of his work was really finished. Each night he would push himself to the edge, separating destruction and creation when he worked past the point of exhaustion trying to find his way to a masterpiece he would never be able to complete.

Less prolific than many of his friends, Bataille possessed a way of thinking that had widespread influence. In the years just before the war his writings focused on how men as a group must join together to face the untouchable and unspeakable—which included corpses, menstruating women, and other pariahs—to arrive at the sacredness of life itself. Writing as a sociologist, Bataille argued that "early human beings were brought together by disgust and by common terror, by an insurmountable horror."[6] He was particularly interested in how an individual reacts in the face of death.[7]

"Joy in the Face of Death" was the title of one of his lectures at the College of Sociology, which he founded in 1937 and where leading French intellectuals, including Sartre, Leiris, Lacan, and Merleau-Ponty, came to speak and listen.[8] (Personal response to death was a popular topic in the late 1930s, and Giacometti would have participated in numerous discussions on the subject.) Bataille's inquiry was always about how to pursue life in its fullest meaning while remaining aware of its end. "Freedom is nothing if it is not the freedom to live at the edge of limits where all comprehension breaks down," he wrote.[9] His strong mystical tendencies fueled his adult search for an "impossible" solution to this question.

During his early surrealist years, Bataille expressed his need to face and surmount the dark aspects of life partly by an interest in alchemy.[10] By the end of the war his alchemical leanings were more disguised but still prevalent. Though the fashion for mystical meandering had been replaced by the exciting new intellectual trend of existentialism, Bataille questioned whatever solution was current, and doubted the value of logic. Though obsessionally tied to internal rules and the orderly activity of a librarian and editor, he publicly dedicated himself to its opposites—disorder, extremity, and *informe* (formless). After the war, in May 1945 Bataille moved to Vézélay, where he began work on a new journal, *Critique*. He often returned to Paris to see his friends, especially Leiris, Masson, Fraenkel, and Teriade as well as Giacometti, to whom he remained close. As we shall see, Bataille's influence on Giacometti's postwar work is significant.[11]

Giacometti's direct experience of the Second World War and its grim horrors was limited to a ten-day bicycle trip toward the south of France with Diego and Diego's lover, Nelly, from June 13 to June 22, 1940, just before the occupation by German troops. It was a grisly journey marked by the sight of decomposing corpses, severed body parts, and panicked refugees, and the traveling companions were nearly victims of machine-gun fire from German planes strafing the roads. After five days, Alberto decided the group was better off in Paris, so they hurried back through the detritus of abandoned vehicles and burning towns.

Back in Paris Giacometti continued to make his little heads and figurines, and Diego went for technical training. By fall 1941, under pressure from their mother, whom they had not seen in two years, and their own consciences, the brothers agreed that Alberto should go to Geneva. No one was dependent on him in Paris, and his two sources of relaxation—cigarettes and late-night prowls around the city—were severely restricted by the curfew imposed by the occupying forces.[12] What was meant to be a short trip turned into a four-year sojourn.

Annetta Giacometti was living in a spacious apartment in Geneva with her son-in-law, Dr. Francis Berthoud, and her little grandson Silvio, Ottilia's child, born in 1937. There she cared for her grandson during the first nine years of his life, spending every summer with him in Maloja.[13] Arriving at the beginning of 1942, Giacometti initially stayed with his family but was uncomfortable with the restrictions of their conventional life. He soon moved into a cheap hotel often used by prostitutes. The comfortless, unheated room measured only ten feet by thirteen feet.

Dependent financially on his mother, Giacometti was also psychologically beleaguered by her. Responding to his obdurate refusal to be neat or to follow her fiscal guidelines, Annetta treated her son like a naughty boy, forcing him to relive childhood experiences of angry compliance and secret rebellion. He was deliberately provocative as he tracked plaster through the spotless Berthoud apartment on his daily visits, while his mother rushed ahead placing newspapers along every path on which he might tread and on every chair on which he might sit. Without his brother as a helper or a dealer to sell his work, Giacometti had no money other than the small allowance his mother doled out at irregular intervals. Securely tethering him to her purse strings, she compelled Giacometti to beg each time he needed additional funds.[14]

When he could bear no more of her tightfistedness, he demanded a lump sum equivalent to a just inheritance from his father. Annetta refused furiously. She disapproved of her son's work as well as his lifestyle. She scolded him for his doodling, called him a "maniac," and told him she hated his tiny figurines. "You don't know how much they displease and trouble me . . . your father never did things like that."[15] Repeatedly making the pieces that his mother so disliked, Giacometti may have retaliated the only way he knew how. To her, working like Giovanni meant the happiness and the security of her marriage with a loving husband. To her son, it meant a failure to be himself. They were truly at cross-purposes.

During his four years in Geneva, Giacometti developed a close bond with his young nephew. He entertained the child with stories from Greek mythology and ancient history and eventually began to use him as a model for drawings and sculpture. Silvio recalled this period: "Occasionally Alberto made me pose, forcing me to remain immobile for interminable periods—fifteen, thirty, forty-five minutes, perhaps even an hour. Despite the charm of his conversation, I have very unpleasant recollections of sitting for him, for it was of utmost importance not to move but to fix him right in the eye and listen to him complain, saying he was getting nowhere. . . . His mother was always present, praising his work."[16] Silvio also remembered that, for several weeks, his uncle persuaded him to pose nude for fifteen to twenty minutes every evening after his bath.[17]

Alberto's rationalization for the lengthy modeling sessions was that he needed to get the portraits right. Silvio recalled: "Things would deteriorate rather quickly, for Alberto would return to his hotel in the evening with a sculpture eight to twelve inches tall under his arm and come back the next day with a piece no more than three or four inches high. He had worked all night, scraping and reducing this artwork. . . . Such a sculpture was not at all to my grandmother's taste, and I would have to pose again, to my great displeasure."[18] Mother and son colluded in the painful exercise in which Silvio was the designated sufferer. Using his young nephew as a model must have evoked for Giacometti childhood memories of posing for his father. On the one hand, these sessions with his nephew, both clothed and nude, probably helped him to reverse the painful and humiliating experience of the earlier time; on the other it likely allowed him to relive the pleasurable connectedness between artist and model.

During the Geneva years, Giacometti's friends were generally younger men whom he knew through Albert Skira, the publisher of *Minotaure*. Skira's office in Geneva had become a gathering place for artists and writers, many of whom were working on his new magazine, *Labyrinthe*. Some of the group were attempting to hold up the banner of surrealism; others were involved in leftist or resistance activities. Giacometti's closest friend in Geneva was Charles Duclos, a geologist fifteen years his junior who espoused surrealism and who was preoccupied with sexuality, death, and a masochistic lifestyle.[19] Giacometti's charm and intelligence entranced Skira's coterie, and he presided over them like a tribal chieftain.[20] Less conventional than Giacometti's family, they were tolerant of his artistic paralysis during the war.

Giacometti's life followed an invariable routine in Geneva. Waking up at noon he would lunch with Duclos and then return to his hotel room to work. Next, he would visit his family, and around five or six o'clock he would stop in at Skira's offices. Then he would dine with Duclos and other friends, after which he would often visit The Parrot, a brothel where Giacometti would drink and joke with the women. Eventually they would move on to a nightclub, the Piccadilly, where he enjoyed watching the striptease dancers.[21] Finally, he would return to his hotel room and work till dawn, unable or unwilling to sleep.

His insomnia could have had a number of causes. The obvious one is the war, which hovered all around, especially at night when bombers could be heard passing overhead. But surely his sleeplessness was also related to the mounting rage he felt toward his family—his mother, his brother Bruno, who worked as an architect in Zurich, and his brother-in-law, Francis Berthoud—all of whom let him know that his tiny figurines were a waste of time.

But insomnia was not the only way the Geneva war years affected Giacometti. In his personal habits and appearance there was a visible change. Usually dirty, badly dressed, and covered with plaster dust, he bathed only occasionally at his brother-in-law's apartment, where his mother would wash his hair. His smoking increased, and he would eventually smoke seventy to eighty cigarettes per day. Likewise he would drink six to ten cups of coffee daily. To be sure, his ostentatiously nonconformist lifestyle was partly an expression of his opposition to his family's conventionality. With his shabby appearance and habits, he could irritate and embarrass his bourgeois relatives. But his punishing lifestyle seems to have a deeper meaning as well. As we have seen, in 1921, following van Meurs's death, he had turned away from the comfortable trappings of middle-class life as a way of castigating himself. In Geneva, face to face with frustration and guilt for the rage he felt toward his family, as well as his fears stirred up by the war, his masochism reemerged and became a permanent feature in his life.

To master the guilt and fear stimulated by his destructive wishes, Giacometti turned to his work. In January 1942, Giacometti visited Maloja. Emboldened by the sight of his old studio filled with his own work, Giacometti was reminded of his father, whose work also surrounded him on the walls.[22] In this productive environment *Woman with a Chariot* (1942–3) (Wilhelm-Lehmbruck-Museum, Duisberg) came forth as a harbinger of Giacometti's future style. In the Maloja studio Giacometti was faced with 1+1=3, his large work commemorating the ancient cult of the fertility goddess at Paphos. Could that earlier sculpture have inspired him to produce a life-size votary for a similar goddess, one combining preclassical with classical legend? *Woman with a Chariot* stands on a large, cubic base, which itself rests on a small woodwheeled platform. Her legs and feet are tightly held together, her body erect and upright, her arms at her sides—the position of many of the small ivory or wooden Egyptian figurines representing concubines of death. The pristine nudity of *Woman on a Chariot* is accentuated by the painted necklace and facial features of the plaster original, lending support to the hypothesis that she was inspired by sculptures of the female servants attending temples in Egypt and the Mediterranean world, who were also nude and bejeweled.[23]

Woman with a Chariot differs from Giacometti's drawn and painted women of the period by her artificial hieratic stance and the way her hands decisively frame her pelvis.[24] As he worked on the little figurines and sketched from life or from imagination, Giacometti's efforts converged on finding a stance that would typify his ideal, the prototypical image of a woman from which he would rarely depart in coming years. Sculpting a young female nude in his father's studio at Maloja must have resonated with a distant memory of Ottilia, posing for her father in the summer sun. Placing the work on a wheeled cart, an obvious allusion to Silvio's wheeled toys, underlines the link to his sister.[25]

As a goddess, or as the servant of a goddess, *Woman on a Chariot* is severely restricted in her movements. She can come closer or go backward, neither of her own accord. Her helplessness resembles that of Alberto and Annetta Giacometti. For decades Annetta would not leave her home base, traveling only between Stampa and Maloja and after Silvio's birth, to Geneva. In a hauntingly similar pattern, her son was also stuck in place, making regular trips between Paris and the Bergel, back and forth with little variation from 1922 until his death in 1966. It is not so surprising to find restricted movement in an elderly woman firmly ensconced in the mores of the late nineteenth century. But in Giacometti, a twentieth-century man with an extraordinarily wide-ranging curiosity, the relative immobility is incongruous and appears to be psychologically based—a product of his obsessional character.

A woman on wheels could also refer to the legend of the Greek god Haephestus (Vulcan), a figure that Giacometti had sketched during adolescence.[26] Haephestus, along with Prometheus, was a patron of artists because he could create living beings, clay figures infused with fire or living breath. Born crippled, or lamed because of his audacious creativity, the divine blacksmith was a magical metallurgist who created golden mechanical servant girls on wheels to help him walk and work.[27] The punishment meted out to especially creative gods seems to fit with Giacometti's habitual feelings of guilt. An automobile "accident" in 1938 (coincidentally at the foot of a gilded statue of Joan of Arc) left Giacometti lame because he neglected the recommended physical therapy. Immediately afterward Giacometti explained that he felt free of his usual tension and anxiety and later reported that the accident had "helped" him.[28] These incongruous facts support the possibility that Giacometti had an unconscious fantasy about lameness being magically connected to artistic powers.

Giacometti's fascination with the magical powers of artists found reinforcement in his reading during the war. While in Geneva he was obsessed by Balzac's *The Unknown Masterpiece*. He kept the book with him constantly, and he underlined many passages, decorated its margins with drawings, and illustrated an article on Balzac in *Labyrinthe*. Balzac's story was about a celebrated older artist, Frenhofer, who was trying to compete with the gods and re-create life on canvas. He was secretly painting the portrait of a beautiful woman, but in his attempt to achieve the highest artistic goal and bring the sitter to life, he overworked the canvas, ending with a thickly chaotic mess of color and line—"a gigantic wall of paint." Giacometti identified with Frenhofer, whose passion matched his own secret desire. In the end, Balzac portrayed his artist as a fool, bewitched by fantasies which inevitably outrun his talent. Balzac's story has captivated many modern artists, including Picasso, who illustrated it, because it portrays a compellingly powerful fantasy—that an artist can create life. Ernst Kris, an art historian and psychoanalyst, has termed this fantasy "image magic," linking it to a belief common in earlier civilizations that artists could indeed create living beings.[29]

Giacometti heeded Balzac's warning insofar as keeping his secret secret, but it did not stop him from being obsessed with his goal. Friends who posed for Giacometti would have recognized him and his behavior in Balzac's depiction of Frenhofer: "Yesterday, toward sunset, I almost thought that my painting was complete. Her eyes seemed moist. Her flesh was agitated. She breathed! . . . But by morning, I realized my mistake. I could not believe that I had failed. . . . However, although I have discovered much, I have terrible doubts about my work."[30] In the same dark period Giacometti was also haunted by Kafka's story The Hunter Gracchus, a parable about a dead man who must wander the earth because he had missed his passage to the afterlife. The hunter's torment and confusion as well as his ambiguous fate fascinated Giacometti, for whom the idea of the undead dead held much power.[31]

Giacometti had told Duclos that his reason for making sculpture was in order not to die.[32] His goal was to make sculpture that was or seemed "alive." Creating living beings (doubles)—to compete with the gods and with woman's biological powers—appears to have been Giacometti's goal in the years after the death of his father and sister. Rational man that he was, Giacometti could not openly admit to such primitive magical thinking, nor could he explain his behavior or reveal his underlying motivations, even to himself. He later explained that he was making work that could give him the feeling of being "with" the model. With the creation of "living" sculpture he could express the loving side of his personality and counterbalance the menace of death and his own rageful destructiveness which he battled against nightly. By continuing to destroy his tiny figures, he was both imitating the gods and inflicting on himself the dangers intrinsic to artists who aspire to be godlike.

Giacometti's articles for Labyrinthe in Geneva provide evidence of this preoccupation as well as his own predominating rage and sadistic fantasies. Giacometti's article for Labyrinthe in January 1945, his first published text since 1933, was nominally about the sculptor Henri Laurens, an older man whom Giacometti had admired in Paris and who had served as a father figure in his imagination.[33] Using the autobiographical and metaphorical style of his surrealist texts, Giacometti wrote of feeling assailed by mental images, recollections, imaginary sensations, and visual events triggered by Laurens's work. Though describing what Laurens's sculpture meant to him, Giacometti is actually describing his own work and conception of art:

> A veritable projection of himself in space, a little like a three-dimensional shadow. His manner of breathing, of touching, of feeling, of thinking has become an object, sculpture. This sculpture is complex, it is real like a glass (I would have said "or like a root") . . . it recalled a reinvented human figure, it was above all the "double" of that which made Laurens identical to himself over time . . . but each of these sculptures is rather a crystallization of a particular moment of this time. . . . Laurens creates simultaneously volumes of space and volumes of clay. These volumes alternate, are balanced and together become the sculpture. And this sculpture is a *clear sphere*.[34]

Giacometti then discusses the "space of indefinable dimension which separates us, that space which surrounds the sculpture and which is already the sculpture itself." It reminds him of exactly the sensation he has often felt in the presence of living beings, especially human heads. The exact limits, the dimensions of this being become indefinable. Laurens's sculpture expresses what Giacometti feels in front of "living reality," by which he means that it is "lifelike" and that lifelikeness is for him one of the reasons he loves it.[35]

The image of the "clear sphere" has long been associated with the occult—from the crystal ball to the alchemical philosopher's stone. And though the author denies mystical undertones in this essay, his many hermetic references belie this. Giacometti's text also reveals his growing obsession with the "double." Through his arcane references to "roots," "crystallization," and the interchangeablility of "space" and "volume," Giacometti's writing discloses how magical "doubles"—his first published reference to this concept—from occult traditions are close to his concept of sculpture and how both underlie his idea of "lifelikeness."[36] He thus establishes, in 1945, the principal aim for his postwar sculpture: to create a living reality or "lifelike" work, a reinvented human figure, a materialization of ephemeral reality. Awareness of the irrationality of such a fantasy can live next to the fantasy itself, and does for many artists. So it seems to have been for Giacometti. This explanation is usually overshadowed by another story he would tell—that he was trying to capture a perceptual likeness—but he stuck by it nevertheless. Few people listened carefully, and fewer understood him.

In his second essay for *Labyrinthe*, "A propos de Jacques Callot" from 1945, Giacometti turned from the occult to the psychology of artistic motivation, which he indirectly describes as sadistic aggression and sexual violence.[37] Although ostensibly about Jacques Callot, the seventeenth-century printmaker, a patriot from Lorraine who refused to take a stand for the king, it is actually about French resistance to the German occupation. Francis Gruber, Giacometti's close friend in Paris who was active in the underground, had painted *Hommage à Callot* in 1942. The canvas depicted the ravages of war and contained a coded signal of resistance.[38]

In addition to Callot, Giacometti discusses Goya and Géricault in his essay, focusing on their depictions of horror. He sees sadistic wishes in their art and claims that all works of art reflect the artist's obsession with his "primordial" subject, which stems from childhood sadism: "It would be necessary to speak of children's pleasure in destruction, their cruelty (killing insects and other animals, mutilating them, making them suffer) and their voracity which is not put off in front of excrement. . . . In all works of art the subject is primordial, whether the artist is conscious of it or not. . . . The form is always the measure of the artist's obsession with his subject."[39]

Is Giacometti telling us that his own work is about his childhood obsessions, particularly his sadistic fantasies? Writing about Callot, Giacometti is entranced with scenes of destruction, massacre, torture, and rape, observing with pleasure that the crowd is involved in killing themselves or each other. He goes on to say that Callot (here we should certainly read this to mean Giacometti himself) may merely be expressing his horror of the war.[40]

In concentrating on the "frenetic desire for destruction in all spheres" in Callot's work and his use of sadistic imagery, Giacometti was employing a classic obsessional way of dealing with trauma, namely, viewing and reviewing a painful scene in an attempt to master the anxiety associated with it. By turning a passively experienced overwhelming event into an active one, the former victim imagines that he can control it.[41]

After Paris was liberated in August 1944, though longing to return to the city he loved and reconnect with his studio and with Diego and other friends, Giacometti was unable to take the active step of leaving Geneva for another year. Even after obtaining a visa and being honored at a farewell dinner hosted by Skira, Giacometti postponed his departure. He later claimed that he needed to make one more tiny figurine.[42] Finally, he left for Paris on September 17, a month after his mother decided to leave Geneva to return to her apartment in Stampa.[43] Giacometti's love for his mother was intermingled with so much anger and frustration that he could not break free until she herself let go. Like many obsessionals, he might have imagined that, without regular contact to undo his hostility, his aggressive fantasies would hurt or even kill her. When he returned to Paris his anger, which had already moved him to destroy most of his sculpture, would continue to drive his work, impelling him to find a new shape, but it would also be tempered by more positive feelings.

ENTER ANNETTE

In October 1943 Giacometti met Annette Arm, who was twenty-two years younger than the artist. A schoolteacher's daughter, brought up in a conventional and somewhat narrow-minded family, Annette was introduced to Giacometti by mutual friends when she was commuting from the suburbs of Geneva for secretarial school. The evening they first met he invited her to stay with him, and he later reported that he was impressed to overhear her lie complacently to her mother about her plans to spend the night in Geneva.[44] She soon moved into his dingy hotel room, and they became lovers and constant companions (fig. 9.1).[45]

Giacometti ordered Annette around, calling her "Little One," teasing her or tapping on her legs with his cane as they walked, crying "Forward, march!" In contrast to his family, Annette's adoring support was a welcome tonic. Not only did she find no fault with his uncomfortable lifestyle, she also liked his work. Her support was more than moral: she had a job with the Red Cross, and her small salary went toward paying their daily expenses; she also bought some of his sculpture.[46]

Choosing Annette as a partner was in character for Giacometti. Her name was similar to his mother's, and she was young, pretty, vivacious, at once compliant and rebellious, and willing to do and be for Giacometti whatever he wanted—all extremely appealing to the middle-aged man, most of whose family viewed him as a failure. Despite his lifelong problems with impotence, in the early years of his relationship with Annette his friends regarded him as happy and believed that he had a gratifying sex life.[47] Annette's parents were at first outraged by her relationship with a man so much older, who was so shabby and poor, but they soon accepted the situation. Annetta, on the other hand, did not meet Annette for six years, largely because Giacometti knew that she would not approve of their partnership.

After living for two years with the adoring Annette in Geneva, Giacometti returned to Paris and resumed his unresolved relationship with the more demanding Isabel Delmer. Meeting Isabel soon after his arrival, he invited her to share his living quarters. Giacometti's positive experience with Annette apparently persuaded him that he could continue the pleasures of domesticity. However, cohabitation with Isabel lasted only a few months. On Christmas Day 1945, without explanation, she went off with another man.

Giacometti's time with Isabel was tormented. He would wake in the middle of the night, terrified at the thought that he might run out of money permanently. Unlike Annette, Isabel was not willing to tolerate his marginal lifestyle or his emotionally withholding behavior. Like his mother, Isabel had a dominating personality and often reduced him to helplessness and rage. It was not until she left him that Giacometti began to find his soul again, and with it his signature style. In the meantime Annette Arm waited in Geneva.

Life in postwar Paris meant long hours in lines to obtain food and fuel, as well as frequent interruptions of electricity. The intellectual and political climate was filled with the aftereffects of the war and the occupation. Denunciations, revenge killings, the settling of old scores and jealousies all went on in

FIGURE 9.1

Giacometti and Annette, c. 1956–57.

the light of public trials in Paris as well as throughout Europe.[48] It would be years before Parisians felt their city had returned from the dark ages into which it had sunk. During this period Giacometti was unrelievedly poor, usually living on borrowed money from old friends like Gruber, Sartre, Balthus, and Picasso in the expectation that he, like other artists and intellectuals dislocated by the war, would eventually get back on his feet.

During Giacometti's sojourn in Geneva, Diego had faithfully cared for his brother's work and work space in Paris, and when he returned four years later Giacometti found everything in order. But artistically he remained as stuck as he was in Geneva. To be sure, the cold of that first postwar winter made it difficult to work; plaster and clay would not behave normally in the frigid studio. For four months he made and destroyed his tiny figures. Claiming that he was trying to regain control over this activity, Giacometti said repeatedly: "It is necessary to make them smaller. If I can make them smaller the way I want to, I'll get to the point where I can make them bigger."[49]

Giacometti's first postwar commission came through Louis Aragon, who had recently visited him in Geneva in 1945 and discussed two possible artworks to be included in a forthcoming exhibition, *Art and Resistance*, due to open February 15, 1946. The first, a memorial for French resistance fighters, would be a sculpted portrait of Colonel Henri Rol-Tanguy, a metallurgist who had been in charge of the resistance in the Ile-de-France region.[50] The second sculpture was to honor the innocent women and children who had died during the war. After his initial frustrating months adjusting to postwar Paris, Giacometti began to work. As the date of the exhibit drew near, the pressure increased.

Giacometti made drawings of Rol-Tanguy's head in two dozen sittings over several months, but he was still working on the sculpture when the exhibition opened. Then, one night at the end of February, everything changed. In an ecstatic letter to his mother, he told of his sudden success with the portrait and with *Night*, the monument for the women and children. He finished both in a manic frenzy over several days.[51] Writing feverishly, Giacometti stated:

> Since Friday I know how to draw like never in my life, and since yesterday I know how to make sculpture, I made in one night the bust of the Colonel from memory and in the morning Diego was completely surprised, because the bust was beautiful like an antique bust. I know how to do everything I want in drawing, sculpting, and painting . . . I am completely frightened by what I have discovered . . . I think about my dear figurines that I made and remade during the years and how they have made this

progress possible. This morning I jumped and cried for joy in the studio. . . . For three days I have seen things the way I have never seen them before.[52]

Why could Giacometti now succeed with sculpture, swiftly and effortlessly? The clues are in his letter. "I see reality for the first time, but in such a way that I can do everything very quickly. I know how to make figures in the void like the Greeks, I know how to make nude sculpture like the Egyptians—of the same quality. Every day I find something new. I almost never sleep. . . . I haven't read a paper for eight days or more."[53]

At least three factors may have helped release Giacometti from his decade-long inhibitions. One was the exhibition itself, where he must have seen works depicting the war's horrors, some painted by Gruber and Picasso as well as others by living witnesses such as Boris Taslitsky, a neighbor, friend, and fellow artist who had been at Auschwitz. The second factor was his reaction to the evidence of the Holocaust.

During the war, Giacometti had heard that Sonia Mossée, an inspiration for his tiny figures, had been interned at Drancy, the internment camp outside Paris, after a jealous concierge revealed her Jewish identity to the authorities.[54] Giacometti believed, as did her other friends, that she had been sent on to a labor camp and was still alive and working in a mine. He remarked to a mutual friend that such an experience would do Sonia some good, a casual comment that would cause him terrible guilt when he learned the truth of her last days. Soon after he returned to Paris, Giacometti heard that Sonia had died of starvation and exhaustion in a concentration camp.[55]

In 1945 the world was at last learning the truth about the "final solution." Reports and photographic evidence were circulating of the unbelievable horrors in the death camps recently liberated by the Allies.[56] With the opening of the Nuremberg trials in November 1945, the enormity of the Holocaust was established well beyond rumors and became regular fare in the press. For the entire month of February 1946 newspapers published the testimony of the war criminals and victims. On February 20, reporting on German atrocities in eastern Europe, the Russian prosecutor Colonel Smirnov showed films and described some of the more barbaric methods of torture: people were forced to walk barefoot on metal planks that electrified them, while others were herded into "trucks" and asphyxiated; one hundred thousand Jews in Minsk were obliged to dance and sing as they waited their turn to die; Serbian prisoners were stripped in the freezing cold and then turned into statues of ice as their tormentors poured water over them. Even *Le Figaro*, the most conservative of the papers read by Giacometti, went beyond its usual laconic report and published a bold headline, "21,000 cubic meters of corpses." *Combat*, the leftist paper written by many of Giacometti's friends, was the most explicit, describing recipes for soap and leather made of human fat and flesh.

Throughout his adult life Giacometti read several newspapers a day, but, according to his letter to his mother, on approximately February 21 he stopped reading the papers for around a week. What compelled him to give up his entrenched habit? Had the news reports become intolerable, particularly Smirnov's graphic testimony? Did visiting the exhibit *Art and Resistance* make the horrific images indelible? Did watching the survivors of the camps, looking like skeletons in their striped pajamas on the streets of Paris, make their suffering undeniable?[57] A person like Giacometti with a lifelong phobia of death would have experienced these images and an awareness of the death of millions of innocent civilians as unparalleled psychic torture. The images and reports of the living dead also forced Giacometti to face himself in the present, to acknowledge his own sadistic urges that had never disappeared.[58]

Giacometti's February letter to his mother also referred to a movie that totally changed his vision and released his creative energy. He talked about the experience often to friends, family, and journalists, and decades later he wrote about its effects:

> The true revelation, the real impetus that made me want to represent what I see came to me in a movie theater. I was watching a newsreel. Suddenly I no longer knew just what it was that I saw on the screen. Instead of figures moving in three dimensional space I saw only black and white specks shifting on a flat surface. They had lost all meaning. I looked at the person beside me, it was fantastic, and all at once by contrast he had assumed an enormous volume. All at once I became aware of the space in which we swim and which we never notice because we have grown used to it. I left. I discovered an unknown Blvd. Montparnasse, dreamlike. Everything was different. Space transformed the people trees and objects. There was an extraordinary almost anguished silence. For the feeling of space breeds silence and drowns the objects in that silence. . . . The unknown was the reality all around me, and no longer what was happening on the screen! . . . I realized that my vision of reality was the polar opposite of the so-called objectivity of the cinema and that it was now essential for me to try to paint this space which I felt so strongly. At the same time, there was a total revalorization of reality to my eyes. It became passionate, unknown, marvelous.

As beautiful as the most wonderful tale in the Arabian nights. That's never stopped since.[59]

All through the first terrible postwar winter, newsreels containing documentary footage collected from the Nazi death camps were shown before every feature film. One movie theater on the Champs Elysées showed the films continuously for over a year, and artists and intellectuals with a conscience considered it a moral duty to see them. Almost certainly Giacometti was among them.[60]

Giacometti's movie experience is a classic instance of the psychological phenomenon known as derealization.[61] When a traumatic stimulus overwhelms a person, relief is sought by turning the stimulus itself into something unreal, a blur of black dots.[62] Because Giacometti's mental life was laced with aggressive fantasies and the guilt these engendered, the shock of seeing so many dead or near-dead people all at once would have been momentarily terrifying. But Giacometti's description of this experience truly makes sense if we conclude that it was a catalyst, not the whole truth. Seeing horrific images of near-dead people and piles of emaciated corpses pushed him backward to his earlier traumatic experiences: the deaths of his grandparents, the near-death of his mother from typhoid in 1911, the death of van Meurs in 1921, and the deaths of his father in 1933 and his sister in 1937. Returning to the world of the living on the boulevard Montparnasse and finding it intact represented joyously rediscovered reality. But it was emancipating for other reasons as well. The newsreels and newspaper reports, the *Art and Resistance* exhibition, and the skeletal survivors on the street all persuaded Giacometti that he was not as evil as he had believed. Unlike the butchers of Bergen-Belsen, he had never implemented his sadistic destructive fantasies on human flesh; he had only imagined them, confining himself to writing about them or portraying them in sculpture and drawings.[63] People who strive to be "good" often feel excessive guilt for their angry wishes, and in the face of mass murder they can feel remarkable relief. The undeniable evidence of other people's hostile behavior puts their fantasies into perspective. I believe that this realization released Giacometti from the guilt that had paralyzed him for so long.

From the time of Ottilia's death nine years earlier, so soon after his father's death, he had been unable to create without destroying. Confronting the difference between his fantasies and grisly reality was a liberation. No wonder he was elated on emerging from the movie theater. No wonder the memory of that elation lasted for the rest of his life, often sustaining him when he drifted back to his habitual self-accusations and guilt.

FIGURE 9.2

Alberto Giacometti, Rol-Tanguy, 1946. Pencil on paper, dimensions unknown. Lost.

Giacometti's new-found freedom was manifested in his sculpture of Rol-Tanguy (1946) (Hirshhorn Museum). The first of the portraits was less than three centimeters high, but the last was nearly thirteen centimeters high—quite possibly the first postwar sculpture Giacometti was able to make "regular" size.[64] A straightforward representational portrait of a head set on a cube within a cube, Rol-Tanguy is an expressive work, succinctly capturing the vitality and dignity of the man while retaining the solidity of his physiognomy.

To Giacometti, Rol-Tanguy was a "proletarian man of action with the magnificent head of a warrior" who had saved countless lives.[65] Able to sit absolutely still and silent for long periods of time, Rol-Tanguy was an inspirational model (fig. 9.2). The artist's scrutinizing gaze was so intense that forty-five years later Rol-Tanguy remembered feeling as though Giacometti's hands were actually touching his face, resulting in "a veritable communion."[66] Giacometti must have felt the communion as well, and the experience of being close to a strong, self-assured, supportive man—another father figure—helped him feel safe and gave him the courage to function as an artist and to resist the compulsion to destroy his work. Just as Giovanni's stable presence posing for his son in 1927 had helped Giacometti make his great leap forward with Gazing Head, Rol-Tanguy's silent support seems to have provided a similar role for the artist in 1946.

In 1946, after his breakthrough with Rol-Tanguy—an event the artist mentioned to his mother and Diego only—Giacometti drew and sculpted portraits of Diego and some of his closest friends, including Jean-Paul Sartre, Simone de Beauvoir, Francis Gruber, Louis Aragon, Picasso, Pierre Loeb, Teriade, Marie-Laure de Noailles, Georges Bataille, Diane Kotchoubey, and, eventually, Annette Arm. Portraiture would soon become one of Giacometti's principal activities. Since the 1920s he had carried on two different kinds of work simultaneously, realistically representational work for home consumption, and his newest stylistic preoccupation for the art world. After the war the two trends began to converge. The painting of Teriade, a commissioned work, was done right after the Rol-Tanguy portrait.[67] Stylistically, it is more strictly representational with fewer distortions than those done later that year or in the following years.

Comments made many years later to his friend Isaku Yanaihara suggest one motive behind Giacometti's impulse to make portraits in the mid 1940s. Many of his friends had died during the war, and when he thought about them they remained alive in his mind, smiling and talking to him.[68] He explained how holding on to mental images of his friends calmed him and robbed their deaths of power. Portraiture was thus his way of possessing the people he loved, of staying close to them and communing with them, as he had with Rol-Tanguy (and, many years earlier, with his father).

Bataille's future wife, Diane Kotchoubey, a flowing-haired beauty from an aristocratic Russian family, provided an important inspiration in the mid 1940s, when Giacometti produced more and larger plaster portraits of her than of any other woman.[69] Her character was familiar to Giacometti—a domineering woman whose commands were taken seriously by her submissive partner.[70] Annette Arm would soon replace her as Giacometti's principal female subject.

ELONGATION, FIRST STEPS

In photographs of Giacometti's studio taken by Marc Vaux in 1946 and published in Cahiers d'art the same year, three styles of human portrayal are visible: tiny figurines of normal anatomical proportions, straightforwardly representational portraits, and tall female figures with elongated headdresses or limbs (fig. 9.3).[71] Vaux's photographs document Giacometti's transition from tiny to tall. In 1947 Giacometti explained himself in his fa-

FIGURE 9.3 *Marc Vaux photograph of plaster heads and figures, 1946 (destroyed).*

mous letter to Matisse: "A large figure seemed to me untrue and a small one intolerable. . . . But head and figures only seemed to me true when small. All this changed a little in 1945 through drawing. This led me to want to make larger figures, then to my surprise they achieved a resemblance only when long and slender."[72]

Allowing for Giacometti's characteristic confusion about dates, I propose that the drawings through which "all this changed" were three versions of his drawing *Standing Woman*, usually dated 1946.[73] The large pencil drawing (50 x 32 cm) illustrated in *Cahiers d'art* (fig. 9.4) is probably the first version. It shows a faceless woman rising up, her body charred and her feet bound. Giacometti added a summarily sketched room around her with suggestive details, such as familiar floorboards recalling the Stampa and Maloja studios, and a door that is too small to allow the woman any escape. She can ascend only through the roof. Her arms are held tightly at her sides, soon to become the prototypical position for Giacometti's standing nudes done from imagination. This *Standing Woman* is spectral, a creature from another world who looks like a person but isn't—she is a skull-faced double.

In all three drawings of *Standing Woman* from 1946, the figures seem to be either footless or standing on their toes about to levitate. The erasures at their bases give the impression that they have risen above the ground. (Before the erasures, the figure illustrated in *Cahiers d'art* stood well within her room, but no longer.) Erasures attack the body and face of the figures in the other two versions, beginning a trend which continued to the end of Giacometti's life.

Each figure has an uncanny air in sharp contrast to the realistic drawings Giacometti had made from models in the late 1930s to mid 1940s, some of which are also illustrated in *Cahiers d'art*. Those were earthy creatures, similar

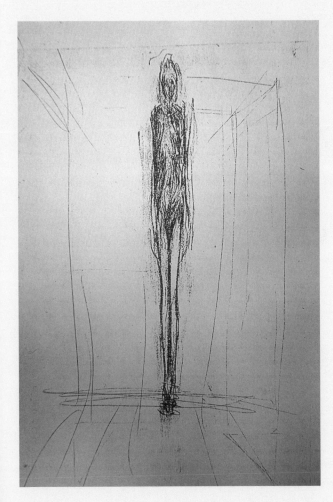

FIGURE 9.4
Marc Vaux
photograph of
Standing Woman,
1946, *from* Cahiers
d'art.

to his tiny figurines, standing firmly on their own two feet, their fertile parts smooth and rounded. The women in the three spectral drawings are also distant from Giacometti's later female figures, whose feet begin to weigh them down.

The three drawings, with their suggestion of upward movement, are forerunners of Giacometti's next phase of sculpted images of women. All the heads, busts, and figurines photographed by Vaux in late 1946 with the exception of some straightforward portraits, are of women with elongated headdresses that lead the viewer's eye upward and intensify the feeling of vertical thrust. In the first photograph of the article, three tiny plaster figurines set on large pedestals appear white and vibrant against the toweringly spacious dark background (see fig. 8.7).[74] The next two photographs in the article are close-ups of the figurines, showing their natural proportions, hieratic stance, and similarity to small Egyptian sculptures at the Louvre.

Night, an evocative monument to the millions of women and children who died in the war, is a slender woman with a skull-like head and angular vitality who strides on skeletal legs atop a sarcophagus (see fig. 9.3, third from right). Her moving arms and spiky fingers suggest an incongruous "lifelikeness" as she walks to her death. Neither is she elongated, nor does she have an elongated headdress, but she moves.

The appearance of movement is paradoxically present in what is probably the first of Giacometti's filiform figures, a *Standing Woman in Process*, prominently displayed in the next two photographs of the article. The plaster figure is twelve centimeters high (without the pedestal), an intermediate stage between the tiny figurines and the one-meter-tall figure also called *Standing Woman in Process* (fig. 9.5). The latter work was presented in a large photograph, and it is positioned next to a chair for scale. By including the photograph of the larger figure Giacometti signaled to the world that he had overcome his inhibition and could now make sculpture of a "respectable" size.

The filiform figures have lost the smooth surfaces of their miniature cousins and unveil, for the first time, the shimmering skin of Giacometti's

FIGURE 9.6 *Marc Vaux photograph of plaster heads, 1946 (destroyed).*

FIGURE 9.7
Maat, Egyptian, 19th
Dynasty. Painted
limestone, h 74 cm.
Archeological Museum
of Florence.

new style. The elongation of the figures and headresses draw the eye upward, while the scintillating surfaces convey their lifelikeness. Taller, thinner, and more skeletal, the new female figures embody a subtle interplay of curves and countercurves designed to launch the eye on a voyage around the silhouette of the whole.

The photographer caught the artist's intention by presenting the artist's bits of plaster, even in their unfinished state, as goddesses. These goddesses survive, remaining resolutely upright, unlike real women, who shrivel and shrink as they age, becoming horizontal in death. Giacometti's new figurines began to reach toward the heights of verticality. The core source here—for verticality and for death—was Egypt, especially the revivified Osiris, who was always symbolized by verticality.[75] Giacometti had told his mother in February: "I know how to make nude sculpture like the Egyptians—of the same quality."

The elongated headdresses visible in the 1946 photographs of Giacometti's studio (fig. 9.6) recall images of Maat, the Egyptian goddess of truth who weighs the heart of the dead with a feather at the moment of final judgment, and Nephthys, the goddess dedicated to death and resurrection. Both goddesses carry their insignias on their heads, as can be seen in a celebrated painted relief of Maat from Florence (fig. 9.7).[76] Though Giacometti soon abandoned the narrow, high headresses of his 1946 figures, the verticality of his work would become even more important.

In late 1946 Giacometti was still some months away from his mature style. The works in Vaux's photographs are still too earthy, too curvaceous, and too hesitant to stand where he needed them to be—on the edge between life and death. He had to take one more step backward (or sideways) in order to arrive at his goal.

CHAPTER 10

1946-1947

GUILT AND HOPE: A DREAM AND THREE SCULPTURES

By 1946 Giacometti had survived the century's greatest atrocity. Sitting safely in Switzerland while many friends and colleagues disappeared and died, he had been touched directly by the war only lightly. Back home in Paris he began his climb out of the depressive state that had kept his work small, but he had not yet found the aesthetic schema for the human form that he would embrace for the next twenty years. That schema would necessarily embody both his guilt and his hope. It is a part of his greatness that he had been the quintessential surrealist sculptor and was now about to become the quintessential postwar artist.

During Easter 1946, shortly after the release from his long artistic paralysis, Giacometti went back to Geneva ostensibly to see his mother, but also to see Annette Arm, the young woman with whom he had shared his daily life during the war. Annette posed for him for the first time during the Easter visit, and this undoubtedly contributed to his decision that she come to Paris and live with him. Her adulation and subservience was a tonic for the middle-aged artist. By Easter he had made many portraits of friends and acquaintances and rediscovered how hard it was for most people to sit patiently through his prolonged struggle to capture them. Annette's willingness to sit still for long periods was a welcome contrast. His drawings of Annette during the Geneva visit show her to be a subtly sensuous young woman who usually sat with her hands resting on her knees and her legs modestly close together. She is portrayed as serious, demure, anxious to please, and willing to assume whatever place in the artist's life that he would allow.

Also while in Geneva Giacometti made three portraits of his mother, and the images of the two women are strikingly divergent.[1] The sketches of the older woman seem to have been obsessively overdrawn, as Giacometti worked the oval of the head, repeating stroke after stroke. The right side of the face has been erased, or was never drawn, and the viewer is confronted with half a head. The one visible eye is only a socket. The lips are pressed tightly together, and the mouth is turned downward as though in a permanent scowl. In two of the three versions, we sense the skull beneath the skin. The portraits are a remarkable embodiment of Giacometti's characteristic ambivalence. He could never face both sides of his feelings about his mother—or, for that matter, about most people. It is as if by eliminating one side of her face he could split off and deny his anger and disappointment. These drawings stand at the beginning of a series of portraits of Annetta, which grow increasingly ominous, hostile, and poignant.

On July 5, 1946, a few months after his visit to Geneva, Annette Arm joined Giacometti in Paris, profoundly changing his life and art. Their interaction on the day of her arrival revealed the dynamic that would characterize their entire relationship. When he met her at the train station he was disgruntled and unfriendly. She responded by disappearing; to a man frightened of separation and loss her deliberate absence, though brief, could have felt like a permanent disappearance—a death. Her intuitive response to his unwelcoming reception made him feel guilty about his rudeness. For Giacometti, her reappearance several hours later was like a resurrection, and he felt a huge relief. His hostility had not killed her or really driven her away. That evening he took her to his usual cafés, where she met Picasso, Balthus, and other of his famous friends. They found her to be an attractive, agreeable, but naive girl-woman.

Giacometti was sometimes protective and fatherly toward Annette, as if she were a not-too-intelligent child. He could also be cruel and sadistic, treating her the way he was used to treating himself. By moving into Giacometti's uncomfortable hovel Annette demonstrated that she could withstand both his masochistic and his sadistic inclinations. Some observers guessed that she occasionally invited his cruelty.[2] Probably because she proved to be so durable, she got along well with Diego, and, like the compliant younger brother, she could tolerate Giacometti's lack of attention to her needs.

Annette was also evidently a satisfactory sexual partner for the artist, at least in the early years. He glowed in her presence, and it was clear to most who knew them that he could enjoy himself with her. His delight in her body seems visible in the many likenesses he made of her over the next decade. The various portraits and images of standing nude women sing a subtle song of sensuous physicality. For the time being Giacometti was comfortable with his own sexuality and was not ashamed to announce it to the world.

THE DREAM OF A GIFTED DREAMER

Three weeks after Annette moved in, a Polish artist named Tonio Poto-sching died in the room adjacent to their sleeping quarters. Tonio, the concierge of that ramshackle warren of buildings in which Giacometti lived and worked, had been seriously ill for several months. His death, so close at hand, turned out to be a momentous event in the artist's life, triggering old conflicts and troubling fantasies.

In October 1946 Skira, to whom Giacometti talked about the event so evocatively and so often, took a group of friends from the Geneva wartime circle to lunch in Paris. They spoke of keeping diaries as the surrealists had done before the war. Giacometti immediately agreed to use the method Breton had taught him to write an article about Tonio's death for *Labyrinthe*, possibly because he needed a way to exorcise his feelings. During the same lunch Giacometti was told that his favorite brothel, the Sphinx, was about to be shut down by the authorities, and he hurried there with his friends one last time.

The Sphinx was unusual even in Paris. It was elaborately decorated in Egyptianate and Pompeian styles, and the women, often in costume, walked around naked to the waist. It was a meeting place for artists and writers, who used it as a café before the evening's regular customers arrived. The theatrical atmosphere made the erotic activity seem antiseptic enough for Parisian men to bring their wives and children to visit the establishment as a local phenomenon.

In rushing to the Sphinx before it closed forever, Giacometti was repeating a habitual behavioral pattern. When a separation was imminent he could overcome his fear of penetrating a woman. After having sex with a prostitute at the Sphinx Giacometti, along with Annette, watched daily for an outbreak of venereal disease. He was expecting immediate retribution for his aggressive act (which is the way he experienced penetrating the prostitute) and the punishment—an infection—arrived as expected. Later in October he had a remarkable dream about the brothel, and he wrote this into the essay for Skira, inviting the reader to join in the experience, along with Annette, of watching his penis.

Giacometti's "The Dream, the Sphinx and the Death of T." was published in December 1946. It consists of many parts: some sections describe the dream—including the closing of the Sphinx and the venereal disease he contracted during his last visit there—and his associations to this experience; other sections resemble earlier surrealist fantasies; still others detail serendipitous coincidences and musings. Ultimately the text refers to most of the artist's long-standing inner conflicts and preoccupations. None of Giacometti's later writings approaches this essay in depth, breadth, aesthetic elegance, or complexity. It is seminal to understanding the man's many facets—his body, mind, emotions, and art—and I propose new ways of comprehending the essay in its entirety (see appendix B for the full English text).

Like all compellingly vivid dreams, Giacometti's "dream" is multilayered. The shimmering surrealist surface of recollected impressions floats above re-experienced memories weaving back and forth in time and ultimately leading to the artist's discovery of a formal way to tell his life story. Themes and forms are woven and interwoven in four dimensions—horizontality, verticality, time, and space. External events are internalized and re-created by the dreamer as awe-inspiring and terrifying works of art.

Giacometti starts by pulling the audience into his own anxious state, dangling scary spiders in the reader's face. Beginning with his most pressing issue—his intense aggression and equally intense guilt—Giacometti presents himself as terrified by "an enormous, brown and hairy spider" at the foot of his bed. "Kill it, kill it," he declares, not being able to accomplish this, either in the dream or awake. Giacometti proclaims how deeply upsetting are his aggressive wishes and how he fights against them but is compelled to face them whenever he feels threatened. Then he wakes within the dream and finds a yellow spider "far more monstrous than the first." How might a psychoanalyst understand this vivid material? Though part of a literary text, it has the feel of an authentic dream, with its origins in an actual nighttime event or the fantasy of such an event.

Some interpreters have noted that the spiders symbolize the disturbing aspect of female genitalia, and other commentators have focused on Oedipal issues, such as desire for his mother.[3] Though possibly true, these interpretations don't reflect the central meaning of the dream as I understand it. Giacometti's imagery refers to a specific trauma, the birth of his sister, Ottilia, which coincided with the death of his grandmother.

To a young boy watching from "the foot of the bed" as his new baby sister and her umbilical cord emerged from the unexpectedly large opening between his mother's outspread legs, the sight may well have resembled an enormous brown, hairy spider dangling from a thread. The yellow spider—described in the dream as scrawny-legged and covered with smooth yellow scales—most likely represents the blond Ottilia, shiny with a moist mix of blood and afterbirth.[4] The birth of a girl in a family of two boys would have made Ottilia seem like a rare specimen. In the essay's dream within the dream, the woman at his side (Annette) reaches out to touch the dreadful object without fear or surprise, just as his mother would have turned to her newborn infant. Now, Giacometti's lover can reach out to the "disagreeable" part of him and touch it with curiosity and pleasure. The dreamer pushes her hand away, asking for the creature to be killed, a typical reaction by an envious two-and-half-year-old toward his newest rival. The dreamer can tolerate hearing the results of his hostile wishes but he cannot bear to watch, so he introduces a stranger whose long, phallic instrument successfully smashes the creature.[5] Only in the aftermath does he see with dismay what his murderous fantasies have wrought: the broken parts labeled with a dispassionate identity: arachnid.

Giacometti then introduces a complaining old housekeeper (symbolic of his finnicky mother) who is searching for the lost spider. Her appearance alerts the frightened boy to keep his hostile fantasies a secret. To do this he goes outdoors and finds another symbolic vagina, "plowed earth hidden by thicket at the foot of a mound," into which he throws the creature's crushed remnants. His host and friend (a symbol for Giacometti's father) suddenly appears with his daughter—a sight that surprises and awakens the dreamer, just as the infant Ottilia had surprised the toddler Alberto by her birth. "All the following day, I had that spider before my eyes, it obsessed me." Since her birth, and especially since her death, Ottilia had obsessed Alberto. He had kept her image before his eyes, making and remaking tiny figurines with her silhouette, especially her fertile silhouette.

Giacometti's next associations in his text almost certainly refer to the illness that resulted from his intercourse with the prostitute. Unable to sleep, he had been waiting for the telltale signs of venereal disease, and after repeated inspections of his penis he finally becomes aware of yellow-ivory traces of pus. It is also likely that any disease involving his genitals would have reminded Giacometti of his adolescent orchitis. His unconscious equating of sexuality, especially phallic penetration, with murder meant that Giacometti faced the possibility of a painful assault of guilt each time he had sexual intercourse. In the essay Giacometti's description of an obscure sense of the usefulness of his illness and how he was temporarily "paralyzed" from "cutting [it] short" bespeaks his masochistic character, even as he, too, vehemently denies that it was "a kind of self punishment."

Annette appears at crucial moments in the essay as the one who listens to him all night long, who comforts him when he is frightened, and who, smiling, looks at his penis with him—even though it was infected by a sexual encounter with another woman. Living with Annette allowed Giacometti to speak and write of his body and sex. Indeed, his associations show her to be calmly unafraid of him, his body, or his fears. In the essay, in his dream within the dream (the truth or the memory of an actual event, according to Freud) she is even unafraid to touch a terrifying little yellow spider. "In bed that evening a little before the dream, my girlfriend [Annette] wanted, smiling, to verify the symptoms of my illness."

How strange that Giacometti would write publicly of an event that is by all rights humiliating. Yet, it is in character for a complicated man who took pride in his "failures" while simultaneously and surreptitiously letting people know the hidden strength behind his masochistic mask. Most interpreters have missed the obvious point that Annette may indeed have been smiling about more than her discovery that her lover's penis was diseased; she may also have been reacting to the fact that he could have an erection.

Giacometti's next paragraph, consisting of one sentence, is filled with reversals and unconscious allusions. "But since the dream, since the illness that brought me to that lunch, T's death has become for me again very much present." By using the initial T instead of Tonio, his neighbor's entire first name, Giacometti seems to be hiding from himself and others an obvious link to the protagonist of Thomas Mann's Death in Venice. Mann's Tadzio is a handsome young man with whom an elderly homosexual falls in love. In an apparent response to the aging swain, Tadzio causes his death—a striking parallel to the death of van Meurs in Madonna di Campiglio. Would the Dutchman's death have occurred if the handsome young Giacometti had not responded to the elderly man's advertisement? One death leads Giacometti backward in time to the recollection of other sequences of death and subsequent guilt.

In his essay Giacometti seems to have intuited or momentarily become aware of his hostile fantasies and the usually unconscious connection in his mind between penetration, murder, and castration. We suddenly hear him abjure responsibility, claiming only to be a passive victim of chance. "I wondered if it were only the coincidence of the timing of Skira's request and the visit to the Sphinx with its attendant consequences to impose on me the memory of T.'s death to give me the desire to write today."

Then he writes that, emerging from the pharmacy with medication to cure his venereal disease, he sees the sign of a café across the street: "Au Rêve." Struck by the sort of coincidence he had learned to take seriously as a surrealist, Giacometti gives himself permission to recall Tonio's death. "While walking I saw T. again the days before his death . . . and I saw him again soon afterwards, at 3 AM, dead, his limbs of skeletal thinness, projected, spread apart, scattered from the body, the enormous bloated belly, the head thrown back, the mouth open." In another conflated condensation, Giacometti writes that Tonio's skin was ivory-yellow, which matches his description of the coloring of the spider—just as the bloated belly of the dead man and the huge belly of his pregnant mother were probably linked somewhere deep in his unconscious. "Standing immobile in front of the bed"—like the toddler fascinated by the extraordinary events of childbirth and death—"I looked at this head which had become an object, a little box measurable and insignificant." Giacometti was using a characteristically obsessional way of denying the overwhelming significance of something frightening: by reversing it and turning it into nothing.

In the next paragraph Giacometti describes helping to dress the corpse and then covering it with a sheet before he returns to his studio, where he works until the next morning. The following night he reports a terrifying experience that takes him across a threshold, where he achieves a new consciousness. After his revelation in the movie theater (see Chapter 9), Giacometti had begun to see "heads in the void," congealed, fixed forever in the surrounding space, and the vision terrified him as he had never before been terrified. Now "it was no longer a living head, but an object that I could see as I might any other object, no, differently, not quite like any other object, but like something simultaneously alive and dead." The men, the objects—everything had undergone a transformation.

Giacometti tells of his elation the following day when he awakens to find that the everyday objects around him were still transformed. "This morning on awakening, I saw my towel for the first time, weightless in a never before perceived stillness and as if suspended in a frightful silence. It had no relation now to the chair or table. There was no relation at all between the objects now separated by immeasurable gulfs of emptiness. I looked at my room with fright and a cold sweat ran down my back."

Terror in the face of otherness was only part of the experience. Jean Genet, Giacometti's model and friend, reported that in the early 1950s the artist described the experience of the empty space between the towel and chair differently, almost ecstatically. "The towel was alone, so alone that I felt I could have removed the chair without the towel moving. It had its own space, its own weight, its own silence, even. The world was light, light."[6] Herein lies the psychological base of Giacometti's spiritual revelation. Separation is a cause for both celebration and fear, even if the cost is occasional terror. True psychological separation is terrifying, especially for someone so ambivalently connected to his parents. A combination of closeness to death, closeness to Annette, sudden relief from guilt, and contemplation of his new life situation released Giacometti from the ties that had bound him for a decade.

For the surrealists, psychological maturity meant philosophical transformation. What did the concept signify to Giacometti's new friends, the existentialists? Could the artist transform a nonliving object into a living one by allowing it space? Space was no longer just a terrifying void, empty of all life, empty because of his destructive fantasies. It could also be a place of productive stillness. He could fill the void with the work of his own hands. He could move from inanimate objects to human beings and back, with the goal of creating "living heads."

Following the manic moment of writing about his ecstatic and terrifying discoveries "at one go," Giacometti reports in his essay that he felt bored and hostile. He couldn't reread his words yet wanted to rewrite them. Feeling the urge to focus on minutiae, he redescribes the concrete details of his dream, the ones that could be seen and touched, but denies the links between them and the hallucinatory material—links that could lead him to a confrontation with his inner life. "I stopped after several lines, discouraged." The defenses that had held him back for a decade were in place again.

Another classic obsessional weapon against anxiety is to break things into small parts and thereby avoid knowing how those parts relate to one another. Giacometti had come face to face with his difficulty, recognizing the contradiction between an emotional rendering of his story (especially his reaction to the visual events) and the facts themselves. "I found myself before a confused mass of time, events, places and sensations." Elements got twisted and confused, leaving him adrift. Strong emotions often threw him off track. Now he wanted to master the problem. "I tried to find a possible solution." As an artist, Giacometti would have to seek a visual solution.

In his first attempt at making a visually coherent narrative of the recent events in his life, Giacometti places the facts in a columnlike format on the page so that their simultaneity could be graphically clear. That doesn't work, because "the time in the ensemble of my story went in reverse from present to past, but with returns and ramifications." No fool about the unconscious, Giacometti knew that time does not adhere to orderly logical sequences. Observing that he hadn't included the lunch at which he recounted the dream in the first draft of the essay, he adds it. For the first time since his experience with van Meurs in 1921, he writes of his terror and melancholy. He tells of specific details as he watched the older man die, and he recalls his confusion and panicky behavior in Venice, where he fled afterward.

Giacometti later claimed that van Meurs's death in 1921 and Tonio's in 1946 touched him in fundamental ways. We have already seen how van Meurs, whose death had touched off phobic rituals, insomnia, and a masochistic lifestyle, can be understood as a replacement figure for a more important person in Giacometti's life, his father. The same is true of Tonio, who, like the Dutchman, was barely an acquaintance. The recollection of the deaths of both men—near strangers—served a psychological purpose for Giacometti at this time. In remembering and seeming to relive the deaths of van Meurs and Tonio, he was actually responding in a delayed way to the traumatic loss of close family members whose deaths had had a profound but inadmissible impact on him: from the time of the deaths of his grandparents in 1904 and 1913, and his mother's close brush with death in 1911, through the more recent loss of his father in 1933 and sister in 1937—Giacometti never publicly acknowledged any of these important events, nor did he adequately mourn them. As a result, he was left with an exceptionally burdensome sensitivity to death. A death in the present evoked one from the past, hence the link between Tonio and van Meurs. The combination of a shift in the artist's recollection from present to past, along with the shift from the deaths of crucial family members to those of relatively unimportant figures in Giacometti's life, helps to decipher his otherwise unaccountably excessive response in 1946.[7]

When the Dutchman died at his side in 1921, Giacometti had momentarily become aware of his competitive rivalry with his father and the homoerotic and murderous wishes he secretly harbored. Only now, with Annette at his side in bed at night, her presence clearly proclaiming his heterosexual orientation, could Giacometti publicly hint at the homoerotic fantasies and conflicts that had held him in thrall for many years. Only now could he describe the homosexual panic he had felt in connection with the aging Dutchman—who had sought a youthful male companion—and his own rapid flight to Venice. Without fully knowing the import of his words he could finally put them down on paper.

The extent to which Giacometti's experience with van Meurs was related to his feelings for his father is suggested when Giacometti next writes about size and dimension, emphasizing the puzzle of objects seeming to be small, large, or on the verge of changing size ("the man appeared to become a giant . . . but the men became like ants"). All children see their parents, especially parents of the same sex, as large and themselves as very small. Creative children can translate this everyday phenomenon into an artistic metaphor.

Nearing the end of his essay, Giacometti tells the reader how much he has struggled with time and chronology. In what order can he best represent his feelings and thoughts? In the end he *sees* a solution. "All the events existed simultaneously around [me]. Time became horizontal and circular." Seated in a café (Giacometti wrote most of his letters in Parisian cafés), he imagines himself at the center of a disc on which he can freely and pleasurably move back and forth in time and space. "I saw it almost simultaneously from two different points of view. I saw it laid out vertically on a page. But I insisted on its horizontality. . . . With a strange pleasure, I saw myself walking on this disc-time-space, and reading the history erected before me."[8]

Here is the artist's triumphant moment of integration. To keep the horizontality of his life while introducing the vertical was the challenge of Giacometti's next two decades. This multilayered metaphor is about his sexuality with his live-in lover *and* his homosexual conflicts, about the reconciliation of his past with his present, *and* about his ability to integrate the warring and diverse sides of his personality—the feminine *and* the masculine, the destructive and the creative.

For the Egyptians, horizontality meant death while verticality meant uprising sexuality and life itself. Giacometti had signaled his awareness of that symbolism in 1932 with No More Play by including his version of the djed pillar, the Egyptian symbol of immortality. From 1946 on, he would focus on verticality, exploring its variants, its thinness and thickness, how long it could stay upright, and how much support it needed. He would celebrate its uprisingness because it had become the meaning of life itself for him. Free to move from present to past, from body to mind and heart, and back again, Giacometti was finally able to confront his own inner depths, thereby liberating himself to find his signature style and true self.

In 1929–30 Giacometti had been torn by his alternating attraction first to Bataille and then to Breton, who represented perversion and sublimation, respectively. Now, after the war, Giacometti tilted toward the aggressive and sadomasochistic side of his personality. His conflicts with his mother and Swiss relatives had worn him down, leaving him only enough tenderness for Annette, whom he could dominate and mistreat if he felt the need.

In postwar Paris the social circles of French intellectuals were small and, despite deep intellectual differences, intertwined. Georges Bataille and Jean-Paul Sartre were at opposite ends of the philosophical spectrum. Sartre was an adamant atheist, now a celebrated existentialist philosopher, novelist-playwright, and editor of a lively journal, *Les temps modernes*. His writing and lectures had caught the imagination of both press and public, and he lived in a whirl of public acclaim that he embraced with gusto. Bataille, in contrast, was a private person living quietly outside Paris, still subscribing to currently unfashionable surrealist ideals.

Never inclined to take sides in the squabbles of his intellectual friends,

Giacometti maintained friendships with both men, doing portraits of them as well as their women. He met Sartre weekly for lunch and saw Bataille either in Vézélay or Paris. As had been true so often, Giacometti needed fatherly support to make major advances in his work, and the charismatic and supremely confident character of Jean-Paul Sartre steadied him.[9] Giacometti and Sartre were both superb conversationalists, exceptionally sensitive to nuances of sentiment, perception, and thought. Sartre would soon write the catalogue essays for Giacometti's forthcoming exhibits that helped to make Giacometti's postwar work legendary.

Schooled in Paris, Sartre had matured intellectually near the milieu of surrealism and shared some of its sensibilities. For both him and Breton, art was the answer to life's emptiness—art and the ongoing effort to face the truth, to search for the absolute. Sartre wrote: "What makes our position original is that the war and the occupation, by turning us into a world in a state of fusion, perforce made us discover the absolute at the heart of relativity itself."[10] Sartre was the new man with new ideas; the writer who writes for his own age, and he had to demolish the previous regime, especially Breton. Was he personally battling Breton for the soul of surrealism's star sculptor?

Early in 1947 Sartre vehemently attacked surrealism, emphasizing its negativity and outdatedness. He decried its occultism, its air of being a secret society, its mystical thrust, and its irrelevance to social, political, and philosophical issues.[11] He had told the world that the war was everyone's war, the occupation everyone's shame—a reassurance to Giacometti, who felt so much guilt already. He claimed to have something more relevant than Breton to offer the thinking man of the day.

Though sympathetic to many of the people and principles of surrealism, by mid 1947 Giacometti had joined Sartre's "family," a coterie of friends and former students who scorned surrealism. Having established his postwar style, Giacometti no longer wanted to be publicly aligned with surrealism. When Breton urged him to participate in the International Exhibition of Surrealism at the Maeght Gallery in July–August 1947, Giacometti initially agreed to make a sculpture and write an essay for the catalogue, thinking the show was going to be a retrospective. However, the exhibition was actually forward-looking and included works by new recruits. Furthermore, it was slanted toward the occult, in keeping with Breton's recent publication of Arcane 17, an openly alchemical work. Once Giacometti realized that his inclusion would put him solidly within the contemporary surrealist camp, he canceled his participation and was furious with Breton for misleading him.[12]

In 1947 Giacometti made from imagination three sculptures that stand apart from his other work done at the time: *Head of a Man on a Rod*, *The Nose*, and *The Hand*. Though made in response to the feelings expressed in "The Dream, the Sphinx and the Death of T.," these works were also influenced by the resurgence of surrealism in Paris in mid 1947. But they could not have been made during an earlier era. The sculptures were too linked with the horrors inherent in war and postwar revelations. Visually simple, the three pieces are complex iconographically and psychologically. One is a skull, another is a skull barely covered with skin, and the third portrays an arm at the crossover point between life and death. All three works reflect Giacometti's thoughts about men, since they either are openly phallic or are associated in Giacometti's writing with a specific man.

The Nose

In his 1947 letter to Matisse, Giacometti sketched two versions of *The Nose*—one freestanding and the other hanging from the scaffolding of a metal cage. In the latter the underlying skull is obvious. The man with the long nose is dead. Did he die of natural causes or was he killed? Is he a killer—in thought or deed? Has he been killed as punishment for murderous wishes?

In both versions, the profile view is gun-shaped; the mouth is a trigger, the nose a barrel, and the neck a hand piece. The work is unabashedly about aggression—Giacometti's own and the world's. It is also about punishment. In the original plaster Giacometti painted a stripe of blood-colored paint spiraling around the nose itself, further emphasizing the hostile, even criminal, nature of the nose.[13] The phallic and lancelike aspects of this work link it to several of Giacometti's earlier sadistic images, notably *Man and Woman* (1929) and *Point to the Eye* (1932). Its excessive length goes beyond the frame and invites castration—or at least a clipping. The jabbing tongue looks as dangerous as the nose but is less at risk of being broken off. Speech, especially a restive jesting and probing, was Giacometti's kind of nosiness, his poking into forbidden areas. Aggressive speech often led Giacometti to feelings of guilt, and guilt was in the air in 1946–47.

That *The Nose* hangs from a metal frame hints at an issue very much on Giacometti's mind. As discussed in Chapter 9, awareness of the difference between his guilty wishes and the actual crimes of the Third Reich had released Giacometti from his paralysis in February 1946. The war criminals convicted at Nuremberg were sentenced on October 1, 1946, and hanged fifteen days later. Sometime during that month Giacometti had his momentous dream, had sex with a prostitute, and was stricken with venereal disease. Once the Nazi murderers were punished by hanging, he might have felt innocent enough by comparison to create these startling sculptures and to write his essay for *Labyrinthe*. In his text Giacometti had identified the death of the Dutchman as the source of his morbid fears. He had even included a passage about a lengthening nose. "I saw the head of van M. transform, the nose became more and more pronounced." But as we have seen, van Meurs's death served as a screen for earlier events and fears.

Many seeing *The Nose* for the first time are reminded of Carlo Collodi's story of *Pinocchio*. It is an amusing moral tale of a puppet whose doting father-creator, Geppetto, lavished him with love only to learn that he had an undisciplined, naughty little delinquent on his hands. And, of course, Pinocchio's nose grew longer with each lie he told. The story was widely known in Giacometti's childhood. Significantly, the Disney film version was released in Paris in May 1946, and the newspaper advertisements featured the boy's long nose. Reluctant to be a good boy, Pinocchio gets into one disastrous scrape after another. At each episode he would have to be rescued and cut back down to size. He barely escapes death by hanging, drowning, starving, and being eaten but is always rescued by mysterious strangers who recognize his good heart. Only when he learns to curtail his selfish wishes and become considerate of others does the little wooden puppet redeem himself and transform into a real person. I believe that the entire tale resonated deeply with Giacometti's view of himself. He had a good heart but sometimes behaved badly and needed to be rescued.

In *The Nose*, Giacometti may have been portraying himself as the liar he had been since childhood. At the same time it is certain that he was burdened by guilty feelings about his own father, who had both assailed and nurtured him. He wanted to be like him *and* be different. In 1932, when he had told the truth about his hostile fantasies disguised as a waking dream, his father died a month later. Now he was left with the spirit of the man whom he wanted to, but could not, propitiate.

The outrageous length of *The Nose* makes it a caricature of masculine prowess. Giacometti had mocked his own sexuality fifteen years earlier with his *Disagreeable Objects*. His renewed friendship with Bataille after the war stirred the cruel side of his nature and loaded his sexual experiences with an expectation of retaliation. His brief liaison with Isabel, who might have left him because of his impotence, would also have reinforced sadistic sexual fantasies.

Giacometti's unconscious equation of penile penetration of a woman with murder was one of his pervasive aggressive fantasies.[14]

When he had made *Woman with Her Throat Cut* in 1932 he was metaphorically illustrating the retaliatory punishment that women could inflict on men who penetrated and murdered them—dismemberment or the threat of being eaten alive. Now, in 1946–47, with a functioning penis Giacometti had something rather specific to lose, and the threat uppermost in his mind, though probably still unconscious, was castration. Unable to contemplate this mutilation directly, he watched nightly for the first symptoms of venereal disease, which he expected but refused to stave off. "Nothing led me to believe that this was a kind of self punishment; I felt instead in a vague sort of way that the illness might be useful to me." Obviously Giacometti knew that he was punishing himself by not cutting short the danger of the illness with prophylactic medication.

For the first time in all the years he had lived in Paris, he was firmly grounded in a lasting and publicly heterosexual relationship. He no longer had to proclaim his impotence to duck out of competitive male storytelling at bars and cafés. He could admit to homoerotic fantasies, albeit disguised. With Annette sharing his bed, he had become a man among men. A war hero admired him—Rol-Tanguy. All his work from here on would proclaim his manhood. Like Pinocchio, he had proven that he had a good heart and deserved to be rescued, redeemed, and brought to life—to verticality.

Head of a Man on a Rod

One of Giacometti's most emotionally evocative works, *Head of a Man on a Rod*, consists of a moon-shaped, open-mouthed, eyeless skull impaled on a metal rod (fig. 10.1). It successfully conveys the screams of terror, which, in 1946–47, were still the preoccupation of the recent survivors of Nazi barbarism. The way the neckless head is mounted on the rod suggests the ancient practice of impaling an enemy's head on a pointed stake as a warning.[15] In "The Dream, the Sphinx and the Death of T." a fly disappears into Tonio's open mouth, terrifying the artist and reminding him of his earlier experience upon emerging from the movie theater:

When . . . I perceived clearly the head that I was looking at congeal . . . I trembled with a terror as never again in my life and a cold sweat ran down my back. It was no longer a living head, but an object . . . not like any other object but like something simultaneously alive and dead. I cried out in terror as if I had just crossed a threshold. All living beings were dead

FIGURE 10.1 Exhibition catalogue photograph of Head of a Man on a Rod, 1947, original plaster version (destroyed).

and this vision was often repeated in the subway, the street, in the restaurant. . . . The waiter at Brasserie Lipp who became immobilized, leaning over me, [his] mouth open, without any rapport with the preceding moment [or] the following moment, mouth open, eyes congealed in an absolute immobility.[16]

Head of a Man on a Rod is usually discussed in terms of the terror Giacometti felt when he saw the Dutchman die, a feeling reawakened by Tonio's death. But the cavernously open mouth of the work may also convey unconscious homoerotic longings to be orally penetrated. In contrast to the extremely active quality of The Nose with its open mouth and thrusting tongue, the back-leaning Head of a Man on a Rod suggests passivity, submissiveness, and vulnerability. The man can only take in. If attacked he cannot defend himself but only stare wide-eyed (or eyeless) with horror.

In another possible interpretation, I propose that The Nose and Head of a Man on a Rod are pendant pieces reflecting once again the themes of sexual identity expressed in the Suspended Ball of 1930 (see fig. 5.4). In that surrealist work male and female body parts and qualities were conflated. By contrast, The Nose with its penetrating extension is quintessentially masculine, while the Head of a Man on a Rod might be seen as feminine, waiting for something to be inserted into its cavity, darkly moonlike and reflecting solar glory.

The Hand

The third in the triad of sculptures done from imagination in mid 1947 is The Hand.[17] Suspended horizontally on a vertical pole (much like Head of a Man on a Rod), a taut, outstretched arm and hand appear as if by magic before the audience's eyes. One gently rounded ovoid end suggests a shoulder. The exquisitely elegant fingers at the other end are thin but not emaciated, as they extend outward from the pleasingly shaped palm. The entire arm is slender but sweetly so, its subtle curves barely noticeable as the eye follows its silhouette and experiences the perfect balance of the limb held up by a finger-thin rod at the point of its elbow.

The Hand had multiple sources of inspiration. They include: the emaciated limbs of prisoners from concentration camps; the dismembered body parts Alberto and Diego saw in June 1940 after the German bombing; a wooden arm from Easter Island that Pierre Loeb displayed in his living room and that the artist coveted; Tonio Potosching's limbs "spare as a skeleton, outstretched, spread apart, cast away from the body,"as Giacometti stated in his essay; images of body parts in the paintings of Théodore Géricault, to which

Giacometti had referred in his recent essay on the artist Jacques Callot; and Giacometti's own surrealist sculpture *Caught Hand*.[18] All these references suggest death, fear, and sadism. I propose, however, that, rather than pointing only to the dark side of the human condition, Giacometti's *Hand* points primarily toward life and hope.

During his student days in Geneva, Giacometti had seen examples of ivory or wooden arms ending in hands that were part of an Egyptian magician's equipment, and he longed to possess one. They represented the divine hand and could be used as a protective device to prevent harmful forces from entering bodies, or as a symbol of creative energy with sexual connotations.[19] In making *The Hand*, Giacometti created his own magical hand.[20] He had done that facetiously in *The Surrealist Table* (1933); now, in 1947, he was serious.

Giacometti immediately had *The Hand* cast in bronze—his choice for the final work. By contrast, *The Nose* and *The Head of a Man on a Rod*, with their unmistakable references to horror and shame, were not cast for several years. Of the three unforgettable sculptures emerging without warning in the midst of Giacometti's stylistic transformation, only *The Hand*, which in the bronze version vibrates with lifelike tension, was about hope and possibilities, about his powers as an artist—that is, the side of Giacometti's personality barely balancing his destructive rage and paralyzing guilt. It leads directly to his filiform figures, which themselves became figures of hope for the survivors of the recent war.

With these three sculptures, Giacometti's detour was complete. He had reconnected with his past and found the strength to step forward into his future. Pierre Matisse's invitation to exhibit new work in a New York gallery was the additional impetus Giacometti needed to assume his place as the sculptor who would best represent mankind at the midpoint of the twentieth century.

CHAPTER 11

1947

THE QUEST FOR THE ABSOLUTE AND ABSOLUTE ELONGATION

Nineteen forty-seven was a year of consolidation for many artists. Most of those who left Paris for safer ground had now returned, taking up their lives and habitual activities. The war's most burdensome memories were beginning to fade, and Europe was starting to recover its hope and strength.

By the middle of the year Giacometti had made The Hand, Head of a Man on a Rod, and The Nose. He had also produced his first tall, elongated figures, whose ravaged surfaces carry the eye upward. Pushing himself and his work to the very edge, Giacometti achieved a novel way of representing the human figure. His powerful evocations of men and women who stood for survival—despite the world's brutality and his own fury—established him as an artist of the first rank.

Giacometti's postwar art grew out of a combination of many factors—talent, superstition, fear, conflict, and an obsessional character. He understood his achievements only imperfectly, usually eschewing explanations. In the vacuum created by his silence, a legend grew up around the man and his art that caught on with both the artist and his followers. Formulated by his eloquent friend Jean-Paul Sartre, the story used terms such as perception, space, and visibility, which had been fashionable since the mid 1930s. In this chapter I unravel the mythic formulation and speculate about the origins of Sartre's interpretation.

For Giacometti, ancient Egyptian beliefs animated the hopeful fantasies he brought to his work. By 1947, after excursions to other systems during his surrealist sojourn and his reversion to his father's way of painting, he returned to Egyptian culture and art (and perhaps to alchemy as well) as a source of solace. As an artist and as a man, he departed from the horizontality of death to approach the verticality of life, both literally and figuratively.

But he could not take this step until he was far from his wartime refuge of Switzerland. Returning to Paris, to his studio, to his friends, and to the truth about the war, Giacometti also came face-to-face with the steady decline of one of his closest friends, Francis Gruber. He watched him grow thinner throughout 1947 and eventually die of tuberculosis at age thirty-six in late 1948.

In 1947 his other tubercular friend, Georges Bataille, invited him to illustrate his latest book, a semiautobiographical novel called A Story of Rats. In his preface, Bataille states: "At times horror had a real presence in my life . . . horror alone still enabled me to escape the empty feeling of untruth."[1] The book's main characters are illustrated by Giacometti and are all recognizable in his straightforward sketches of the men's heads and the woman's bust: Bataille is the gaunt, physically ill, masochistic, and lustful hero named D.; Diane Kotchoubey, soon to be Bataille's wife, is his beautiful, uninhibited aristocratic lover B.; A., an ascetic priest stimulated by sadistic activities, either represents another aspect of Bataille or is Alexander Kojève, the Russian intellectual who was Bataille's philosopher mentor.[2] The story line takes the hero, his lover, and his priestly alter ego through a series of erotic adventures, which include sadomasochistic sex, near-death experiences, memories of torture, and sexual release while a rat is stabbed to death.

As we have seen, violent pleasure, horror, and death were poetic concepts for Bataille, opening the way to inner truths. "True poetry was reached only by hatred," he explained. "How great is the silence of death in the recollection of debauchery, when debauchery itself is the freedom of death!" By making his characters face and embrace these dark ideas with bravado, Bataille dealt with the scars of his childhood. "Nakedness is only death and the tenderest kisses have an aftertaste of rat."

Did Bataille choose Giacometti to illustrate A Story of Rats because he recognized in him a kindred soul who would understand and visually express the central ideas of his book? He knew that Giacometti had made sadistic sculpture and drawings in his surrealist period. The coalescing of Giacometti's filiform figures at a moment of close professional and personal association with Bataille is probably not coincidental.[3]

Both Bataille and Giacometti held to a redeeming vision of creation, or "possibility," as a counterweight to aggression. In Bataille, the redeeming vision took the form of analogical thinking, alchemy without the overt trappings.[4] It also took the form of a wish for a social order in which men related to each other around excess—not material goods, success, or "project," as he called activities tainted by useful purposes.

Bataille saw a particular role for art, one that stood apart from anything conventional and even apart from the exalted status Breton had always given it. Instead of existing as objects which could be admired, possessed, bought, and sold, paintings and art, he argued, could *"as it directs a dark light onto a point . . . [can] direct our attention towards a part of the horizon where everything is in flux."*[5] The "point on the horizon where everything is in flux" is the same location where Giacometti's filiform figures are positioned. Art was to stand at the very place where creation (life) turned into destruction (death) and back again into creation (life)—transformation crystallized.

Bataille had always seen himself as surrealism's enemy from within, criticizing the movement's follies and foibles. In the postwar era, he was one of its serious supporters from without and decried its antagonistic successor, existentialism.[6] Surrealism "is life itself, precarious, elusive, which cannot be defined by death . . . and whose infinite difficulty recalls the wretchedness—and the muteness—of giving birth," Bataille wrote in 1948.[7] His postwar version of surrealism was more appealing to Giacometti than Breton's and provided a rationale for what he was already doing. Through Bataille, Giacometti came to see that the destruction he was compelled to wreak on his work was not only equal to creation, but was its essential counterpart.

THE ARTIST'S INTENTION

Giacometti could never explain why he worked in the strange way he did, or why his figures had to be so elongated and thin. He did not address the issue of thinness in writing or conversation until well after the establishment of his new style and, almost always, only in response to specific questions. His most frequent explanation over the next twenty years was that the elongation was beyond his control. In the early 1950s he stated: "One does things through mania, through obsession, through a need more automatic that escapes the understanding."[8] In 1955 he claimed: "There's nothing voluntary about it. They've always surprised me."[9] As late as 1964, he said: "I never tried to make thin sculptures. . . . They became thin in spite of me."[10]

Most artists are unaware of the complex motivations behind their stylistic choices. They usually have conscious intentions with a vague sense that other factors beyond their awareness may also be playing a role. Having come to artistic maturity with surrealism, Giacometti was used to accepting his unconscious as an important source of his behavior and artistic choices.

In 1949 Leiris, who had known Giacometti for many years, said that the artist's current intentions and goals were: "To set up votive stones, to materialize experiences, to give a lasting consistency to whatever is fugitive or impossible to grasp in any happening, to fix realities by borrowing . . . from naturalism only what is indispensable to carry conviction."[11]

A few years later Alexander Liberman, the sculptor/photographer and a relative stranger, astutely observed that Giacometti wanted "to solve the question of how thin, how immaterial can the human body be and still exist? How small, how infinitesimal and still be? . . . One must use the minimum of material substance, reduce the quantity of substance to express an idea to the limit."[12]

While these comments provide insight into Giacometti's artistic goals, his elongated and emaciated figures, and his use of a minimum of substance, they merely hover on the surface—they are descriptive rather than truly explanatory. To arrive at a more profound understanding of the multilayered motivations behind his artistic choices, we must translate his words and work into two related questions. First, how close can one get to total destruction and still permit life to persist? and second, how to make lifelike sculptures out of dead materials—plaster, clay, or bronze?

In 1946–47 Giacometti's distant and recent past collided. No single factor motivated him. It was the combination of stimuli and memories, along with his characteristically complex responses to them, that impelled him to develop the filiform figures. The films of the Holocaust and the camp survivors in Giacometti's neighborhood, dying or nearly dead of typhoid fever, drew him back to the visual memory of his mother's grave illness from typhoid when he was nine. Her narrow escape and the feelings associated with that early trauma came back to him in postwar Paris. Giacometti always denied vehemently that the death camp survivors were the inspiration for his filiform figures, but he was only half wrong. It was the *visual memory of his mother's near death triggered by the sight of the Holocaust survivors, and not merely the survivors themselves, that influenced him.* The recent vision of life at the edge of death broke through the crust which had held back his memories and feelings for so long and unleashed both his rage and creativity.[13]

In an interview in 1950 Giacometti explicitly connected the tense forms of his elongated figures with violence. "I am most touched by sculpture where I feel there is contained violence. . . . If I want to draw, paint or sculpt a head, all that is transformed into a tensely stretched form which always seems to me a kind of extremely restrained violence. It is as if the form of the person is . . . above all a sort of nucleus of violence."[14] Violence was the motor that drove his postwar work. Giacometti saw it in others just as he felt it in himself, and it inspired him to elongate, to draw out and almost destroy the figures he created. Leiris, who saw what he was doing, noted: "I have often wondered whether sculpture is not for him simply a way of making something which can at once be destroyed."[15] As did Liberman: "There is a destructive quality in Giacometti. Intensely proud, he has a high concept of his mission. He is never satisfied with what he does. He smashes it and discards it."[16]

INTEGRATION AT LAST

Giacometti's struggle with rage and aggression was lifelong. The war years had rekindled those intolerable feelings, and only after the war was he able to transform them into great art. He was angry at his mother for her unmaternal harshness and at his father for his multiple abandonments and exploitation. His life and work were ruled by his ambivalence and the contrary currents inside him. His rage at his parents was counterpoised against his desire to be close to his father and to win his mother's approval, and against his love for both. Sadistic wishes and behavior oscillated with masochism and kindness. The destruction of his work alternated with his wish to create art that would live forever. They were necessary counterparts. Giacometti's postwar work—like his life—was the outcome of a consummate balancing act— whatever emerged and survived had to contain both life and death, creation and destruction.

To balance his need to ravage and annihilate, Giacometti had long sought a way to give voice to the competing wish—to give birth or bring to life. As with the tiny figurines, the underlying aim of the filiform figures was to portray the *aliveness* of the image. "What is important is to create an object capable of conveying the sensation as close as possible to the one felt at the sight of the subject," he often said.[17] The sensation to which the artist was referring was that of being with someone *alive*, of sensing the breath and movement that represented life itself—the same closeness he had recently experienced with Rol-Tanguy. To reproduce that closeness—which I believe derived from the daily experience during childhood of being with his father in the warm studio they shared as fellow artists—as well as the miraculous discovery of life at the edge of death (his mother's survival from typhoid) were Giacometti's oldest and deepest needs. They are also fundamental human needs, and Giacometti's genius was his ability to make them visible in his art.

All of Giacometti's figures after 1947 have two things in common—flickering surfaces and subtle asymmetries—both of which served his principal purpose of making them look "like," or "life-like," terms that he used interchangeably. I have discussed his treatment of the sculptures' surfaces in Chapter 9 as they are illustrated in the 1946 article in *Cahiers d'art*. Similarly, the asymmetries of the figures' profiles force the mind's eye to kinetically shift back and forth, stirring the viewer to sympathetically feel the images' vital energy. Whether we study the constantly shivering profile edge of a bust or a body, or the scarred surface of the sculpture's skin, we see traces of movement, traces designed to let us believe that art can imitate life, and breathe. The sculptures stand as eloquent proof that Giacometti had mastered his profound conflict. By creating lifelike images, he could repair the damage he had imagined with his kernel of rage. Probably without conscious awareness the artist was trying to make sculpture that was or seemed "alive"—just as he believed the ancient Egyptians had done. He once even told an interviewer that the Greeks believed that Egyptian standing sculptures would come to life and walk away if they were not attached at night.[18] His comment is another instance of his simultaneously knowing and not knowing the truth about his fantasies of magical transformation. To create life was an old, secret wish that emerged again at this critical moment.

CAREER AND REPUTATION

Despite the lack of a one-person show for fifteen years and his long-standing preoccupation with figurines he could neither exhibit nor sell, Giacometti had developed an enormous underground reputation. The high repute of his surrealist sculptures, his famous turn away from them, and the unceasing seriousness of his labors from 1935 on had made him the contemporary prototype of the pure artist willing to abandon all mundane pursuits in order to follow an impossible quest. The story of his minuscule figurines and their daily destruction was widely known among European artists and intellectuals, though not many had actually seen the sculpture he had been obsessively making and unmaking.

The 1946 article in *Cahiers d'art*, illustrating Giacometti's recent sculpture and drawings, had captured the imagination of the art world hungering for new work and new ways to see.[19] A short time later Giacometti began searching for a dealer. In early 1946, Pierre Matisse, whose gallery in New York was growing in prestige, paid a call to Giacometti at his studio. He left after the briefest of visits, saying that he found the works too small. By year's end Giacometti's studio contained a number of "respectably" sized works. When Matisse revisited the studio in early 1947, he offered him a one-person exhibition the following January.[20]

THE MYTH

Each night (or each day) Giacometti worked on the filiform figures, building up and carving away until he had reduced them to the barest essential, leaving only enough on the metal armature to suggest a glimmering flicker of life. Creating life with one's hands and mind has been the secret goal of artists since the beginning of art. As we have seen, it was also the semisecret aim of the surrealist coterie into which Giacometti had been introduced by Masson, Breton, and Ernst. Though Giacometti gave up the trappings of surrealism he never abandoned this goal. But in the contemporary intellectual atmosphere of existentialism and phenomenology, Giacometti found it impossible to acknowledge that intention, or the magical thinking that lay beneath it. It contained too much raw emotion and too much reliance on unconscious fantasies and irrational wishes. He needed a simpler, less-incriminating explanation to present to the world. Enter Jean-Paul Sartre.

Bataille might have been Giacometti's soul mate in the realms of obsession, sado-masochism, guilt, and spiritual aspirations, but it was Sartre, the most celebrated intellectual of his time, whom he selected to speak for him and who explained what Giacometti's work was all about, or at least he helped people orient themselves in the artist's strange new style.

An important element of the existential philosophy current in postwar intellectual circles was an old surrealist idea that the attempt to achieve is more important than the goal itself. In 1945 Sartre had written: "Existence precedes essence . . . man first of all exists, encounters himself, surges up in the world and defines himself afterwards. . . . Man is nothing else but that which he makes of himself."[21] When Sartre applied this notion to Giacometti's sculpture and sculpting, it fit. Giacometti's men and women do indeed surge up in the world. At least that is what Giacometti was continually trying to accomplish with his art and through his nearly constant obsessional actions and ruminations.

Though few sculptures were sold at Giacometti's 1948 exhibition at Pierre Matisse's gallery in New York, the show and its unusual catalogue were a masterstroke of public relations. One section of the catalogue was a copy of Giacometti's letter to Matisse about his artistic journey. Written in the artist's laconic, surrealist style, it was a poetic autobiography, illustrated with sketches of the major works of his surrealist and pre-surrealist years.[22] The catalogue also contained an essay by Sartre titled "Search for the Absolute."[23] Even more than Giacometti's own words, Sartre's text set a course for interpretations of Giacometti's postwar work that has rarely been challenged in fifty years. Imported copies of the catalogue were reverentially passed from hand to hand.[24] It established Giacometti as an existentialist artist and placed him at the vanguard of new art.

Since 1937–38 Giacometti had been focused on size and scale as he worked on his tiny figurines (see Chapter 8). Sartre took what Giacometti had been saying repeatedly about scale and the variance in the size of people seen from a distance and applied it to the artist's filiform figures, transmuting Giacometti's very specific preoccupations into his own larger battle with perception and the experience of being seen.[25] In his effort to make Giacometti an existentialist, Sartre made an eloquent claim that immediately became a central part of the Giacometti myth. "Each of them [Giacometti's sculpted figures] offers proof that man *is* not at first in order to be *seen* afterwards but that he is the being whose essence is in his existence for others."[26] Sartre argued that Giacometti's accomplishment is revolutionary. "Before him men thought that they were sculpturing *being* and this absolute dissolved into an infinite number of appearances. He chose to sculpture *situated* appearance and discovered that this was the path to the absolute."[27]

Sartre's explanation of how Giacometti achieved his goal is both subtle and contradictory. Whether or not he understood all of Giacometti's intentions, he chose to make sense of the filiform figures by arguing that the artist's main goal was to situate the viewer at a specific remove from the art, in order to create "an imaginary, indivisible space."[28] He described the arbitrary distance necessary to see the filiform sculptures as "a leap into the realm of the unreal."[29] We are forced to know the imaginary woman in the artist's mind by looking at his vision of her, by understanding that we can only see his vision of her and never see her, herself. "His creatures, which are wholly and immediately what they are, can neither be studied nor observed."[30]

Sartre's interpretation of Giacometti's elongated filiform figures in terms of distance and nearness was a brilliant argument by a brilliant philosopher and caught on almost immediately. It explained not only the oddness of the works themselves but why they appealed to so many people. But was Giacometti truly attempting "to sculpt man as he is seen from a distance"? I think not, at least not at this point, and perhaps not ever. Giacometti was absorbed by problems of size and scale—a subtle but important difference.

At fifteen Giacometti lectured his schoolmates on painting, saying that "the artist must be rigorous and conscientious in his work. He must present the subject as he sees it not as others make it."[31] He did not write another word on the subject of perception until the mid 1940s. When Giacometti met Sartre in 1938, his recorded comments on perception to that time were limited to discussions of size and scale. Sartre, like other writers and thinkers of the times, was plumbing the philosophical depths with arguments about the role of perception in man's ability to understand himself and the world around him.[32] His argument was a prop for his own philosophical scheme of the moment. He, not Giacometti, was preoccupied with man as *situated*, seen by others in a certain place, at a specific distance. On these grounds, then, I think it is fair to conclude that Giacometti's claims to have been constantly preoccupied and troubled by the way things looked or by his inability to capture his subjects' appearance are mostly retrospective and date from after Sartre's essay and not before.

That Giacometti eventually let Sartre's arguments creep into his own discussions was typical of the passivity that formed an important part of his character. Sometimes he rebelled and exploded with anger when others would describe him falsely or build a case about him that suited their own needs. But more often he let things go as long as it went to his advantage and didn't interfere with his work.[33]

GIACOMETTI'S SPACE AND DISTANCE

As we have seen, Giacometti had been preoccupied since childhood with the distance between objects. His ritualistic placement and replacement of physical objects, like his socks and shoes, had been reported at various points in his biographies from the mid 1930s to the end of his life.[34] Giacometti himself describes one version of the ritual in a notebook entry dated 1947: "There was never an end, I was overtaken, crushed by that task. I abandoned it always with dissatisfaction, but it began again often a moment later with the socks, the shoes, the doors which I closed too weakly or too strongly, or with no matter what objects touching each other on a table, a piece of paper a string, an inkwell. . . . I distanced the objects from each other, but how much? They were always slightly too near or too far apart . . . then I moved them imperceptibly, I knew I would always have to begin again."[35] It is easy to see how a friendly observer of such rituals, such as Sartre, might believe that Giacometti's obsession with the distance between objects also invaded his artistic activity and was translated into the distance between the artist and subject. But I think another explanation is more likely.

Giacometti alludes to space in intriguing and contradictory ways in three essays in 1945–46. In the first, on the sculptor Laurens, Giacometti recounts how a frequently recurring mental image of himself in space existing simultaneously with objects around him *"fills him with joy."*[36] He observes that space is just like the space created by Laurens's sculpture, which reminds him exactly of "the sensation he has often felt in the presence of living beings, especially human heads." It was Laurens's ability to express *likeness*—what it feels like to be in the presence of living reality—that Giacometti so loved.[37] Here, the idea of joy-filled space leads directly to Giacometti's later statements about his desire to create an object capable of conveying a sensation as close as possible to the one felt at the sight and in the presence of the subject.[38]

The space surrounding Jacques Callot's tiny figures catches Giacometti's attention in his second essay: "The only permanent and positive element in Callot is the space, the large gaping space in which his figures gesticulate, annihilate and do away with themselves."[39] Here, space is connected to helpless self-destruction and sadistic fantasies.

Giacometti's third and most frequently cited statement on space comes from his 1946 essay "The Dream, the Sphinx and the Death of T.," in which he describes seeing his towel, table, and chair suddenly immobile, suspended, and separate: "[T]here was no relation at all between the objects now separated by immeasurable gulfs of emptiness."[40] I observed in Chapter 10 that in describing the aloneness of the towel Giacometti was probably referring to his discovery of the liberating experience of a new kind of psychological space which allows for room between people and objects.

Taken together, the three examples suggest that Giacometti had recently shifted from experiencing space as a terrifying void or abyss to something more benign. How and why did he need to take this step? As a psychoanalyst, I believe that Giacometti's difficulty in seeing space as a benign separation between people and objects can be traced to two factors. The first relates to very early anxieties about being alone. Giacometti had been the firstborn who was soon displaced at his mother's side by two younger siblings. As a child he had also been very close to his father, and, as discussed earlier, to survive Giovanni's many absences he would "forget" him. Sometimes, as we have already seen, this strategy was so successful that he was unable to summon a memory of the beloved face; he would then be confronted with a terrifying emptiness and would feel completely alone.

The second reason for Giacometti's difficulty with space and distance concerns some observations and feelings about the female body, especially the part that is usually hidden, the vagina. It is likely that as a sensitive, introverted toddler he was traumatized by the experience of watching his mother give birth to his sister, Ottilia—the blood, the pain, and the violence of the birth process would have been terrifying. Later, the two childhood fears—of feeling alone in space and being frightened by the vagina—merged into one.

On one level, the vagina stood for distant but intrusive women—like his ambivalently loved mother—from whom Giacometti usually kept his distance. On another level, it represented danger or death.[41] According to either metaphor, the vagina was a malevolent abyss or void, and the idea of penetrating it frightened him to the extent that he became impotent.[42] Giacometti's obsession with the vagina had been evident in his outspoken surrealist sculptures and drawings. That obsession would grow more obvious in the years that followed. But by 1946, as a result of his relationship with Annette, the vagina was no longer only a frightening void he could not fill. Nor was it just a battleground for his sadistic fantasies. It had attained new significance. It was now also a safe place where he could connect with another human being.

Giacometti's ability to be close to a woman, physically and emotionally, represented an enormous psychological achievement. It allowed him unprecedented freedom of movement—a big step, both figuratively and literally, for someone constantly beset by fear and guilt whenever he was separated from a loved one. At the same time, it allowed him to achieve a breathtaking advance in his artistic work, creating the men who could walk away and the large standing women. Both creator and viewers could approach and retreat from the women Giacometti had made, free now to find a comfortable distance.

MAN WALKING

The catalogue illustrations for Giacometti's 1948 exhibition at Matisse's gallery, and the best record of his work during that period, are the photographs taken by Patricia Echuarren (later Matisse), a young, pretty, vivacious American heiress who had met Giacometti before the war. She was part of the small circle, including Balthus and Isabel Delmer, who saw him regularly, and just after the war she bought some of his most important surrealist sculptures, including Invisible Object.[43]

Patricia Echuarren's photographs show several preliminary versions of Man Walking—one is resolute, the other more hesitant.[44] Though the figures are thin to the point of emaciation, their vitality is clear. The ghostly images captured on film appear to rise up from shards of plaster, their arms seeming to swing back and forth as they stride against the dark background (fig. 11.1).

FIGURE 11.1 *Patricia Matisse photograph of* Study for Walking Man, 1947, *plaster (destroyed).*

In the last version the figure's arms are locked into position at his sides. The final bronze sculpture of *Man Walking* (1947) is large (170 x 23 x 53 cm) and conveys a solemn mixture of hesitancy and conviction.[45] With his bald, skull-like head, wasp waist, and fleshless body, the figure resembles a Holocaust survivor. Seen straight on, he appears graceless and impassive, too frail to survive; his limbs are too thin to bear the weight of his head and body. In profile, he is a different man. There is no longer any question about his durability. A subtle play of curves creeps up and down his sinuous silhouette, the broken lines of its rugged surface enlivening rather than stopping the eye's journey. Despite his skeletal frame, he is sure-footed, solidly set on his chunky feet. He will walk, the clearest indication that he has been brought to life by the artist.

Obstinately unlike the Egyptian prototypes of idealized youthful figures that inspired it, Giacometti's *Walking Man* is a gaunt, ageless wreck, a double of himself. The artist seems to have believed that the Egyptian standing position for the male, which looked like a walking stance, symbolized movement and life.[46] In keeping with his oppositional character, he reversed the traditional positions of the legs, making the right leg move forward rather than the left. By making a personal *ka* figure—a man who could be reborn after a decade of paralysis, a man who could finally walk erect with dignity, melding ancient magic with modern myth—Giacometti transformed an Egyptian formula into an icon for his own times.

MOVEMENT

Many of Sartre's arguments about Giacometti's goals center on the sculptor's ability to create a convincing image of movement, to "write movement into the total immobility . . . to prove that sculpture is possible." Sartre's references to movement were connected to one of his favorite concepts—the idea that man is nothing more than the sum of his actions. He took an old philosophical argument and found a way to make it contemporary. "I recognize man, the first cause, the absolute source of movement. Giacometti succeeded in giving to his substance the only truly human unity: the unity of action."[47]

Walking Man was a man who could put existence before essence because Giacometti created an object that appeared to come to life and would therefore never be a static object. By achieving "contingency" and by depicting movement Giacometti had become Sartre's ideal existentialist—one who had achieved the only absolute Sartre accepted: art. "The passion of sculpture . . . is that the statue of a man may sally forth."[48]

Movement implies aliveness, hence the question of how was creating movement in painting or sculpture related to the fantasy of image magic underlying so much of Giacometti's postwar work. The closest Sartre comes to grasping that point appears in his discussion of the appearance of upward movement in Giacometti's elongated figures in his 1948 essay.

But to the bodies of Giacometti something has happened: do they come . . . from the fountain of youth, or from a camp of displaced persons? At first glance we seem to be up against the fleshless martyrs of Buchenwald. But a moment later we have a quite different conception; these fine and slender natures rise up to heaven. . . . And when we have come to contemplate this mystic thrust, these emaciated bodies expand, what we see before us belongs to earth. This martyr was only a woman. But a woman complete, glimpsed, furtively desired, . . . a woman whose delicious plumpness is haunted by a secret thinness, and whose terrible thinness by a suave plumpness, in danger on this earth, and yet not utterly of this earth, and who lives and tells us of the astonishing adventure of the flesh, our adventure. For she, like us, was born.[49]

The text is not mere rhetoric to fit the occasion of the war's aftermath. Sartre understood that Giacometti's art of 1946–47 was about the perilous adventure of life on earth and the necessity of opposing an horrific vision with something hopeful—an almost mystic apparition allowing rarefied matter to ascend upward, leaving behind a double, a scarified surface with a hint of "delicious plumpness." The sculpture, Sartre believed, spoke to the profound needs of an audience numbed by a decade of horror and burdened by guilt.

WOMEN STANDING

Leoni and *Tall Figure* are two of the few female figures from 1946–47—also in the 1948 Pierre Matisse Gallery exhibition—that survived Giacometti's destructive impulses. With their elongated headdresses or coiffures, slanted bases with triangular masses in place of separately articulated feet, and subtle asymmetries, *Leoni* and *Tall Figure* have become signature works of Giacometti's postwar style.[50] Here we shall be considering the artist's studies for these works as photographed by Patricia Echuarren for the catalogue of his 1948 Matisse gallery exhibition.[51]

In the studies for *Leoni* we can already see the exquisitely subtle and complex combination of flowing curves circumnavigating the figure's outer edges (fig. 11.2). The silhouette is asymmetrical, but this is barely noticeable. The slight variations in the left and right edges of her body are felt by the viewer rather than seen. They create a sense of movement that will become more pronounced in later works. Though her face has been left featureless (in the final version), inviting us to impress the mental image of an adored face into the ready space, *Leoni* has a sensual particularity. She is a goddess of youth

FIGURE 11.2 *Photograph (probably by Patricia Matisse) of* Standing Female Figure, *1947, plaster (destroyed).*

FIGURE 11.3 *Photograph (probably by Patricia Matisse) of* Study for Tall Figure, *1947, plaster (destroyed).*

and love, an immortal beloved brought to life with an extraordinary sense of presence by the artist.

This work marks the beginning of the experience that most viewers of Giacometti's postwar sculpture have noted but usually misinterpret: the sculptures seem to disappear if approached from the wrong distance or angle, becoming shards of messy material. This feature has several possible explanations, the most important of which is Giacometti's characteristic ambivalence, which seeped into the form and format of his art. To see a person as whole and integrated, both loved and hated, was rarely possible for him. He split his friends, lovers, and family into idols or demons, goddesses or prostitutes.[52]

Tall Figure (1947) is Giacometti's largest figurative work after *Large Figure* (1930–31). Goddesslike and iconic, if only partly because of its size, it stands nearly seven feet tall on a coffin-shaped base. The feet have a crevice echoing the pudenda above, and one feels the subtle equivalences the artist characteristically found in the human form. *Tall Figure* has three remarkable features: the hourglass torso of his tiny figurines with their hint of inner plumpness and fertile future; thin limbs emphasizing a deathlike fragility; and an elongated head, which keeps the viewer's eye moving upward. As with *Leoni* the asymmetry of the body is subtle; the right shoulder higher and rounder than the left one, the left arm lumpier and closer to the waist.

In one *Study for Tall Figure* (fig. 11.3) the figure is luscious and curvaceously lifelike, enticing and recognizably womanly. In other studies she is fleshless and skeletal. In the final version (if such a word can ever be applied to Giacometti's postwar works), the two states are subtly combined. We sense the figure's sensuality, but only fleetingly. Her starkness arrests us before we can follow the seductive traces.

The profile views of both sculptures differ dramatically. From the front, *Tall Figure* looks formidable, even frightening. Some of her body seems to have been eaten away, and we wonder that it has survived at all since we can practically see her bones beneath the flesh. From the side, she appears elegant, Italianate, and full of life, almost too ordinary. (A similar instance of this type of disparity is visible in figure 11.4, in which front and profile of two separate works appear in the same photograph.)

SEARCH FOR THE IMPOSSIBLE, FOR THE ABSOLUTE

In 1946 *Combat*, one of the many newspapers Giacometti read, contained a story about some newly discovered cave paintings. Around this time, Giaco-

FIGURE 11.4 *Marc Vaux photograph of* Two Standing Women and Head *(Marie-Laure de Noailles), 1946–47, plaster (destroyed).*

metti pondered the impossibility of drawing movement from life. He wrote in his notebook: "[C]ave drawings, caves, caves, . . . there and only there, movement has succeeded. Look to see why, to find the possibilities. Look to see for sculpture, painting, reliefs."[53]

Giacometti probably spoke about the recent discovery with Sartre during one of their weekly lunches. Following Giacometti's lead, Sartre wrote in his catalogue essay: "For three thousand years, sculpture modelled only corpses. . . . So one must begin again from scratch. The task of Giacometti and of contemporary sculptors is . . . to prove that sculpture itself is possible. There is a single problem to be solved: *how to mold a man in stone without petrifying him?* It is all or nothing."[54]

"To mold a man in stone without petrifying him" might sound like art talk, signifying the appearance of vitality in a work of sculpture. But suppose the artist really felt that he was trying "to bring to life or to keep alive." That would explain why it would feel like "all or nothing"; why Giacometti would inevitably fail but always have to try again. Sartre becomes more specific: "He has chosen for himself a material without weight, the most perishable, the most spiritual to hand: plaster. Never was matter less eternal, more fragile, nearer to being human." Here Sartre seems to be signaling his understanding that Giacometti was trying to create life in sculptural form, like the cave artists whose images were designed to help with the hunt or with the continuation of the tribe. By cloaking it in existential garb, he made Giacometti's fantasy palatable to a larger public, even to unbelievers like himself. Sartre fathomed Giacometti's goal even as he disagreed with some of his inclinations, especially anything smacking of mysticism.

Did Sartre surmise that Giacometti's filiform sculptures hovering on the edge of nonbeing were as close as an artist could come to making life itself? "His figures, by the very fact that they have been fated to die in the very night wherein they were born, are, of all the sculptures I know, the only ones able to keep the ineffable grace of seeming perishable. Never was matter less eternal, more fragile, nearer to being human."[55] That the figures were only meant to last a few hours—because they would soon be destroyed by the artist himself—made them the ultimate instance of contingency for Sartre.

In the aftermath of World War II, the intellectuals, writers, and artists around Giacometti were seeking ways to deal with the consequences of the war. Sartre was calling for writers (and artists) to address the current situation as only they could—by making their art. Though the surrealists had put their faith in an alchemical program, neither they nor the atheistic existentialists would have abided a return to organized religion. Nevertheless, many in both groups were searching for the sacred in everyday life—or at least its moral equivalent.[56] An adamant atheist, Sartre would have looked askance at Giacometti's spiritual leanings, which were particularly near the surface in these years, in the guise of superstitiousness and magical thinking. Yet in his essay on Giacometti the philosopher seems to grant immunity to the artist, supporting him for his attempt to "make contact with the eternal."[57] Sartre understood that Giacometti's works reflected his belief that through art, living beings could be made whose transcendence would alternate with presence in a never-ending cycle of birth and death. What disturbs Giacometti, he wrote, "is that these [sculptures] always mediating between nothingness and being, always in the process of modification, perfection, destruction and renewal, have begun to exist independently."[58]

In choosing "The Search for the Absolute" as a title for his essay on Giacometti, Sartre was playing with words.[59] On the one hand, he was declaring that one of the "remarkable things" about the artist is "his intransigence in his quest for the absolute." On the other hand, he was invoking a classic figure in French literature, Balthazar Claes, the central character in Balzac's novel The Quest for the Absolute.

In midlife, Claes, a good-hearted Flemish burgher, a student of chemistry, became obsessed by a desire to discover the life-giving principle beneath all natural phenomena. Refusing to abandon his search, the success of which he repeatedly asserts is only millimeters away, Claes depletes a vast fortune, ruins his family, and drives his wife to despair and death.

In his appearance and in various particulars of quotidien life, Giacometti had much in common with the beleaguered Claes, down to the presence of a faithful servant (Diego) and daily alternations of hope and disappointment. There seems little doubt that Sartre was poking gentle fun at his friend. But Sartre particularly admired Giacometti's—and Claes's—uncompromising attitude and way of working.[60] He could identify with it because it fit with his idea of how an existential man should lead his life—with total commitment. De Beauvoir, who saw Giacometti and Sartre together often during the late 1930s and mid 1940s, observed: "There was a deep bond of understanding between them: they had both staked everything on one obsession—literature in Sartre's case, art in Giacometti's—and it was hard to decide which of them was more fanatical."[61]

It was perhaps inevitable that Sartre would use his own philosophical views on perception, visibility, and indivisibility when writing about artists.[62] Sartre felt capable of explaining anything and everything. He told his story about Giacometti, relieving the artist of the need to clarify his thinking about his own work, which was always driven more by intuition and feeling than by rational thought. Giacometti was obliging, as he had been with Breton. In time, he even took up some of Sartre's positions, tackling the perceptual problems alleged to be at the center of his work.

Yet, for those who understood, Giacometti's quest for the absolute had

hidden meaning, and the metaphor of making magic in an alchemical laboratory was compelling, especially if it could heal the horrible wounds of war.
With his art, Giacometti embraced the tattered souls of the survivors and gave
them hope. His means were remarkably subtle. Embodying the image magic
in which he secretly believed, his figures passed on their coded secrets
through pulsating profiles, shivering surfaces, and vitalizing asymmetries.
With his filiform figures Giacometti won his struggle with mortality. He acknowledged the power of death to carve away at people until they were almost
defeated, but he showed that it was also possible for the human form and
spirit to prevail. Giacometti's tall elongated figures showed the world that human aggression, especially the artist's urge to destroy, could be halted or reversed by the slightest curve, the smallest shape indicating that breath still
flows, that life goes on. This, I believe, is the principal reason for their astonishing success.

CHAPTER 12

1948-1954

EXUBERANCE AND MATURITY

In this and the following chapter I discuss subjects and themes stretching over the last period of Giacometti's life, 1946–66. Here, I take up the themes of standing women, walking men, heads of men cut off at the neck, and especially the interrelationship of the three. In Chapter 13 I consider the portraits that formed a significant part of his postwar work.

Throughout his career, Giacometti looked for ways to express his feelings and fantasies about the human body. During his apprenticeship and surrealist years he sought prototypes for his mental images of man and woman in the art of ancient civilizations, primitive societies, and contemporary culture. After World War II his primary models were his intimates—Diego and Annette. Whatever he could not put into his more representational portraits of them emerged in his iconic portrayals of man and woman. When he could feel fondness for his brother and wife he could depict them in idealized or idolized ways. Even when he was angry he could represent them in this way to protect them from his rage. During such times, however, he could also sketch or sculpt them as ugly or mutilated. Sometimes, when he had destroyed them mentally or symbolically, he could rescue their images from the trash heap and start over again in an attempt to bring them back to life.

Like all profound artists and thinkers, Giacometti understood that his feelings for other human beings, both male and female, could also be a reflection of what he felt about himself—not a mirror image, but a refracted one. It is rightly assumed that Giacometti was the voyeur of the images he created, and that his models, even when they were imaginary, were objects who had to submit to his gaze. That he also identified with the figure being portrayed is not usually recognized. The sculptures and drawings he made of women, for example, especially the androgynous images, expressed not only his identification with his mother, but some of his feelings about his own body.

EXUBERANCE

Beginning in the late 1940s and continuing through 1954 Giacometti's work was marked by a new, buoyant mood. At last he had begun to achieve the professional success and financial stability which had so long eluded him; no longer did he have to borrow money from friends or turn to his mother for help. Moreover, dealers and collectors sought him out, reversing a decades-long trend.

For at least fifteen years, Giacometti's work had been admired and collected by a circle of influential friends and colleagues, and photographs of some of it had been published in important art journals. After his 1948 show at the Pierre Matisse Gallery in New York he became known to the larger world. The exhibition was his first one-man show since 1932 and provoked a resoundingly positive response. With Matisse's enthusiastic and inspired sponsorship, his work began to be featured in major museums and collections. By 1951 he also had a formidable and energetic dealer in Paris, Aimée Maeght, with whom Matisse reluctantly divided the artist's annual production. Between the two dealers, Giacometti's reputation among European artists and intellectuals was transformed: no longer was he just an artist's artist, he was now an international celebrity. Another factor affecting Giacometti's state of mind was the experience of being close to women who enthusiastically supported him and his art. In addition to Annette Arm, there was Patricia Echuarren, who had already bought some of his most important works and who came to his studio almost every day during 1946–47, photographing each stage of his work in progress.

Giacometti married Annette Arm on July 19, 1949. He had always resisted a legal union, but Annette's pressure, combined with Annetta Giacometti's insistence that he not return to Stampa with an unwed partner, finally pushed him to act. He might also have hoped that Annette's adoring docility would act as a counterbalance to his mother's domination. The marriage had an unexpectedly positive psychological effect on Giacometti, and the engulfment he had always feared did not materialize. Moreover, as a wife, Annette was— for a while, anyway—the same relatively obedient young woman she had been when he met her six years earlier in Geneva.

As a result of his new emotional and financial security, Giacometti could work infused with the fresh breath of success. Between 1946 and 1951 he took up the themes that had preoccupied him since childhood, specifically the ways in which men and women could stand on their own or relate to each other.

In 1947, practically for the first time, Giacometti made sculptures of adult men. His representations of man as a subject could take two forms: a full figure on the move or an unmoving head and neck. I will explore below in greater depth how the head and neck conveyed Giacometti's feelings about himself as a subject looking out on the world. Sometimes that glance could make him feel small and bodiless, amputated from the neck down. At other times his perceptions could fill him with potent vitality. Walking man, by contrast, was about movement expressing the artist's belief that mankind, himself included, had a new footing—that he could be alive in the world. In subsequent years the artist's iconic walking man would become striding man and be repeated in increasingly magisterial versions as Giacometti understood ever more deeply the meaning of his ability to move. And for the next several years there was no stopping the artist.

"MAN WITH A FINGER"

Man with a Finger is the title Giacometti preferred for the most realistic male figure he ever made. Pierre Matisse changed the name of this sculpture to Man Pointing, presumably to tone down the rawness of Giacometti's turgid title. Created in October 1947, the life-size sculpture of a naked man—the bronze version stands 1.8 meters tall—is a unique image in Giacometti's sculptural oeuvre (fig. 12.1). It is also one of his rare sculpted self-portraits. Beckoning to an unseen other with his left arm, he points forward with a sure but shaky right arm. The elongated finger at the end of his outstretched arm makes an unforgettable impression. Like the wasp-waisted walking man made at the same time, Giacometti had created another icon. Whether the sculpture is beckoning us to join him in the pedestrian present or to travel with him to some loftier spiritual locale, we know that we are being summoned. Our eyes follow his silhouette as he turns on his small base, and we are drawn along through the current of his slight oscillation.[1]

With its explicit phallic content—a penis and penislike arm and finger—Man with a Finger is about masculine mastery, in the studio and in the world.[2] Like Giacometti himself, the figure aims toward the unknown, directing his gaze toward a point on the horizon with the expectation of a successful arrival. Poised between Giacometti's walking men and standing women, Man with a Finger represents a rare moment of freedom: a man who simply stands in readiness to act.[3]

FIGURE 12.1 *Patricia Matisse photograph of* Man Pointing, *1947, plaster (destroyed).*

In 1947 Giacometti began producing his images of walking figures, and soon *Walking Man* was everywhere in his sculptures, paintings, and drawings. By 1948 his walking men had developed a sprightly step and more flexibility. Many scholars and critics have noted the marked transition from the earliest *Walking Man* of 1947 to the later versions, including *Man Walking in the Rain* (1948). It is my belief that the first frightening image that hesitantly placed one faltering foot before the other was triggered in part by the artist's observation of refugees from the death camps walking on the streets of Paris. But soon, like the artist himself, his sculpted walking figures developed confidence in their stride and could be found out in different weather—in the sun and in the rain, in company with other men, even women. They lope along, heads up, as Giacometti himself must have done on his long daily walks throughout Paris.[4]

When he was working on the *Walking Man* of 1947 for his exhibit at Matisse's gallery, Giacometti wrote to his dealer that he hadn't sent the sculpture to the foundry yet because "he walked way too much."[5] Two years later, in October 1949, he jested about possible titles for a similar sculpture he had just sent Matisse: "I don't know what title to give the walking man—Walking Man III . . . his own name, Jean or Paul, doubting man . . . too literary, or man *coincé*—that's what he is."[6] After the war, coincé was the word Giacometti most frequently used to describe himself. Literally translated, it means cornered, inhibited, or stuck. Knowing that he often felt "stuck," Giacometti always closely monitored the representation of movement in sculpture. For him, it was equivalent to freedom—an important value for a man who felt so unfree. When the artist made a man on the move it represented a part of himself—the active, empowered man who could stride to success and who could connect and separate. During his glory years—1948–52, the most artistically free period of his life—he succeeded. His paintings and drawings of walking men show the same kind of physical energy and buoyancy as the sculptures.

Though he kept making walking men after 1953, these later works do not break new ground and are essentially repetitions of earlier successes, little changed even in 1959–60, when, for the Chase Manhattan Plaza project, Giacometti made his largest *Walking Man*.[7]

"CAPSIZING MAN"

The first years of married life were happy for Giacometti and Annette. Their friends and family observed that the two were in love and openly affectionate. Giacometti's art of 1949–50 suggests that during this idyllic period they also shared a gratifying sexual life. It seemed as though an inhibited man whose sexuality was largely mental had, for a brief time, become physical. When Giacometti could depict what his mind and body presented directly to him, he created masterpieces of spontaneity. *Capsizing Man* (1950) (Kunsthaus Zurich) is one such work, the most liberated and liberating of all of his sculptures.[8] It shows a confident leaper making an open-armed fall as he prepares to vault into the flow of movement that will carry him into a world-space ready to catch him. No adequate English translation exists for the French title, *L'Homme qui chavire*. *Chavirer* means to be turned upside down, to be moved. "Head over heels" more accurately expresses the feelings this sculpture connotes than do any of the tragic, or existential, interpretations that have been assigned to it. Though most usually translated as "falling," *chavirer* has also been rendered as "tottering" or "staggering," lending a subtle weight to the tragic reading.

The smallness of the high, rounded base serves as a springboard to release the man. On tiptoes, he reaches out toward the unknown rather than bracing himself against it. It is the uncontrollable, rule-less world of life and love. From every angle, the sculpture speaks to spontaneous, even joyous movement, epitomizing all the enjoyable letting go that the inhibited Swiss artist had ever allowed himself.

MULTIFIGURE GROUPS

Bruno Giacometti believes that all of his brother's male images are autobiographical, and certainly his depiction of men on the move in 1948–49 relates to his own life actions. The figures in *Three Men Walking* and *City Square* from that time are simultaneously a reference to his own differing states of mind and body and to his creative reconstruction of Giacometti family life as prototypical human relationships.[9]

In *Three Men Walking*, filiform figures who could represent Alberto, Diego, and Bruno or Giovanni move on a platform as small as Switzerland itself (72 x 32 x 31.5 cm). Despite their narrow terrain each one strides energetically in a different direction. They cannot go far and must be particularly attentive to each other's movements lest they collide. As formal figures they are alike as peas in a pod, as they might have seemed to themselves when painted by their father. Each figure is also the artist testing the margins of his limited freedom and reveling in his capacity to walk. When the platform on which the men meet is larger, more complications are possible.

In *City Square* (1948–49) a woman stands alone near the center of the sculptural platform at the rear of the group of men, unmoving like Annetta Giacometti anchored to her Swiss home. All four men walk. They seem more connected to each other than to her, because they could actually meet at the intersections of their paths. Even if he were not consciously aware that he was depicting his own history and inner life, Giacometti was expressing a universal perception about how powerful a woman can be in the minds of men who know her.

Sartre and various existentially inclined reviewers saw man's condition in Giacometti's urban landscapes. Giacometti did not contradict their interpretations, but they had little to do with the origins of his multifigured groups. Giacometti's art was always too closely connected with his state of mind to be strictly a reflection of contemporary society or philosophy. His prime achievements were grounded in his ability to transmute his inner life in accordance with the times. That gift of attunement makes it possible for widely diverse audiences to discover their own concerns and feelings in his work.

WOMAN AS AN AWESOME APPARITION

Since his arrival in Paris, Giacometti had struggled to find an image of woman to match that which he carried in his mind. At first he avoided her sexual parts and drew primarily her foot, her head, her back—but he repeatedly returned to the genital area by making coded images of it. Switching to abstraction with his flat plaques in 1927–28, Giacometti combined his inner vision with a schematic image of woman's sex—*Observing Head*. After the war, in the course of developing his iconic figures, Giacometti transposed the admiration, fear, and awe he had always felt toward his mother (as well as his sister and all subsequent women) and female bodies into the core image of an imaginary woman around whom most of his work revolved.

Giacometti's postwar figurines are two-sided (best seen from either profile or front view) and consequently give mixed messages to the viewer. Their boyish masculinity is visible from their profiles and contrasts sharply with their full-bodied womanliness evident in frontal views. Viewed head on, the upper part of their bodies often forms a single shape—a shield or a keyhole through which one could glimpse an extraordinary sight, a phenomenon visible in several figurines from the late 1940s. To this shield shape Giacometti sometimes summarily attached breasts, an apparent afterthought since their feminine nature was already determined by their passive receptivity and gentle un-

FIGURE 12.2 *Ernst Scheidegger photograph of Two Figurines, c. 1950, plaster (destroyed).*

dulations. Several new features appeared in the 1950s and remained: hands cradling crotches, an increasing emphasis on rounded pelvic areas, and—in a shorthand as old as prehistory—the slit between the figurine's legs and feet resembling a genital crevice (fig. 12.2)

"THE CAGE"

During his surrealist period, in such works as *Disagreeable Object* and *Suspended Ball*, the artist had played freely with undisguised genital symbols, usually containing an aggressive connotation. By the 1950s the male's overt hostility disappears; instead, sexual seduction and possession are expressed by the gaze alone. *The Cage* is the key unlocking the remaining principal mysteries in the Giacometti oeuvre. A woman standing in a cage or on a stage, platform, or altar is part of the formula epitomized by the idea of a woman as a startling apparition—a frightening and exciting goddess who appears suddenly. The point of Giacometti's *Cage* is that man must not look directly at her, as though she were too dazzling for his eyes. *The Cage* demonstrates Giacometti's fantasy of what the sight of a young woman can do to a man. He figuratively loses his head, and in doing so he loses his entire body—a symbolic castration, and only his head and neck remain to indicate his manhood. Here is the bodiless man who, from now on, will represent either the artist himself, Diego, or an archetypal man constantly striving and failing not to gaze at Woman.[10] Is she the truth, away from which Giacometti must turn to avoid seeing too much and repeating the trauma that transformed his childhood from paradise to purgatory? She has cut him down, sliced off his sex, and appropriated it for herself.

The Cage (1950) was the culmination of four years of effort (fig. 12.3). On a high, four-legged pedestal—the bronze sculpture stands nearly 1.8 meters tall—an open rectangular frame with a solid platform contains a filiform figurine and the bust of a man with a long neck. Before settling on the form for the woman, Giacometti experimented with many alternatives, including nine undated sketches in a notebook, a pair of drawings, a drawing on the wall of his Paris studio, a chandelier, and an initial sculptural version.[11] Central to each of the preparatory works is an unashamed display of female nudity. In the sketches, the woman appears imposing and awesome. With her large, rounded belly, big breasts, wide hips, and accentuated pubic triangle, she is no nubile acrobat; she is the Great Goddess, the Mediterranean fertility figure who had preoccupied Giacometti for so long (as discussed in chapters 4 and 6). As he developed the theme, the man's head and neck grew larger in relation to the woman's body. By the final version she looks small, though still triumphant, but he now dominates by size, weight, and position.

The man has gained in stature but is still not whole. His head is large and bald, and his long, thin neck rests on sturdy shoulders. Placed behind the woman on the platform they share, the man actually looks past her, not at

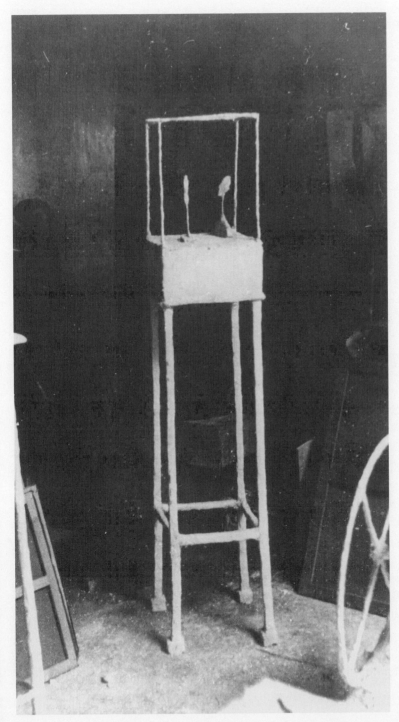

FIGURE 12.3 *Patricia Matisse photograph of* The Cage, 1950, *plaster (destroyed).*

her, because of his perpendicular position. She is to his left, and he can see her only with his peripheral vision. We cannot see both simultaneously at their most characteristic, because she should be seen face front and he in profile. Regarded any other way, one of them disappears, she becoming a beanpole and he a bulky bust with a bizarre face and head. The diminished woman, who has been reduced to a passive but complete object, still rises above him. Though his head and neck are proportionately much larger than hers, he is, by virtue of his missing body, dwarfed by her. She is mindless, and he is bodiless—the essence of the formula. The woman with her disproportionately small head towers triumphantly over the man. Her body fills his mind, but the two figures can never connect.

In both his first version of The Cage (Galerie Beyeler, Basel) (where the woman holds the bars of her cage) and the definitive final version (where she stands with her arms at her sides) Giacometti presents a goddess with her worshipper. But from one version to the next he transforms the goddess from a celebratory figure, arms outstretched as if giving adoration, to a phallic form, both male and female, rising ever upward until she towers over her acolyte. For Giacometti, when man is trapped within a space (physical or emotional) that keeps him too close to a woman, he is terrified and paralyzed. He can no longer act. What is there for him to do or be in the face of her power? How can he tame that power? These questions would obsess Giacometti for the rest of his life.

In a letter to Matisse, Giacometti referred to the figurine in The Cage as the maiden who left the man with only his head, but, he added, "it is difficult to call [the sculpture] Judith and Holofernes." Understandably, Giacometti did not choose Judith and Holofernes as a title for his cage sculptures. The biblical story about a beautiful woman who seduced a man into letting down his guard and then cut off his head was too close to the artist's fears and fantasies.[12] Only with his vivid imagination could Giacometti fully (and safely) express his desire. The combination of a naked female torso and a disproportionately large, phallus-shaped male head, his eyes level with her crotch, would appear with escalating frequency in the last twenty years of his life. He returned to the theme repeatedly, sometimes with exceptional verve, at other times like an exhausted warrior returning one more time to the battlefield.

When Giacometti encaged women, either as portrait subjects or as universal figures, their stuckness also suggested an inability to separate, to leave home or be left, echoing his observations about a mother who could not, or would not, leave her home base. Encaging the women also made them less dangerous. Implicit in my interpretation about dangerous women and the frightened men who watch them is the idea that when Giacometti depicted women, he was also representing his identification with them. He too had been watched, had felt exposed, and had experienced the power and powerlessness of the posing model. When he tightened the bonds around the feet of the women he drew and painted, he was also portraying his own constraints and fetters.

In the deep Alpine valley of his childhood, he had been both embraced and trapped within the tight circle of his family—partly by the father he adored, partly by the mother to whom he was ambivalently attached, and partly by the memory of his sister whose birth gave him his first and most lasting view of a miraculous event in an enclosing structure.

"FOUR FIGURINES ON A PEDESTAL" AND "THE CAGE"

Giacometti completed a version of *Four Figurines on a Pedestal* by fall 1948, at around the same time he was working on *The Cage*. Four large-footed filiform females are lined up equidistantly on a narrow platform. In some versions the platform is coffin-shaped, in others it is pyramidal and placed at the top of a very tall, cagelike pedestal. In December 1949, when he was searching among his associations and memories for ways to explain this work to his dealer, Giacometti wrote: "I have often thought of the four figures on the base somehow as the devils that came out of the box and of the women that I saw sometimes in reality, attractive and repulsive at the same time."[13] The next year he wrote of *Four Figures on a Pedestal* (1950): "Several nude women seen at the Sphinx, at the end of the room. The distance which separated us (the shining parquet floor) and which seemed uncrossable despite my desire to cross it made a great impression on me. I saw them often, above all one night in a little room rue l'Échaudé all near and menacing."[14]

Giacometti encouraged people to think that his caged and pedestaled women were based on the many prostitutes he knew. In these sad, often proud women whose courage he admired, Giacometti found goddesses—sacred servants of the ancient goddesses he revered. Always a man of opposites, he took the lowly women who were the antithesis of his mother and turned them into idols.

For Giacometti, as for Bataille, the ultimate aim of art was the arrival at the sacred through the profane—prostitutes to be seen as goddesses.[15] "Profanation is the sacred . . . it is the truth of sacrifice. . . . [The surrealist act] can be performed only if it is accepted as a sacred act (in the *profanatory* sense of the work): *against the unacceptable world of rational utility*."[16] Giacometti's comfortable habit of visiting prostitutes before the war had been transformed into a "higher principle" as he elevated and placed them on altars.

Like goddesses, prostitutes are anonymous objects of desire or worship. In *Four Figurines on a Pedestal* they stand in a row or lineup, similar to the way the four Giacometti children had stood when they dutifully posed for Giovanni. Proud display was combined with enforced exhibitionism, and the powerful object of desire was simultaneously a tool for someone else's pleasure. The artist could have felt kinship with the women who were subjected to so much excitement and degradation.[17] The Basel version of *Four Figurines on a Pedestal* is painted so that each figure has a slightly different skin color, reminiscent of Giovanni's *Boys on the Beach at Torre del Greco* and the paintings of his children in the nude.[18]

Four Figurines on a Pedestal and *The Cage* express two sides of the same theme. The man in *The Cage* is a sculpture about *not watching*—about being tantalizingly close to what the artist wants—and doesn't want—to see. *Four Figurines on a Pedestal* addresses the theme from a distance. Giacometti could safely view a nude woman—or perhaps be viewed by a woman in the nude—only when there was space between them.[19] Closeness represented danger. The pedestal increased the distance and consequently the safety for the viewer. Having found a satisfactory expression for his old theme of man watching woman, the artist repeated it insistently.

ANDROGYNY

A reductionist Freudian interpretation connecting Giacometti's obsessionally repeated filiform figures with phallic images contains a kernel of truth, but it does little justice to his art. If his figurines are phallic images, they are also considerably more—at their core is a fantasy about androgyny. From the beginning of his career Giacometti had conflated male and female, skating on the knife edge of sexual differentiation. The earliest manifestation of his merging male with female occurred in the 1920s, when he was most influenced by primitive and prehistoric art—*Torso* (1925), *Little Crouching Figure* (1926), and *The Couple* (1926) being prime examples. The most outspoken and least disguised instances of his combining the sexes were an undated surrealist *Drawing* of an androgynous sexual organ, and the *Large Figure* commissioned for the Count de Noailles, both discussed earlier.

The image of two sexes merged into one was a plausible construct for a man who had fears about his sexual potency and who felt his masculine and feminine aspects merged through an identification with both parents.[20] Giacometti's last surrealist sculpture was 1+1=3 (see fig. 6.11), last probably because the androgynous combination of male and female left him stranded. Soon after making it during his transitional period (1935–45), Giacometti whittled his figurines into tiny sticks that, from a distance, could be taken for phallic shapes. Giacometti's postwar work contains a range of "solutions" to his ongoing dilemma about the anatomical difference between men and women, but it is an emphatically phallic one. Both men and women, with their elongated limbs and torsos, become impressively vertical. Women often lose substance in their heads, leaving their bodies to carry the symbolic burden, while the heads and necks of men become engorged or elongated beyond measure.

Giacometti knew from his family history that his mother survived the many losses in her childhood by imitating her father's asceticism—in other words, by taking on his manly or phallic strength. Having grown up with a strong, masculine mother, Giacometti could imaginatively transform the mythic figure of Osiris boxed in a coffin into an encaged phallic woman, which appears in his many images of caged women. By incorporating his penis or phallic power, she becomes strong. Though Giacometti's vertically rising female figures grew taller and more imposing, they were often fragile, brittle, and vulnerable like their original model, his mother. Sometimes they were so narrow that from a distance they did not appear to be women at all—just girls who have not developed into full womanhood. Yet sometimes Giacometti's women seemed to soar, free and liberated, triumphant and mobile. One glorious example is The Chariot of 1950.

"CHARIOT"

Giacometti's 1943 Woman with Chariot had ironically combined playful childishness in the form of the little wheels from one of his nephew's wheeled toys with memories of his sister, Ottilia. In The Chariot, made seven years later, Giacometti clearly had something else in mind (fig. 12.4). Despite (or because of) his characteristic formal contradictions, the sculpture has an enchanted spirit—a magical momentum. She is about to move, to take off for another realm. The huge wheels, resembling those of ancient Egyptian chariots, are ready to carry away this lightest of light figurines.[21] She is on the verge of departure but can go nowhere. Held back by the funereal stele-shaped blocks on which the large wheels are placed, her equivocal triumph is established. With her proud stance and slight sinuosities, she turns as though to survey her kingdom, but she will never move beyond this point.

FIGURE 12.4
*Patricia Matisse
photograph of* The
Chariot, 1950, *plaster
version (destroyed).*

The probable model for this work was Annette Arm, whom he had met shortly after he made *Woman with Chariot*. Though still restrained like the earlier charioteer, here she seems much more vital and liberated. Giacometti claimed that this chariot reminded him of the wheeled cart at the Bichat Hospital, where he was taken to recover from his foot injury in 1938 after a fall. Another instance of a humorous disguise containing a kernel of truth (as we saw in his various stories about *Invisible Object*), Giacometti's claim reveals a forgotten association. When he fell and injured his foot, he landed at the base of the gilded statue of *Joan of Arc* in the place des Pyramides. Perhaps the significance of the piece is highlighted by the fact that he wanted all casts of the work to be patinaed in gold.[22] As I observed in Chapter 9, gold was the substance of the magically alive mechanical servant girls of Vulcan who helped the lame smithy walk.

Implying movement in the charioteer cost Giacometti much effort, and he repeatedly revised the position of her arms.[23] By raising her above the multitude, Giacometti made the woman of *The Chariot* into an object of worship. She stands in direct contrast to his numerous immobile or encaged women of that year who were simultaneously enticing and threatening. Like *Night* (visible in fig. 9.3), her direct predecessor, she is one of the very few female figures Giacometti shows in movement—metaphorically alive.[24] With his second *Chariot* Giacometti momentarily triumphed over death with his contemporary image magic, just as ancient Egyptians believed that the shining sun triumphed every day over the darkness of night and death. *Night* had been a memorial to the dead Ottilia and Sonia and, in 1950, at the height of his powers he could afford to carry out a project that secretly celebrated one of his profoundest fantasies—an apparently inanimate creature could be seen as vital.

LITTLE MONSTERS

Giacometti had stopped sculpting from live nude models when he left Bourdelle's academy. Only for a brief period (1953–54) did he make sculpture from a live model—his wife, Annette.[25] Her splayed breasts, narrow waist, and distinctive hairstyle give the works a naturalistic look. Soon, however, the figurines turn into small, hideous caricatures whose protruding breasts and bulging buttocks recall some of the exaggerated aspects of prehistoric fertility figures. Giacometti's little figurines were so grotesque and unexpected that dealers called them "Little Monsters."[26] *Standing Nude IV* (ca. 1953) (Hirshhorn Museum) and *Standing Nude III* (1953) (Alberto Giacometti-Stiftung) are two such examples.[27]

Why, after more than three years of making elegant, eloquent paintings, drawings, and sculptures that celebrated his young wife's shapely body, and the pleasures it provided him, did Giacometti suddenly switch gears and produce pieces that made Annette look grotesque? I think the answer lies in the fact that, sometime in 1953, Annette announced that she wanted to have a child. She was thirty and feeling the pressure of her biological clock. Despite having heard about her husband's inability to father children and having observed his obdurate unwillingness to be a parent, Annette pushed him repeatedly on the subject.[28] His failure to fill her heartfelt longings opened a gulf between the artist and his heretofore compliant girl-wife, awakening a forgotten trauma and energizing old pain. He seems to have displaced his experience of her relentless pressure and applied it to the sculptures. By dividing his depictions of women—young and nubile or rageful and ugly—the same way he divided his ambivalent feelings for Annette, he protected her from his wrath and disappointment.

Woman, or Figurine on a Cube (1953), a work made in painted bronze (Alberto Giacometti-Stiftung) and painted plaster version, persuasively represents the transforming power of maternal urges.[29] The woman's important parts are presented to us—her head diminished and her lower limbs truncated by the small, square cube on which she is placed. In the bronze version (recognizably Annette by virtue of the narrow waist and characteristic hairstyle), oversized, chunky hands and arms frame the figure's pelvis. The delicate pinkish tints of the flesh and purplish black of her pubic hair humanize the figure and distract us from the grotesqueness of her torso. But in the plaster version, with its drastically reduced head, the bursting belly and crotch are the undisguised focus of the artist's rage. Seemingly overcome by inner demands, the face in both versions looks angry and perturbed, like a scold staring back at her maker, or a woman who has lost her mind. Like her model, the figure is dominated by her wish to reproduce. She must conceive and be fertile.

Adding to the tension between husband and wife, Giacometti forced Annette to make sacrifices that she considered unnecessary. For example, though he was now successful, Giacometti insisted on maintaining the lifestyle of an impoverished artist, refusing to buy more comfortable quarters across the street from the studio complex where they worked. His sadistic withholding from his wife contrasted greatly with his generosity with his brother, Diego; his mother; and many other individuals who were virtual strangers. Furthermore, Giacometti responded to Annette's various demands for sexual and emotional attention by urging her to turn to other men, even to have a child with another man.[30] This started a train of liaisons and betrayals that would eventually unravel their previously harmonious domestic life.

Though Giacometti soon regained his balance and could again see his wife as the stalwart shapely model of womankind she had previously been, his representation of the female body would never be the same. From 1954 on, almost all of his sculptures of women accentuate the pelvic area. In Annette (Nude from Nature) (1954) the hands frame the pelvis in a way that foretells the

Women of Venice series two years hence.[31] The reproductive center of his female sculptures will grow in size, until the artist achieves his transmuted version of the Great Goddess for the twentieth century—but one whose hands cradle a yawningly empty space.

Though Giacometti made many sculptures of standing women between 1954 and his death, two groups exemplify his aesthetic mastery of the childhood trauma reawakened by his wife's wish to be a mother. The series called Women of Venice is the first. The second consists of four very large standing women he made in 1960 for the Chase Manhattan project.

For sculptures he was simultaneously preparing for the French pavilion at the Venice Biennale and for an exhibit in the Kunsthalle in Bern, both scheduled to open in June 1956, Giacometti began by using his wife as the model for the female figures. Annette's familiar hairstyle and figure indicate that Giacometti had her in mind, at least at the outset. But photographs of the artist working on the figures show no model present, thereby confirming Lord's supposition that he worked from imagination—it was the image of his wife he kept in his mind's eye.[32]

According to David Sylvester, Giacometti worked on a single standing figure for five months using the same armature and the same clay for all revisions.[33] He worked and reworked the figure repeatedly, a pattern reminiscent of his most troubling projects. On a single afternoon he might modify the figure up to forty times.[34] When pleased with a particular version, he would ask Diego to make a plaster cast of it and then continue. All of the casts were provisional for the artist—merely a means of seeing his work more clearly—never a final version. The series of fifteen figures, only nine of which survive, are now called Women of Venice, and their subject is the continuity of life—fertility.[35]

At the outset of the series, as seen in Woman of Venice I, it is clear that the artist was inspired by prehistoric models with their jutting pelvises and exaggerated profiles.[36] What the first four women have in common is the space between their arms and waist, and this has the effect of aggressively highlighting the pelvic area, which seems to screech its suctioning power. About halfway through the series Giacometti resolved to close the open spaces and used the entire torso to attract the viewer's eye. The figures' overall stance has been tamed, making them seem more discreet. Yet the viewer drawing near is stopped cold. Slim, elegant, and self-contained, these women may be ready to receive whatever the viewer can give, but they neither greet nor use their hands to reach out. They cannot be moved or unbalanced because of their ballast—their feet a triangular mass qualifying the openness of the invitation above.

With the *Women of Venice*, Giacometti overcame the conflicts, expressed in the little monsters, that had made it so hard for him to sculpt the female figure with equanimity between 1953 and 1956. Many of the resulting sculptures have the elegance and power of the artist's first filiform figurines. But in contrast to those earlier works, these are not ghosts come to life. They are instead ancient goddesses transformed into icons.

Giacometti had one more step to take to arrive at his last major sculptural statement, an outdoor monument commissioned for the Chase Manhattan Plaza in New York City in 1958. He worked on the project primarily in the second half of 1959, cast one large standing woman (2.7 meters tall), a head (1 meter tall), and two walking men (each 2 meters tall) in March 1960 and then left for Stampa. He was disappointed when he returned at the end of April and saw the results in bronze, and he wrote to Matisse that he could not send any of them. He explained that he would probably be unable to get them right until he saw the site for which they were intended. Giacometti continued to work on the project through 1965, and by the time of his death he had completed four large women, at least one monumental head, and two walking men.[37]

It is unclear how many of the men and women were intended for the final monument, as they were exhibited during his lifetime in various combinations. In spite of Giacometti's claim that his problems with these large works was formal—"a question of dimension, proportion, figuration, etc."—he later stated that he didn't much like the large women and that the commission required them to be bigger than he wanted.[38] As usual, there were other factors at play, not the least of which was the fact that their great size could have pierced the wall of denial he usually kept around his deeper motives.

In all four versions, the *Large Standing Woman*'s largeness is emphatic and imposing. The woman towers over the *Walking Man*. One meter shorter, the walking men are on a more human scale and must feel helpless in the face of her enormity and pulsating power. But if the sculpted men are *us*, she is *other*, and her otherness is goddesslike. She seems divinely serious with her masked face and Cycladically simple head. A plaster version of *Large Standing Woman IV* that was photographed next to Giacometti's studio eloquently conveys both her ancient and divine status as his Great Goddess (the bronze version is 2.7 meters tall) (fig. 12.5).

The demure elegance of the figure's curvilinear silhouette is strangely augmented by her rough surface textures and the jagged negative spaces between her arms and torso. Three of the four versions accentuate the hourglass torso, suggesting her function as a fertility goddess (very similar to the figurines in *No More Play*). In contrast, *Large Standing Woman III* recalls the stark emaciation

FIGURE 12.5 *Ernst Scheidegger photograph of* Large Standing Woman IV, 1959, *plaster (unfinished).*

of Giacometti's 1946–47 figures. She is shorter than the others, and when she and the walking man are placed side by side, she is his perfect partner. Their emaciations match. But they should never be seen next to each other, and Giacometti usually placed them at right angles where *he* appears to be moving and *she* standing stock still.

FIGURE 12.6 *Ernst Scheidegger photograph of* Bust of Man, *c. 1950, plaster (destroyed).*

"MAN'S MONUMENTAL HEAD"

Giacometti was a charismatic conversationalist and a dominating gazer. He once told Leiris that he would be happy to be left with only his head sitting on a mantelpiece, as long as he were able to participate in conversation.[39] The power of his mind, expressed through his verbal gifts and his vision, was Giacometti's most potent mode of phallic mastery.

FIGURE 12.7 *Ernst Scheidegger photograph of* Monumental Head (Large Head of Diego) and Walking Man *(both unfinished), 1959, plaster.*

The rocketing upsurge of many of Giacometti's postwar male heads and busts is their most startling aspect. Ostentatiously upright, they thrust their way into our consciousness. As with the filiform figures he made in 1946–47, the uprising quality served as an ingenious way to show lifelikeness. In many of these busts, whether sculpted, drawn, or painted, the shoulders curve asymmetrically and smoothly upward toward the narrowing neck and advance the accelerating upward momentum, as can be seen in a lost work from 1950 (fig. 12.6). When the head is reached its ovoid shape seems a perfect culmination and masculine triumph.

Toward the end of his life Giacometti transmuted that vision into a commanding image of a *Monumental Head* (1960) (fig. 12.7). The sculpture, which was originally part of his Chase Manhattan project, could easily be a subject of scorn, since it is so overtly phallic. Instead, the sturdy base stolidly supports the elongated, thick neck of a substantial man. Though it is often compared to the gigantic head of the Roman emperor Constantine, which Giacometti had sketched during his visit to Rome in 1959–1960, the Roman work is a minor factor among the influences behind this powerful sculpture.[40] In the profile, the close-cropped hair, and the sternly stoic stance we vaguely recognize Diego, but *Monumental Head* is not one man, he is everyman. As the epitome of the artist's concern about how to portray a man with a mind and no body, *Monumental Head*, unlike many of Giacometti's other male busts, is optimistic and complete. We are heartened and hopeful. Compared with male embodiment as a walker, this head seems surpassingly surefooted.

CHAPTER 13

1955-1966

PORTRAITS: REPRISE AND REPRISAL

Giacometti is almost invariably presented as a strongly independent man who withstood years of isolation and daily solitude, an artist whose "stark skeletal figures evoked alienation and solitude."[1] Yet near the end of his life he claimed that he had no intention of being "an artist of loneliness. . . . I don't have the slightest tendency in that direction . . . but if so many people feel it then there must be a reason. I believe that all of life is the opposite of loneliness because it consists of a net of relationships with others."[2]

I have already noted Giacometti's exceptional sensitivity to loss and separation. It was always hard for him to say goodbye to a person or a place—whether for an evening out or a trip to Switzerland. He repeatedly postponed his departures from both Paris and Stampa, and he was usually the last to leave the bar or the restaurant.[3] Returning home in the early hours of the morning he could comfort himself by looking in at his wife asleep in their tiny bedroom, where the light was always left on at his insistence.[4] Giorgio Soavi recalled: "Before he goes to bed he has tremendous desire to stay up, to talk as if the explanations of people, of friends were the most original, essential that he couldn't miss for anything."[5] Reluctant to be alone with his thoughts and feelings, Giacometti devised many ploys to avoid that discomfort—and even more rationalizations to hide the unpalatable fact of his fear, often wandering the streets at night to find company and stave off the moment at which he would be left alone.

Giacometti's most fundamental conflicts were fear of abandonment and fear of engulfment—roughly translated into how to find the right degree of nearness or distance from another person—and the arena for wrestling with these demons was portraiture. From the time of the artist's tumultuous emotional and spiritual growth during and just after the war until the end of his life, portraiture was a linchpin in both his mental and artistic life.

In his youth Giacometti learned his father's methods of portraiture as he painted and drew his family and schoolmates, and his portraits from that era show more accomplishment than his landscapes and still lifes.[6] In Giacometti's surrealist period portraiture was put aside except on visits home. After his return to figuration in the mid 1930s, he began making portraits in Paris as well as in Switzerland. The experience could take the artist back to his connection with his father and make him relive past feelings: a pleasurable communion as the object of loving attention, and sadomasochistic fantasies of capture.

Giacometti's models often described posing for him as a form of psychological possession. When the work went well the artist might proclaim, "I've got you, you can't escape me now." Knowing his reputation as a tyrant, many relatives and friends avoided posing for the artist, whose "failure to make heads the way he saw them" justified for him the endless posing sessions. The artist's youngest brother, Bruno, described the experience of posing for his brother during childhood: "I felt like I was his slave. He, who by character was so sweet, gentle, rarely difficult to be with, became a tyrant from the moment he was before the model. One couldn't move an inch."[7]

Giacometti's insistence that his models sit completely immobile, in exactly the place and position he determined, reflects his terror of losing them. It is as though he felt that movement would break the spell of connectedness, and his painted portraits often convey the rock-solid attachments he needed for himself to feel emotionally safe. As he grew older Giacometti developed plausible explanations for his insistence on his subjects' immobility; at least, they seemed plausible to some of his sympathetic sitters. Whatever other factors and themes might become part of a given portrait, the underlying theme was always about how to hold on to someone, especially his three principal models from 1946 to 1956—mother, brother, and wife. Between 1956 and his death he added two new figures to his pantheon, Isaku Yanaihara and Caroline.[8]

Giacometti expressed a fear of losing emotional balance through his reluctance to finish anything. Rather than let his work leave his studio, the artist would simply declare a painting or sculpture unfinished. This trait is usually romanticized when Giacometti is discussed or written about, since it fits with the image of the artist as an ever-unsatisfied seeker. "Every canvas or sculpture must be torn away from him by force, he will work right up to the moment of an exhibition and alter its contents even after it has begun."[9] Toward the end of Giacometti's life this tendency increased, and his rationalizations for not finishing work became exaggerated. He would declare that completing his work is an impossible goal. "If I put myself in front of you to paint what I see . . . it will be endless. I will be there for ten years, a thousand years, all my life."[10]

Though formal similarities are apparent within his unfolding painting style, Giacometti treated Diego, his mother, and Annette differently, focusing on the very distinct emotional relationships he had with each—an issue usually obscured by his insistence on discussing formal and perceptual problems whenever he spoke to anyone about his portraits. Like Cézanne, his principal mentor in painting and drawing, Giacometti created paintings that are exquisitely complex; the figures are woven into compositions with lines, color, and perspectival thrusts.

Giacometti placed his portrait subjects into cagelike structures, an electrifying network of lines similar to the sculpted cages he was making during the same period. Using feats of legerdemain he often makes us feel what he feels—he is pushed in and pulled out of closeness to his sitters, as we feel pushed into and pulled out of the canvas.[11] Wrapping his figures with lines, or fixing them within a fascinating grid, Giacometti also brings his figures into our space, keeping them and it alive.

Giacometti almost always uses the same rooms, either the stua (the living-dining room) in Stampa or his studio in Paris, to frame his sitters. Staying with known spaces and their interior furnishings allowed the artist to incorporate the contents as visual elements to suit his formal or emotional needs, playing the horizontals, verticals, and diagonals like an instrumentalist. In the earliest examples he seems enamored of the space he could create and the way he could make his figures feel at home within it. Sometimes the people blend with the background in color and line. More often, their diagonals and volumetric roundness are proof of their stature as live human beings—his great postwar discovery.

ANNETTA GIACOMETTI

The artist's portraits, especially those of his mother, are overwhelming evidence that Giacometti's alleged perceptual difficulties almost invariably express emotional meaning. They represent a common psychological phenomenon—all seeing is contingent, colored by feelings and fantasies, whether conscious or unconscious.[12] When Giacometti couldn't "see" someone clearly, it was because his feelings interfered with his visual perception.

Of his three major portrait subjects Giacometti's mother receives the harshest treatment. Though we do not know how much he could admit to himself about his feelings, he could not lie with his art. His postwar portraits of her tell a consistent story. In today's world, Annetta Giacometti, with her commanding intelligence, organized mind, and dominating will could be a successful executive. Her goals were mostly constructive, and she nurtured the stoic sides of her children. Giving backbone to the men in her family, she was a prototypical phallic woman—upright, tough, and strong. That was how her husband usually painted her, how her children experienced her, and how her eldest son sometimes depicted her. Attached to her by indestructible bonds, he also revealed his disappointment and rage by sometimes making her look awful (when he positioned her up close) or unreachably distant (when he set her far back on the canvas, away from the artist).

The most frightening known image he made of his mother is an infrequently reproduced portrait from 1947–48 (Musée des beaux-arts, Montreal) showing a woman's head and shoulders on a roughish red background. Her face and neck are mostly white, and her features cursorily conveyed with the same sienna that outlines her shoulders and hair.[13] Bloody strokes surround her eyes and also seem to drip out of her mouth and down her neck. The splashes of red paint, which course down her face from a gash at the base of her hairline, evoke the image of a stabbing victim.

Giacometti was a passionate man who both loved and hated. Did he hate his mother at the moment he portrayed her thus? The work was probably painted during a visit at the end of 1947. He had spent most of that year in Paris preparing for his first exhibit at the Pierre Matisse Gallery in New York and didn't go to Switzerland until just before the new year. Between his arrival there on December 27, 1947, and his departure just after February 16, 1948, Giacometti wrote nine letters to Matisse in which we catch glimpses of his state of mind. (The artist's relationship to Matisse was very close, as can be discerned from their extensive correspondence spanning two decades.) In one of his first letters, he claims to be unhappy with his name, especially his family name; "I don't like to sign it and I don't have a close relationship to it, it is strange to me I have often looked for another."[14] This, at the moment he is ensconced in his family home after an extended absence. By the end of January, his mother is posing regularly "every morning and afternoon, even Sundays," and he is impressed that she does this even at age seventy-five.[15] A casual remark in one of his letters to Matisse suggests that it may be she who is driving the work on her portrait(s). After telling about his flu and the doctor's report that it was only the result of "neurosis and overwork" he writes: "I am working on a portrait of my mother, it is snowing which makes me sleepy but then she comes to pose and I have to try to work."[16] On January 11 he repeats his urgent wish to return to Paris to make more sculpture and says how pleased he is that Matisse is "not discontent" with his work, as "everything else is secondary."[17] On February 16, 1948, he explains that he is waiting for his mother to be ready to leave for Geneva because he is "anxious to get back to Paris and to sculpture since all that I've made is only a beginning."[18]

Giacometti was having his first major exhibit in sixteen years and wanted to be closer to his studio and the center of action.[19] Having spent two months surrounded by his father's paintings, he would have been particularly mindful of the professional consequences of his father's isolation in a beautiful backwater. Was he feeling trapped in Switzerland with a mother who tried to keep him from leaving by insisting on posing for him?

Giacometti also wanted to be with his supportive young mistress whom he had left in Paris, as well as with Patricia Echuarren, his admiring friend.[20] Could the contrast between the two appreciative young women and his critical mother explain the hideousness of Annetta's depiction? Arriving back in Paris, Giacometti immediately wrote Matisse that two months in Switzerland had done him good and that he would no longer need to destroy his things.[21] Could this mean that, having exhausted his destructive impulses in the process of portraying his mother, he could preserve his work in Paris?

Giacometti's most famous pair of painted portraits done in the period between 1948 and 1952 are his 1950 paintings of his wife (Neumann Collection) and mother (Museum of Modern Art, New York) on the same chair and in the same room in Stampa.[22] Giacometti placed the two primary women in his life smack in the middle of each canvas. Hands folded in their laps, they are seated on a hard chair directly in front of a red door before a niche between Giovanni's desk (filled with his mementos) and wall on the left, and a large decorated oven that fills the right side of the room. By posing his two women identically, Giacometti took his concept of the cage back to Stampa, where it had begun. Giovanni had designed both the desk and the oven with its attached bench and clock. He had also painted and carved the decorations on the oven and adjacent wall. The red door directly behind both figures opened into his mother's bedroom, which had been the room Alberto originally shared with his two brothers and sister—the cage of his childhood.

Alberto had not been able to produce a happy family in a home of his own, but he could transform a setting associated with his father into two masterworks of such vitality that they enchant strangers a half century later. Overcoming both the joys and traumas of his childhood, Giacometti transmuted the memory-laden room into a magical domain.

The younger woman is larger, firmer, and more mobile. She swings her leg in the space provided for her. Unlike Annetta, Annette has the power of the diagonal, and the oriental rug under her feet does not block her movement. The thin tracery in the mother's immediate vicinity touches her dress and chair, whereas similar lines are stopped before they can confine his wife. The lines radiating around Annette give her the vibrating liveliness of youth, while similar lines tie Annetta to her chair, her room, and her memories. Annette seems closer to us and to the painter, whereas Annetta, who had already demonstrated that she did not want to leave this room or her position in it, is kept at a discreet remove. Small variations in color tell the same tale. Annette is darker and, by implication, stronger, the door behind her is redder, the hues in the rug beneath her feet are not as overlaid with white.

There are only hints of his father's works in these two portraits. Alberto has reduced Giovanni's paintings to design elements, which work as part of a weave of rectangles, squares, horizontals, and verticals. Above the door one of Giovanni's paintings is turned into a horizontally oriented rectangle, slowing the vertical rise of the door and its occupant. The converging lines of rug, table, and bench rush back toward that door and are stopped by the light color on the floor behind the sitter, the red door, and the unexpected rectangle above.

In 1951 Giacometti pushed his mother away again in his now-famous *The Artist's Mother in the Bedroom* (Musée nationale d'art moderne).[23] Here she is not horrible but small and distant, surrounded by a mist of dusky colors and a light overlay of thin black lines, a captive of the surrounding walls and furniture. The sweetness of the rose, gray, and white on her bed compensates for the fact that she is so far away.

A few years later Giacometti painted his mother again in the *Stampa stua* (1954) (Krugier Gallery, Geneva).[24] In this work, he places her next to Giovanni's desk. She is legless, and her eyes stare directly at us. The bravura brushwork on the door behind her and to her right is the closest he comes to honoring her. But might he actually be paying homage to his paternal heritage more than honoring his mother? She seems almost transparent, and the slashing marks that define her in black and white do not feel as sympathetic as his rendering of the domestic setting.

In almost all of Giacometti's late portraits of his mother he delineated her grasping eyes and intense need to possess and command. That need, visible

FIGURE 13.1 *Giacometti with his mother, Annetta, 1961 (Henri Cartier-Bresson photograph).*

as early as the famous 1909 family photograph, is especially discernible in her son's late drawings, where she seems to diminish him with her steely gaze. There are many examples, and one of the most splendid is the lithograph *Face of the Artist's Mother* (1963, Alberto Giacometti-Stiftung), in which Annetta's small, frowning face and staring eyes appear like a condensed kernel of grim energy at the very heart of a vast expanse of white paper. In his drawings and lithographs, more obviously than in the paintings, Giacometti shows her devouring gaze. That gaze is also notable in a well-known photograph taken by his old friend Henri Cartier-Bresson in 1964 in the Stampa stua (fig. 13.1). She looks up at her son with an intensely bright-eyed hunger.

Annetta had always idolized her painter-husband and had tried to make her artist son behave like him. "Why can't you be a good artist like your father?" she still carped in 1960. That same year, Herbert Matter went to Stampa to take photographs for a book on Giacometti. His wife, the painter Mercedes Matter, who wrote the text, accompanied him. Matter reports: "His mother Annetta looked with dismay at her son's way of life and made sardonic comments which amused Alberto. However proud she was of her son she managed to conceal this beneath her disparaging manner. When he won the Carnegie prize for sculpture in 1961, she remarked: "At least you'll never win the beauty prize!"[25]

When Matter observed that Giacometti was the outstanding artist of his time, his mother responded: "Oh, you know, he's absolutely worthless around the house!" And when Matter told him about his mother's comment, he said: "She treats me like a child, just like a small child!"[26] I believe that Giacometti, who was as tough as his mother, concealed his pain and embarrassment at her unrelentingly acrid remarks by using laughter and feigned delight. By 1960 Giacometti had been playing the role of obedient but tormented son for six decades. His "boundless devotion" to her, as Mercedes Matter described it, was a complicated mix of shame, rage, concern, and respect.

ANNETTE

Portraying his wife gave Giacometti the scope that portrait sessions with his mother wouldn't allow. He could show Annette as she was: youthful, obedient, loyal, and lovely; he could also show her as shallow, strident, and frightened. Since she was willing to be anything for him, he could present her as the universal female he had been depicting since his twenties.

In the early years of their partnership Giacometti's portraits of Annette are restrained and decorous. She sits sedate and clothed in his studio, at a window, or within a grid he designs for her. She often looks very Swiss, her legs demurely held together, her hands clasped obediently in her lap. By 1949 Annette began to pose for paintings nude, standing or seated in the studio. In his magnificent painting *Annette* (1953) (Carnegie Museum of Art), her face is barely legible, but her stilted position and figure are recognizable.[27] Sitting firmly upright, Annette and her shadow configure the gray composition, heightened by white and warmed by touches of salmon and ocher. At other times, especially when isolated from a specific setting—as in a number of canvases from 1951 and 1953—she becomes a universal figure, closer to the sculpted figurines that had been obsessing him since the 1930s.

In 1953, one of Giacometti's most consistent gestures was to gouge out the eyes of the little monsters who were so clearly angry effigies of his wife. (Could she not literally see how much her demands made him suffer?) The following year he gave them back to her, now enormous and emphasized in three painted portraits. Giacometti had allegedly been first attracted to Annette because of her unwavering eye contact. In these paintings her eyes are so large, dark, and open that they seem almost lidless—like the Egyptian Fayoum funerary paintings (which date from the first through fourth century A.D.) he always admired.[28]

In *Annette* (1954) (Stuttgart), an exceptionally sensual portrait of his wife, he shows her nude and nicely near, a pleasure to have up close.[29] Like his mother, Giacometti's wife was always thin, yet here he paints her firmly fleshed body with a rounded belly using radiating lines and white highlights that attract the viewer's attention. Such an incongruous stomach on a slim woman recalls the rounded belly Giacometti included in the 1937 portrait of his mother after his sister's pregnancy and death and hints at his struggle with his wife's demands to have a child. This work, along with five other paintings of Annette (some very large) in 1954, are evidence of Giacometti's victory over his destructive impulses. By making Annette into a new icon—a woman with wide-open eyes—he compensated not only for his aggressive sculptural outbursts directed at her from the previous year, but also for personal losses of that year—Laurens, Derain, and Henri Matisse had died.[30]

Between 1955 and 1960 Giacometti tended to place his wife farther back in the canvas so that the powerful fixity of her gaze was not so noticeable. It wouldn't be prominent again until the 1960s, when she regained her distinction after his detours with guest subjects. Giacometti's portraits of Annette in the 1960s focused on her material reality. She is present and forward—her eyes increasingly the crux of his inquiry. In a series of six startling pencil drawings made in 1962 Giacometti used his wife's wide-open, staring eyes as the primary feature of the portraits. Her head is isolated in the middle of a large piece of paper. We sense that there could or should be more of her showing. Other features—flesh, muscle, and hair—disappear and reappear—but Annette's anxious eyes remain unchanged, and we are caught in their lidless grip.[31]

With the exception of one small bust in 1946, Giacometti did not have Annette pose as a model for sculpture. This changed, however, in 1960. Why? By then Annette had reached the limit of her tolerance for unconventional lodging and posing in the cold, dirty studio. At the same time, Giacometti had met a new woman, Caroline, who was willing to sit for a fee and for the many gifts he generously gave her. Annette at first was glad to be relieved of some of her tasks, but she soon grew jealous. He offered to buy an apartment for Caroline. When Annette objected, Giacometti bought her an apartment too, but swore he would never live in such a bourgeois setting. Husband and wife saw less of each other. Yet, no matter how fascinated he was with other models, Giacometti still needed his Annette, and she came to his studio daily.

DIEGO

Of the artist's three principal models, Diego was treated most kindly. He had been Giacometti's model for everyman since childhood, as can be seen from a sculpted portrait *Diego* (1914) that the artist often cited as the best he had ever made (fig. 13.2). Shortly after the war, the depictions of Diego insistently captured his physical reality with little distortion. Between 1949 and 1955 Giacometti made many sculpted portraits of his brother. Some are strongly representational, others only slightly so. Soon, the physiognomy would grow attenuated and ghostlike, and some of the busts ceased to be portraits at all.

In the two most representational sculpted portraits of his brother from 1954, *Diego in a Coat* and *Bust of Diego*, Diego is supremely recognizable.[32] In each, the man is firmly anchored by his heavy body. His clothing wraps him in a stupendous solidity without reducing the power of his head. Proud, certain, and dour, Diego looks at us from his smooth-haired head through eyes as able as his brother's to hold a gaze. In these works we feel the presence of the model and applaud the artist for his achievement in capturing Diego's physical reality with little distortion, presenting him to the world as a figure of absolute stability.

But he also had other feelings about his brother, and these, too, needed expression. Indeed, frequently over the next decade, some of the sculpted

portraits of Diego have scratch marks on the face and clothes that range from gentle scrapings to deeply scored scarring.[33] Might these mutilating marks convey Giacometti's ambivalence toward his mostly beloved brother? At the same time, trailing finger marks—akin to the bravura brushwork of the painted portraits—enliven the busts even while they recall painful scarifications that primitive artists used to keep the magic in or out.

Giacometti created some of his most splendid painted portraits with his brother as subject. *Diego in a Red Plaid Shirt* (1954) (Maeght Collection, Paris) is one example.[34] Seated under the staircase in his Paris studio, Diego adopts a relaxed pose that shows a casual insouciance, his wounded hand in his pocket, the other draped over his leg. Against a peachy, warm background, Diego's somber head crowns the rounded body, which is wrapped with lines encircling his arms and chest. A classically Italianate contrapposto has been transformed by the Swiss-Italian artist. Following the head, which leans slightly to the left, the viewer's eyes whip around the body from the model's left hand and sweep across his shoulders and into his right-hand pocket. The head is the top part of a snaking, curvilinear movement brought into focus by the bright red, vertically curving line of the shirt. Giacometti's compositional mastery is at its peak in this painting. He plays the soft peach and whitish beige of the upper-right quadrant against the dark black, brown, and gray of the lower left. The entire canvas seems much brighter than it actually is because the frame around the scene is gray, bringing out the colors ever more sharply.

Through the years the artist found new ways of representing his brother. He erased, blackened, or painted over Diego's face. Sometimes he brought him back from the abyss and remade him; at other times, he left him in tatters, broken shards, or pale marks barely visible on the paper. Could it be that despite his best intentions, Giacometti was less than wholehearted in his support for his brother's growing success as an artist and designer? With this in mind, let us consider the mysterious black heads of Diego done in the late 1940s and early 1960s.

Giacometti's black portraits are dark in many meanings, and his *Head of a Man (Diego)* (1961) is a stunner.[35] The subject looks out from his black face, uncannily recalling Giacometti's 1927 flattened portrait of his father. Diego's eyes show white, as do a few lines defining the tip of his nose, the bone structure under the skin, and the shape of his lip and chin. It does not matter that the "man" is Diego, since he has become what all the important men around Giacometti would become in the last years of his life—bald Egyptian funerary priests who attend to temples and tombs. He stares, but not with fright or even sorrow. Certain knowledge of the future seems etched in his eyes, saying "I am here with you. I know you: I am you. Forever."

What better way than this to tell of the end, the everlasting end—the darkness flecked with light, the light of the night sky in the Bregaglia valley, the light of art continuing into the dark and unknown future. Thusly, the Egyptians still made their funerary masks in Fayoum, even as the Romans and Christians were appropriating their kingdoms and their gods. Nothing could take away the everlastingness of eternal afterlife—the Egyptian solution to mankind's deepest fear—the silent nothingness of death.

GUEST MODELS AS SURROGATES

Toward the end of their lives, artists often return to emotional themes from childhood, tackling unresolved dilemmas. Giacometti always was prone to hero-worshipping with men and usually found someone ready to take on the mantle of confidant, beginning with Giovanni Giacometti and progressing from Lucas Lichtenhahn in adolescence to Breton, Ernst, Derain, Bataille, and Sartre. By 1954 one of them was dead, two were on the other side of an intellectual divide, one had moved away, and the fourth was busy with his own fame. These losses left Giacometti especially vulnerable to longings for a new father figure. The shadow of death was further cast over Giacometti in his last decade since he was well aware that his mother, already in her mid eighties, could not live much longer and that his own health was deteriorating. He believed that his life span would not exceed his father's or grandfather's—sixty-five years.

Chance provided Giacometti with an exceptional new father figure at this moment of need—Isaku Yanaihara, a Japanese philosophy professor and arts writer. Never before had the artist found someone so ready to be a close companion as well as a reliable portrait subject. Having come to Paris to study existentialism, Yanaihara encountered Giacometti indirectly through Sartre.[36] They met in November 1955 but the relationship between the two men did not flower until 1956 during the frenzied time that Giacometti was working on *Women of Venice*. Posing sessions for Giacometti's first portrait of Yanaihara began in September 1956 at Giacometti's invitation and continued uninterrupted until December, when Yanaihara finally departed for Japan, two months behind schedule. The tale of Giacometti's herculean efforts to paint Yanaihara and the consequent artistic "crisis" of 1956–57 expands in several directions our understanding of the artist's psychological relation to memory and beloved objects. Hanging over all the posing sessions with Yanaihara was a series of repeatedly delayed departure dates.[37] Each potential postponement—there were many—became the subject of exceptional tension between the two men. The artist had convinced his model that there was a compelling need to continue their work together despite the growing pull of Yanaihara's commitments to family and professional life in Japan.

At its core, Giacometti's relationship with Yanaihara was a reliving of the intimate bond between himself and his father: endless posing; respectful and lively conversations about anything and everything; and a shared love of art and devotion to that muse with a willingness to forgo ordinary comforts as well as obligations. The two men were also talented sons of celebrated fathers, and both were unconventional truth seekers. They formed an attachment based upon strong similarities and mutual affinities.[38] The artist's decision to ask Yanaihara to begin posing so close to the time of his intended departure was surely not coincidental; Giacometti was accustomed to keeping someone attached to him this way. It was torture for Giacometti to lose Yanaihara each time he left for Japan, and it becomes obvious in retrospect that the philosopher's inevitable departures were part of the attraction. It made Yanaihara even more like Giacometti's father, who had traveled so much during his son's childhood.

Giacometti was immediately excited by Yanaihara's ability to sit immobile, and he wrote to Matisse about his "Japanese friend who poses unmoving, like a statue."[39] Yanaihara returned to Giacometti four more times, in the summers of 1957, 1959, 1960, and 1961, and the relationship that developed between the two men surprised Giacometti's friends.[40] Not only did they meet every day for lunch, after which Yanaihara would pose from 1 P.M. until around midnight, they also dined together almost every evening. They also shared the same woman: with Giacometti's consent, Annette and the Japanese philosopher became lovers a month after Yanaihara started posing. Annette and Yanaihara's affair, beginning in November 1956 and continuing to the end of his last visit to Paris in 1960, was open and very public. They became a threesome and frequently dined together (fig. 13.3). Giacometti encouraged the relationship and professed to be delighted that his close friend could make his wife so happy.[41] However content they were at the outset of the affair, it caused more conflict and distress than Giacometti had anticipated. It eventually fractured the uneasy peace between Giacometti and his wife. Even more problematic, the affair, and especially Diego's unhappiness about it, broke up the triumvirate of artist, wife, and brother, which had served as a safe haven for Giacometti for seven years.

Yanaihara was a man after Giacometti's own masochistic heart. As long as Giacometti could sit or stand for uncomfortably long periods, so could the stalwart Japanese philosopher, matching pain for pain, sacrifice for sacrifice. At the end of each day with Giacometti, Yanaihara took notes on their dis-

FIGURE 13.3 *Alberto and Annette Giacometti with Yanaihara in Stampa.*

course. The Japanese philosopher's descriptions of the artist's thoughts, along with his extensive direct quotes from Giacometti, provide an intelligible picture of the artist's mental and emotional processes.[42]

Through the lens of Giacometti's relationship with Yanaihara the psychological connection between truth and separation becomes clear. Yanaihara reports Giacometti's near-panicked reaction at the thought of "finishing" a portrait: "If I had to finish up today," the artist said, "I would never be able to do good work; if I only thought of only finishing up I would abandon everything."[43] The crescendo of hysteria invades the modeling sessions as any of Yanaihara's departure dates nears. Once a separation is postponed the artist's relief is palpable, almost comic. Reminded that he had ten more days to work before one of Yanaihara's scheduled departures, Giacometti responded: "Today progress will be twice as fast as yesterday, and tomorrow four times as fast as today and the day after eight times as fast." Giacometti tried to comfort himself by spouting obsessional formula as though they could help him through the painful interval. The inevitable separation once a portrait was completed was comparable to a death and was linked in Giacometti's mind with truth. As he drew closer to the moment of completion, the artist felt that he also grew closer to the truth. Unfortunately, as he discovered, Giacometti could not have one without the other.

Giacometti told Yanaihara about the ways he protected himself against intolerable feelings of loss connected to death. "After suffering so much I came to think that . . . even a dead man is not different from a live man as long as I can see his face and hear his voice."[44] Memory protected Giacometti, but intense feelings (especially "bad" ones) for someone he loved could keep him from holding on to the memory image of that person. When he could not remember the image, the person seemed to disappear, not only from his mind, but from life itself, just like his father when Giovanni went away from home.

Two factors characterizing the way Giacometti functioned psychologically are finally clear. First, he felt that his loss of memory could kill, making his chronic terror comprehensible. Second, Giacometti tried to conquer his terror and helplessness by repeatedly erasing and redrawing a face. Painting or drawing a person in or out of existence was the artist's way of killing and then reviving another human being. Psychoanalysts describe this way of defending oneself against pain as turning passive into active. This was how Giacometti reassured himself that his power to bring a person to life was still intact, and that he was not as guilty as he felt whenever he destroyed someone in effigy. "Everyday he painted and erased. 'I should not be afraid to lose the face' he repeatedly said: 'I am going to erase everything. I won't be able to make any progress if I don't. Your face is going to be disappeared. . . . Your face will come back soon with many times as much power as before.'"[45]

Years earlier Giacometti had used almost the same words with Jedlicka, an old friend and willing subject: "Here you sit. With every stroke I make, you become more foreign. With every stroke I push you away from me! . . . If I continue, you will disappear."[46] Giacometti had been destroying and re-creating his portrait subjects for most of his life. His work with Yanaihara seems to have brought the meaning of his own behavior close enough to his conscious awareness so that he could finally reveal his hidden fantasies and magical beliefs.

After a meandering series of thoughts, which included a fantasy of carrying Yanaihara off to Stampa where they could "work quietly in a safe place, surrounded by mountains," Giacometti had a vision of a "beautiful lake behind the model, a lake which reflected the brilliant light of sunset—bright and endlessly wide. The firmer I see your face the more huge the surrounding space becomes."[47] Between these two observations Giacometti drew a tiny head of Yanaihara on one end of a newspaper, and a dot-sized figure representing Madame Yanaihara in Tokyo at the other end, stating how far away and small she looks. He was using dramatically reduced size to deal with Yanaihara's separation from his wife. The artist then impishly told his model that he had just painted and erased his eyes, saying they were false eyes and had to be eliminated. Immediately he had a fantasy of permanent attachment to the model whom he had just destroyed in effigy: "If only I could continue painting like now for at least one year. I envy those painters serving in Renaissance palaces. If you were a king I would want to serve you, to keep painting your portraits for my entire life."[48]

Giacometti was reliving with Yanaihara his youthful experience of a seemingly endless but loving enslavement as his father's model. Yanaihara described Giacometti's tortured work and his role in the dynamic interaction: "[He] twisted his body, screamed and kicked the floor. It is crazy to keep up this unreasonable work any longer. . . . The king should change his painter." To which Yanaihara replied: "If I were a king I would order you to continue the work." The dialogue between them continued: "Then I'm relieved. I cannot deny the king's order. . . . I am only a slave who follows the king, whatever the result is, the king has to take responsibility for it." "No," replied Yanaihara, "I am your slave, you order me to pose." Giacometti did not like that at all. "I haven't forced you, whenever you want to quit you can . . . you are the king." The astute philosopher concluded: "Both he and I were slaves for each other, but slaves who chose to serve with their own wills."[49]

Whereas Yanaihara was willing to accept responsibility for his part in their mutual attachment, Giacometti was not. Never comfortable with an active role, he refused to be responsible for feelings and actions he did not like. Nine days before one of Yanaihara's scheduled departures a crisis erupted. Giacometti begins the afternoon posing session with the usual complaints:

"It doesn't proceed at all. It is as if I were forced to eat stones. I don't know what to do." Suddenly he screamed: "Damn, God damn it." He withdrew his hand, and with clenched teeth he looked at me with a dreadful glance. He stretched his arm out to paint again and pulled it back at the moment when the tip of the brush touched the canvas. "I don't have the courage to touch the canvas," he uttered: He kicked the floor and tried again to touch the canvas. Again his hand was pulled back. This was repeated a few more times. "It is impossible." He sat on a chair, his head hanging down, without moving for a long time. . . . He had spoken pessimistically but had never stopped painting or moving his hand.

When Yanaihara approached, he saw that Giacometti was sobbing and so tried to comfort him, but he failed to get a response. After a long time the artist calmed down and apologized for crying:

"Your face on the canvas looked like a bomb and I felt as if it would explode everything the moment I touched it even slightly. I couldn't touch the canvas in any way . . . everything would blow up in the air. Everything is destroyed and absorbed into some deep place that I cannot reach. Look at it, there are no eyes, nose or ears. What there is on the surface is only a mass—a vague cloud-like thing. If I continued there would be nothing left. . . . Not only my art work but also my life itself is collapsing." The artist started to work again but hit the same crisis. The very moment his brush was to touch the canvas, he pulled it back like an electric shock; he crouched down, his head buried in hands, screaming and sobbing. It continued this way for three days.[50]

Giacometti's panic about not being able to capture the image of his subject was only a mask for his deeper dismay about not being able to hold on to the subject himself. Yanaihara wisely recognized that the crisis had to do with his own impending departure. By agreeing to stay two more weeks, he made the crisis disappear.[51]

By experiencing Yanaihara's face as a "bomb" ready to explode at the artist's merest touch, Giacometti demonstrates how he projected his anger directly on someone else, *while at the same time retaining the sense of himself as ex-*

FIGURE 13.4
Yanaihara photograph of one of Giacometti's 1956 portraits of him (oil on canvas, 81.3 x 65 cm) (unfinished version).

traordinarily *dangerous*—the trigger for the bomb of anger. His touch, via his penetrating finger, or its extension, the tip of the brush or pencil, is as dangerous as it had been when it was symbolized as the male lance in *Man and Woman* (1929) or the point aimed at the eye in *Point to the Eye*.

There are three frontal paintings of Yanaihara dating from 1956 (fig. 13.4).[52] Unlike the portraits of Yanaihara done the following year, these works epitomize Giacometti's ability to capture absence and longing. A golden glow, heightened by a whitish arc, surrounds the subject with a luminous halo, suffusing the canvas with an atmosphere of astonished nostalgia. Yanaihara is present (little else matters) but we feel the imminence of his departure into the dusky gray-beige background—as well as the gravity of his presence. He is here by some miraculous intervention—why else would he be surrounded by a heavenly light? The artist picks out a few details of the face and clothes with the now-familiar black brush strokes and touches them with white highlights. He had already constructed his subject with a gray, claylike foundation. In the version pictured here his arms rest on the bottom of the canvas, and the background fades from view. In another version (Musée national d'art moderne, Paris) Yanaihara's horizontally held hands—the artist's coded reference to his model's Oriental serenity and meditative posture—make a firm anchor for his formal shirtfront.

When Yanaihara came back to Paris in subsequent summers, Giacometti returned to his task. Judging from the works themselves, portraying Yanaihara grew easier as the years passed, apparently because the artist became more adept at handling his model's appearance and subsequent disappearance. As a result, the works convey a changed mood with a lower emotional pitch. Yanaihara's face is very dark in three paintings from 1959. No glow lightens the canvases. He seems shadowed, saddened perhaps, with barely enough white highlights to define him.

Following the initial sittings with Yanaihara in 1956 and 1957, Giacometti's "crisis" spilled over to portraits of his wife and brother, who became more distant and harder to see than ever before. They both seem to recede into the canvas, farther and farther away from the abandoned artist. They either fade into a gray background or barely emerge out of a darkness.[53]

CAROLINE

In the last two years of his relationship with Yanaihara, Giacometti realized that he would not be able to keep his model and friend from returning to his own family and his country after each visit to Paris. Giacometti found a replacement for him—someone local who would devote her valuable time to his art. In October 1959 Giacometti met Yvonne Marguerite Poiraudeau, a prostitute, in a café-bar. She called herself Caroline, and she was twenty-one years old. Giacometti was fifty-eight. There was an instantaneous mutual attraction. As with any woman who had interested him in the past, Giacometti was drawn into the orbit of her gaze. Caroline was particularly adept at using her eyes seductively. As a friend of Giacometti's related: "Her eyes were so big they just sucked you in, as she lit my cigarette, her eyes went right into and through me."[54] Soon she began to pose for Giacometti.

Caroline lived nearby in Montparnasse. The artist was impressed with what the young woman had made of herself, given her childhood. She was an unwanted child in a large family; her father had been an unsuccessful pimp who eventually killed himself. Caroline was sent away to boarding school and then went off on her own. After landing in a reform school and attempting suicide, she took to the streets.

As discussed earlier, Giacometti always had a weak spot for prostitutes, and Caroline was clever and zestful. She took chances with her life. Addicted to gambling, she was a thief who associated with pimps and gangsters, drove incredibly fast, and always lived at the edge of the underworld. Through her own wits she had survived her past and seemed strong; Giacometti felt inferior, having had so much help and so little courage. By 1959, after ten years of modeling in a cold and dirty studio, Annette was tired of posing. The bourgeois apartment Giacometti had just bought for her made her seem more like his mother, giving him reasons to seek a woman who was both unconventional and who would sit for him.

In addition to Caroline's availability at night and willingness to sell her time, she had a prescient grasp of Giacometti's exquisite sensitivity to loss and abandonment and understood his emotional weaknesses. From the beginning of their relationship she played on his vulnerability. She would disappear regularly, returning to describe her adventures with other men as her new lover listened attentively. Locking him firmly into the relationship, Caroline vanished from sight in April 1960. Puzzled at her absence from her usual haunts, Giacometti searched frantically for her, writing plaintive, agonized letters: "It seems to me that I have become you who is writing! as if I were myself Caroline, here at this table."[55] The psychological boundaries between himself and the other person are gone. He feels completely merged with his latest love, and this sense of oneness with Caroline is meant to protect him from feeling the pain of her absence. It is a powerful way to avoid feeling alone or abandoned.

Caroline had been arrested for robbery and sentenced to prison. Despite (or because of) stern warnings from the police and judge about her dangerous companions and activities, Giacometti fervently persisted in the relationship. It is clear from her correspondence with him that Caroline knew how to keep him attached. One of her letters is a masterful play of threats to abandon him; it ends by promising to stay close forever. She begins: "I say goodbye to you. I must leave, absolutely. I see you on the sidewalk. You were very handsome and it annoys me to leave. . . . I would like to be with you here, Alberto. We should see each other soon, for we have been separated a very long time. Do you desire to see me? I have a great desire. . . . You will have to wait to write to me til I get to a hotel in Sicily. I leave tomorrow . . . you are very dear to me, it's true, I embrace you again, til soon, Caroline."[56] She had his number—veiled threats to leave "absolutely," coupled with implied promises of intense connectedness.

Caroline's status as a lower-class woman and her unconventionality and youth made her an apparently unlikely surrogate for Annetta, which contributed even more powerfully to her psychological hold on him. But some similarities existed under the surface—in her concern for money, her demandingness, and her insistence on getting her way. However, it was primarily her presence and her willingness to *be there* for him—just as he was acutely aware of his mother's approaching death—which passionately connected him to Caroline. The younger woman could wind him around her finger and swallow him up with her eyes, and she would not die soon, nor would she ever publicly demean him or compare him with his father.

Giacometti's paintings of Caroline are puzzling. She is the beautiful and sexually charged woman of Giacometti's last years, but ironically almost none of the artist's known portraits of her show her as beautiful or focus on her body. Rather they present her fully clothed, upright and hard-headed. We rarely see her legs, arms, or even hands. In most of his paintings her face is dark, and her eyes convey a sense of menace. Why does Giacometti paint his last lover so unlovingly? Could it be that when Giacometti was painting Caroline, his awareness of his mother's impending death pervaded some part of his mind? His mad infatuation with an unlikely woman masked his panic about his mother's imminent death.

FUSION PORTRAITS: SELF AND OTHER

Like his father, Giacometti made self-portraits that record his evolving state of mind and moods from childhood to the end of his life. Beginning with his youthful candor and belligerence, they continue through his sadness and despair at moments of mourning in the 1930s and arrive eventually at his last statements about himself—coded as images of someone else.

During the postwar experimental years, as his filiform style and impulse for elongation evolved, Giacometti began to make knifelike heads and busts with ultrathin, flattened faces, which are distinguished by their bushy-haired profiles, long necks, and jutting chins. His first, *Little Bust on a Pedestal*, was likely completed in 1948, and Giacometti marks its importance, or perhaps its otherness, by placing it on a pedestal. Over the next twelve years he continued to experiment with male busts and heads, claiming that Diego was his model but often working from memory or imagination. I propose that while these knife-blade heads and busts contain the artist's feelings about the man he knew best, his brother, they are also self-portraits.

In 1953–55 he made a series of these sculptures, including *Large Head of Diego* (1954) (Alberto Giacometti-Stiftung) and several smaller works titled *Amenophis*.[57] Though listed as portraits of Diego, they are not modeled after him. In each instance the figure has an attenuated neck and a strikingly thin head when seen from the front. The unusual profile of these works is characterized by a protruding chin and a shock of bushy hair, recognizably Alberto's.

The singularity of the profile recalls that of Akhenaten (Amenophis). Titling some of the heads after the heretic ruler of Amarna forty years after seeing the astounding portraits emerging from the Amarna workshop suggests a return to Giacometti's earliest motivations for making sculpture: to keep alive the original of the sculpted double. By presenting himself to the world as his inspiring alter ego—an ancient pharaoh—Giacometti could have been attempting his own version of life-giving portraits. Amenophis IV was the name given to Akhenaten by his father, Amenophis III, which the young man later rejected. In using Amenophis as a title for work that resembled Giacometti, there was a reference, perhaps unconscious, to the relationship of a son to his father.

The most magisterial version of Giacometti's knife-blade portraits is the *Large Head of Diego* (1954) (figure 13.5 illustrates a similar but somewhat smaller work from approximately the same period). Compositionally, all these knife-blade heads are a triumph of triangles, as the head, nose, chin, and shoulders all take that shape. The rugged surfaces almost obscure the elegant linear outline with their curves and countercurves. That such a man—with his open mouth, jagged nose, jutting jaw, and saw-toothed hair—is totally convincing as a human being seems amazing, given his insubstantiality from the front. In profile he seems about to speak, to listen closely with his huge ears, or to spring up out of his collared crown. When we see him straight on, he looks completely different. Now we feel the pathos of his open mouth and his blind eyes; his vanishing features are sucked back into space, and his head seems ready to return to its shouldery shell.

In the knife-blade sculptures, Giacometti makes us focus on the stunning difference between the human profile and frontal view. He insists that we come to terms with it. It is not so much visual distortion that we see in the frontal view of the flat heads as it is their essential disappearance; consequently, we experience Giacometti's emotional state—how easily he could lose his visual memory of another person (or himself). Giacometti spoke often of

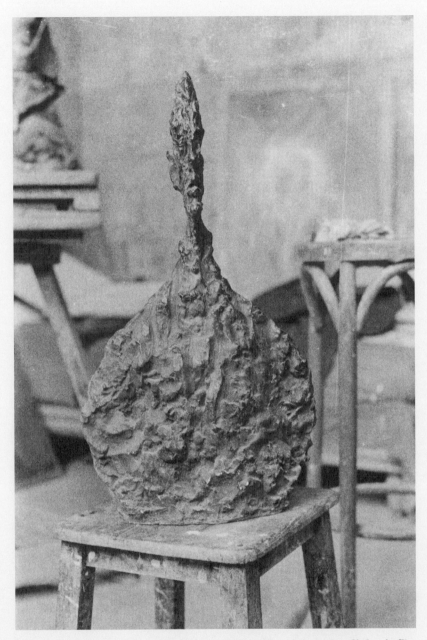

FIGURE 13.5 *Yanaihara photographs of Bust of Diego (frontal view and profile [overleaf]),*
1956, clay (destroyed).

his difficulty uniting side and frontal views: "If I look you in the face I forget the profile. If I look at the profile, I forget the face. *All becomes discontinuous.*"[58]

On first reading this seems like art talk, but it is actually a vivid description of Giacometti's old problem of memory loss and loneliness transmuted into a justification for a style. The artist has conveyed his experience of forgetting a person's face—the dramatic difference of here and gone, so present from one view and absent from the other—into a startling formal device. In the radical difference between an arrestingly recognizable profile and the nearly invisible frontal view, the onlooker becomes insignificant in the face of his subject. He is knowable only when he himself is the subject of another's gaze—self and other mirrored into eternity.

As we have seen, Giacometti often could not connect his model as a person in his daily life with the individual before him during the act of painting or sculpting. Thus he could say to Yanaihara: "I know who you are when I talk with you at the cafe, but, surprisingly enough, once I start to work I don't know who you are."[59] Having disconnected his feelings from his perceptions he could not hold on to the memory of the person he perceived.

Reconsidering Giacometti's problem with "memory" from the perspective of magical thinking, we have more insight into his laments. Telling Yanaihara of his experience at Bourdelle's academy: "I had done a lot of sketches there for four years in vain. I could not make whole images after elaborating the details in a face. I could not connect each side of the face. So I left the academy and started to work depending on my memory. With this practice I became able to make objects a little more similar to what I saw. . . . But I've never made the same objects as those I see with my eyes."[60]

Giacometti had never been able to re-create life *as he saw it with his eyes*—to hold a detailed, seen image in his mind or match a memory of one side of the face with another. This is both a psychological problem and the essence of Giacometti's magical wish. By not remembering the profile when facing the front view of a person of a model, or vice versa, Giacometti was covertly expressing an aggressive wish. He was eliminating one side of the person from his mind—a process similar to his destructive diminutions of the late 1930s and early 1940s. Necessarily, his own aggression and its result frightened him. Hence he had to re-create the whole person magically.

In Giacometti's later years his words continued to conceal and reveal his underlying goals—to create life, to make doubles—especially in his sculpture. In a late interview with Sylvester, his meaning comes closest to the surface when he speaks of "dead clay":

If I copy exactly the surface of a head in sculpture, what has it got inside it? A great mass of dead clay! In a living head, the inside is as organic as the surface? So a head that looks real . . . is in fact like a bridge, in that its surface looks like a head but you have the feeling that the inside is empty, if it's in terracotta . . . [t]he fact that it's empty . . . makes it false; because it isn't at all *like*, since there isn't a millimetre inside your skull that isn't organic. Therefore . . . heads that are narrow have just enough clay to hold them together: the inside is absolutely necessary. It's necessarily more like a *living head* than if it were a copy of the outside.[61]

In this strange mix of logical and illogical remarks—rationalized descriptions of his magical thinking heavily couched in art talk—Giacometti is saying that he aims to reproduce life and keeps coming upon proof that he has failed. His insistence that the inside of a skull is organic and "necessary," and that the clay or stone inside a sculpted head is not "necessary" and therefore not true to "life," suggests a fantasy about making doubles out of the elements necessary to life itself: organic coherence, or living tissue.

"At the British Museum, looking at the Greek sculptures, I felt, that they were great boulders, but dead boulders. . . . One of the reasons I have made life-size figures that became extremely thin must be that for them to be real they needed to be light enough for me to be able to pick them up, pick them up with one hand and put them in a taxi next to me," said Giacometti in the last year of his life.[62]

Why must a life-size figure be light enough to pick up with one hand? Because it must be able to move, stand on one foot—in short, be *alive*. The stone substance of the Greek sculpture was clearly not organic flesh and muscle. Yet it purported to be real. This falsehood is the lie of symbolism, that one object can stand for another. At times Giacometti could not tolerate this notion: symbol and referent had to be exact equivalents. Thus his sculpted head, like a real, organic head, had to be no thicker than necessary for life.

Yanaihara's diary notes reveal the artist's meaning when he speaks about a portrait of a young woman he barely knows: "It's impossible to draw a person whom I don't know well in a couple of times. It would be easy to make a drawing look like her but it is important to make a drawing of the face itself rather than to make a similar face."[63] Frequent repetition of this sentiment in Giacometti's recorded conversations finally persuades us that with part of his mind he wanted to reproduce life itself, not mere likeness. He did not find his goal strange or illogical and reconciled it with old hopes and wishes.

In a particularly clear passage Yanaihara described what he has come to understand as Giacometti's purpose: "It was to actualize reality on canvas—to transfer a real human being, his face with its own atmosphere around it and its eyes looking back at [the viewer]. The goal was not to make a picture but to approach reality."[64] To succeed in this goal, Giacometti asserted to Yanaihara, "I need to find some new methods . . . like a revolutionary finding that changes the basic method, like the tactical switch from arrows to guns. There must be some principle to capture the reality. It must have some simple rules to follow. I do need to find them." Yanaihara responded: "[T]here is no rule," but Giacometti insisted: "Yes there is, otherwise it is impossible to work." The canny Yanaihara responded: "It is possible to work because there is no rule. If you found it you would lose interest and be done." Giacometti insisted: "It wouldn't happen; only after the rule were found could the real work begin. Until then everything is preparation. Oh, if only I could find the way to copy the endlessly prolonged line of your cheek, then I finally would be able to paint everything."[65]

In this passage (which came right after a discussion of hari-kari and the promise that Yanaihara would help him commit suicide if he were to fail as an artist) we find links between many aspects of the artist's psychology. The magical thinking of his lifelong nightly ritual of lining up his shoes and socks is translated into the search for an imagined rule that will allow him to remake life. The same motivation makes him wish for a "method" to draw the

FIGURE 13.6 *Patricia Matisse photograph of Elie Lotar III, 1965, clay (destroyed).*

FIGURE 13.7 *Giacometti approximately a year before his death in 1965 (Henri Cartier-Bresson photograph).*

undrawable—an endlessly prolonged line caressing and capturing the cheek of his model.

Not for the first time we hear in Yanaihara's writing a clear and repeated refrain about "preparation and the beginning of the real work." Such are the words of alchemists. The "great work" in that ancient practice was the magical transformation of dross to gold for puffers, of matter to spirit for the philosophical alchemists, and of words, paint, and clay into art and surreal acts for their twentieth-century descendants—the surrealists.

Giacometti's last sculpture was a "portrait" of the photographer *Elie Lotar III* (1965) (fig. 13.6).[66] The two men had known each other in their surrealist days when Lotar's photographs of a Paris abattoir, celebrated by Bataille, were included in *Documents*.[67] They met again in 1964 in a Montparnasse bar. Lotar, long since impoverished and alcoholic and with little else to do, became a willing companion and do-all for Giacometti.

Giacometti knew his own death was imminent—he believed that no man in his family was supposed to live beyond age sixty-five, and he had just entered his sixty-fifth year. For years he had looked much older than his age (fig. 13.7).

Up to now he rarely made sculpted portraits of any but his closest friends and relatives. But since time was now short, anyone would do, as long as he or she could sit stock-still, like an Egyptian funerary priest watching over the needs of the dead, fulfilling the small ceremonial requirements to keep the *ka* alive and to protect the dead on his journey through the underworld.

He knew the Egyptians had found the best answers to the mystery of death—an eternity of afterlife. The sculpture of *Elie Lotar III* is severe and sombre and was fittingly chosen by Diego to mark his brother's grave.[68] It shows a kneeling man with his barely indicated hands upon his knees; his bald head will keep watch with large, staring eyes. With his magic Giacometti has kept himself, his images, and his art alive for all of us.

APPENDIX A *Chronology*

For more exhaustive chronologies see Christian Klemm's 2001 *Alberto Giacometti* (exhibition catalogue) as well as Reinhold Hohl's *Giacometti: A Biography in Pictures.*

1901

October 10   Alberto is born in Borgonuovo; Cuno Amiet named godfather.

1902

November 15   Diego is born in Borgonuovo.

1904

May 31   Birth of Ottilia in Stampa.

June 6   Death of paternal grandmother, Ottilia, in Stampa.

1905

May 10   Family moves to new apartment.

1907

March   Diego suffers accident in which his hand is mutilated.

August 24   Birth of brother Bruno; Hodler named godfather.

1908

Summer   Family summers in Maloja for the first time; Giovanni begins nude paintings of children.

1911   Annetta almost dies in typhoid epidemic.

1913

May 13   Death of Giovanni Stampa, maternal grandfather.

Spring   Fechheimer articles about Akhenaten appear.

Summer   Giovanni paints *Children of the Sun.*

1915

August   Alberto begins attending the Evangelical Secondary School in Schiers and remains a student there until April 1919; learns German.

1917–18   Stricken with mumps-orchitis at Schiers.

1919   Returns to Stampa before completing school; studies in Geneva from autumn 1919 until spring 1920.

1920
March–April   Visits the Amiets at Oschwand.
May   Visits Venice with Giovanni.
1920–21   Second trip to Italy; stays in Rome.
1921
March   Travels to Pompeii and meets van Meurs.
September 3   Travels with van Meurs in the Tyrol, where van Meurs dies
                   suddenly; flight to Venice.

1922
January   Moves to Paris.
November   Tutankhamen tomb discovered.
                   Attends sculpture classes at Bourdelle's Academie de la
                   Grand-Chaumière until 1927.
1925   Begins affair with Flora Mayo, fellow student at
                   Bourdelle's academy, which lasts until 1929.
February   Diego moves to Paris.
October 11   Death of Giovanni's youngest brother, Otto.
1927
Spring   Moves to studio at 46, rue Hippolyte-Maindron, where he
                   lives for the rest of his life.
Summer   Travels to Switzerland, makes series of portraits of
                   Giovanni.

1929
June   Exhibits *Gazing Head* and figure at Jeanne Bucher Gallery,
                   resulting in immediate attention; meets Masson, Prevert,
                   Miro, Ernst, Leiris, Bataille, and Conte de Noailles.
September   Leiris publishes article on Giacometti in *Documents*.
1930   *Suspended Ball* on exhibit at Gallery Pierre [Loeb] and is
                   bought by Breton, marking the beginning of their
                   friendship.
Summer   Appendectomy in Switzerland.
1932
May   First solo exhibition at the Pierre Colle Gallery.
December 23   Death of Giovanni's brother Giacomo Arnoldo.
1933
April 9   Ottilia marries Francis Berthoud and moves to Geneva.
May   "Yesterday Quicksand" published.
June 7–18   Participates in "Exposition surréaliste" at the Pierre Colle
                   Gallery.
June 25   Death of Giovanni Giacometti.

1934
February 3   Death of Giovanni's brother Silvio Alberto.

Summer   Ernst stays with Giacometti family in Maloja; Alberto designs tombstone for father.

December   Solo exhibit at Julien Levy Gallery, New York.

1935
February   "Excommunicated" from surrealists; friendship with Derain begins; circle also includes compatriots Gruber, Balthus, Tal Coat; meets Isabel Rawsthorne.

1937   Nuremberg rally; Austrian Anschluss begins.

October 10   Birth of nephew Silvio Berthoud.

October 11   Death of Ottilia; approximate date of friendship with Picasso.

1937–9   Begins experimenting with producing tiny figures.

1940
June 13–17   Travels French countryside with Diego and Nelly.

1941
Spring   Meets Sartre.

December 31   Leaves Paris for Geneva, where he remains until the war ends.

1943
October   Meets Annette Arm; they move in together in 1944.

1945
September 18   Returns to Paris.

September–
December 25   Lives with Isabel Rawsthorne.

1946
February   Art et résistance exhibition; makes Rol-Tanguy portrait *Night*.

July 6   Annette arrives in Paris and moves in with Giacometti.

July 25   Death of Tonio, the concierge of the building where the artist lives.

October   The brothel Sphinx closes; writes "The Dream, the Sphinx, and the Death of T."

October 1   End of Nuremberg trials; sentence of death by hanging; *Cahiers d'art* article (first publication of works in postwar style).

1947   Exposition internationale du surréalisme at Maeght Gallery, Paris; illustrates Bataille's *A Story of Rats*.

1948

January 19–

February 14   First solo exhibition at Pierre Matisse Gallery, New York; Sartre writes catalogue essay.

1949

July 19   Marries Annette Arm, and they honeymoon in Venice; writes "May 20" afterward.

1950

December 12   Second exhibition at Pierre Matisse Gallery.

1951

June–July   First solo exhibition at Maeght Gallery, Paris.

1954

May   Second exhibition at Maeght Gallery; Sartre writes essay on paintings for catalogue; Death of Laurens.

September   Death of Derain.

November   Death of Henri Matisse.

1955

June–July   Retrospective exhibitions at London Arts Council and Guggenheim Museum, New York.

November   Meets Isaku Yanaihara.

1956   Works on *Women of Venice* early in the year while the relationship with Yanaihara develops; exhibits at Kunsthalle Bern and at Venice Biennale-French pavilion.

September   Begins Yanaihara portrait.

November   Annette and Yanaihara begin affair.

1958

May   Third exhibition at Pierre Matisse Gallery.

1959

October   Meets Caroline; works on Chase Manhattan Project.

1962

Summer   Solo exhibition at the Venice Biennale.

December   Solo exhibition at the Kunsthaus Zürich.

1963

February   Has operation in Paris for stomach cancer.

1964

January 25   Death of mother, Annetta; Lotar begins posing.

1965   Retrospective exhibitions at Tate Gallery and Louisiana Museum in Denmark; visits both; exhibition at Museum of Modern Art, New York, which he also visits.

1966

January 11   Dies of inflammatory heart condition.

The Dream, the Sphinx, and the Death of T.

Translation by Terri Gordon

Terrified, I noticed an enormous, brown and hairy spider at the foot of my bed. The filament it was holding onto led to a web hanging just above the bolster. "No, no!" I cried, "I won't be able to make it through the night with such a menace hanging over my head, kill it, kill it," and I said this with the same repugnance at the idea of doing it myself in my dream as I would if I were awake.

I woke up at that moment, but I woke up in the dream that continued. I found myself in the same place at the foot of the bed and at the exact moment at which I was telling myself, "It was just a dream," I noticed, as I searched involuntarily with my eyes, I noticed a yellow spider, an ivory yellow spider far more monstrous than the first. This one, however, was smooth and seemed to be covered with smooth, yellow scales and had long legs which were thin and smooth and hard in appearance like bone. It appeared to be splayed out over a bit of earth and the fragments of a plate or of small, flat stones. Terrorized, I saw my girlfriend's hand move forward and touch the scales of the spider; apparently, she felt neither fear nor surprise. With a cry, I pushed her hand away and, as in the dream, I asked for the beast to be killed. Somebody that I hadn't yet noticed crushed it with a long stick or a spade, the person struck with great violent blows and, my eyes averted, I heard the scales cracking and the strange sounds of soft parts crushing. Only afterwards, as I looked at the remains of the spider gathered on a plate, did I read a name written very clearly in ink on one of the scales, it was the name of this species of arachnid, a name that I would no longer know how to pronounce, that I have forgotten, I see only the letters now, detached, the black color of the ink on the ivory yellow, the kinds of letters that one sees on stones and shells in museums. Obviously, I had just brought about the destruction of a rare specimen belonging to the collection of the friends with whom I was staying at the time. This was confirmed a moment later by the complaints of an old housekeeper who came into the room in search of the lost spider. My first impulse was to tell her what had happened, but I saw the trouble that would ensue, the bad feelings that would arise toward me on the part of my hosts; I should have realized that it was a rare insect, I should have read the name and alerted them instead of killing it, and I decided not to mention it, to pretend to know nothing about it and to hide the remains. I went out to the park with the plate and took care to remain out of sight, the plate in my hands might seem strange, I went to a bit of plowed earth which was hidden by a thicket at the foot of a mound, and sure that I couldn't be seen, I threw the remains in a hole and stamped on it, telling myself, "The scales will spoil before they can be discovered." At that moment, I saw my host and his daughter passing above me on horseback; without stopping, they said a few words to me, which surprised me, and I woke up.

All the following day, I had that spider before my eyes, it obsessed me.

Late the night before, I had realized from the ivory yellow traces of pus on a sheet of glossy, white paper that I had the illness I had been expecting for several days. As I registered this, I was troubled by an initial, involuntary mental paralysis which prevented me from cutting short the threat of illness, which would have been very easy to do, but which I didn't bother with. Nothing led me to believe that this was a kind of self-punishment; I felt instead in a vague sort of way that the illness might be useful to me, that it might afford me certain advantages the nature of which I was unaware.

In bed that evening a little before the dream, my girlfriend wanted, smiling, to verify the symptoms of my illness.

I had been expecting this sickness since the preceding Saturday when, at six o'clock in the evening, upon learning that they were going to close the "Sphinx" permanently, I had run there, finding it unbearable that I would never again see this place in which I had spent so many hours, so many evenings since the opening, and which was for me the most wonderful place of all.

I went there that last time a bit drunk, after a lunch with friends. At this lunch we had spoken, in passing, of the pros and cons of keeping a daily journal. My immediate—and unexpected—desire was to begin right away with this journal, beginning from the exact moment in which we found ourselves, and, to this end, Skira asked me to write for *Labyrinthe* the story of the death of T. that I had recounted to him some time before. I promised to do it without very clearly discerning the possibility of realizing it.

But since the dream, since the illness that brought me to that lunch, T.'s death has become for me again very much present.

As I returned from a visit to the doctor this afternoon, I wondered if only the coincidence of the timing of Skira's request and the visit to the Sphinx with its attendant consequences were enough to impose on me the memory of T.'s death to give me the desire to write today. I must add that in leaving the pharmacy, tubes of *Thiayzomides* in my hand, the first thing that struck me as I stood in the doorway of the pharmacy on the avenue Junod, two steps from the house of my doctor, was the sign of a small café across the street, "Au Rêve."

While walking, I saw T. again in the days before his death, in the bedroom adjoining mine, in the small house at the back of the somewhat dilapidated garden where we lived. I saw him again, at the foot of his bed, immobile, the skin ivory yellow, curled up into himself and already strangely far away, and I saw him again soon afterwards, at three A.M., dead, his limbs of skeletal thinness, projected, spread apart, scattered from the body, the enormous, bloated belly, the head thrown back, the mouth open. Never had any corpse seemed so negligible to me, some wretched remains to throw into a rut like the corpse of a cat. Standing immobile in front of the bed, I looked at this head which had become an object, a little box, measurable and insignificant. At that moment, a fly approached the black hole of the mouth and slowly disappeared into it.

I helped dress T. in the best manner possible, as if he had to make an appearance at a fancy social event, at a party perhaps, or as if he had to leave on a big trip. By lifting, lowering, and moving the head like some sort of object, I managed to put a tie on him. He was dressed oddly, everything seemed ordinary, natural, but the shirt was sewn at the collar, and there was no belt nor suspenders and no shoes. We covered him with a sheet and I left to work until morning.

As I entered my room the following night, I noticed that, through a bizarre coincidence, there was no light. A., invisible in bed, was sleeping. The corpse was still in the room next door. This lack of light was disturbing to me, and, as I was about to cross naked the black hall which led to the bathroom and which passed by the room of the deceased, I was seized by terror, and all the while not believing it, I had the vague impression that T. was everywhere, everywhere except in the miserable corpse on the bed, this corpse that had seemed so insignificant to me; T. no longer had any limits and, in terror at feeling an icy hand touch my arm, I crossed the hall with an enormous effort, came back to bed and, keeping my eyes open, I talked with A. until dawn.

In an inverse sense, I had just experienced what I had felt a few months earlier in the presence of living beings. At that time, I started to see heads in the void, in the space that surrounded them. When for the first time I clearly perceived the head that I was looking at congeal, freeze in an instant, definitively, I trembled with fear like never before in my life and a cold sweat ran down my back. It was no longer a living head, but an object that I could see as I might any other object, no, differently, not quite like any other object, but like something simultaneously alive and dead. I let out a cry of fright as if I had just crossed a threshold, as if I was entering into an unknown world. All living beings were dead, and this vision was often repeated, in the subway, in the street, in restaurants, with friends. That waiter at chez Lipp who became perfectly still, leaning over me, the mouth open, lacking any rapport with the preceding or following moment, the mouth open, the eyes fixed in a state of absolute immobility. But just as the people underwent a transformation, so did the objects—the tables, the chairs, clothing, the street, even the trees and the scenery.

This morning on awakening, I saw my towel for the first time, weightless in a never before perceived stillness and as if suspended in a frightful silence. It had no relationship now to the chair or table. There was no relation at all between the objects now separated by immeasurable gulfs of emptiness. I looked at my room with fright and a cold sweat ran down my back.

A few days after having written the above at one go, I wanted to pick up the story again, to rework it. I was in a café on the boulevard Barbès-Rochechouart where the prostitutes have strange legs—long, thin and tapered.

A feeling of boredom and hostility prevented me from rereading what I had written and in spite of myself I began by describing the dream differently. I tried to describe what had affected me in a more precise and more vivid manner; for example the volume, the thickness of the brown spider, the density of the hairs which would seem to be pleasant to touch, the position and the exact form of the web, the unexpected and fearsome appearance of the yellow spider, above all the form of its scales, their flat, slippery wave-like form, the strange conjunction of the head and the acuteness of its right foot forward. But I wanted to say all this solely in an affective manner, to render certain points surreal without trying to establish links between them.

I stopped after several lines, discouraged.

Black soldiers were passing by outside in the fog, this fog which had already filled me with a strange pleasure the day before.

There was a contradiction between the affective way to render what had sent me into an altered state and the succession of facts that I wanted to recount. I found myself before a confused mass of time, events, places and sensations.

I tried to find a possible solution.

First, I tried to designate each fact with two words that I placed in a vertical column on the page, this didn't lead to anything. I attempted to design small compartments vertically as well that I would have filled in little by little, seeking through this to situate all the facts on the page simultaneously. There were temporal problems, so I made an attempt to lay out the whole thing chronologically. Each time I came up against this tube form of the story that I didn't like. On the whole, the time in the ensemble of my story went in reverse, from present to past, but with returns and ramifications. In the first account, for example, I hadn't found the means to introduce the lunch with R.M. on Saturday at noon, which preceded the visit to the doctor.

I had recounted my dream to R.M., but when I reached the moment when I bury the remains, I saw myself in another meadow, surrounded by bushes at the edge of a forest. Brushing the snow off my feet, digging a hole in the hardened soil, I buried a piece of barely-touched bread (a theft of bread in my childhood) and I saw myself again running in Venice holding tightly in my hand a piece of bread I wanted to get rid of. I crossed all of Venice looking for remote and solitary areas and there, after numerous failed attempts on the most obscure, small bridges, at the side of the darkest canals, nervously trembling, I threw the bread into the rotting water of the last arm of the canal closed in by black walls and I ran away in a panic, scarcely aware of myself. This led me to describe the state in which I found myself at that moment. By dint of recounting the voyage to Tyrol and the death of van M., see note, (that long rainy day when I sat alone by a bed in a hotel room, a book by Maupassant on Flaubert in my hand) I saw the head of Van M. transform (the nose became more and more pronounced, the cheeks hollowed out, the nearly immobile, open mouth barely breathed and toward evening while trying to sketch this profile I was taken by a sudden fear that he was going to die), the stay in Rome the preceding summer (the newspaper that fell into my hands by chance and which carried an ad seeking my whereabouts), the train at Pompeii, the temple at Paestum.

But also the dimensions of the temple, the dimensions of the man who loomed up suddenly between the columns. (The man between the columns appeared to become a giant, the temple doesn't get smaller, the actual size no longer matters. And this stands in contrast to what happens at the church of Saint Peter in Rome. The empty interior of this church seems small [this is very clear in a photograph] but the men become like ants and Saint-Pierre doesn't get bigger, only the metric dimension counts).

This led me to speak about the dimension of heads, about the dimension of objects, of the links and differences between inanimate objects and living beings and through this I arrived at what concerned me above all, at the same moment when I told this story on Saturday at noon.

Sitting in the café of the boulevard Barbès-Rochechouart, I thought of all of this and searched for a way to say it. Suddenly, I had the feeling that all the events existed simultaneously around me. Time became horizontal and circular, it was space at the same time, and I tried to depict it.

Shortly afterward, I left the café.

This horizontal disc filled me with pleasure and, while walking, I saw it almost simultaneously from two different points of view. I saw it laid out vertically on a page.

But I insisted on its horizontality, I didn't want to lose it and I saw the disc become an object.

A disc with a radius of about two meters and divided into sections by lines. On each section was marked the name, the date and the place of the event to which it corresponded and on the edge of the circle before each section stood a panel. These panels of different widths were separated from each other by blank spaces.

The story corresponding to the sections was developed on the panels. With a strange pleasure, I saw myself[1] walking on this disc—time—space, and reading the story erected before me. The freedom to start where I wanted, to start, for example, with the dream of October 1946 in order to end up after an entire rotation a few months earlier in front of the objects, in front of my towel. The location of each fact on the disc was very important to me.

But the panels are still empty; I know neither the value of words nor their reciprocal relationship to be able to fill them in.

Note: This trip that I took in 1921 (the death of van M. and all the events surrounding it) constituted for me a sort of break in my life. Everything became different and this trip obsessed me continually for a whole year. I have recounted it untiringly and often I have wanted to describe it in words, this was always impossible for me. Only today, through the dream, through the bread in the canal, has it become possible for me to record it for the first time [Note of Alberto Giacometti].

NOTES

Preface

1 Giacometti, *Écrits*, 130.
2 For an extended discussion of my methodology see Wilson, "Alberto Giacometti's *Woman with Her Throat Cut*."

Chapter 1. Down in the Valley

1 Letter to Althaus, in Althaus, "Zwei Generationen," 34.
2 Stampa, "Reminiscenze," 87.
3 Gilot, interview, 1990.
4 Clay, "Le long dialogue," 137.
5 Bruno Giacometti has been censoring any story of his brother's life that does not exactly match his own ideas. His "view of my brother's work rests entirely on the works themselves and not on why they were made." B. Giacometti to author (9 Oct. 2000).
6 Giovanni Giacometti in Zendralli, *Giovanni Giacometti*, 23.
7 Giovanni made a number of self-portraits in van Gogh's style; with his brilliant blue eyes and red hair he obviously identified with the Dutch artist. He also carved van Gogh's words on his studio wall as ever-present inspiration: "However hateful painting may be and however cumbersome at the present time, the artist who still pursues his chosen profession with a passion is a solid and loyal man of duty."
8 Decades later, whenever his sons complained of their struggles in Paris, they would be reminded that the only Giacometti who had ever been truly poor was Giovanni, especially during his time in Torre del Greco. B. Giacometti, interview by author, 1988.
9 G. Giacometti to Meng, 16 March 1900, in Stampa, "Dieci lettere," 38.
10 Amiet and Giacometti, *Briefwechsel* (no. 136, 3 Feb. 1900), 286–87.
11 In forty years of letters to Amiet he was never combative. In one case he apologized when he felt his previous letter had been too assertive. G. Mauner, personal communication.
12 Her weekly churchgoing contrasted starkly with Giovanni's sporadic attendance on major holidays. The local brand of Protestantism was particularly ascetic.
13 In 1871, the year of Annetta's birth, her maternal aunt died; almost exactly one year later her paternal aunt died. When she was four and a half, her mother died. Less than three years later, her paternal grandmother died. Finally, when she was fourteen, her Aunt Clara died.
14 Dolfi-Giacometti, interview, 4 May 1990.
15 Given her lifelong desire to be enveloped by the known, it is no surprise that Annetta Stampa married a man with the same name as her father.
16 Alberto was weaned at four months, probably as a result of Annetta's next pregnancy. Doc. 511 James Lord papers, hereafter referred to as JLP.

17 See her extensive correspondence with Anna Amiet. Amiet correspondence.

18 The mother had been exposed to a gas leak, which the family believed had a fatal effect on the fetus. Despite many medical efforts to help Anna Amiet conceive again, she had no subsequent pregnancies. The Amiets later adopted five children, all over the age of five. George Mauner graciously assisted me with biographical details about Cuno Amiet and his relationship to his godson. Mauner, "Kopf Alberto Giacometti," 97.

19 According to the Canton records, Ottilia was born in Stampa, and close family members recall being told that Ottilia was born in the Piz Duan; Dolfi-Giacometti to author, 7 Oct. 1990. Since the Giacomettis did not fully relocate to the Piz Duan until mid October 1904, they may have briefly returned to Borgonuovo after spending the summer in Maloja as they had the previous year, and Giovanni may have used their apartment in Borgonuovo as a studio. On the day of Ottilia's birth Giovanni wrote to Amiet stating that his mother was dying, his sister was getting married and moving away, and Annetta was about to give birth. Amiet and Giacometti, *Briefwechsel* (no. 219, 31 May 1904), 373–74.

20 Bruno and Odette Giacometti, interview by Lord, 1985. JLP.

21 Such family myths can color a person's memories of his childhood. For Giovanni's travels, see the exhibition record in Müller and Radlach, *Giovanni Giacometti*, 594–95.

22 An early portrait, *Annetta and Alberto* (1903) (Kunsthaus Zürich), shows the wide-eyed gaze of the infant in his mother's arms. The painting hung over his parents' bed to the end of Alberto Giacometti's life.

23 Annetta Giacometti to A. Amiet, 2 Sept. 1904, Amiet correspondence.

24 Dolfi-Giacometti, interview by author, Stampa, 4 May 1990.

25 The theme of motherhood dominated Segantini's work, influencing Giovanni to make domestic images a central theme.

26 See Müller and Radlach, II:1, 266. Giovanni made a number of paintings with older siblings watching the most recently born sibling being nursed by Annetta. See *Mother and Child* in Müller and Radlach, *Giovanni Giacometti* I: 306–7.

27 This photograph is included in most books on Giacometti. See, for example, Lord, *Biography*, opposite 178. B. Giacometti, interview, 1988.

28 B. Giacometti, interview, 1988.

29 Schneider, "Au Louvre," 30.

30 D. Giovanoli to Lord, JLP, Doc. 411.

31 B. Giacometti, interview, 1988. Stoppani, interview by Lord, 1971, JLP.

32 Silvio Berthoud told Lord that he had heard this story from his grandmother, Annetta Giacometti, insisting that Diego said he couldn't remember the incident but had heard it often. Berthoud, interview by Lord, 24 June 1971, JLP.

33 Lord, *Biography*, 8.

34 Lord, *Biography*, 16.

35 Afterward, they were further impressed that Diego asked often and with great interest how the cogs turned on the machine that had maimed him, describing that very machine with pleasure. Amiet and Giacometti, *Briefwechsel* (no. 279, 24 March 1907), 435–38.

36 A. Giacometti to A. Amiet, 28 June 1906 (author's emphasis).

37 A. Giacometti to A. Amiet, 28 Feb. 1906, Amiet correspondence.

38 Personal communication with Michael Brenson, who was well acquainted with Diego Giacometti in the 1970s.

39 Though the Giacometti family was apparently free of the superstitions believed by many who still live in the mountainous areas of Switzerland, a closer look reveals tendencies to magical thinking. Giovanni's observation that his brother Sammuele died "at exactly the same moment" a month after his father is one example.

40 Diego's lifelong respect for this ritual indicates both its importance to Alberto and the depth of Diego's devotion to his older brother.

41 A. Giacometti, "Hiers, Sables Mouvants," *Le Surréalisme au service de la révolution* 5, (15 May 1933): 44–45. Hereafter referred to as "Yesterday Quicksand." Later we shall explore the fantasy in detail because it connects with a sculpture Giacometti was making at the time. Here the fantasy serves as a pointer to the kinds of hostile thoughts and feelings behind the boy's behavior.

42 B. Giacometti, interview, 1988.

43 His taste for sensual images of nudes went back at least to his student days in Paris when his favorite paintings were Manet's *Olympia*, Rembrandt's *Bathsheba*, and works by Titian and Velázquez.

44 Hodler visited Giacometti in Stampa in 1907 and was Bruno Giacometti's godfather.

45 The German Expressionists with whom Amiet and Giovanni were associated also painted nudes in nature—Heckel and Kirchner. See also Green, *Mountain of Truth*, which details a Swiss bohemian movement, Monte Verita, with which Amiet and Giovanni must have been familiar.

46 Amiet and Giacometti, *Briefwechsel* (no. 327, 1 Dec. 1909), 482.

47 See Müller and Radlach, 308–9.

48 Amiet and Giacometti, *Briefwechsel* (no. 369, 27 Sept. 1913). Giovanni used several figures from the triptych in woodcuts as New Year's cards in 1913.

49 By 1909 the Giacometti family owned a house in Maloja, inherited from one of Annetta's uncles, and from at least 1905, they regularly rented or borrowed summer quarters there.

50 See Müller and Radlach, II:2, 354–55.

51 See Müller and Radlach, II:2, 426–27, 434–35. The painting was probably done at Cavloccio where a shallow lake in a relatively private spot makes bathing in the otherwise frigid Alpine waters bearable.

52 B. and O. Giacometti, interview by Lord, 1970, noted in manuscript draft. JLP.

53 Phallus is the Greek word for penis and is used by psychoanalysts in two ways: anatomically, it usually refers to the penis; symbolically, it refers to personality traits usually associated with masculinity, such as strength, assertiveness, aggression, and potency. For a more extensive discussion see Moore and Fine, *Psychoanalytic Terms*, 143–44.

54 The text was written in Maloja 5 Sept. 1919, in Zendralli, *Giovanni Giacometti*, 27.

55 Zendralli, *Giovanni Giacometti*, 24.

56 Clay, "Le long dialogue," 136.

Chapter 2. Coming of Age

1 This event came to light only sixty years after the fact in interviews conducted by Giacometti's biographer, James Lord, with the artist's brothers. Diego and Bruno misremembered the date of the typhoid epidemic that almost killed their mother as 1913, the year of their grandfather's death. Lord, manuscript draft *Biography*, 149–50, JLP and B. Giacometti, interview, 1988. Cantonal records for the death of her neighbor, Clemente Faschiata, from the same disease confirm unequivocally that the typhoid epidemic occurred in 1911.

2 During and after her illness, Annetta Giacometti often said that God would not let her die because she had four children to care for. Dolfi-Giacometti, interview, 4 May 1990.

3 Schneider, "Long Walk."

4 Lord, *Biography*, 19.

5 He recalled this drawing in an interview with Schneider, "Ma Longue Marche," 48–50.

6 I am grateful to my psychoanalytic colleague Joann Turo for calling my attention to this psychological factor in Giacometti's history.

7 See Jacob Arlow, "Disturbances of the Sense of Time," about time confusion resulting from the need to wish away the existence of a frightening event.

8 Althaus, "Zwei Generationen," 36.

9 Carluccio, *Sketchbook*.

10 Giacometti in Carluccio, *Sketchbook*, "Notes sur les copies," 4 Oct. 1965, vii.

11 Letter to Althaus in Althaus, "Zwei Generationen," 35.

12 A few years earlier Amiet had sent his nine-year-old godson a note thanking him for his drawing of a soldier the boy had sent. Remarking that the younger Giacometti was making good progress, Amiet jokingly chided him: "just don't go too quickly or you will surpass your godfather (maybe even your Papa)." C. Amiet to A. Giacometti, 29 Dec. 1910, Amiet correspondence.

13 Diego Giacometti in Lust, *Complete Graphics*, 214. Upon completing his carefully wrought copy of Dürer's *Knight, Death and the Devil*, Giacometti immediately began a second copy "spurred by the hope of arriving at an absolute perfection." Carluccio, *Sketchbook*, xxxiii. Dürer's print was associated with Erasmus's *Manual of the Christian Knight*. Eisler, *Dürer's Animals*, 240–42.

14 See *La Mamma a Stampa*, 84.

15 See Wilson, "Copies."

16 Fechheimer, "Königsbüste," 373–75. The author found early issues of this journal in the Giacometti studio on a visit to Stampa in 1990.

17 Fechheimer, "Die neuen Funde," 228.

18 Baikie, *Amarna Age*, 289. For a more accurate presentation of Akhenaten's story see Aldred, *Akhenaten*.

19 Schneider, "Ma Longue Marche," 48.

20 Schaefer, *Principles*, 17.

21 The notebook containing Giacometti's talk was originally kept in the Amicitia clubhouse but has disappeared. I am grateful to Hans Hitz, a former art teacher there, for providing a copy.

22 Years later Giacometti dated the drawing 1913–15.

23 See Bonnefoy, *Alberto Giacometti*, 13, fig. 7.

24 The other side of the locket contains a design made up of her mother's hair, a common practice in the late nineteenth century.

25 See Bonnefoy, *Alberto Giacometti*, 9, fig. 2.

26 The piece was actually completed in 1915. A. Giacometti to C. Amiet, 19 March 1915. Giacometti described how he effortlessly captured the likeness after having been inspired by a photograph of a sculpture on a pedestal in one of his father's books. Clay, "Dialogue with Death," 136. See Bonnefoy, *Alberto Giacometti*, 25, fig. 23.

27 Notebook of Alberto Giacometti written at Schiers. The original is now at the Bündner Kunstmuseum, Chur.

28 Like all well-educated Swiss citizens, Giacometti learned to read and write in three languages: German, French, and Italian.

29 Giacometti to C. Amiet. 25 Dec. 1915, Amiet correspondence.

30 Bernoulli, "Jungenderinnerungen," 20–21.

31 Stampa, "Reminiscenze," 82.

32 Giacometti to C. Amiet, 19 March 1915, Amiet correspondence.

33 Giacometti's illness is not mentioned in the available correspondence, thus making the date uncertain. I am grateful to John Marks, M.D., for information about mumps/orchitis, an affliction long known to adversely affect the fertility of adult men. See Glenn, "Testicular," 353–62.

34 Giacometti to Lichtenhahn, June 1918, AGS.

35 Giacometti to Lichtenhahn, 28 Jan., 15 June 1918, AGS.

36 Giacometti to Lichtenhahn, Geneva, 8 Oct. 1919, AGS.

Chapter 3. Travel Is Broadening

1 The date is written 23 Aug. 1920 but was probably a month later. This sort of time confusion occurred whenever he was anxious. Giacometti to Lichtenhahn, Geneva, 23 Aug. 1920, AGS.

2 Giacometti to Lichtenhahn, Geneva, 10 Dec. 1919, AGS.

3 Personal communication from Martika Sawin, 1993.

4 Bruno Giacometti described his older brother's closeness to Seligmann in the context of Alberto's fears and phobic rituals. Referring to a vacation Seligmann spent with the Giacomettis in Stampa, he said: "Alberto was interested in everything occult; we had an aunt who was very sensitive and made the tables spin, this fascinated Alberto and Seligmann, [it was] right after Schiers, Alberto took certain things very seriously and we teased him." B. Giacometti, interview, 1988. Seligmann eventually built a vast library of occult literature and wrote an erudite history of magic. Seligmann, *Magic*.

5 Giacometti to Lichtenhahn, Maloja, 16 Aug. 1918, AGS.

6 Stampa, "il centenario," 130.

7 Sylvester, *Looking*, 126–27. Most of the citation comes from the newly revised translation of Sylvester's 1964 interview with Giacometti. Some sentences come from an earlier translation.

8 Sylvester, *Looking*, 127.

9 I am grateful to Jules Glenn, M.D., for alerting me to the importance of the testicles, especially in men who have had orchitis and often feel that the illness is a punishment for their sexual fantasies and/or masturbation.

10 Courthion, "Alberto Giacometti," 7.

11 Giacometti to C. Amiet. 6 March 1920, Amiet correspondence.

12 Kornfeld, interview, 1989.

13 Giacometti to A. and C. Amiet, 10 April 1920, Amiet correspondence.

14 Giacometti, "Mai 1920," 33–34. Lord, *Biography*, 38–41, and Bonnefoy, *Biography*, 88–97, interpret this text very differently; Lord sees Giacometti's crisis as aesthetic and Bonnefoy views it as moral and spiritual.

15 Giacometti, "Mai 1920," 34.

16 Giacometti. "Mai 1920," 34.

17 We shall see in the next chapter that Giacometti's mother was represented by a black-draped figure in his imagination.

18 Giacometti, "Mai 1920," 34.

19 For Giacometti, the painter Cimabue was like Giotto. Both had absorbed the lessons of sculpture to make paintings that were solid and "true." He later said: "It is impossible to be truer to life [than Cimabue's *Virgin Surrounded by Angels*] . . . it is those Roman excavations that changed Giotto." Giacometti in Pierre Schneider, "Au Louvre," 37.

20 Giacometti to family, 11 June 1921, JLP. Doc. 21.

21 Giacometti, "Mai 1920," 34.

22 Giacometti, "Mai 1920," 34.

23 Giacometti, "May 1920," 33.

24 Jedlicka, "Fragmente aus Tagebüchern," 1. Giacometti must have told the same story repeatedly because the first article on him by Leiris (1929) contains precisely the same words—"a painter *or* a sculptor."

25 Giacometti to family, Rome 18 Feb. 1921, JLP. Doc. 18.

26 Giacometti to family, Rome 4 Feb. 1921, JLP. Doc. 14.

27 Giacometti to family, Rome, 4 Feb 1921, JLP. Doc. 14.

28 Lord, *Biography*, 45–47; 50–52.

29 Lord, *Biography*, 50.

30 Giacometti to Pierre Matisse, Paris 1947, and checklist of early works. In the exhibition catalogue *Alberto Giacometti: Sculptures, Paintings, Drawings*. New York: Pierre Matisse Gallery. 1948. Hereafter referred to as Giacometti to Matisse, 1947.

31 Lord, *Biography*, 96.

32 Giacometti to Matisse, 1947.

33 Lord, *Biography*, 51.

34 Giacometti to family, Naples, 1 April 1921, JLP. Doc.19.

35 Giacometti to family, Rome, 8 April 1921, JLP. Doc. 20.

36 Giacometti to family, Rome, 11 June 1921, JLP. Doc. 21.

37 Clay, "Giacometti, un sculpteur à la recherche," 53.

38 Clay, "Le long dialogue," 136–37.

39 Lord, manuscript draft of *Biography*, 134 JLP. The young Giacometti frequently

turned to his father rather than his mother for solace and advice, especially when at school in Schiers.

40 Clay, "Giacometti, un sculpteur à la recherche," 53.

41 Giacometti told the story many times to Bianca, each time adding new and different details. Galante to Lord. 28 Feb., JLP. Doc. 578.

42 Giacometti to family, Venice, 7 Sept. 1921, JLP. Doc. 582.

43 Giacometti to Lichtenhahn, 10 Dec. 1921, AGS.

44 Giacometti, "Le rêve, le Sphinx, et la mort de T," *Labyrinthe* 22–23 (15 Dec. 1946): 12–13. An English translation of the entire text can be found in the appendix.

45 The choice of Venice as a place from which to recover from the fear of death is apotropaic, like wearing the image of an eye to ward off the evil eye. Giacometti knew about the successive waves of cholera that had devastated Venice in recent decades, and the influenza epidemic that raged through Europe in 1918 and 1919 had been very present in Stampa and at Schiers. Each member of the Giacometti family was afflicted, and Giacometti had written to Lichtenhahn about its effect on citizens of the community as well as on his own body. Giacometti to Lichtenhahn, 18 Oct.; 1 Nov.; 17 Dec. 1918, AGS.

46 Bruno Giacometti confirmed that Alberto knew Mann's novel. B. Giacometti, interview, 1988.

47 Giacometti, "Le rêve." The next, and much more complete public versions of this experience do not appear until 1963, nine months after Giacometti's operation for cancer and a few months before the death of his ninety-three-year-old mother. One is part of a radio interview with Drôt and the other is from an extended interview with Jean Clay in Stampa, where Giacometti was visiting his ailing mother. Drôt, "Alberto Giacometti." Interview for television.

48 These are the words Giacometti used to describe van Meurs in a letter to Lichtenhahn, 10 Dec. 1921, AGS.

49 Clay, "Giacometti, un sculpteur à la recherche," 137.

50 Drôt, "Alberto Giacometti." Imitation was one of Giacometti's ritualistic defenses which started around the time of his grandfather's death. Seligmann or his own researches could have educated Giacometti about Egyptian beliefs on the magical power of imitative gestures. One of the central funerary customs in ancient Egypt was the "opening of the mouth" ceremony, which allowed the image of the dead person to partake of the offerings provided for afterlife by the descendants and priests who tended the tomb.

51 B. Giacometti, interview, 1988.

52 I am grateful to Joann Turo for this insight.

53 Schneider, "Survivors of a Shipwreck," 42.

54 Such superstitious thinking probably underlaid Giacometti's general avoidance of new clothes. Until Rome, Giacometti often wore his father's old clothes. After September 1921, his preference for family hand-me-downs returned, persisting for the rest of his life. B. Giacometti, interview, 1988.

55 In 1921, Giovanni made a portrait of Alberto entitled *The Painter* (113 x 81 cm), his largest portrait that year. Done the year his son had left home to study sculpture, Giovanni's portrait might be seen as a father's wistful statement of his own wishes.

Chapter 4. Paris, Prehistory, and Sexuality

1 This trait continued until the last year of his life but had not been true earlier. He had stayed contentedly at Schiers during several vacations and did not go home while studying in Geneva.

2 Giacometti to family, Basel, 7 Jan. 1922, JLP.

3 Diego Giovanoli, interview by author, Chur, 1990.

4 Ruth Buol to Lord. JLP. Doc. 483.

5 In a letter to his father at the end of 1922 Giacometti described his difficulty sleeping, noting that what he started early in the evening tended to go on all night. Giacometti to G. Giacometti, Stampa, Dec. 1922, JLP. Doc. 25.

6 Elizabeth Geissbuhler, interview by author, Dennis, Massachusetts. July 1990. Arnold Geissbuhler, one of Giacometti's first friends in Paris, was another Swiss student and Bourdelle's studio chief.

7 Gilot, interview by author, New York 1990. Gilot vividly recalled Giacometti's idealization of his parents, as did Michel Leiris, interview by author, Paris, 8 April 1988.

8 Lord, interview by author, New York, 23 May 1990.

9 Schneider, "Au Louvre," 25, 29. Photographs of the Giacometti children can be seen in Bundner Kunstmuseum, Von Photographen, 12,13.

10 As a child, Giacometti had painted the portrait bust of his father done by his friend Rodo von Niederhäusern (1905). He later recalled: "The white color was unbearable. How little it resembled my father! once when my father had left the house for a short time I decided to paint the bust. I took my palette and brush and painted the eyes blue, the hair, mustache and beard red and the skin pink . . . only then was the bust finished, only then was it a portrait of my father." Jedlicka, "Fragmente," 1.

11 See Bonnefoy, Alberto Giacometti, 123, fig. 112.

12 Dormoy, "Bourdelle," 22.

13 See Wilson, "Copies."

14 Giacometti to family, 29 Dec. 1923. In Die Sammlung, 38.

15 Giacometti, "Yesterday, Quicksand," 44.

16 Giacometti, "Je ne puis parler," 46. He was describing the elements of his Surrealist sculpture, Palace at 4 AM.

17 Lord, Portrait.

18 Selz, New Images, 68.

19 I am not suggesting that Giacometti's orchitis was the sole or even most important motive for becoming an artist. That sort of reductionistic observation does a grave disservice to the complexity of a psychoanalytically informed approach.

20 Freud, "infantile neurosis." Esman, "primal scene."

21 Lord, Biography, 77.

22 Giacometti, "Yesterday, Quicksand," 45.

23 What Giacometti actually publicized was his failure to complete a portrait of Bianca—a transmuted version of lovemaking.

24 Leiris, interview by author, 1988.

25 Schneider, "At the Louvre," 36. It is highly improbable that Giacometti would have taken a prostitute "home" to the Italian branch of the Giacometti family with whom he was staying at the time.

26 Gerd Schiff. Communication, 1988. Schiff learned from a close friend of the artist about Giacometti's weekly meeting with an old woman who would fellate him. Giacometti later spoke to Genet about the same woman. Genet, L'atelier.

27 Serge Brigoni (quoting Giacometti) to Michael Brenson, cited in Lord. Biography, 77–78.

28 Lord, manuscript draft, Biography, 752. JLP.

29 B. and O. Giacometti, interview by Lord, 1985. JLP.

30 Lord, Biography, 373–74.

31 Lord, interview by author, 7 April 1989.

32 Lord has provided a number of references to Giacometti's public announcements of his impotence and his aversion to intimate relations with women of his own class. Lord, Biography, 77–78.

33 Mayo to Lord. 1972, JLP. Doc. 540.

34 Writing to Lord, Flora admitted that she used alcohol to numb herself to the anxiety she felt about her precarious existence since her funds were dwindling. Op. cit.

35 Lord, Biography, 87–89, 94–96, 106–7. Elisabeth Geissbuhler. Unpublished diary, 13 May 1960, JLP. Doc. 549.

36 Giacometti, Écrits, 134.

37 Lord, Biography, 84.

38 Giacometti's grasp of the formal implications of Mexican and African art are cogently discussed by Krauss, "Giacometti," 502–33.

39 Brenson, Early Work, 58.

40 Courthion, Campigli, 6.

41 Little Man is illustrated in Bonnefoy, Alberto Giacometti, 149, fig. 141.

42 Stampa, Bregaglia, 7–14.

43 Campigli was also an avid visitor there.

44 Reinach, "L'art et la magie," 135.

45 See the diagrams in Leroi-Gourhan, Prehistoric Art, 513–14. The schemata are drawn from works on exhibit at the Musée des antiquités nationales in Saint-Germain-en-Laye.

46 The visible sexual innuendo may have been responsible for Bourdelle's remark about the work when Giacometti chose to include it in his first round of participation in the Salon des Tuilleries. "One can do things like that at home but one doesn't show them." Cited in Jouffroy, "Portrait d'un artiste," 9.

47 For an illustration of Woman and the Bakota figure see Hohl, Biography, 57, 44.

48 B. Giacometti, interview, 1988.

49 Establishing the exact dates of Giacometti's work is always problematic since the artist continued to revise his work long past its initial inspiration.

50 Giacometti to Matisse, 1947.

51 Huber, Giacometti, 12–13; Brenson, Early Work, 27; Krauss, 503–533; Hohl, Giacometti, 79, 291; Bonnefoy, "Etudes comparées," 643–55. Bonnefoy takes a psychophilosophical approach to the quality of emptiness in this work.

52 Freud, Screen memories, 303–22. Greenacre, "Study of screen memories," 73–84. Both papers provide illuminating discussions on the psychological reconstruction of memory.

53 C. Amiet to A. Giacometti, 20 Nov. 1901, Amiet correspondence.

54 As an adult, Giacometti usually visited his godfather when he came to Bern. Korn-feld, interview by author, 1989.

55 A related set of meanings for spoons and spoon women is associated with Giaco-metti's sentiments about nurturance. His eccentric eating patterns—dining at odd times of day and night, never having a kitchen in his home in Paris—especially his regular return to his mother in Stampa to be renourished after months of alleged deprivation in Paris, the center of haute cuisine, is characteristic. The artist's in-tense ambivalent connection to his mother suggests that a "spoon woman" could also refer to his lifelong wishes to be fed and nurtured.

56 The first two heads of Giovanni are illustrated in Hohl, *Biography*, 54. The second is stylistically related to a granite head dated 1925, also done at Maloja. Its rough sur-face and simplified features echo figures from Easter Island, Eskimo art, and the Oceanic work.

57 Diego Giacometti told Brenson in 1971 that *Gazing Head* was Giacometti's first plaque and was conceived while he was part of the Italian group and best friend of Campigli. Brenson, *Early Work*, 58, n. 44.

58 In many cultures the eye symbolically represents both penis and vagina since it is an organ which can play either an active or passive role.

59 Zervos was the first to note the connection to Cycladic idols. Zervos, "Notes sur la sculpture contemporaine," 472. Giacometti would have seen prophetic prototypes of his plaques in Geneva where simple, abstract Cycladic and Boetian female fig-ures were on display in the Musée d'art et d'histoire.

60 Jean Soldini is the only other scholar who has noted that these shapes symbolize female genitals, though he does not connect them to prehistory. Soldini, *Il colossale*, 74.

61 Giacometti, *Écrits*, 137.

62 Two additional references to a "drop of blood" appear in Giacometti's writings from 1933; "Charbon d'herbe," 15; and "Poeme en sept espaces," 15.

63 Giacometti describes it in his 1933 text, "Yesterday, Quicksand."

64 Greenacre, "The Childhood of the Artist." Even more pertinent for Giacometti is Greenacre's article on the profound and usually traumatic effect on young children (under three years) when they witness a sexual event, whether it is intercourse, birth, or miscarriage. Greenacre, "The primal scene."

65 Leiris, "Giacometti," 210.

66 Charbonnier, interview, April 1951, in Giacometti, *Écrits*, 243–44.

67 As was characteristic for Giacometti, there are multiple sources for such an impor-tant theme. Some are well known in the Giacometti literature. See, for example, Clair, "La pointe a l'oeil."

Chapter 5. One of the Boys

1 Lord, *Biography*, 15–17. See Chapter 1.

2 R. Stampa, "Per il centenario," 118.

3 The surrealists gave numerous apologies about how their interest was not weird like the more naive followers of stargazing necromancers. Leiris refers critically to Papus and Eliphas Lévi in his review of Grillot De Givry's book on magic. M. Leiris,

"A Propos," 111. To avoid the ridicule of their "rational" friends and acquaintances, many surrealists and their sympathizers—Picasso and Miró as well as Giacometti—simply kept silent about their magical leanings.

4 A rare but welcome exception is the work of M. E. Warlick on Ernst. As Franklin Rosemont states in his introduction to *Max Ernst and Alchemy*: "Conventional wisdom has regarded alchemy as a pitiably misguided prescientific form of chemistry, or a greedy form of charlatanry, or a purely idealistic spiritual exercise. Surrealists, however, have long recognized it as a highly energizing art of transmutation that draws equally on the real and the imaginary, matter and mind, praxis and *symbolique*—and consequently as both confirmation and inspiration for the surrealist project itself." Warlick, *Ernst*, xvii.

5 I am indebted to the pioneering work of Anna Balakian on Breton and the surrealists for my entry into the study of alchemy as it relates to Giacometti. A. Balakian, *André Breton*. See also E. Maurer, *In Quest of the Myth*, E. Legge, *Max Ernst*; M. E. Warlick, *Max Ernst's collage novel*; D. Hopkins, "Hermetic and philosophical themes" were also helpful in comprehending the importance of alchemy in the work and life of Max Ernst.

6 An article has since appeared in *Apollo* discussing the alchemical symbolism in the *Suspended Ball*. The article's author, John Finlay, astutely observes some of the same links between the alchemical interests of Ernst, Leiris, and Breton and Giacometti's 1930 sculpture as outlined in this chapter, but without explanation as to why Giacometti would have been drawn to the occult at this time. Finlay, "Giacometti, Surrealism, and the Occult."

7 Breton, *Manifestoes*, 128.

8 Breton, *Manifestoes*, 26.

9 He may have learned about Freud even earlier through his medical studies in 1913–14. Balakian, *Breton*, 27.

10 F. B. Davis, "Three letters," 127–34; C. Chiland, "Psychoanalytic movement," 55–68.

11 Breton, *Manifestoes*, 26.

12 Breton, *Communicating Vessels*, 86.

13 Breton, *Manifestoes*, 141.

14 Ibid., 159.

15 Though Freud wrote extensively about artists and writers he claimed that he could not understand creativity. "Before the problem of creative artist analysis must, alas, lay down its arms." S. Freud, "Dostoyevsky," 177.

16 Breton, *Communicating Vessels*, 17–22.

17 Breton, *Manifestoes*, 126.

18 According to the public announcement in "Avis," *La Révolution Surréaliste*, no. 2 (15 Jan. 925): 31.

19 Breton, *Manifestoes*, 178.

20 Nadeau, *History*, 136.

21 Silberer, *Hidden Symbolism*, 216.

22 Silberer, *Hidden Symbolism*, 216.

23 Silberer, *Hidden Symbolism*, 229.

24 Ibid., 239, 241.

25 Ibid., 256.

26 Ibid., 263.

27 Warlick, Ernst, 131–33.

28 Silberer, Hidden Symbolism, 325.

29 See M. McInnes, Taboo and Transgression.

30 Masson had been gravely wounded during World War I and spent his life trying to work his way past that trauma. Horrified at the evidence of "civilized" man's bestiality in the trenches, Masson searched for a new mythology which could reconcile him to the twentieth century. The amalgam which worked was alchemical, archaic, primitive, and preclassical.

31 Leiris, "Giacometti," 209–10.

32 Leiris, Manhood, 63 ff.

33 Ibid., 65.

34 Ibid., 66. Giacometti's orchitis may have had a similar impact on him.

35 Ibid., 5.

36 "Eye Put Out" presages some of Giacometti's later works and focus on the gaze.

37 Leiris, "A propos," 116. The text is from Leiris's review of the book Le Musée des sorciers, mages, et alchimistes by the popular occultist Grillot de Givry. The book summarized a variety of hermetic disciplines and was illustrated with works by Cranach, Breugel, Goya, and Rembrandt.

38 Surrealists interested in the occult who became Giacometti's lifelong friends include Bataille, Masson, and Leiris, all of whom continued their interest after World War II.

39 Under each photograph, Leiris included the words "photograph composed by the author." Leiris, Giacometti. Marc Vaux was the photographer guided by Leiris. Giacometti always paid close attention to photographs of his work. Russell, Matisse, 148.

40 Fletcher points to the continuity between the more abstract Composition: Man and Woman of 1927, which bears strong resemblance to The Reclining Woman Who Dreams. In the earlier work two undulating horizontal forms already appear with several empty spoons. Fletcher, Giacometti, 84–88.

41 Giacometti's recollection of this work, visible in two sketches drawn from memory twenty years later (Giacometti to Matisse, 1947), includes a penis, showing that the man's vertical body extended all the way to the base. See the illustration in Bonnefoy, Alberto Giacometti, 152, fig. 144.

42 Shifting from a sexual part of the body to a similarly shaped nonsexual part, for example using the nose as a symbol for the penis, was typical. "Defense Mechanisms," in Moore and Fine, Psychoanalytic Terms, 48–49. Giacometti could talk his way into intimacy with women, and he may have experienced his tongue as his most potent erotic equipment. There are numerous accounts of Giacometti's charismatic conversational ability. He entertained both men and women late into the night with conversation.

43 Lord, Biography, 95, 106–7.

44 Only when he moved to Paris in 1922 did Giacometti master French. The wordplay

of the surrealists, in combination with his still imperfect grasp of French, would have reinforced the association, thus "couchée" could sound like "accoucher" to the freshly arrived foreigner.

45 Nestled inside the larger concavity are three small hemispheres. Heading toward them are the familiar parallel diagonal lines; hence the entire work suggests male penetration and fertilization of eggs.

46 Fletcher, *Giacometti*, 86.

47 Bataille's embrace of Sadean sexual mores included group sex and other transgressive sexual activities. Gilot, interview by author, 1990. Engel, interview by author, 1990. Engel lived next door to Bataille in Paris. The man's ogling eyes could also symbolically represent the testicles so obviously missing from his body—perhaps another coded reference to the artist's orchitis.

48 See illustration in Geneva and Paris, "Retour a figuration," 65.

49 See illustration in Bonnefoy, *Alberto Giacometti*, 40–41, fig. 38. Pressly, "The Praying Mantis."

50 The spherical eyes are perhaps another encoded symbol for Giacometti's eroticized visuality and its relation to his adolescent illness.

51 Though he took a public stand against homosexuals, Breton knew that several of his close colleagues and friends were homosexuals, and his position against perversions could have presented problems for Giacometti. Through Masson and Leiris he met Jean-Michel Frank, a homosexual interior designer for the very wealthy, for whom Giacometti made various decorative objects for a number of years.

52 Breton, *Manifestoes*, 184.

53 Breton, *Manifestoes*, 178.

54 Cited in Bonnefoy, *Alberto Giacometti*, 191.

55 Most scholars date the work from the winter because it was supposedly exhibited at Galerie Pierre in 1930 with works by Arp and Miró. Breton was so impressed he allegedly bought the work immediately and invited Giacometti to join the orthodox surrealists.

56 Jean illustrates *The History of Surrealist Painting* with a photograph of *Suspended Ball* titled *Hour of Traces* (see p. 226).

57 This phrase was selected by Man Ray out of Lautréamont's long book, suggesting the important role Man Ray played in the formulation of surrealism. I am indebted to Milly Heyd for this information.

58 Balakian, interviews, 1992, 1997.

59 Breton, *Manifestoes*, 174–75.

60 According to his brother Bruno, Giacometti's tendency to hero-worship lasted all his life. B. Giacometti, interview, 1988.

61 Breton, *Manifestoes*, 136–37. Freudian psychoanalysts usually mean something different from Breton by "the dizzying descent into ourselves," but so many parallels exist between Breton's conception of truth's lair and the Freudian understanding of the unconscious that some scholars see Breton as one of Freud's disciples.

62 Russell, *Max Ernst*, 13–14. Greenacre, "Childhood of the artist," 479–505.

63 Ernst, "Youth of M. E.," 28–30.

64 Ibid., 29.

65 Ernst was familiar with Freud's 1910 essay *Leonardo da Vinci and a Memory of His Childhood*, in which Freud discussed the significance of a bird and explained how the mind uses condensation and other psychic mechanisms in dreams. Freud, SE 11:59–137.

66 Maurer, *Quest of Myth*, 278.

67 Ernst, "Beyond Painting," 13.

68 Ernst, "What Is Surrealism," 3–7.

69 Ernst discussed the painting with Maurer in 1974, acknowledging its alchemical foundation. Maurer, *Quest of Myth*, 279. See also G. Hinton, "Max Ernst," 292–99.

70 From the inscription on back of canvas, cited in Maurer, *Quest of Myth*, 279.

71 Ernst wrote a cryptic inscription on the back of the canvas to help Breton decode the message of the painting. He was referring to the unity of macrocosm and microcosm—"what is below is like what is above, and what is above is like what is below to accomplish the miracles of one thing." Hermes Trismesgistus in Maurer, *Quest of Myth*, 282.

72 Hinton, "Max Ernst," 294.

73 With or without Giacometti's consent, Breton and Ernst may have decided to keep silent about their new friend's occult leanings. Might they have recognized, at Giacometti's urging, how distressed his family (especially his mother) would be to learn of another unconventional aspect of his life? To have it publicly known that Alberto was not only an atheist but also involved in alchemy seems beyond Annetta's tolerance for unconventionality. Giacometti might have believed in the occult, but he would never have jeopardized good relations with Stampa for his beliefs.

74 Seeing man as a passive vehicle through whom deeper truths could be found led the surrealists to mediums and mediumistic methods. The poet Robert Desnos, a part of the group since 1921, was particularly good at going into trances, as was René Crevel, a writer and one of Giacometti's few close surrealist friends and whose friendship would extend beyond Giacometti's participation in the movement. Breton and others visited local Parisian mediums. Crevel, "The Period of Sleeping-Fits."

75 The use of "hour" in the title could also refer to the Egyptian concept of death and the passage of the twelve hours of the night through which all souls must pass on their way to the afterlife. See Hornung, *Ancient Egyptian Books*.

76 Jack Spector has explored this notion in his book on Surrealism, *Surrealist Art and Writing*.

77 We can't know when Giacometti saw the movie but he could not have missed seeing the still photograph of the grisly scene in *Varietés*, 15 July 1929, or reading a description of it in *La Révolution Surréaliste*, 15 Dec. 1929.

78 Dali, "Objets" 16–17.

79 Ibid.

80 See, for example, Krauss, "Giacometti," 503–33.

81 Giacometti's orchitis with its painful symptoms suggests an additional underlying meaning of a suspended ball. Furthermore, the gender reversals many scholars have noted in *The Suspended Ball* might be seen as echoing what I have proposed as the Giacometti family drama.

82 Giacometti, *Écrits*, 41–42.

83 Balakian, Interviews, 1992, 1997.

84 Hopkins, "Ramon Lull," 391–94.

85 See illustration in Breton, *La peinture*, 278.

86 Such pairings were common in the seventeenth-century alchemical engravings known to the surrealists.

87 Breton, *Communicating Vessels*, 108–9.

88 Giacometti, "Aube," 8.

89 Breton, *Communicating Vessels*, 109.

Chapter 6. Surrealist Sculpture

1 D. Giacometti, interview by Lord, 1978.

2 Casimiro di Crescenzo discusses Giacometti's political inclinations in di Crescenzo, "Artist and Revolutionary."

3 See Bonnefoy, *Alberto Giacometti*, 539, fig. 559, and Hohl, *Biography*, 75. Klemm, *Alberto Giacometti*, 89, fig. 40.

4 Giacometti, *Écrits*, 130.

5 See Bonnefoy, *Alberto Giacometti*, 204, fig. 184. Klemm, *Alberto Giacometti*, 97, fig. 47.

6 For *Drawing* see Hohl and Koepplin, *Alberto Giacometti*, fig. 42; for *Large Figure* see Bonnefoy, *Alberto Giacometti*, 539, fig. 558. Klemm, *Alberto Giacometti*, 95, fig. 45.

7 Bruno Giacometti often repeats an anecdote about Ernst's visit to Maloja. "In the morning at breakfast . . . [Max] told us all his dreams and talked about all his affairs with women. Alberto's mother . . . said how glad she was that her sons weren't like that. Ernst started to protest and wanted to talk about Alberto's [sexual] adventures but Alberto kicked him under the table to shut him up!" Interview by Patrick Elliott, Edinburgh, National Galleries of Scotland, August 1996. Giacometti told me the same story in 1988.

8 It immediately followed Dali's 1931 article on the surrealist object in *Le Surréalisme au service de la révolution.*

9 Alberto Giacometti, "Objets mobiles et muets," trans. Wolf, *Art Magazine* (May 1974): 40.

10 See Hall, *"Woman with Her Throat Cut."* See also Wilson, *"Woman with Her Throat Cut."*

11 The opening of the cave in which Giacometti often hid as a child has a sawtoothed upper edge, the memory of which may have played some role in the artist's visual thinking about this sculpture.

12 The head is shaped like a violin handle and serves as a familiar pun: the French word for rape (*violer*) is similar to the French word for violin (*violon*).

13 An essential step in the alchemical process is the separation of metals into their component parts, often represented metaphorically by dismemberment. This alchemical step allowed for the expression of aggression as part of a natural process of growth and sublimation. An analogy often used among initiates was the cutting of Osiris's body into many pieces by his evil brother, Seth.

14 For an illustration of the drawings see Musée d'art moderne Saint-Étienne, 91, fig. 22.

15 The same title was still assigned to the sculpture in a second reference by Zervos in *Cahiers d'art* (1938): 446. The change of title occurred after the war, when Giaco-

metti listed his early works in the famous 1947 letter to Pierre Matisse. He retitled the work *Point Menacing the Eye of a Skull*, which he soon shortened to *Point to the Eye*. Like the transformation of *Suspended Ball/Hour of Traces*, Giacometti changed the original symbolic title to a descriptive one. For an illustration, see Bonnefoy, *Alberto Giacometti*, 200–1, figs. 179–81, or Klemm, *Alberto Giacometti*, 107, fig. 55.

16 See Clair, "La pointe à l'oeil." Among the meanings he attributes to the sculpture is the idea that a view of female genitals fills the viewer with fear, echoing the myth of the Medusa and that Giacometti's sculpture was apotropaic.

17 An ink sketch for the sculpture reveals more clearly that the line with the ball-cup at its end is very similar to the vagina shape of the 1928–29 *Femmes*. Tériade, a publisher of art books and magazines, owned the sketch, which he obtained from Pierre Colle. Lord, interview by author, 1992.

18 Zervos, "Quelques notes," 337–42.

19 Levy considered *No More Play* the artist's best work and kept it as recompense for financing the exhibit. Giacometti was pleased that it went to a sympathetic owner, who later described his sculptures as magical fetishes with all the mystery of a dream made concrete. Levy, *Memoir*, 156–57, and Levy, *Surrealism*, 21.

20 For illustrations not included here see Wilson, *No More Play*.

21 These two figurines have almost invariably been interpreted as one male and one female.

22 I am indebted to James Romano, curator of Egyptian, Classical, and Ancient Middle Eastern Art at the Brooklyn Museum of Art, who suggested the *Sit-Shamshi* as a possible source for some Giacometti sculptures. The artist repeatedly declared his admiration for Chaldean art, by which he meant a variety of Semitic, non-Egyptian cultures in ancient Mesopotamia such as Elam and Babylon.

23 The right-hand panel of *No More Play* with its twelve caverns could be read as the realm of the sun. In Egyptian mythology, the sun must pass through the twelve hours of night in darkness before its rebirth at dawn the following day. Erman, *Handbook*.

24 Giacometti would also have seen Egyptian offering tables and sculpture with false doors in the Egyptian collection of the Vatican Museum, which he visited during his Roman sojourn.

25 Erman, *Handbook*, 86. There are many theories about the *ka*, but for those cited in this book I have relied primarily on sources available to Giacometti.

26 Nan Rosenthal, "No More Play," cited in J. Strick, "No More Play," cat. entry, *Art for the Nation*. Washington D.C.: National Gallery of Art, 1990. See Bonnefoy, *Alberto Giacometti*, 224, fig. 207.

27 See Karageorghis, *La Grande déesse*. Though scholars have usually identified the figures as male and female, Giacometti consistently referred to these standing "game" pieces as *figurines* in his twenty-year correspondence with Pierre Matisse. Pierre Matisse Gallery Archives.

28 Giacometti, "Je ne puis parler," 46.

29 Kapolny, "Ka." Figures with upraised arms appear throughout prehistoric, archaic, and Egyptian art. Mirrors from el-Amarna, for example, have handles in the form of nubile women holding up polished discs representing the sun god. The stance has often been associated with sun worship.

30 The women who served in her temples were the sacred prostitutes who appear in Giacometti's postwar work.

31 The symbols of Osiris and Isis were frequently produced as amulets: the djed (backbone of Osiris) and the tyt (blood of Isis). Erman, Handbook, 144. According to the Book of the Dead, whoever wears the djed may enter freely into the realm of the dead, eat the food of Osiris, and be justified, or that he on whom the tyt is hung will be guarded by Isis and Horus, and welcomed with joy.

32 Clark, Myth and Symbol.

33 Erman, Handbook, 50–51.

34 Hopkins, La Toilette, 237–44. The sources for these three surrealists were primarily a combination of alchemical and psychoanalytic.

35 Silberer, Hidden Symbolism, citing the central text of Rosicrucians' The Chemical Wedding of Christian Rosenkreutz, 133.

36 Grillot de Givry, Magic & Alchemy, 350.

37 Silberer, Hidden Symbolism, 137.

38 For illustrations see Bonnefoy, Alberto Giacometti, 203, fig. 183; 538, fig. 554. Klemm, Alberto Giacometti, 98–99, figs. 48–49.

39 Silberer, Hidden Symbolism, 116.

40 Giacometti renamed the work in his list for Pierre Matisse in 1947 as Type of Landscape—Reclining Head.

41 Breton, Communicating Vessels, 39.

42 "The grave changes imperceptibly into the vessel where the bridal pair . . . are united and securely locked in" is an alchemical parable cited by Silberer, Hidden Symbolism, 133.

43 For an illustration see Musée d'art moderne Saint-Étienne, 115, fig. 36.

44 Balakian noted this interpretation in a personal communication, 1997. The brutality of Giacometti's image struck his colleagues as excessive, too sadistic even for Aragon and Sadoul, co-editors of the journal. Only his friend the surrealist filmmaker Buñuel supported its inclusion, and his minority position was overruled. Aragon, "Grandeur nature,"16.

45 Aragon suggested the use of a pseudonym to disguise Giacometti's identity, because his livelihood was coming from interior designer Jean-Michel Frank's wealthy customers, who were the subjects being attacked in the cartoons. As an artist working for Frank, he could not afford to be identified as a radical.

46 There was a contemporary trigger for Giacometti's interest in murdered infants. In March 1932, Charles Lindbergh's twenty-month-old baby son was kidnapped, setting off a manhunt and worldwide furor. Two months later the baby's body was found.

47 For an illustration of the sculpture see Klemm, Alberto Giacometti, 101, fig. 50.

48 Giacometti, "Je ne puis parler," 109.

49 Giacometti, "Je ne puis parler," 109.

50 Freud, Interpretation of Dreams, 353–54.

51 Lord, Biography, 126.

52 Alberto Giacometti, "Charbon d'herbe," 15; Wolf translation in Arts Magazine (May 1974): 39. Carola Gideon-Welcher, a friend of the artist and an art historian, included this poem in her discussion of the "Palace."

53 Beckett told Giacometti scholar Michael Brenson about the incident. Personal communication.

54 Birds are associated with the soul (holy spirit) and death in both Egyptian and Christian art. Familiar with these meanings, Giacometti used a bird on his father's gravestone two years later.

55 Seventeenth century alchemical engravings familiar to the surrealists show the old king in his open coffin, with a background scene of Isis recovering the dismembered parts of her brother-husband, Osiris.

56 Hohl, "Alberto Giacometti's Atelier," 83. On the first page of a laudatory article about Lurçat in Cahiers d'art, Drieu La Rochelle writes, "Lurçat ne joue plus" (Lurçat plays no more). The author refers to the painter as having grown up and become a serious artist. Reading this in 1930 or later, Giacometti could have found further motivation for his self-analysis via sculpture. He would also have found a title for No More Play.

57 Especially an androgyne holding the philosophic egg in its hands such as the one illustrated in a seventeenth-century manuscript republished in the 1920s. Trismosin, Splendor Solis.

58 Frazer describes the worship of Astarte-Aphrodite in The Golden Bough, 330–31, a book known to Giacometti and a favorite of Masson. Paphos was one of the most celebrated shrines of the ancient world. Swedish archaeological expeditions in Cyprus during the mid 1920s were widely reported and revived interest in ancient Cypriot art. See Maier and Karageorghis, Paphos, and Blinkenberg, Le Temple.

59 Giacometti to Matisse, 1947.

Chapter 7. A Double Loss

1 Lord, Biography, 147–496; B. Giacometti, interview, 1988.

2 Giacometti to Noailles, July 1933, responding to his condolence letter and saying that he was leaving for Paris the following Monday. Bach, "Giacometti's Grande Figure," 278–80.

3 Giacometti, Écrits, 154.

4 In a series of frantic letters shortly after his father's death in 1993, Giacometti invited Breton to visit Maloja. Giacometti to Breton, Zurich, 3 Aug.; Maloja, 8 Aug.; 11 Aug. Breton correspondence.

5 These deaths included: his paternal uncle, Giacomo Arnoldo Giacometti (December 1932); his father (June 1933); and his last living paternal uncle, Silvio Alberto (February 1934).

6 Giacometti, Écrits, 165.

7 Ibid., 168.

8 Ibid., 178 (Giacometti's emphasis).

9 Freud observed that mourning usually includes identification with the deceased person as a means of holding on to the lost individual. Freud, "Mourning and Melancholia."

10 Giacometti, Écrits, 158.

11 See Klemm, Alberto Giacometti, 122, fig. 64, for a comparable portrait.

12 B. and O. Giacometti, interview by Lord, 7 Dec. 1985, JLP. Ernst interview by Lord,

1970. Despite Bruno Giacometti's recent attempts to revise his brother's chronology the 1934 date of Ernst's visit is confirmed in his response to a 1970 questionnaire about his sculpture, an untitled *Painted Stone* in the Museum of Modern Art in New York. Ernst wrote that "the *Stone* was found in Maloja and painted in Giacometti's place where the artist has spent a month (summer 1934)."

13 Ernst, letter from Maloja to Giedion-Welcker.

14 B. and O. Giacometti, 1985 interview by Lord. They remembered Ernst being present in 1934 when Giacometti designed his father's tombstone. See Hohl, *Giacometti*, 1998, 81, for illustration.

15 Treasuring the small spherical rock, Ernst called it *The Sphinx Eye/The Stone of Knowledge* (1930) and kept it with him, always in a plush jeweler's box. In Egypt on their honeymoon, Roland Penrose and his wife consulted with a Spanish mystic who taught them about alchemy. There they obtained the "eye-stone" that they gave to Ernst on their return. Penrose, *Scrapbook*, 35. Silberer described the philosopher's stone as: "The Egyptian stone—an ancient alchemic symbol of the philosopher's egg. Silberer, *Hidden Symbolism*, 116.

16 Warlick, *Ernst and Alchemy*, 128–31.

17 B. and O. Giacometti, interview by Lord, 1978, JLP.

18 For an illustration of *Tombstone* see Hohl, *Biography*, 81.

19 I am indebted to James Romano for this information.

20 Yanaihara, *With Giacometti*, 118.

21 Russell, *Max Ernst*, 204; Giacometti wrote to his mother in Stampa about seeing Ernst often. Giacometti to Mother, 21 Oct. 1936, JLP, Doc. 44.

22 Giacometti's interest in crystals signaled his closeness to Breton, who was fascinated by them. He saw crystals as a version of the philosopher's stone and wrote a celebrated elegy to them in his 1934 article in *Minotaure*. Breton, *Mad Love*, 11.

23 See Klemm, *Alberto Giacometti*, 103, fig. 52.

24 Caws, Mary Ann (trans.), essay in Breton, *Communicating Vessels*, 124.

25 Giacometti's *Man Inside a Polyhedron* was probably also related to the images in Leiris's article on alchemical figures in "Deux figures."

26 The work was completed by May 1933 when it was included in an exhibition at the Pierre Colle Gallery titled *Exposition surréaliste*. Its original title was simply *Table*. Centre nationale, *Alberto Giacometti*, 98–101. See Klemm, *Alberto Giacometti*, 115, fig. 61, for an etching of *The Surrealist Table*.

27 Leiris wrote of a visit to Mme. Sacco in his diary for 1925. *Journal*, 105, 848. Breton often visited clairvoyants who "saw" his future in their crystal balls. Tanning, *Birthday*, 21.

28 Cooper, *Illustrated Encyclopaedia*.

29 In a drawing of *The Surrealist Table*, but eliminated from the sculpture, is an element the artist labeled *glace*. It is probably a reference to Marcel Duchamp's famous *Large Glass*, which may also have an alchemical meaning. Personal communication with David Hopkins, Edinburgh, 1996.

30 Giacometti acknowledged that Dürer's *Melancholia* inspired his polyhedron in a letter to Breton, 8 Aug. 1933.

31 There are many references to the occult in the Dürer print—the magic square, the

bell, and the sphere—which hint at the artist's magical beliefs and fears, especially concerning death.

32 Man Ray's collage sculptures, including the colored polyhedron, were exhibited in spring 1933 at Gallerie Pierre.

33 Giacometti to Breton, 8 Aug. 1933, Breton correspondence.

34 Unsigned review of exhibition *Thèse, antithèse, synthèse,* in *Cahiers d'art,* nos. 9–10 (1934): 272.

35 For an especially sensitive discussion of this work, see Didi-Huberman, *Le Cube et le Visage.* He persuasively argues that it is Giacometti's funerary object—a creation of his own through which he can identify with his dead father and eventually come out on the other side as himself. See also *Giacometti: Collection Pompidou,* 104–6.

36 For an illustration of *Lunaire* see Bonnefoy, *Alberto Giacometti,* 214, fig. 194.

37 This mysterious work has an Ernstian precedent. In Ernst's collage-novel, *Une semaine de bonté* (A Week of Kindness), the *"Second visible poem"* (1933) begins with Breton's words: "a man and a woman absolutely white" and an image of an open-mouthed, bearded bald head shining down from a dark sky on two disembodied hands gently placed on a large, mysterious book. The black background of *Lunaire* resembles the printed page of Ernst's collage though Giacometti's cross-hatching makes the blackness sparkle in a way the mechanically made image of Ernst's work could not.

38 The sharp-edged polyhedron could also represent the mother whose emotional brittleness would have been most evident while she mourned the loss of her husband.

39 For illustrations see Bonnefoy, *Alberto Giacometti,* 226–27, figs. 209–20, or Klemm, *Alberto Giacometti,* 113, fig. 58.

40 D. Giacometti, interview by Lord, January 1970, JLP.

41 Selz, *Giacometti,* 43. Giacometti's comment cited in the catalogue originated in a conversation with Selz. Selz to author.

42 Dupin, *Giacometti,* 38.

43 See Bonnefoy, *Alberto Giacometti,* 231, fig. 214.

44 A photo by Emile Savitry shows the original sad, expressive face of the woman. Bündner Kunstmuseum, *Von photographen,* 44.

45 Breton, "L'equation."

46 Krauss cites a Malanngan spirit figure from New Ireland, which she identifies with a hovering maternal force simultaneously associated with death and birth. Krauss, "Giacometti," 519–20. Brenson believes that Giacometti's enigmatic figure refers to loss and incompleteness, the male child who has disappeared from the hands of the Madonna. Brenson, *Early Work,* 186–87. Lord proposes the most abstract meaning: a metaphysical opposition of being and nothingness that places the artist's thinking squarely within the milieu of existentialism. Lord, *Biography,* 151. Bonnefoy claims that this work is a dream object, Giacometti's childless version of Cimabue's Madonna seated on a tomb instead of on a throne as well as the actual but as yet inaccessible work he will produce in the future. Bonnefoy, *Alberto Giacometti,* 226–34.

47 Jean, *History.*

48 Brenson, *Early Work*, 186.

49 Leiris, "Pierres," 2.

50 Giacometti to Pierre Matisse from Paris, May 1956, L. 127, Pierre Matisse Gallery Archives, hereafter referred to as PMGA.

51 In German, "guter Hoffnung sein" means to be pregnant.

52 Despite many medical efforts to help Anna Amiet conceive again, she had no subsequent pregnancies.

53 George Mauner. Personal communication with author, 1990.

54 Mauner, "Hoffnung," 113–16; and *Cuno Amiet: Hoffnung und Vergänglichkeit*. Both works also have double titles.

55 Giacometti's biographer observed that the artist often retained precise memories of artwork seen decades earlier. Lord, *Portrait*, 28.

56 Breton, "Qu'est-ce que," 19.

57 The exhibition included a portrait of Giacometti's father, landscapes with flowering apple trees, and very probably a version of *La Toilette*. Galeries Georges Petit, *Exposition Cuno Amiet*, Paris, 1932.

58 Guggenheim Museum, *Alberto Giacometti*, 22.

59 In the artist's native Italian, "bird" (*uccello*) is also a slang word for penis.

60 Lord, *Biography*, 151–52.

61 Chevalier, "Giacometti," 36.

62 Giacometti's self-analysis had consisted largely of letting his unconscious become conscious, which bypassed other therapeutic aspects of a clinical analysis. When his father died Giacometti lost the stabilizing influence of his identification with the older artist, leaving him unprotected from some overwhelming regressive impulses that had been stirred up by his self-analysis. Quite naturally, extreme anxiety followed and he needed to ward off his frightening feelings and fantasies by keeping them out of his awareness.

63 Kornfeld, interview, 1989; Jean, *History*, 228–29. The connotation of the word *masturbation* in French intellectual circles at that time was both literal and metaphorical, referring to a self-indulgent narcissistic preoccupation. Such a meaning is consistent with Giacometti's renewed effort to look outward at external reality, exemplified by his work from models. It is also possible that Giacometti's surrealist work was influenced by masturbation fantasies he would later wish to keep hidden.

Chapter 8. Transition and Timelessness

1 Giacometti to Breton, 16 Feb. 1935, Breton correspondence.

2 In *Mad Love* Breton makes several observations that refer to Giacometti's sadness. Breton, *Mad Love*, 26, 32.

3 Giacometti's enthusiastic response to the invitation is chronicled in a letter describing his method of closely reading the poem to capture the author's meaning. Giacometti to Breton, 17 Sept. 1934, Breton correspondence.

4 Given Breton's continuous praise and inclusion of Giacometti's art, it seemed to be a break Breton did not really want.

5 De Beauvoir, *The Prime of Life*, 387.

6 Some of Breton's allies were breaking with him. Aragon and Breton had a dispute that turned into a permanent, acrimonious breach, and Giacometti chose to maintain his friendship with Aragon.

7 The first was in 1919 when Breton dedicated a poem to Derain, which he sent to Appollinaire, and the second was in 1928 when he discussed the artist at length in *Surrealism and Painting*. Breton, *Le Surréalism et la peinture*, 21–23.

8 Hilaire, *Derain*, 9–12, 14–15.

9 Derain, "Critérium," 8. Though the surrealists used tarot cards like a parlor game, many knew of its foundation in the Kabbalah and alchemy.

10 Hilaire, *Derain*, 15.

11 Tériade, interview by Lord, JLP.

12 Giacometti to Matisse, 1948, 43–44. The letter, written in 1947, became part of the catalogue for Giacometti's 1948 exhibition at the Pierre Matisse Gallery in New York.

13 Mahler, Pine, and Bergman, *Psychological Birth*.

14 Giacometti, interview by Sylvester, in *Looking*, 134.

15 Parinaud, "Entretien," 1.

16 Giacometti to mother, fall 1936, JLP (author's emphasis).

17 B. Giacometti, interview, 1988. Having come to maturity during the height of fin-de-siècle spiritualist fever, Giovanni Giacometti was more tolerant of his son's superstitiousness.

18 *The Book of the Dead* (a compilation of funerary inscriptions) provided formulae and prayers for the descendants to recite for protection from the vengeful spirits of the deceased.

19 Giacometti to parents, 4 Feb. 1921 (author's emphasis).

20 Giacometti, "Mai 1920," 34.

21 The bust in Florence, which greatly resembles Annetta Giacometti, is probably the plaster bust of a woman illustrated in Fechheimer, *Plastik*, 64. In guidebooks available to Giacometti during his visit he would have read that this portrait of a princess was of an "incomparable fineness and artistic sensibility without equal in all Egyptian art." Milani, 117.

22 Giacometti to parents, n.d. (ca. 1921), JLP. He bought the first book in Rome and kept both in his studio until he died. They contained many of the photographs he knew from the earlier articles. Fechheimer, *Kleinplastik*; Fechheimer, *Plastik*.

23 Berthoud, "Personal Memories," 15.

24 Campbell, "Alberto Giacometti," 47.

25 The three groups differ in style and mood but all are part of his response to death. See Wilson, "Giacometti's Copies," 26–30. See also the essays by Soldini and Di Crescenzo in *Alberto Giacometti: The Dialogue with the History of Art*.

26 Aldred, *Akhenaten*, 110–13.

27 Petrie, *el-Amarna*, 41.

28 Scholars still debate the actual relationship between Akhenaten and Tutankhamen.

29 Frayling, *Tutankhamun*, 223 ff.

30 The interest in Carter's discoveries and excavations was kept current by the serial

publication of his three volumes in 1923, 1927, and 1933. Each illustrated the tomb's contents in detail. The artifacts remained in Cairo so Carter's photographs enabled the rest of the world to see them.

31 It was illustrated in Carter's second volume.

32 Schaefer, Erman, and Sethe were the chief members of the Berlin School, which, until the 1930s, was the most prestigious group of Egyptologists in the world.

33 Schaefer, *Principles* and *Amarna* (1931). Schaefer wrote in German for a German-speaking audience. Giacometti was fluent in German as a result of his years at Schiers.

34 Fechheimer, *Plastik*, 8–9.

35 Schaefer, *Principles*, xi.

36 Fechheimer, "Neuen Funde," 228.

37 Fechheimer, *Plastik*, 13.

38 Schaefer, *Principles*, 37–38 (Schaefer's emphasis).

39 Maspero was credited with firmly establishing the concept of the *ka* as the "double" in the French scholarly community in 1878. His writings and those of his students helped spread the concept. Weynants-Ronday, *Les statues vivantes*, 1 ff. Fraser cites Maspero in his discussion of Egyptian magic and religion in *The Golden Bough*, 53, a book that Giacometti had read.

40 Maspero, *Manual*, 128.

41 Maspero, *Manual*, 241 (author's emphasis).

42 According to Freud, unconscious fantasy plays a primary role in mental life, expressing itself in dreams, symptoms, and the psychopathology of everyday life. See Freud, "The Unconscious." Most psychoanalysts see a pervasive role for unconscious fantasy. See, for example, Arlow, "Unconscious Fantasy and Disturbances of Conscious Experience," 1–27, and the work of Melanie Klein, for whom unconscious fantasy is ubiquitous and continually present in mental functioning.

43 Schaefer, *Principles*, 16.

44 Aldred, *Akhenaten and Nerertiti*, 53–54.

45 Petrie, *el-Amarna*, 41.

46 Schaefer, *Principles*, 18.

47 Schaefer, *Principles*, 91.

48 Schaefer, *Principles*, 86–90.

49 Schaefer, *Principles*, 90.

50 Schaefer, *Principles*, 312.

51 Schaefer, *Principles*, 316.

52 Yanaihara, *On Giacometti* (14 Oct.), 147.

53 For illustrations see Bonnefoy, *Walking Woman*, 539, fig. 557; *Isabel*, 250, fig. 229.

54 Intended to celebrate one of Breton's favorite writers, *Bizarre Tales* was published for the centenary of Arnim's birth. Giacometti to Breton, Maloja, 8 Aug. 1933, citing his having read the book once and expecting to reread it. Breton correspondence.

55 She soon came to be known as one of the three most beautiful women in Paris. Lord, *Biography*, 161.

56 In 1936, *Le Golem*, a French-Czech movie directed by the renowned Julien Duvivier and cast with leading actors of the day, opened in Paris. Based on a Jewish myth

about a double made of clay, it was set in the time of Rudolph II, the great but deranged Renaissance ruler and collector of art who was obsessed with alchemy and the occult. At a spine-chilling moment in the movie, the clay golem is brought to life when the Hebrew word for truth is written on the creature's forehead. After it had caused massive mayhem, saved the Jews, and punished the evildoers, the clay creature was destroyed by the removal of one letter from the word on its forehead, transforming "truth" into "death." An avid moviegoer, Giacometti is unlikely to have missed it, especially since it depicted so many of his fantasies about image magic, doubles, truth, and death. I am grateful to Michael Brenson for suggesting the possible relevance of the golem myth to Giacometti.

57 Schneider, "Au Louvre," 26.

58 Drôt, *Les heures chaudes*, 246.

59 Diego was a "secret sharer" for his brother. A term coined by Joseph Conrad and taken up by the psychoanalyst Bernard Meyer, who used it to describe the special twinship between two individuals whose closeness led to creative productivity. Meyer, *Joseph Conrad*, 154–67.

60 Giacometti's relationship with women differed from that of many of his friends, who were finding female partners and making commitments to them. In the mid 1930s even his brother Diego began to live with Nelly and her young son in a kind of domestic harmony that lasted twenty years.

61 Giacometti to B. Giacometti, 1937, reference in manuscript draft, JLP.

62 Ottilia was warned that she would have a difficult time giving birth and was advised to have a cesarean section, which she refused. Thus the toughness she had learned from her mother may have contributed to her death.

63 For an illustration see Bonnefoy, 259, fig. 236; and Klemm, *Alberto Giacometti*, 174, fig. 114. The work may allude to Cézanne's portraits of his wife because of her sense of presence and stolid appearance. Fletcher, *Giacometti*, 112.

64 Giacometti's first known very small sculpture is probably the bronze bust *Ottilia* (5.3 x 4.6 x 2.3 cm), dated from 1935 to 1937. Francis Berthoud commissioned his brother-in-law to make a bust of Ottilia shortly after her death. This may be that bust. See Musée d'art moderne de la ville de Paris, *Alberto Giacometti*, 161, fig. 69. The overall shape is dense and schematic, and except for the arched forehead and long neck the features are without delicacy or grace. It is likely that the small sculpture was done shortly after her death as a memorial and that his sorrow and anger overshadowed his recollected image of his sister.

65 Soavi, "Il mio Giacometti," 51.

66 In an extended interview with Jean Clay in 1963 while he was recuperating from abdominal surgery in Stampa, Giacometti first publicly named Isabel as the model he was compelled to miniaturize. Perhaps the nearness of the artist's aged mother also helped Clay pierce the defensive mantle of myths Giacometti usually wore in Paris. Clay, "Le long dialogue." The other report is in Dumayet, "La difficulté," 1963.

67 Clay, "Le long dialogue," 142.

68 Copies of some of Giacometti's letters to Isabel can be found in the James Lord papers. The letter cited by Sylvester is not among them.

69 Just as he never mentioned the traumatic losses and near losses in his childhood and adolescence, nor his grief after the deaths of his father and sister.

70 Gilot, interview by author, 1989.

71 Giacometti to Isabel, Paris, undated (c. 1938), JLP, Doc. 76.

72 De Beauvoir, *Prime of Life*, 278.

73 Engel, interview by author, 1992. Nina Engel, a German woman who was part of the Parisian scene of intellectuals and artists, was a close friend of Sonia's and, at one time, her roommate. Engel was introduced to Giacometti by Sonia Mossée.

74 Engel, interview by author, Paris, 1992. In 1938–39 Giacometti made this remark often to Engel.

75 The photograph was included by the artist in the 1946 *Cahiers d'art* article—which included illustrations but no text—that represented Giacometti to the art world after the war.

76 Ottilia was a weaver and Sonia designed objects such as perfume bottles and buckles for Schiaparelli and other houses of haute couture. Engel, interview by author, 1990. Giacometti was also working with Schiaparelli at the time.

77 Erman, *Handbook*, 131, 144.

Chapter 9. The War Years

1 Bataille, "Attraction and Repulsion," 114.

2 Surya, *Bataille, la mort*, 608–10.

3 Dupin, interview by author, 1998.

4 See "Surrealism from Day to Day," from Bataille's unpublished text in *Absence of Myth*, 38.

5 See S. Freud, "Three Essays," and Novick and Novick, *Fearful Symmetry*, 14–48.

6 Bataille, "Attraction and Repulsion I," 106.

7 Bataille and Giacometti both lost a beloved woman in the late 1930s. Giacometti's sister died in 1937; Collette Peignot, Bataille's lover and muse in both social issues and alchemical passions, died in 1938.

8 Bataille, "Joy in the Face of Death," 322–28.

9 Bataille, "A Story of Rats," 40.

10 Bataille's selection of articles for *Documents* provides ample evidence for this interest. See also Richardson, *Bataille*.

11 In his manuscript draft Lord cites Bataille as one of Giacometti's close friends, *Biography*, 1712, JLP. Most biographical accounts (see especially Krauss) note the connection between Bataille and Giacometti during the late 1920s. None addresses their later relationship.

12 D. Giacometti, "Some Conversations," 215.

13 Berthoud, interview by Lord, 3 July 1970, JLP.

14 Duclos, interview by Lord, 1970, JLP.

15 Lord, *Biography*, 223–25.

16 Berthoud, "Some Personal Memories," 16. Though Annetta is usually remembered as deprecating Giacometti's work during this period, Silvio's recollection suggests how she might have used her approval of specific endeavors to make her son comply. Silvio's reminiscence also casts light upon Annetta's role in her children's

early life and suggests that, at the very least, she had not disapproved of their use as Giovanni's models thirty years earlier.

17 Lord's manuscript draft (p. 1418) included this information from an interview with Berthoud by Lord on 24 June 1971 and 3 July 1970, JLP. The sculpture did not survive. Silvio's birth on Giacometti's birthday made an identification of the older man with the boy even easier.

18 Berthoud, "Some Personal Memories," 16.

19 Teicher, "Du 'Minotaure' au 'Labyrinthe'," 22. Duclos, interview by Lord, Lord papers. Duclos had been alerted to Giacometti's imminent arrival by Geiger, a lover of Sonia Mossée and a leader of the French resistance.

20 Weber, "Thinking Back," 25–34.

21 Giacometti told Duclos of his attraction to a particular dancer whom he claimed was the model of his tiny figures and whose physique resembled that of Sonia Mossée. Duclos interview by Lord, 1970, and Teicher, "Du 'Minotaure'," 22.

22 Since Ottilia's death in October 1937 it is unlikely that Giacometti had visited Maloja in any condition to be productive. His guilt and depression, in addition to the buildup of the war, were not conducive to the creative spurts that usually signaled Giacometti's changes of style.

23 Those young women were the sacred prostitutes of the ancient world, whose service to the goddess was extolled in the historical fictions of writers, such as Pierre Louys, whom Giacometti admired and mentioned in his notebooks in the 1930s. Giacometti, Écrits, 183.

24 A painted version on the studio wall differs in several ways from the sculpture: her face is sadder, her belly rounder, her hips wider, and her pubic triangle more clearly accentuated.

25 The freshness and sense of stylistic departure of Woman with Chariot raises the question of whether it might have been inspired by the artist's having already met Annette Arm, a possibility as yet undocumented.

26 Klemm, Die Sammlung, 25; 171, fig. 97. Study after Velázquez's "Apollo in Vulcan's Smithy," c. 1917–1918. Giacometti was familiar with Greek and Roman mythology from his classical education, and thirty years later he could tell his nephew stories about the ancient gods and goddesses. Berthoud, "Some Personal Memories," 15–16.

27 "Haephestus," in Mythologies, vol. I, 384–86.

28 Lord, Biography, 198–99.

29 Teicher, "Du 'Minotaure'," 22–23. Kris, Psychoanalytic Explorations in Art, 47–50, 75–78, 203.

30 Balzac, Masterpiece, 23–24.

31 Kafka's portrayal of inner persecution gripped the guilt-ridden artist as it did many others during and after the war, when new translations of Kafka's works and monographs on him became available. Articles on Kafka in Labyrinthe focused on him as writer of terror and guilt with a special interest in the mysteries of the last moments of life.

32 Duclos, interview by Lord, 1970.

33 Giacometti, "Laurens." Skira, "Giacometti à labyrinthe," 11–12.

34 Giacometti, "Laurens," 5 (Giacometti's emphasis).

35 Giacometti, "Laurens," 5.

36 That the double is associated in Giacometti's mind with a homunculus is suggested by his statement: It is real like a glass (I would have said "or like a root"). A glass that is transparent or mirrorlike shows the double of what stands before it, along with mandrake roots, which have been linked to magical doubles of human beings. Both appear as doubles in von Arnim's "Isabelle of Egypt," which Giacometti read in 1933. Giacometti to Breton, 8 Aug. 1933, Breton correspondence.

37 Giacometti, "Jacques Callot," 3.

38 Gruber depicted France as a pale nude woman, dying on the battlefield holding a bouquet of red, white, and blue flowers. Reproductions of Gruber's painting were available during the war. Gilot, interview by author, 1990. See Cone, *Artists Under Vichy,* 176–77.

39 Giacometti, "Jacques Callot," 3.

40 Dupin is one of the few writers on Giacometti's work who has noted the artist's intense rage. Dupin, *Giacometti,* 17–19.

41 Psychoanalysts call this phenomenon counterphobia, referring to the unconscious effort to deny or overcome a phobic tendency by seeking contact with the dreaded object or situation. See Moore and Fine, ed., *Psychoanalytic Terms,* 145. In a similar manner Giacometti dealt with his frustrated rage in Geneva by often looking at a photograph of the dead bodies of Mussolini and his lover, Clara Petacci. Jean Starobinski in "Retour a la figuration," 16. Bataille had written of a similar experience in *Guilty,* 46, where he described repeatedly studying a newspaper photograph of torture.

42 Lord, *Biography,* 241–44.

43 Berthoud to Lord, 31 March 1990, and Lord, interview by author, 1990.

44 Lord, *Biography,* 230. Duclos, interview by Lord, 1970.

45 Yanaihara, *With Giacometti,* 201.

46 Palmer, presentation at Hirshhorn Symposium, 1988.

47 Duclos, interview by Lord, 1970.

48 Wilson, "Paris Post War," 27.

49 Tailleux, interview by Lord, 1970.

50 Rol-Tanguy first fought in the Republican army in Spain. For his leadership during the war, he was awarded the Legion of Honor and Medal of the Resistance.

51 Giacometti to Mother, Paris, 28 Feb. 1946, Doc. 69, JLP. Lord made copies of two versions of this letter, written hours or days apart, listing them as docs. 69–70.

52 Giacometti to Mother, 1946, Doc. 69, JLP.

53 Giacometti to Mother, Paris, Feb. 1946, Doc. 70, JLP (author's emphasis).

54 Unwilling to abandon her parents, who insisted on staying in the city, Sonia resisted all opportunities to save herself. Proud and convinced that her blond hair and beauty would save her, Sonia refused to wear the obligatory yellow star or observe any other Nazi regulation. Engel, interview by author, 1990.

55 Engel, interview by author, 1990. In fact, Sonia Mossée was sent in a convoy from Drancy to the extermination camp at Sobibor in March 1943, where all were killed upon arrival.

56 Though many French Jews and non-Jews refused to believe in the reality of Hitler's "final solution," word of the real destination of the trains leaving Drancy was known and discussed, especially by leftists. Hence Giacometti's friends knew the truth.

57 At the Hôtel Leutetia near the Metro Sèvres-Babylone, not far from Giacometti's neighborhood, the French survivors from the concentration camps of central and eastern Europe were housed until they could be identified and claimed by their families. Gilot, interview by author, 1991.

58 Perhaps only by turning to the writing of Bataille, whom he saw often at this time, could Giacometti find relief from his guilt. In all his texts from this period, Bataille was celebrating laceration, disequilibrium, sacrifice, and the ecstasy of pain, seeing death as the only truth.

59 Clay, "Le long dialogue," 144.

60 Gilot, interview by author, 1992. See also Amishai-Maisels, "The Influence of the Holocaust," and De Beauvoir, Force of Circumstance, 45–46.

61 See Hinsie and Campbell, Psychiatric Dictionary, 205.

62 Overwhelming trauma is one of the possible determinants of derealization. Others exist.

63 Giacometti had long been aware that his staring at people had an aggressive component. His surrealist sketches revealed that piece of self-knowledge and he must have fantasized for years that his look could kill—a common fantasy.

64 Rol-Tanguy to author, 1991. Four small versions of the portrait exist.

65 Giacometti to Mother, Paris, Doc. 69, JLP.

66 Rol-Tanguy to author, 1991.

67 Giacometti to Mother, Doc. 69, JLP. Teriade may have been another significant paternal figure for Giacometti during this crucial period.

68 Yanaihara, With Giacometti, 141–42. Yanaihara was recalling a conversation in mid October 1956. The newspapers frequently reported devastating typhoid epidemics in the camps just after the war, and Giacometti would have learned that Robert Desnos, a close friend from surrealist days, died of typhoid in a camp on 17 October (Combat, 18 Oct. 1945). The death of Desnos a few days before liberation of the camp affected the entire artistic and intellectual community. Gilot, interview by author, 1990.

69 Lisa Palmer, communication with author, 1998. His largest portrait, Diane Bataille, was the first postwar work he exhibited, and this occurred in The Exposition d'art moderne au Palais des Papes in Avignon in 1947. Bataille and Diane Kotchoubey lived together beginning in 1945; they married in 1951.

70 Dupin, interview by author, Paris, 1998.

71 "Alberto Giacometti, Sculptures et Dessins Récents," Cahiers d'art (1946): 253–68 (Paris). The article has no text and includes works from the late 1930s as well as drawings and sculpture done in Geneva. It reintroduced the art world to Giacometti's recent productions.

72 Giacometti to Matisse, 1947, 44.

73 One of the drawings was dated 1946 by Giacometti (Krugier) and the other given and inscribed to Max Ernst in 1950, at which time it was erroneously dated 1950.

Giacometti's practice of dating drawings at the time they were sold has led to numerous dating errors. For the Krugier Gallery figure see Hohl, *Biography*, 110.

74 This article made these tiny figurines (discussed in Chapter 8) available to a large public for the first time.

75 To the end of his life Giacometti kept an Egyptian image of Osiris in his Paris bedroom, one of the few items adorning that room.

76 Giacometti would have seen the work during his 1920 visit. As the sister of Isis and goddess of coffins, Nephthys participated in the Osirian rites celebrating the rebirth of her brother-in-law, the god of the underworld.

Chapter 10. Guilt and Hope

1 See Bonnefoy, *Alberto Giacometti*, 309, fig. 282; Klemm, *Alberto Giacometti*, 143, fig. 87.

2 Lord, manuscript draft, 1867, JLP. B. and O. Giacometti, interview by Lord, 1973, JLP.

3 Lord, *Biography*, 276; Bonnefoy, *Alberto Giacometti*, 45.

4 In describing the spider, Giacometti mentions yellow three times—in close succession—a suggestive emphasis and likely link to Ottilia's blondness.

5 Could this represent the fatal penetration Giacometti could not often accomplish, and might the stranger be one of his many self-representations? The fantasy is remarkably like Melanie Klein's hypothesized fantasy of all young boys, that the father's penis will destroy whatever is inside the mother. Klein, "Intellectual Inhibition," 243–44.

6 Genet, "Giacometti's Studio," 23.

7 Giacometti's depiction of himself face to face with death has an historical context. By telling the world of his own sweaty encounter with death, Giacometti had again found a way to be one of the boys. See Chapter 9.

8 Giacometti's horizontal disc with its vertical panels around the edges resembles the megaliths of prehistoric Stonehenge in the United Kingdom, especially an illustrated reconstruction of Stonehenge from an article titled "Le centre féminin sacré" in *Documents* (1930, 7: 377), the surrealist journal he kept in his studio throughout his life. The ancient solar monument seemed to celebrate horizontality and verticality simultaneously as well as the round shape of the sun.

9 They had become friends in the late 1930s.

10 Sartre, "Situation of the Writer," 177.

11 Sartre, "Situation of the Writer," 338–45. See, especially, the long footnote attacking the 1947 surrealist exhibition.

12 Giacometti to Breton, 1947. Breton correspondence.

13 See Clair, *Le Nez*, 1992. For illustrations see Bonnefoy, *Alberto Giacometti*, 294, fig. 270; Klemm, *Alberto Giacometti*, 147, fig. 90.

14 This sexually explicit member was horizontal, not vertical, which may explain in part why it is associated with disease, cruelty, and criminality. It could not participate in the grand scheme of nature and uprising creativity.

15 The sculpture is often compared to a specific Oceanic sculpture, a human skull covered with chalk, wax paint, and beads from New Ireland that is in the Ethno-

graphic Museum in Basel. An additional source might be Puccini's last opera, *Turandot*, which was performed fourteen times in Paris in 1928–29. The opening scene presents the grisly sight of the many decapitated heads of Turandot's would-be suitors, either on poles or hung from standards. Giacometti was enough of an opera lover in those years to have sung his favorite aria from Verdi's *Rigoletto* to Bianca when she visited in Maloja. Lord, original manuscript, 189, JLP. (See chapters 3 and 4.)

16 Clay, "Le long dialogue," 143–44.

17 For illustration see Klemm, *Alberto Giacometti*, 149, fig. 92.

18 Klemm, *Die Sammlung*, 86, 159. Fletcher, *Giacometti* (1988), 126.

19 Pinch, *Magic in Ancient Egypt*, 84.

20 Hands also have an obvious association with masturbation; this would have been especially relevant for a man who was frequently impotent.

Chapter 11. The Quest for the Absolute

1 Bataille, *Rats*, 9.

2 Dianus—"D."—was one of Bataille's pseudonyms. In Surya, *Bataille*, the three illustrations are identified as Bataille, Diane, and Kojève. See illustrations in Lust, *Graphics*, figs. 81–83.

3 After two years of creating portraits of his many Parisian friends, Giacometti made a deliberate statement to the world of his closeness to Bataille by including his portrait in the 1948 exhibit at the Matisse gallery. The only other portrait in the exhibit was the 1937 painting of his mother. See an additional drawn portrait of Bataille from the period in Hohl, *Biography*, 125.

4 Richardson asserts that the connection between Bataille's analogical thinking and alchemical ideas began during his involvement with surrealism and was later reinforced by his relationship to Colette Peingan. Richardson, *Bataille*, 110–12.

5 Bataille, "Surrealism and How It Differs from Existentialism," 63 (author's emphasis).

6 Never comfortable within someone else's movement, Bataille declaimed his beliefs ironically and idiosyncratically. In 1946, when Bataille reviewed Breton's new book *Arcane 17*, he also reviewed surrealism itself. He found great value in Breton's attachment and interest in "magic," which he (correctly) expected would encounter unfavorable prejudice. Bataille, "Surrealism and How It Differs from Existentialism," 64.

7 Bataille, "Surrealism," in *Absence*, 1994 (1948), 56. Bataille's words echoed what Breton had written in 1929: "[T]here exists a certain point of the mind at which life and death, the real and the imagined, past and future, . . . cease to be perceived as contradictions . . . one will never find any other motivating force in the activities of the Surrealists than the hope of finding and fixing this point." Breton, *Manifestoes*, 123–24.

8 Liberman, "Giacometti," 146–51, 178–79. An artist as well as a writer/journalist, Liberman interviewed Giacometti in the early 1950s.

9 "Ordeal by Sculpture," *Time*, 20 June 1955.

10 "The Champ of the Prize Winners," *Life Magazine*, 29 May 1964, 95.

11 Leiris, "Thoughts Around Giacometti," 413.

12 Liberman, "Giacometti," 151.

13 Psychoanalysts call the incidence of a later trauma recalling an earlier one and being invested with exceptional significance *deferred action* (Nachträglichkeit). Freud used the term repeatedly, as did Lacan. The concept involves the revising of past events at a later date and investing them with exceptional significance—allowing an individual to rework the earlier experience for maturation or regression. See Laplanche and Pontallis, *Language of Psychoanalysis*, 111–14, and Turo and Wilson, forthcoming.

14 Charbonnier, "Entretien avec Alberto Giacometti," 164. Fifteen years later, Giacometti used almost the same words to acknowledge the power of his aggression. "In the softest, most insignificant of men there is a kernel of violence . . . it's normal. . . . [Man] contains a force, something which sustains him from the inside." Clay, "Giacometti, un sculpteur à la recherche," 56.

15 Leiris, "Thoughts," 416. Leiris had been the first arts writer to report Giacometti's extraordinary talent and sculptural sensibility (1929), and by 1948 he was the director of the Musée de l'homme and a well known ethnologist. His years of close observation of other cultures had added to his exceptionally sensitive attunement to art.

16 Liberman, "Giacometti," 178.

17 Parinaud, "Entretiens," 1, 5. Lord confirms that Giacometti repeated this comment frequently. Lord, interview by author (1989).

18 Charbonnier, "Entretien avec Alberto Giacometti," 168.

19 Sylvester, *Looking*, xi, 96.

20 In November 1946 Giacometti wrote to Matisse, assuring him that he was now making larger work. "Don't be too worried about the sculptures you saw! Their appearance was misleading . . . they were only beginnings. Now, they're quite different. . . . The largest of them is about 48 inches high." Russell, *Matisse*, 152.

21 Sartre, "Existentialism Is a Humanism," 289–91.

22 In addition, Giacometti included an illustrated list of those sculptures.

23 Sartre, "The Quest for the Absolute," in *Essays in Existentialism*, ed. Wade Baskin. For some parts of Sartre's essay I have cited a recent translation (Baskin) for clarity. For the balance I have used Sartre's text as it was translated in 1948. "The Search for the Absolute," in *Alberto Giacometti: Sculptures, Paintings, Drawings* (New York: Pierre Matisse Gallery, 1948), 2–22. Sartre published his essay, along with two photographs from the catalogue, as the lead article in his new journal, *Les temps modernes*. Sartre, "La recherche de l'absolu."

24 Sylvester, *Looking*, xi. Sylvester argues that Sartre's essay was based on conversations with Giacometti and expresses the artist's views.

25 Martin Jay has an especially useful discussion of Sartre's relationship to perception. "Sartre, Merleau-Ponty," 143–85.

26 Sartre, "Quest," 398 (emphasis in original).

27 Sartre, "Quest," 398 (emphasis in original).

28 Sartre, "The Quest," 395–96.

29 Sartre, "Quest," 395.

30 Sartre, "Quest," 397.

31 Giacometti, lecture to Amicitia, Schiers, 1917.

32 One of Giacometti's diary entries, dated loosely to 1944, may allude to a transformation of his ideas about alchemy into those on perception. Giacometti, Écrits, 184.

33 Dali's misreading of The Suspended Ball is an earlier instance of the same phenomenon.

34 Breton, "L'equation de l'objet," 17–24; Yanaihara, "Pages de journal," 18–26. His ritualistic placement of his socks and shoes went back to early childhood. B. Giacometti, interview, 1988.

35 Giacometti, Écrits, 190.

36 Giacometti, "Laurens," 5.

37 Giacometti, "Laurens," 5 (Giacometti's emphasis).

38 Parinaud, "Entretiens avec Giacometti," 1, 5.

39 Giacometti, "Callot," 26.

40 Giacometti, "Le Rêve" in Écrits, 31.

41 The fantasied danger of a woman's vagina (vagina dentata) was discussed by Ferenczi in 1925, "Psychoanalysis of Sexual Habits," 278–81. That the concept was known to, or intuited by, the surrealists is evident from Picasso's paintings of dangerous women in the 1930s. Melanie Klein also addressed the subject of children's fantasies about the vagina extensively in The Psychoanalysis of Children (1932), 1975. See also Bertram Lewin on the oral triad (to eat, be eaten, and to sleep) as a regressive expression of castration fear. Lewin, "The Sleep, the Mouth."

42 In A Story of Rats, and in his other books, Bataille alludes often to the abyss or void as the vagina.

43 The installation photographs of the exhibition reveal a conventional display of interesting—even fascinating—works, but their presentation was ordinary and expectable. Not so with Patricia's photographs in the catalogue, which tell a tale of life magically emerging out of chaos and darkness. Born Patricia Kane, she was married during the war to Matta Echuarren, who was a Chilean painter championed by Breton as a new surrealist and who was also a trusted friend of Giacometti. The two divorced, and she later married Pierre Matisse.

44 Matisse relied heavily on Patricia's photographs to track Giacometti's progress in the months before the exhibition. Following Giacometti's directions, Matisse accorded Matta and Patricia much leeway as trusted advisers and intermediaries in both the preparation of the catalogue as well as the installation of the exhibition. Russell, Matisse, 156.

45 For illustrations see Bonnefoy, Alberto Giacometti, 318–19, fig. 292; Klemm, Alberto Giacometti, 159, fig. 101.

46 A few years later Giacometti told an interviewer that the Greeks believed that Egyptian standing sculptures would come to life and walk away if they were not attached at night. Charbonnier, "Entretien," 168. The reason for the extended left leg in Egyptian art mostly concerns the legibility of the body structure. Schaefer, Principles, 293–95. See also Romano, "An Introduction," 25–26.

47 Sartre, "Quest," 397–98.

48 Sartre, "Search," 3.

49 Sartre, "Search," 16, 20.

50 The final versions of both sculptures are widely illustrated; see Bonnefoy, *Alberto Giacometti*, 334, fig. 306; 336, fig. 309; Klemm, *Alberto Giacometti*, 154–55, figs. 96–97. The title, *Leoni*, was assigned to the work in 1957 by Giacometti when Peggy Guggenheim commissioned a cast in bronze. The artist then named the work in honor of Guggenheim's home in Venice, Palazzo Venier de Leoni. Rudenstine, "Femme debout ('Leoni')," in *Peggy Guggenheim Collection*, 348.

51 For illustrations of the final versions of *Tall Figure* see Bonnefoy, *Alberto Giacometti*, 334, fig. 306; and Klemm, *Alberto Giacometti*, 155, fig. 97; of *Leoni* see Klemm, *Alberto Giacometti*, 154, fig. 96. Some of the titles of the studies are inaccurately labeled in the catalogue.

52 It was not in Giacometti's character to be comfortable with conflicting feelings. He could feel them in alternating cycles but he could almost never bring them together. His family and friends often observed him arguing strenuously on both sides of any topic. Bruno Giacometti recalled: "In discussions, if someone said this is white, he [Alberto] would say: it's black. He always needed to construct an argument even if he did not believe what he was saying." B. Giacometti, interview by author, 1988.

53 Giacometti, *Écrits*, 188.

54 Sartre, "Search," 4.

55 Sartre, "Search," 6.

56 Leiris, "The Sacred," 24–31.

57 Sartre had written that "by taking part in the singularity of our era, we ultimately make contact with the eternal, . . . man is an absolute." Sartre, "Introducing *Les Temps Modernes*," in *What Is Literature? and Other Essays*, 254–55. Ever since his first novel, *Nausea*, Sartre had placed artistic creation in a privileged position as one of the few activities that could lift man above the mundane and deliver him from despair.

58 Sartre, "Quest," 391.

59 In traditional philosophy, the absolute generally refers to the one independent reality of which all things are an expression. For the spiritually minded, the absolute was God. For atheists, it represented a transcendent being or, at least, a highly valued activity or object, such as art. Hegel, to whom Sartre and most twentieth-century philosophers were deeply indebted, defined the absolute as spirit, a kind of self-knowledge that reflected a complex social inheritance. In the twentieth century, art became the last place for the absolute as a locus for transcendence. See Menke, *Sovereignty*.

60 Lord, *Biography*, manuscript draft, 1355, JLP.

61 De Beauvoir, *Prime of Life*, 387.

62 Sartre's ideas on perception were undoubtedly influenced by Merleau-Ponty, who placed human perception at the center of his philosophical project. Indeed much of what he wrote about Giacometti's perception was probably directed at Merleau-Ponty, his old friend and colleague. For a discussion of the relationship between Giacometti, Sartre, and Merleau-Ponty, see Fletcher, *Paintings*, especially Chapter 5, "Phenomenology and Existentialism in Giacometti's Aesthetics."

Chapter 12. Exuberance and Maturity

1 His stance and manly might is perhaps inspired by *Poseiden of Artemision*, a large Greek sculpture discovered and raised from the sea in 1928 during Giacometti's formative years.

2 Ironically, *Man with a Finger*, which has no nose to speak of, was produced in the same year as *The Nose*—as phallic-aggressive an image as Giacometti ever created. Equally notable is the absence of testicles next to the man's explicit penis.

3 In 1951, for his first exhibition at the Maeght Gallery, Giacometti added a second figure to *Man with a Finger*, calling the two-man composition *Group of Two Men*. He destroyed the second figure almost immediately after the show. Did the second man seem too passive, too much at the mercy of the first—too open to misinterpretation in the naughty Parisian art world? While it was always true that Giacometti's most intimate emotional and intellectual relationships were with men, at this point in his life he had a woman and was attentive to his reputation, careful to avoid impressions he did not want to make.

4 He never took the Métro and for many years could not afford taxis.

5 Giacometti to Matisse, Paris, 19 Oct. 1947, L. 15, PMGA.

6 Giacometti to Matisse, Stampa, 18 Oct. 1949, L. 54, PMGA.

7 Matisse wrote to Giacometti in 1952, warning him about the danger of repeating himself, especially in the walking men. Matisse to Giacometti, 29 Sept. 1952, PMGA.

8 For illustration see Bonnefoy, *Alberto Giacometti*, 326, fig. 300; Klemm, *Alberto Giacometti*, 186, fig. 126.

9 B. Giacometti, interview, 1988. These two well-known works exist in several versions and can be found in most books on the artist. See Bonnefoy, *Alberto Giacometti*, 331–32, figs. 304–5; Klemm, *Alberto Giacometti*, 161, fig. 102.

10 Iconographic sources for naked women from whom men avert their eyes include many ancient Mediterranean goddesses. In classical philosophy truth was rendered as a naked woman and in the ancient Near East the proper dress of gods and goddesses was nudity. Their nudity was sacred. An example closer to home was Ferdinand Hodler's *Truth II* (1903) in the Kunsthaus Zürich, which Giacometti had known since childhood. Hodler's nude woman stands at the center of the large canvas on a flower-bedecked grassy mound, an obvious reference to her sexuality and fertility. She holds up her arms in a gesture exposing her body. The men surrounding her turn away, covering their faces, unable or unwilling to look at her and her "truth." In 1929, the year of Giacometti's entry into the group, Magritte had painted a mysterious standing nude with her head coyly turned away and her hand simultaneously concealing and revealing her breasts. Breton acquired the painting and then created a surrealist icon by framing it with photographs of surrealist men with tightly closed eyes. *La revolution surréaliste*, no. 12 (15 Dec. 1929).

11 *The Cage* (first version) was first exhibited posthumously in 1990 (Gallerie Beyeler, Basel). The chandelier is in the collection of the Musée nationale d'art moderne, the sketches at the Bündner Kunstmuseum at Chur.

12 Giacometti to Matisse, 27 Dec. 1950, L. 76, PMGA. Leiris had used the subject of Judith and Holofernes to address memories of wounds suffered in childhood and the

lifelong feeling of vulnerability they created. "The Head of Holofernes," a chapter in *Manhood*, contains sections titled "Throat Cut," "Penis Inflamed," "Hurt Foot," "Bitten Buttock," and "Cut Head"—all provocative references to castration fears.

13 Giacometti to Matisse, in Pierre Matisse Gallery, *Alberto Giacometti*, exh. cat. (November 1950), 16–17. That *The Cage* and *Four Figurines* were usually linked in his mind is evident from the fact that many of his sketches include both images; and when he wrote to Matisse about one, he usually mentioned or sketched the other on the same page.

14 Giacometti, *Écrits*, 56–57. Though the Sphinx closed right after the war, it was always Giacometti's prototypic image of a brothel.

15 The vision of prostitutes as goddesses was also a prevalent theme in Bataille's essays. Bataille, *Guilty*, 12–13.

16 Bataille, "Surrealism in 1947," 69–79 (emphasis in original).

17 This view of seer and seen as a sadomasochistic interchange was central to Sartre's vision of perception—see Martin Jay's *Downcast Eyes*.

18 Giacometti would have been reminded even more forcefully of his father's works in 1949–50 as he helped prepare for Giovanni's exhibitions in Chur (1949) and St. Gallen (1950).

19 Most of Giacometti's comments about the four figurines on a pedestal refer to the distance between the seer and the seen.

20 Giacometti's little surrealist drawing was predictive of his postwar women, who are also simultaneously phallic and feminine. The androgyne of alchemy, so much a part of the surrealist credo, expresses a similar bisexual identity.

21 Giacometti was familiar with the style of chariot wheels found in Egyptian tombs, including that of Tutankhamen, because illustrations were widely exhibited and written about since the beginning of the twentieth century. See, for example, Maspero, *New Light*, 246, in which the chariot of a young girl from a barely disturbed tomb is illustrated. The large wheels could also be a condensation of Egyptian wheels and the wheels of the *Sun Chariot* from Trundholm that Giacometti admired; Clayeux, "Notes."

22 According to interviews with Diego Giacometti by Lord, 11 Jan. 1978 and 15 March 1981, *The Chariot* was the only sculpture for which Giacometti insisted on having all casts done with a gold patina. JLP.

23 D. Giacometti, interview by Lord, 11 Jan. 1978, JLP.

24 *The Chariot* was created in response to a commission to replace a monument that had been destroyed in the war. Though the work was not accepted for the commission, Giacometti had it cast and included it in his 1950 exhibition at Pierre Matisse Gallery. Unlike *Night*, which was also originally intended as a public monument, Giacometti allowed this figure to be celebrated. Lord, *Biography*, 197–98, 304–6.

25 According to Fletcher, Giacometti had never made sculpture of a female figure from a model before this date. *Giacometti: The Paintings*, 516–17.

26 Matisse's letters to Giacometti refer to them as monsters but there is no evidence suggesting that the artist himself used that title.

27 For illustrations see Bonnefoy, *Alberto Giacometti*, 385, fig. 360; Klemm, *Alberto Giacometti*, 219, fig. 158.

28 Lord, *Biography*, 327. Around this time Diego's companion, Nelly, became pregnant and, at Diego's (and probably also Alberto's) urging, had an abortion. She soon left him, and Diego never again invited a woman to share his life.

29 For the plaster see Musée d'art moderne de la ville de Paris, *Alberto Giacometti*, 321, fig. 220.

30 Lord, *Biography*, 328.

31 For illustrations see Bonnefoy, *Alberto Giacometti*, 384, fig. 358; Klemm, *Alberto Giacometti*, 219, fig. 156.

32 Lord, *Biography*, 355.

33 Sylvester, "An Inability to Tinker," 23–25.

34 Lord, *Biography*, 355.

35 When Giacometti was writing to Matisse about his work on these figures he recalled a long anecdote about *The Invisible Object*, suggesting yet another link between the underlying subject of both—human creativity symbolized by woman's fertility. Giacometti to Matisse, May 1956, L. 127, PMGA.

36 For illustrations see Bonnefoy, *Alberto Giacometti*, 400–4, figs. 374–82; Klemm, *Alberto Giacometti*, 220–21, figs. 159–61. The earlier versions of *Women of Venice* have been misnumbered IV and V and are less frequently illustrated or exhibited because they are far less appealing. Fletcher, *Giacometti*, 200.

37 See the correspondence between Giacometti and Matisse, especially letter 169, PMGA. Though Giacometti decided at the last minute that they were still not satisfactory for the project, in the last year of his life he intended to do one more version for New York. He included I and II in the 1962 Venice Biennale and all four of them in his 1965 exhibition at the Museum of Modern Art in New York.

38 Giacometti to Matisse, 2 Feb. 1960, L. 166, PMGA.

39 Leiris, interview by Lord, 10 Nov. 1971, JLP.

40 Giacometti's copy is in Carluccio, *Sketchbook*, no. 52.

Chapter 13. Portraits: Reprise and Reprisal

1 Ken Bensinger, *Wall Street Journal* (3 March 2000), 12. Almost exactly the same words were written about Giacometti's 1948 New York exhibit in popular magazines such as *Time* and *Life*.

2 Conversation with Giacometti at the 1962 Venice Biennale. In de Micheli, "E morto."

3 Campbell, "Personal reminiscence," 47. Gilot, interview, 1989.

4 Giacometti's insomnia was directly related to his fear of being alone.

5 Soavi, "Il mio Giacometti," 52.

6 Working within a venerable artistic tradition, he imitated his father and his godfather and their common artistic heroes: Rembrandt, Cézanne, van Gogh, and Hodler. He added Dürer, Rodin, Munch, and the Egyptian sculptor Thutmose to the list.

7 B. Giacometti, "Souvenirs fraternels," 38. Bruno Giacometti has proudly proclaimed that, as soon as he was old enough to refuse, he would no longer pose for his brother.

8 Valerie J. Fletcher's recent dissertation, *Alberto Giacometti: The Paintings*, provides a

thorough discussion of Giacometti's painted portraits: style, dating, history, and iconography.

9 Schneider, "Survivors," 44.

10 Clay, "Giacometti à l'Orangerie," 126.

11 For an illuminating discussion of Giacometti's stylistic treatment of this feature see Fletcher, *Paintings*, chapters 3 and 5.

12 This idea, fundamental to psychoanalysis, is also one of the principal ideas of postmodernism—proposed most cogently by Merleau-Ponty, who was familiar with the psychology of perception. See Fletcher's *The Paintings*, especially Chapter 5, "Impact of Existentialist Phenomenology," for a thorough discussion of its importance for Giacometti.

13 A color reproduction of this painting can be found in Madrid, *Alberto Giacometti*, 593.

14 Giacometti to Matisse, Maloja, 4 Jan. 1948, L. 24, PMGA.

15 Giacometti to Matisse, Stampa, 16 Feb. 1948, L. 29, PMGA.

16 Giacometti to Matisse, Stampa, Jan. 1948, L. 26, PMGA.

17 Giacometti to Matisse, Maloja, 11 Jan. 1948, L. 25, PMGA.

18 Giacometti to Matisse, Stampa, 16 Feb. 1948, L. 29, PMGA.

19 "I want a Paris show; It's very necessary to situate myself here." Giacometti to Matisse, Paris, 25 Feb. 1948, L. 30, PMGA.

20 Giacometti to Isabel Rawsthorne, Feb. 1948, Doc. 78, JLP.

21 Giacometti to Matisse, Paris, 25 Feb. 1948, L. 30, PMGA.

22 From letters it is clear that these works were done in spring 1950 when Giacometti had come to visit with his new bride to Stampa before going to Venice for the Biennale. The two paintings are frequently reproduced, see Bonnefoy, *Alberto Giacometti*, 358–59, figs. 330–31; Klemm, *Alberto Giacometti*, 174–75, figs. 114–15.

23 Illustrated in Centre Georges Pompidou, *Giacometti*, 145, fig. 57; Klemm, *Alberto Giacometti* 177, fig. 117.

24 Illustrated in color in Madrid, *Alberto Giacometti*, 595, fig. 277.

25 Matter, *Giacometti*, 196–97.

26 Matter, *Giacometti*, 196–97.

27 For illustration see Bonnefoy, *Alberto Giacometti*, 414, fig. 394.

28 In his youth he had seen them in Geneva and Florence and much later made drawn copies of Fayoum portraits.

29 For illustration see Klemm, *Alberto Giacometti*, 238, fig. 176.

30 Giacometti had always admired Henri Matisse and made a series of drawn portraits of him shortly before his death.

31 See Musée d'art moderne de la ville de Paris, *Alberto Giacometti*, 356–57; Klemm, *Alberto Giacometti*, 239, figs. 177–78.

32 For illustrations see Bonnefoy, *Alberto Giacometti*, 442, figs. 424–25; Klemm, *Alberto Giacometti*, 204–5, figs. 142–43.

33 In *Bust of Diego* (1954) the eyes are gouged out as they were in the "little monsters" of 1953. But rather than blinding the portrait subject as it had the figurines, this feature actually accentuates the power of his gaze.

34 See Bonnefoy, *Alberto Giacometti*, 422, fig. 402; Klemm, *Alberto Giacometti*, 207, fig. 144.

35 For illustration see Bonnefoy, *Alberto Giacometti*, 516, fig. 525.

36 Yanaihara had come to Paris to study and met Giacometti because he wanted to write an article on him for a Japanese journal.

37 Some postponements were external, such as the 1956 Suez crisis and an airline strike.

38 Yanaihara's father was a progressive academic who became a university president in Tokyo. Not long afterward Giacometti said to Lord: "He seemed just like me. . . . I came to accept his as the norm because I was with him so much." Lord, *Portrait*, 21.

39 Giacometti to Matisse, 15 Oct. 1956, L. 129, PMGA.

40 Pierre Matisse was concerned that Giacometti's preoccupation with Yanaihara would interfere with his portraits of Diego and Annette, as well as with some landscapes and still lifes in process. Matisse to Giacometti, 18 Oct. 1956, PMGA.

41 Lord, *Biography*, 373–76.

42 Yanaihara's *With Giacometti* is a transcription of Yanaihara's diaries, which have been translated privately for the author by Rumi Ito Purcell. Akihiko Takeda is undertaking a new publication of the diaries.

43 Yanaihara, *With Giacometti*, 133.

44 Yanaihara, *With Giacometti*, 355–56.

45 Yanaihara, *With Giacometti*, 145.

46 Jedlicka, "Tagebüchern," 1.

47 Yanaihara, *With Giacometti*, 211.

48 Yanaihara, *With Giacometti*, 213.

49 Yanaihara, *With Giacometti*, 215.

50 Yanaihara, *With Giacometti*, 264–68. According to Takeda in conversation with Fletcher, 1995, this is a somewhat exaggerated version of the actual events. Takeda's new edition of Yanaihara's diaries will present the material as originally written.

51 Similar scenarios may have occurred with other sitters but were never recorded in such detail.

52 For illustrations see Bonnefoy, *Alberto Giacometti*, 449, fig. 432; 450, fig. 434.

53 Fletcher has recently observed that Giacometti seemed to regain his footing with painting in 1958, refinding form. Fletcher, *Paintings*, Chapter 4. I propose that, without Yanaihara's arrival to disturb his recovery from the emotional difficulties stirred by their separation, the artist could regain equilibrium.

54 Herbert Lust, interview with author, 1988.

55 Giacometti to Caroline, Paris, 6 May 1960, Doc. 458, JLP.

56 Caroline to Giacometti, Naples, dated 1962 but probably summer 1961, JLP.

57 For illustrations see Bonnefoy, *Alberto Giacometti*, 433, fig. 415; 441, fig. 423; and Klemm, *Alberto Giacometti*, 203, fig. 140. He made others in 1952, 1955, and 1957–58 and often placed them on top of tall pedestals. Giacometti's narrow knife-blade heads were related to the man in *The Cage* (1950), and at least three of them (two on pedestals) were made as independent sculptures.

58 Parinaud, "Entretiens," 1, 5 (my emphasis).

59 Yanaihara, *With Giacometti*, 143.

60 Yanaihara, *With Giacometti*, 14 (8 Nov. 1955).

61 Sylvester, *Looking*, 130 (1964 interview) (author's emphasis).

62 Sylvester, *Looking*, 130.

63 Yanaihara, *With Giacometti*, 36.

64 Yanaihara, *With Giacometti*, 347.

65 Yanaihara, *With Giacometti*, 209.

66 Giacometti made three portraits of Lotar, a bust, and two half figures. Giacometti's portraits of Lotar are similar to his last sculpted portraits of Diego, *New York Bust I and II*. In both, the balding figures are stern and monastic.

67 *Documents* 6 (Nov. 1929): 328, 330.

68 It has since been moved to a museum in Stampa.

Appendix B

1 Word added.

SELECTED BIBLIOGRAPHY

Years appearing in brackets refer to original publication date.

COLLECTIONS

Amiet correspondence: Correspondence between Cuno and Anna Amiet with Annetta and Alberto Giacometti. Landesbibliothek, Berne, Switzerland.

James Lord papers: These encompass the original manuscript of James Lord's biography of Alberto Giacometti, numerous letters, interviews, transcripts, and other archival documents. Beinecke Rare Book and Manuscript Library, Yale University, New Haven. Hereafter referred to as JLP. Some documents referred to in Lord's original manuscript, particularly transcripts of interviews, are actually in his possession in Paris.

Breton correspondence: Letters by Alberto Giacometti to André Breton. Jacques Doucet Library, Paris.

Alberto Giacometti-Stiftung (AGS): Photographs and correspondence from Alberto Giacometti to Lucas Lichtenhahn. Kunsthaus Zurich, Switzerland. Hereafter referred to as AGS.

Pierre Matisse Gallery archives (PMGA): Includes correspondence between Pierre Matisse and Giacometti as well as photographs and other archival material. Hereafter referred to as PMGA.

Écrits: A collection of Giacometti's previously published writings as well as notebook jottings and unpublished fragments of prose and poetry.

"*Alberto Giacometti: Retour à la figuration 1934–1947.*" Exhibition catalogue. Essays by Pierere Bruguière and Jean Starobinksi. Geneva and Paris: Centre Georges Pompidou, 1986.

Aldred, Cyril. *Akhenaten and Nerertiti*. New York: The Brooklyn Museum and The Viking Press, 1973.

———. *Akhenaten: King of Egypt*. London: Thames and Hudson, 1988.

Althaus, Peter. "Zwei Generationen Giacometti." Du 205 (March 1958): 32–38.

Amiet, Cuno, and Giovanni Giacometti. *Briefwechsel*. Edited by Viola Radlach. Zurich: Scheidegger and Spiess, 2000.

Amishai-Maisels, Ziva. *Depiction and Interpretation: The Influence of the Holocaust on the Visual Arts*. Oxford: Pergamon Press, 1992.

Anonymous. "Alberto Giacometti, Sculptures et Dessins Récents." *Cahiers d'art* (1946): 253–68.

Arlow, Jacob. "Unconscious Fantasy and Disturbances of Conscious Experience." *Psychoanalytic Quarterly* (January 1969): 1–27.

———. "Disturbances of the Sense of Time; Timelessness." *Psychoanalytic Quarterly* 53 (1984): 13.

Bach, Friedrich Teja. "Giacometti's Grande Figure Abstraite und Seine Platz-Projekte." *Pantheon*, no. 3 (July–August–September 1980): 269–80.

Baikie, James. *The Amarna Age*. New York: Macmillan, 1926.

Balakian, Anna. *André Breton: Magus of Surrealism*. New York: Oxford University Press, 1971.

———. Unpublished interviews by author. New York, 1992, 1997.

Balzac, Honoré de. *The Quest of the Absolute*. Translated by Ellen Marriage. Sawtry, Cambridge: Dedalus, 1997 [1834].

———. *The Unknown Masterpiece*. Translated by Michael Neff. Berkeley, Calif.: Creative Arts Book Company, 1984 [1837].

Bataille, Georges. *Story of the Eye*. New York: Urizen Books, 1977 [1928].

———. "Attraction and Repulsion I" (22 Jan. 1938). In *The College of Sociology*, edited by Denis Hollier. Minneapolis: University of Minnesota Press, 1988.

———. "Attraction and Repulsion II: Social Structure" (5 Feb. 1938). In *The College of Sociology*, edited by Denis Hollier. Minneapolis: University of Minnesota Press, 1988.

———. "Joy in the Face of Death" (6 June 1939). In *The College of Sociology*, edited by Denis Hollier. Minneapolis: University of Minnesota Press, 1988.

———. *Guilty*. Translated by Bruce Boone. Venice, Calif.: Lapis Press, 1988 [1944].

———. "A Story of Rats." In *The Impossible*. San Francisco: City Lights Books, 1991 [1947].

———. *Georges Bataille: The Absence of Myth: Writings on Surrealism*. Edited and translated by Michael Richardson. London and New York: Verso, 1994.

———. *Georges Bataille: choix de lettres, 1917–1962*. Collected letters of Bataille. Compiled and edited by Michel Surya. Paris: Gallimard, 1997.

Bernoulli, Christoph. "Jugenderinnerungen an die Familie Giacometti." *Du* 252 (February 1962): 16–22.

Berthoud, Silvio. Unpublished interviews by Lord. 3 July 1970, 24 June 1971, JLP.

———. "Some Personal Memories." In *Alberto Giacometti*, by Valerie Fletcher. Washington, D.C.: Smithsonian Institution Press, 1988.

Blinkenberg, Chr. *Le temple de paphos*. Copenhagen: Bianco Lunos Bogtrykkeri, 1924.

Bonnefoy, Yves. "Études comparées de la fonction poétique." In *Annuaire du collège de France*. Paris: Collége de France, 1982.

———. *Alberto Giacometti: A Biography of His Work*. Paris: Flammarion, 1991.

———. *Mythologies*. Chicago and London: University of Chicago Press, 1991.

Brassai. "Alberto Giacometti." In *The Artists of My Life*. Translated by Richard Miller. New York: The Viking Press, 1982.

Brenson, Michael. *The Early Work of Alberto Giacometti: 1925–1935*. Ph.D. diss., Johns Hopkins University, 1974. Ann Arbor: University Microfilms, 1986.

———. Unpublished interview by author. New York, 1991.

Breton, André. "A Letter to Seers." Essay in *Manifestoes of Surrealism*. Translated by Richard Seaver and Helen R. Lane. Ann Arbor: University of Michigan Press, 1969 [1925].

SELECTED BIBLIOGRAPHY

————. *Le Surréalisme et la peinture*. Paris: Gallimard, 1928.

————. *Nadja*. Translated by Richard Howard. New York: Grove Press [1928].

————. "First Manifesto of Surrealism 1924," "Second Manifesto of Surrealism 1929." In *Manifestoes of Surrealism*. Ann Arbor: University of Michigan Press, 1969. [1929].

————. *Communicating Vessels*. Translated by Mary Ann Caws and Geoffrey T. Harris. Lincoln and London: University of Nebraska Press, 1990 [1932].

————. "L'equation de l'objet." *Documents* 34, N.S. 1 (June 1934): 17–24.

————. "Qu'est-ce que le surréalisme?" *Documents* N.S. 2 (November 1934): 19.

————. *Mad Love*. Translated by Mary Ann Caws. Lincoln and London: University of Nebraska Press, 1987 [1937].

————. *L'art magique*. Paris: Club francais du livre, 1957.

Breton, André, and Paul Eluard. *The Immaculate Conception*. Translated by Jon Graham. London: Atlas Press, 1990 [1930].

Brignoni, Serge. Unpublished letter to Michael Brenson (fragment), JLP, Doc. 448.

Bundner Kunstmuseum and Kunsthaus Zürich. *Von Photographen Gesehen: Alberto Giacometti*. Zürich: Bündner Kunstmuseum, Chur and Kunsthaus Zürich, 1986.

Buol, Ruth. Unpublished letter to James Lord, JLP, Doc. 499.

Campbell, Robin. "Alberto Giacometti. A Personal Reminiscence." *Studio International*, no. 2 (1966): 47.

Carluccio, Luigi. *Giacometti: A Sketchbook of Interpretive Drawings*. New York: Harry N. Abrams, 1967.

Caroline. Unpublished letter to Alberto Giacometti from Naples, 1961 (probably 1962), JLP, Doc. 331.

Carter, Howard. *The Discovery of the Tomb of Tutankhamen*. Vol. 3. London, 1933.

Carter, Howard, and H. C. Mace. *The Discovery of the Tomb of Tutankhamen*. Vol. 1. London, 1923.

Carter, Howard, and P. White. *The Discovery of the Tomb of Tutankhamen*. Vol. 2. London, 1927.

Centre national d'art et de culture Georges Pompidou. *Alberto Giacometti: La collection du centre Georges Pompidou, musée national d'art moderne*. Exhibition catalogue. Paris: Éditions du centre Pompidou et réunion des musées nationaux, 1999.

Centro de arte Reina Sofia, *Alberto Giacometti*. Exhibition catalogue. Madrid, 1990.

Charbonnier, Georges. "Entretien avec Alberto Giacometti." First interview for Radio Télévision Française (RTF), 3 March 1951. In Charbonnier, *Le monologue du peintre*. Paris: Juillard, 1959, 159–70. Also in *Écrits*.

————. "[Deuxieme] Entretien avec Alberto Giacometti." Second interview for Radio Télévision Française (RTF), 16 April 1957. In Charbonnier, *Le monologue du peintre*. Paris: Juillard, 1959, 171–83.

Chevalier, Denys. "Giacometti: Je ne pouvais faire autrement." *Equilibre* 22 (July 1966): 35–42.

Chiland, C. "The Psychoanalytic Movement in France." *French-Language Psychology* 2 (1981): 55–68.

Clair, Jean. "Alberto Giacometti: 'La pointe a l'oeil.'" *Cahiers du musée national d'art moderne* 11 (1983): 62–99.

———. *Le nez de Giacometti*. Paris: Gallimard, 1992.

Clark, R. T. *Myth and Symbol in Ancient Egypt*. London: Thames and Hudson, 1959.

Clay, Jean. "Alberto Giacometti: Le long dialogue avec la mort d'un très grand sculpteur de notre temps." *Réalités* 215 (December 1963): 135–45.

———. "Giacometti, un sculpteur à la recherche de la vie." *Lectures pour tous* (March 1966): 52–59.

———. "Giacometti à l'Orangerie." *Realités* 285 (October 1969): 124–29.

Clayeux, Louis. "Notes sur Alberto Giacometti." *Les cahiers du musée national d'art moderne* 31 (spring 1990): 5–13.

Cone, Michèlle. *Artists Under Vichy: A Case of Prejudice and Persecution*. Princeton, N.J.: Princeton University Press, 1992.

Cooper, J. C. *An Illustrated Encyclopaedia of Traditional Symbols*. London: Thames and Hudson, 1978.

Courthion, Pierre. *Massimo Campigli*. Paris: Chroniques du jour, 1938.

———. "Alberto Giacometti." *Art-Documents* 10–11 (July–August 1951): 7.

Crevel, René. "The Period of Sleeping-Fits." *This Quarter* (Surrealist Number) (1932): 181–88.

Dali, Salvador. "Objets surréalistes." *Le surréalisme au service de la révolution* (December 1931): 16–17.

David, Rosalie A. *The Ancient Egyptians: Religious Beliefs and Practices*. London: Routledge and Kegan Paul, 1982.

Davis, F. B. "Three Letters from Sigmund Freud to André Breton." *Journal of the American Psychoanalytic Association* 21 (1973): 127–34.

De Beauvoir, Simone. *The Prime of Life*. Translated by Peter Green. Cleveland and New York: The World Publishing Company, 1962.

———. *La force des choses (Force of Circumstance)*. Harmondsworth, England: Penguin Books, 1968 [1963].

de Micheli, Mario. "E morto lo scultore Alberto Giacometti." *L'Unita* (13 Jan. 1966).

Derain, André. "Critérium des as." *Minotaure* 3–4 (1933): 8.

Di Crescenzo, Casimiro. "Giacometti: Artist and Revolutionary." *Alberto Giacometti 1901–1966*. Exhibition catalogue. Edinburgh, Scottish National Gallery of Modern Art, 1996: 35–39.

Didi-Huberman, Georges. *Le cube et le visage: Autour d'une sculpture d'Alberto Giacometti*. Paris: Éditions Macula, 1993.

Dolfi-Giacometti, Sina. Unpublished interviews by author. Stampa, Switzerland, 4 May 1990, 6 May 1990.

———. Unpublished letter to author, 7 Oct. 1990.

Dormoy, Marie. "L'enseignement du Maître Bourdelle." *L'amour de l'art* (January 1930): 22.

Drôt, Jean-Marie. "Alberto Giacometti." Interview for Paris television. Office de Radio Télévision Française (ORTF), 19 Nov. 1963. Published as *Les heures chaudes de Montparnasse*. Paris: Fondation Électricité de France, Hazan, 1995.

Duclos, Charles. Interview by James Lord, 1970.

Dufrêne, Thierry. *Alberto Giacometti: Les Dimensions de la réalité*. Geneva: Albert Skira. 1994.

———. La pointe à l'oeil d'Alberto Giacometti "objet a fonctionnement symbolique." *Iris: L'oeil fertile.* Centre de Recherche sur l'Imaginaire. Hors Serie 1997, 153–64.

Dumayet, Pierre. "La difficulté de faire une tete: Giacometti." *Le nouveau candide* (6 June 1963).

———. "Les Giacometti." *Paris-Match* 1079 (10 Jan. 1970): 39–45.

Dupin, Jacques. *Alberto Giacometti.* Paris: Maeght, 1962.

———. Unpublished interviews by author. Paris, 8 April 1988, December 1998.

Dupin, Jacques, and Michel Leiris. *Alberto Giacometti.* Paris: Maeght, 1978.

Eisler, Colin. *Dürer's Animals.* Washington, D.C.: Smithsonian, 1991.

Engel, Nina. Unpublished interviews by author. Paris, 8 May 1990, 22–24 Feb. 1992.

Erman, Adolf. *A Handbook of Egyptian Religion.* Boston: Longwood Press, 1977 [1907].

Ernst, Max. "What Is Surrealism." In Zürich Kunsthaus exhibition catalogue (11 Oct.–4 Nov. 1934): 3–7.

———. "Beyond Painting." *Cahiers d'art* II, 6–7 (1936).

———. "Some Data on the Youth of M.E., as Told by Himself." *View,* no. 1 (1942). In *Max Ernst: Beyond Painting* (New York: Wittenborn, Schultz, 1948), 28–30.

———. Letter from Maloja to Carola Giedion-Welcker. In *Sculpture of the 20th Century.* New York: Wittenborn and London: Faber and Faber, 1955, 242.

———. Unpublished interview by Lord, 31 Jan. 1970, JLP.

Esman, A. The primal scene. *Psychoanalytic Study of the Child* 28 (1973): 49–81.

Fechheimer, Hedwig. "Die neuen Funde aus Tell el-Amarna." *Kunst und Kunstler* (1913): 228.

———. "Eine Ägyptische Königsbüste." *Kunst und Kunstler* 11, no. 8 (May 1913): 373–75.

———. *Kleinplastik der Ägypter.* Berlin: Cassirer, 1922 [1921].

———. *Die Plastik der Ägypter.* Berlin: Cassirer, 1922.

Ferenczi, Sandor. "Psychoanalysis of Sexual Habits." In *The Theory and Technique of Psychoanalysis.* New York: Basic Books, 1925.

Finlay, J. "Giacometti, Surrealism and the Occult." *Apollo* (2001): 10–16.

Fletcher, Valerie J. *Alberto Giacometti.* Exhibition catalogue. Hirshhorn Museum and Sculpture Garden. Washington D.C.: Smithsonian Institution Press, 1988.

———. *Alberto Giacometti: The Paintings.* Ph.D. diss., Columbia University, 1994.

Frayling, Christopher. *The Face of Tutankhamun.* London and Boston: Faber and Faber, 1992.

Frazer, James. *The Golden Bough: A Study in Magic and Religion.* New York: Macmillan, 1928.

Freud, Sigmund. "Screen memories"(1899). In *Standard Edition (SE).* Vol. 3. London: Hogarth Press, 1962.

———. "Interpretation of Dreams" (1900). In SE. Vol. 5. London: Hogarth Press, 1962.

———. Three essays on the theory of sexuality (1905). In SE. Vol. 7. London: Hogarth Press, 1962.

———. "On the Sexual Theories of Children" (1908). In SE. Vol. 9. London: Hogarth Press, 1962.

———. "Leonardo da Vinci and a Memory of His Childhood" (1910). In SE Vol.

———. "The Unconscious" (1915). In SE. Vol. 14. London: Hogarth Press, 1962.

———. "Mourning and Melancholia" (1917). In SE. Vol. 14. London: Hogarth Press, 1962.

———. From the history of an infantile neurosis (1918). In SE, vol. 17: 3–23. London: Hogarth Press, 1962.

———. "Dostoyevsky and Parricide" (1928). In SE. Vol. 21. London: Hogarth Press, 1962.

Galante, Bianca. Unpublished letter to Lord, 28 Feb., JLP, Doc. 578.

Galerie Georges Petit. *Exposition Cuno Amiet.* Exhibition catalogue. Paris: Galeries Georges Petit, 1932.

Geissbuhler, Elisabeth. Unpublished diary including conversations with Giacometti in Paris, 1960, JLP, Doc. 549.

———. Unpublished interview by author, Dennis, Mass., July 1990.

Genet, Jean. *L'atelier d'Alberto Giacometti.* Paris: Decine: Barbezat, 1958. English translation: "Alberto Giacometti's Studio." In *Alberto Giacometti—The Artist's Studio.* Liverpool: Tate Gallery, 1991.

Giacometti, Alberto. Unpublished letter to C. Amiet, 19 March 1915, Amiet correspondence.

———. Unpublished letter to C. Amiet, 25 Dec. 1915, Amiet correspondence.

———. "Which Culture Is More Sublime, Ours or the Egyptians'?" Initiation speech, Amicitia, Schiers. October 1917.

———. Unpublished letter to Lichtenhahn, Maloja, 16 Aug. 1918, AGS.

———. Unpublished letters to Lichtenhahn: Schiers, 28 Jan.; 24 May; 15 June; 18 Oct.; 1 Nov.; 17 Dec. 1918, AGS.

———. Unpublished letters to Lichtenhahn: Geneva, 8 Oct.; 10 Dec. 1919, AGS.

———. Unpublished letter to C. Amiet, 6 March 1920, Amiet correspondence.

———. Unpublished letter to Anna and Cuno Amiet, 10 April 1920, Amiet correspondence.

———. Unpublished letter to Lichtenhahn, Geneva, 23 Aug. 1920, AGS.

———. Unpublished letter to family, Rome, 4 Feb. 1921, JLP, Doc. 14.

———. Unpublished letter to family, Rome, 18 Feb. 1921, JLP, Doc. 18.

———. Unpublished letter to family, Naples, 1 April 1921, JLP, Doc. 19.

———. Unpublished letter to family, Rome, 8 April 1921, JLP, Doc. 20.

———. Unpublished letter to family, 11 June 1921, JLP, Doc. 21.

———. Unpublished letter to family, Venice, 7 Sept. 1921, JLP, Doc. 582.

———. Unpublished letter to Lichtenhahn, 10 Dec. 1921, AGS.

———. Unpublished letter to family, Basel, 7 Jan. 1922, JLP, Doc. 23.

———. Unpublished letter to Giovanni Giacometti, Stampa, late December 1922 or January 1923, JLP, Doc. 25.

———. "Aube," unpublished notebook, c. 1924–32. Musée national d'art moderne, centre Pompidou, Paris, 8.

———. "Objets mobiles et muets." *Le surréalisme au service de la révolution* 3 (December 1931): 18–19.

———. "Charbon d'herbe." *Le surréalisme au service de la révolution* 5 (15 May 1933): 15.

———. "Hier, sables mouvants." *Le surréalisme au service de la révolution* 5 (15 May 1933): 44–45.

———. "Poeme en sept espaces." *Le surréalism au service de la révolution* 5 (15 May 1933): 15.

———. Unpublished letter to Breton, 3 Aug. 1933, Breton correspondence.

———. Unpublished letter to Breton, 8 Aug. 1933, Breton correspondence.

———. Unpublished letter to Breton, 11 Aug. 1933, Breton correspondence.

———. "Je ne puis parler qu'indirectment de mes sculptures" (I can only speak indirectly about my sculptures). *Minotaure* 3–4 (12 Dec. 1933): 46.

———. Unpublished letter to Breton, 16 Feb. 1935, Breton correspondence.

———. Unpublished letter to mother, Paris, 21 Oct. 1936, JLP, Doc. 44.

———. Unpublished letter to mother, Paris, 1936, JLP, Doc. 139.

———. "Un sculpteur vu par un sculpteur [Henri Laurens]." *Labyrinthe* 4 (15 Jan. 1945): 5.

———. "A propos de Jacques Callot." *Labyrinthe* 7 (15 April 1945): 3.

———. *Écrits.* Compiled and edited by Michel Leiris and Jacques Dupin. Paris: Hermann, 1990 [1945].

———. Unpublished letter to mother, Paris, 28 Feb 1946, copied by Lord, JLP, Doc. 69.

———. Unpublished letter to mother, Paris, 28 Feb 1946, copied by Lord, JLP, Doc. 70.

———. "Le rêve, le sphinx, et le mort de T." *Labyrinthe* 22/23 (15 Dec. 1946): 12–13.

———. Unpublished letter to Breton, mid June 1947, Breton correspondence.

———. Unpublished letter to Matisse, Paris, 19 Oct. 1947, PMGA, L. 15.

———. "Letter to Pierre Matisse." Text with thirty-five sketches of the works in *Alberto Giacometti: Sculptures, Paintings, Drawings.* Exhibition catalogue. New York: Pierre Matisse Gallery, 1948, 29–39.

———. Unpublished letter to Matisse, Maloja, 4 Jan. 1948, PMGA, L. 24.

———. Unpublished letter to Matisse, Maloja, 11 Jan. 1948, PMGA, L. 25.

———. Unpublished letter to Matisse, Stampa, January 1948, PMGA, L. 26.

———. Unpublished letter to Matisse, Stampa, 16 Feb. 1948, PMGA, L. 29.

———. Unpublished letter to Matisse, Paris, 25 Feb. 1948, PMGA, L. 30.

———. Unpublished letter to Isabel Rawsthorne, February 1948, JLP, Doc. 78.

———. Unpublished letter to Matisse, Stampa, 18 Oct. 1949, PMGA, L. 54.

———. Unpublished letter to Matisse, 27 Dec. 1950, PMGA, L. 76.

———. Unpublished letter to Matisse, December 1950, PMGA, L. 77.

———. "Lettre à Pierre Matisse." Twelve sketches of works with accompanying texts in *Alberto Giacometti.* Exhibition catalogue. Pierre Matisse Gallery.

———. "Mai 1920." *Verve* III, 27–28 (December 1952): 33–34.

———. Unpublished letter to Matisse, Paris, May 1956, PMGA, L. 127.

———. Unpublished letter to Matisse, 15 Oct. 1956, PMGA, L. 129.

———. Unpublished letter to Matisse, 2 Feb. 1960, PMGA, L. 166.

———. Unpublished letter to Caroline, Paris, 1960, JLP, Doc. 458.

———. Interview with David Sylvester in London in *Alberto Giacometti: Thirteen Bronzes.* Exhibition catalogue. London: Thomas Gibson Fine Art, 1977 [1964].

———. "Notes sur les copies [Texts of 4 and 18 Oct. and 30 Nov. 1965]." In *Giacometti: A Sketchbook of Interpretive Drawings.* New York: Abrams, 1967.

Giacometti, Annetta. Unpublished letter to A. Amiet, 24 Nov. 1901, Amiet correspondence.

———. Unpublished letter to A. Amiet, 2 Sept. 1904, Amiet correspondence.

———. Unpublished letter to A. Amiet, 28 Feb. 1906, Amiet correspondence.

———. Unpublished letter to A. Amiet, 28 June 1906, Amiet correspondence.

Giacometti, Bruno. Unpublished interviews by Lord, Zurich, 9 July 1978; 1989. JLP.

———. "Souvenirs fraternels." In *Alberto Giacometti*. Exhibition catalogue. André Kuenzi, Foundation Pierre Gianadda, Martigny, 1986.

———. Unpublished interview by author. Tape recording. Zurich, 1988.

———. "Ein Gespräch mit Bruno Giacometti." Interview with Christian Klemm in *La Mamma a Stampa: Annetta—Gesehen von Giovanni und Alberto Giacometti*. Exhibition catalogue. Chur, Zurich: Bündner Kunstmuseum; Chur: Kunsthaus Zürich, 1990.

Giacometti, Bruno and Odette. Interview by Lord. November 1973. 10 July, 20 Oct. 1978, JLP.

———. Interview by Lord. Tape recording. 7 Dec. 1985, JLP.

Giacometti, Diego. "Some Conversations with Diego Giacometti" (interview with Herbert Lust, 12 Dec. 1969). In *Giacometti: The Complete Graphics*, by Herbert Lust. New York: Tudor Publishing Company (1970).

———. Unpublished interviews by Lord. 26 Jan. 1970, 11 Jan. 1978, 6 Feb. 1978, 8 Feb. 1978, 15 March 1981, JLP.

Gilot, Françoise. Interview by author. New York City, 1989; 27 March 1990; 1991.

Giovanoli, Diego. Unpublished interview by author. Chür, Switzerland, 1990.

———. Unpublished letter to James Lord, n.d., JLP, Doc. 411.

Glenn, Jules. "Testicular and Scrotal Masturbation." *International Journal of Psycho-Analysis* 50, no. 3 (1969): 353–62.

Green, Martin. *Mountain of Truth: The Counterculture Begins, Ascona, 1900–1920*. Hanover, N.H. and London: University Press of New England, 1986.

Greenacre, Phyllis. "A contribution to the study of screen memories." *Psychoanalytic Study of the Child* 3/4 (1949): 73–84.

———. "The Childhood of the Artist: Libidinal Phase Development and Giftedness." *Emotional Growth*. Vol. 1. New York: International Universities Press, 1957.

———. "The Primal Scene and the Sense of Reality." *Psychoanalytic Quarterly* (1973): 10–41.

Grillot de Givry, *Witchcraft, Magic & Alchemy*. Paris, New York: Dover Publications, 1971 [1929].

Guggenheim Museum. *Alberto Giacometti: A Retrospective Exhibition*. Exhibition catalogue. New York: Solomon R. Guggenheim Foundation, 1974.

Hall, Douglas. *Alberto Giacometti's "Woman with Her Throat Cut."* Edinburgh: Scottish National Gallery of Modern Art, 1980.

Hess, Thomas B. "Giacometti: The Uses of Adversity." *Art News* (May 1958): 34–35, 67.

Hilaire, Georges. *Derain*. Geneva: Pierre Cailler, 1959.

Hinsie, L., and R. Campbell. *Psychiatric Dictionary*. New York and London: Oxford University Press, 1970.

Hinton, Geoffrey. "Max Ernst: 'Les hommes n'en sauront rien'." *Burlington Magazine* cxvii (1975): 292–99.

Hohl, Reinhold. "Alberto Giacometti's Atelier Im Jahr 1932." *Du* (May 1971): 352–65.

———. *Alberto Giacometti.* New York: Abrams, 1971.

———. *Giacometti: A Biography in Pictures.* Ostfildern-Ruit, Germany: Verlag Gerd Hatje, 1998.

Hohl, Reinhold, and D. Koepplin. *Alberto Giacometti: Zeichnungen und Druckgraphik.* Niederteufen, Switzerland: Verlag Arthur Niggli, 1981.

Hollier, Denis, ed. *The College of Sociology (1937–39).* Minneapolis: University of Minnesota Press, 1988 [1979].

Hopkins, David. "Max Ernst's 'La Toilette de la Mariée'." *Burlington Magazine* 133, no. 1057 (April 1991): 237–43.

———. "Hermetic and Philosophical Themes in Max Ernst's 'Vox Angelica' and Related Works." *Burlington Magazine* 134, no. 1076 (November 1992): 716–23.

———. "Ramon Lull, Miro, and Surrealism: The Link with Medieval Philosophy." *Apollo* 139, no. 382 (December 1993): 391–94.

Hornung, Erik. *The Ancient Egyptian Books of the Afterlife.* Ithaca and London: Cornell University Press, 1999.

Huber, Carlo. *Alberto Giacometti.* Lausanne, Switzerland: Editions Rencontre, 1970.

Hugelshofer, Walter. *Giovanni Giacometti 1868–1933.* Monographien Zur Schweizer Kunst. Vol. 8. Zurich–Leipzig, 1936.

Idel, Moshe. *Golem: Jewish Magical and Mystical Traditions on the Artificial Anthropoid.* Albany, N.Y.: State University of New York Press, 1990.

IVAM Centre Julio Gonzales, *El dialogo con la historia del arte Alberto Giacometti.* Exhibition catalogue, with essays by Simone Soldini and Casimiro di Crescenzo. IVAM Valencia d'art modern, 2000.

Jakovski, J. "L'art du style; en marge du salon des surindépendants; 1934." *Cahiers d'art* (1934): 264.

Jay, Martin. "Sartre, Merleau-Ponty, and the Search for a New Ontology of Sight." In *Modernity and the Hegemony of Vision,* edited by D. Levin. Berkeley: University of California Press, 1993, 143–85.

———. *Downcast Eyes.* Berkeley: University of California Press, 1993.

Jean, Marcel. *The History of Surrealist Painting.* Translated by Simon Watson Taylor. New York: Grove Press, 1960 [1959].

Jedlicka, Gotthard. "Fragmente Aus Tagebüchern" (conversations with Giacometti of 30 March, 1 April, and 3 April, 1953; and 1958). In *Neue Zürcher Zeitung* (4 April 1964.).

Jouffroy, Allain. "Portrait d'un artiste: Giacometti." *Arts-Lettres-Spectacles,* no. 545 (1955): 9.

———. "Rétrospective 1978 à la fondation Maeght: L'oeuvre impossible." *XXe siècle* 51 (1978): 4–8.

Kaplony, Peter. "Ka." In *Lexikon der Ägyptologie,* compiled and edited by W. Helck, E. Otto, and W. Westendorf. Vol. 3. Wiesbaden: Otto Harrassowitz, 1980, 275–82.

Karageorghis, Jacqueline. *La grande Déesse de Chyphre et son culte.* Lyon: Maison de l'orient, 1977.

Klein, Melanie. "The Theory of Intellectual Inhibition." In *Love, Guilt, Reparation and Other Works.* New York: Delta, 1975 [1931].

———. *The Psychoanalysis of Children.* Translated by Alix Strachey. New York: Delta, 1975 [1932].

Klemm, Christian. *Die Sammlung der Alberto Giacometti Stiftung*. Zurich: Zürcher Kunstgesellschaft, 1990.

Klemm, Christian, in collaboration with Carolyn Lanchner, Tobia Bezzola, and Anne Umlan. *Alberto Giacometti*. Exhibition catalogue. New York: Museum of Modern Art; Zurich: Kunsthaus Zürich, 2001.

Kornfeld, Eberhard. Unpublished interview with author. New York, 1989.

Krauss, Rosalind. "Giacometti." In *"Primitivism" in 20th Century Art*, edited by William Rubin. Exhibition catalogue. Vol. 2. New York: Museum of Modern Art, 1984, 503–33.

Kris, *Psychoanalytic Explorations in Art*. New York: International Universities Press, 1952.

Kuenzi, André. *Alberto Giacometti*. Exhibition catalogue. Martigny: Foundation Pierre Gianadda, 1986.

Kunsthaus Zürich. *"La Mamma a Stampa: Annetta-Gesehen von Giovanni und Alberto Giacometti."* Exhibition catalogue. Chur: Bündner Kunstmuseum; Zurich: Kunsthaus Zürich, 1990.

Laplanche, J., and J.-B. Pontalis. *The Language of Psycho-Analysis*. 1967. New York: W. W. Norton and Co., 1973.

La révolution surréaliste (15 Dec. 1929): n.12.

La Rochelle, Drieu. Lurçat in *Cahiers d'art*, 1930.

Legge, Elizabeth. *"Max Ernst: The Psychoanalytic Sources."* Ann Arbor and London: U.M.I. Research Press, 1989.

Leinz, Gottlieb. "Das Bein von Alberto Giacometti: Errinerungen an dem Tod." *Pantheon* 55 (1997), 172–88.

Leiris, Michel. "Alberto Giacometti." *Documents* (1929): 209–14.

———. "A propos du *musée des sorciers*." *Documents*, no. 2 (1929): 111.

———. *Manhood*. New York: Grossman Publishers, 1963 [1929].

———. "Notes sur deux figures microcosmiques des XIVe et XVe siècles." *Documents* 1 (1929): 48–52.

———. "Thoughts Around Alberto Giacometti." *Horizon* 19, no. 114 (June 1949): 411–17.

———. "Pierres pour un Alberto Giacometti." *Derrière le mirroir*, nos. 39/40 (June 1951).

———. Unpublished interview by author. Paris, 8 April 1988.

———. "The Sacred in Everyday Life." Lecture in *The College of Sociology*, edited by Denis Hollier. Minneapolis: University of Minnesota Press, 1988.

———. "Journal 1922–1989," edited by Jean Jamin. Paris: Éditions Gallimard, 1992.

Leroi-Gourhan, André. *Treasures of Prehistoric Art*. New York: Harry Abrams, 1967.

Levin, David M., ed. *Modernity and the Hegemony of Vision*. Berkeley: University of California Press, 1993.

Levy, Julien. *Surrealism*. New York: The Black Sun Press, 1936.

———. *Memoir of an Art Gallery*. New York: G. P. Putnam's Sons, 1977.

Lewin, Bertram, "Sleep, the Mouth and the Dream Screen." *Psychoanalytic Quarterly* 15 (1946): 419–34.

Liberman, Alexander. "Giacometti." *Vogue* 218 (January 1955): 146–51, 178–79.

Limbour, Georges. "Giacometti." *Magazine of Art* 41, no. 7 (November 1948): 253–55.

Lord, James. *A Giacometti Portrait*. New York: The Museum of Modern Art, 1965.

SELECTED BIBLIOGRAPHY

———. *Giacometti: A Biography.* New York: Farrar, Straus, Giroux, 1983.

———. "Sartre and Giacometti: Words Between Friends." *New Criterion* 1 (June 1985): 45–55.

———. Telephone interview by author. 10 Dec. 1989.

———. Unpublished interviews by author. New York, 7 April 1989; 16 April, 23 May 1990; 9 May 1992.

———. Unpublished manuscript draft. *Alberto Giacometti,* JLP.

Lurker, Manfred. *The Gods and Symbols of Ancient Egypt.* London: Thames and Hudson, 1988 [1974].

Lust, Herbert. *Giacometti: The Complete Graphics.* Catalogue raisonné. New York: Tudor Publishing, 1970.

———. Unpublished interview by author. New York, 1988.

Mahler, Margaret, Fred Pine, and Anni Bergman. *The Psychological Birth of the Human Infant.* New York: Basic Books, 1975.

Maier, F. G., and V. Karageorghis. *Paphos: History and Archeology.* Nicosia: A. G. Leventis Foundation, 1984.

Maspero, Gaston. *Manual of Egyptian Archeology.* New York: G. P. Putnam's Sons, 1926 [1886].

———. *New Light on Ancient Egypt.* Translated by Elizabeth Lee. New York: Appleton and Company, 1909.

Matisse, Pierre. Unpublished letter to Giacometti, 29 Sept. 1952, PMGA.

———. Unpublished letter to Giacometti, 18 Oct. 1956, PMGA.

Matter, Herbert and Mercedes. *Alberto Giacometti.* New York: Harry N. Abrams, 1987.

Mauner, George. *Cuno Amiet, Giovanni Giacometti, Augusto Giacometti: Three Swiss Painters.* Exhibition catalogue. Museum of Art, Pennsylvania State University, 1973.

———. "Die Hoffnung (Auch Die Vergänglichkeit)." In *Kunstmuseum Olten Sammlungskatalog.* Zurich: Schweizerisches Institut für Kunstwissenschaft, 1983, 113–16.

———. *Cuno Amiet.* Zurich: Orell Füssli, 1984.

———. "Kopf Alberto Giacometti," *Bündner Kunstmuseum Chur: Gemälde und Skulpturen,* Chur: Stiftung Bündner Kunstsammlung, 1989, 97.

———. Telephone interview by author. 1990.

———. *Cuno Amiet Hoffnung und Vergänglichkeit.* Aargau: Aargauer Kunsthaus, 1991.

———. *Amiet's Apfel-Zuden "Obsternten" von 1912.* Zurich: Schweizerische Institut für Kunstwissenschaft, 1999.

Maurer, Evan. *In Quest of the Myth: An Investigation of the Relationships Between Surrealism and Primitivism.* Ph.D. diss., University of Pennsylvania, 1974.

Mayo, Flora. Unpublished letter to James Lord, 4 April 1971, JLP.

———. Unpublished letter to Lord, 30 Sept. 1972, JLP, Doc. 540.

McInnes, Mary. "Taboo and Transgression: The Subversive Aesthetics of Georges Bataille and 'Documents'." Ph.D. diss., Boston University, 1994. Ann Arbor, Mich.: UMI, 1995.

Menke, C. *Sovereignty of Art,* Cambridge: MIT Press, 1998.

Merleau-Ponty, Maurice. "Cézanne's Doubt." In *Sense and Non-Sense,* translated and edited by Hubert and Patricia Dreyfus. Northwestern University Press, 1964 [1945].

———. *Phenomenology of Perception*. Translated by Colin Smith. London: Routledge, 1989 [1945].

Meyer, Bernard. *Joseph Conrad: A Psychoanalytic Biography*. Princeton, N.J.: Princeton University Press, 1967.

Milani, Luigi Adriano. *Il R. museo archeologico di Firenze*. Vol. 1. Florence: Tipografia Enrico Ariani, 1912.

Moore, Burness, and Bernard Fine. *Psychoanalytic Terms and Concepts*. The American Psychoanalytic Association; New Haven and London: Yale University Press, 1990, 48–49.

Müller, Paul, and Viola Radlach. *Giovanni Giacometti: Werkkatalog der Gemälde*. Zurich: Schweizerisches Institut für Kunstwissenschaft, 1997.

Musée d'art moderne de la ville de Paris. *Alberto Giacometti: sculptures, peintures, dessins*. Exhibition catalogue. Paris: Paris-Musées, 1991.

Musée d'art moderne Saint-Étienne. *Alberto Giacometti: La collection du centre Georges Pompidou, musée national d'art moderne*. Exhibition catalogue. Paris: Éditions du centre Pompidou et réunion des musées nationaux, 1999.

Musée national d'art moderne, Centre Georges Pompidou. *André Breton, la beauté convulsive*. Exhibition catalogue. Paris: Éditions du centre Pompidou, 1991.

Museum of Modern Art. *Alberto Giacometti*, Exhibition catalogue. New York: Museum of Modern Art, 1965.

Nadeau, Maurice. *The History of Surrealism*. Translated by Richard Howard. Cambridge: Belknap Press of Harvard University Press, 1989 [1944].

Novick, J., and K. K. Novick. *Fearful Symmetry: The Development and Treatment of Sadomasochism*. Northvale, N.J.: Jason Aronson, 1996.

Orangerie. *Alberto Giacometti*. Exhibition catalogue. Paris: Orangerie des Tuileries, 1969.

Palmer, Mary Lisa. Paper presented at Giacometti Symposium, Hirshhorn Museum and Sculpture Garden, Washington, D.C., 1988.

Parinaud, André. "Entretiens avec Giacometti: Pourquoi je suis sculpteur." *Arts—lettres—spectacles* 873 (13 June 1962): 1, 5.

Penrose, Roland. *Scrapbook, 1900–1981*. New York: Rizzoli, 1981.

Petrie, W. M. Flinders. *Tell el-Amarna*. London: Methuen, 1894.

Pinch, Geraldine. *Magic in Ancient Egypt*. Austin: University of Texas Press, 1995 [1994].

Pressly, William L. "The Praying Mantis in Surrealist Art." *Art Bulletin* (December 1973): 600–15.

Reinach, Salomon. "L'art et la magie." In *Cultes, mythes et religions*. Paris: Éditions Erest Leroux, 1922.

Richardson, Michael. *Georges Bataille*. London, New York: Routledge, 1994.

Rol-Tanguy, Henri. Unpublished letter to author, 1991.

Romano, James F. "An Introduction to Ancient Egyptian Art." In *Art for Eternity: Masterworks from Ancient Egypt*, by R. Fazzini, J. Romano, and M. Cody. New York: Brooklyn Museum of Art, 1999, 15–27.

Rosemmont, Franklin. Foreword to *Max Ernst and Alchemy*, by M. E. Warlick. Austin Texas: University of Texas Press, 2001.

Rosenthal, Nan. "Giacometti's 'No More Play' 1931–32." Paper presented at symposium on modern sculpture: "Talk at Viewpoints and Visions," Southern Methodist University, Dallas, 1987.

Rotzler, Willy. "Alberto Giacometti and His Times." In *Alberto Giacometti and America.* New York: Graduate School and University Center, City University of New York, 1984.

Rudenstine, Angelica Z. "Giacometti: Projet pour une place 1931–32. Femme qui marche 1932. Femme égorgée 1932. Femme leoni 1947. Piazza 1947–48." In *Peggy Guggenheim Collection.* New York, 1985.

Russell, John. *Max Ernst: Life and Work.* New York: Abrams, 1967.

———. *Matisse: Father and Son.* New York: Harry N. Abrams, 1999.

Sartre, Jean-Paul. "Existentialism Is a Humanism." In *Existentialism from Dostoyevsky to Sartre,* edited by Walter Kaufmann. New York: Meridian Press, 1956 [1946].

———. "La recherche de l'absolu." *Les temps modernes* 3, no. 28 (1948): 1, 153–63.

———. "Situation of the Writer in 1947." In *What Is Literature? and Other Essays.* Cambridge: Harvard University Press, 1988 [1948].

———. "The Quest for the Absolute." In *Essays in Existentialism,* edited by Wade Baskin. Secaucus, N.J.: Citadel Press, 1997 [1948].

Schaefer, Heinrich. *Principles of Egyptian Art.* London: Oxford University Press, 1986 [1919].

———. *Amarna in Religion und Kunst.* Berlin: Deutsche Orient-Gesellschaft, 1931.

Scheidegger, Ernst. *Traces d'une amitie.* Paris: Maeght, 1991.

———. *Das Bergell: Heimat der Giacometti.* Zurich: Verlag Ernst Scheidegger, 1994.

Schiff, Gerd. Communication with author, 1988.

Schneider, Angela, ed. *Alberto Giacometti.* Munich: Prestel, 1994.

Schneider, Pierre. "'Ma longue marche' par Alberto Giacometti." *L'express* 521 (8 June 1961): 48–50.

———. "Au Louvre avec Alberto Gaicometti." *Preuves* 139 (September 1962): 23–31.

———. "His Men Look Like Survivors of a Shipwreck." *New York Times Magazine,* 6 June 1965, 34–37, 39, 42, 44, 46.

Seligmann, Kurt. *The History of Magic and the Occult.* New York: Crown Publishers, Harmony Books, 1975 [1948].

Selz, Peter. *New Images of Man.* New York: Museum of Modern Art, 1959.

———. *Alberto Giacometti.* Exhibition catalogue. New York: Museum of Modern Art, 1965.

———. Unpublished letter to author, July 1990.

Silberer, Herbert. *Hidden Symbolism of Alchemy and the Occult Arts (Problems of Mysticism and Its Symbolism).* Translated by Smith Ely Jelliffe. New York: Dover Publications, 1971 [1914].

Skira, Albert. "Giacometti à labyrinthe." *Les lettres françaises,* no. 1115 (20 Jan. 1966): 11–12.

Soavi, Giorgio. "Il mio Giacometti." In *Protagonisti. Giacometti, Sutherland, De Chirico.* Milan: Longanesi, 1969 [1966].

Soldini, Jean. *Il colossale, la madre, il sacro.* Bergamo: P. Lubrina, 1991.

Spector, Jack. *Surrealist Art and Writing, 1919–1939.* Cambridge and New York: Cambridge University Press, 1997.

Speiser, Felix. "L'art plastique des nouvelles hébrides." *Cahiers d'art* (1929): 91–94.

Stampa, Renato. "Alberto Giacometti: Reminiscenze." *Quaderni Grigionitaliani* (Poschiavo) 35, no. 2 (1966): 82–86.

———. "Per il centenario della nascita de Giovanni Giacometti." *Quaderni Grigionitaliani* (Poschiavo) 37 (April 1968): 118–32.

———. "Dieci lettere de Giovanni Giacometti," *Quaderni Grigionitaliani* (Poschiavo) 38, no. 1 (January 1969): 38.

———. *Storia della Bregaglia.* Poschiavo: Pro Grigioni Italiano: Società Culturale di Bregaglia, 1991, 7–14.

Stoppani, Rita. Unpublished interview by Lord, September 1971, JLP.

Surya, Michel. *Georges Bataille, la mort à l'oeuvre.* Paris: Gallimard, 1992.

Sylvester, David. "Giacometti: An Inability to Tinker." *Sunday Times* (London), July 1965, 23–5.

———. "An Interview with Giacometti by David Sylvester, Autumn, 1964." In *Alberto Giacometti: Arts Council Exhibition, Manchester, Bristol, London.* 1981, 3–11.

———. *Looking at Giacometti.* New York: Henry Holt and Company, 1994.

Tailleux, Francis. Unpublished interview by Lord, 11 May 1970.

Tanning, Dorothea. *Birthday.* San Francisco: Lapis Press, 1986.

Turo, J., and L. Wilson. "An Essay on Freudian Temporality: Deferred Action of Memory and Nachtraeglichkeit." *Clinical Psychoanalysis.*

Trismosin, Salomon. *Splendor Solis.* 1616.

Warlick, M. E. *Max Ernst's Collage Novel, "Une Semaine de Bonté": Feuilleton Sources and Alchemical Interpretation.* Ph.D. diss., University of Maryland, 1984.

———. *Max Ernst and Alchemy.* Austin: University of Texas Press, 2001.

Weynants-Ronday, M. *Les statues vivantes.* Brussels: Edition de la fondation egyptologique reine Elisabeth, 1926.

Wilson, Laurie. "Alberto Giacometti's Copies of Egyptian Art: The Louvre or Not the Louvre." *Source* 13, no. 1 (1993): 26–30.

———. "Alberto Giacometti's *No More Play*: A Monument to Ancient Magic, Fertility Goddesses, and Universal Ambivalence Toward Women." In *Psychoanalysis and the Humanities,* edited by Jack Szaluta and Laurie Adams. New York: Brunner Mazel, 1996.

———. "Alberto Giacometti's *Woman with Her Throat Cut*: Multiple Meanings and Methodology." *The Annual of Psychoanalysis* 26/27 (1999): 143–71.

———. "A Touching Subject: Parent/Child Images in the Art of Giovanni and Alberto Giacometti." In *Psychoanalysis and Art: The Artistic Representation of the Parent/Child Relationship.* Madison, Conn.: International Universities Press, 2003.

———. "Giacometti's Thin Figures: Dead Men Walking." *Art in America* (May 2002): 134–43.

———. *Giovanni and Alberto Giacometti: The Good Father and the Better Son.* Florence: Nincomp. L.E. 2003.

Wilson, Sarah. "Paris Post War: In Search of the Absolute." In *Paris Post War: Art and Existentialism 1945–55.* Exhibition catalogue. London: Tate Gallery, 1993, 25–52.

Wolf, Marian. "Giacometti as a Poet." *Arts Magazine* (May 1974), 38–41.

Yanaihara, Isaku. *On Giacometti.* Tokyo: Misuzu Shobo, 1958.

———. "Pages de journal." *Derrière le mirroir* 127 (May 1961): 18–26.

SELECTED BIBLIOGRAPHY

———. *With Giacometti*. Tokyo: Chikuma Shobo, 1969.

———. *Album Giacometti*. Tokyo: Misuzu Shobo Publishing, 1999.

Zendralli, A. M. *Giovanni Giacometti nell'occazione del 60 di sua vita*. Lugano, 1928.

Zervos, Christian. "Oeuvres d'art océaniennes et inquiétudes d'aujourd hui." *Cahiers d'art* (1929): 57–58.

———. "Notes sur la sculpture contemporaine, a propos de la récente exposition internationale de sculpture, galerie Georges Bernheim, Paris." *Cahiers d'art* (1929): 472.

———. "Quelques notes sur les sculptures de Giacometti." *Cahiers d'art* (1932): 337–42.

———. *Histoire de l'art contemporaine*. Paris: Editions cahiers d'art, 1938, 444–47.

INDEX

Page numbers in boldface indicate artwork and photographs. Giacometti's artworks are listed under either Paintings and drawings or Sculptures.

PHOTO CREDITS

Alberto Giacometti-Stiftung (figs. 2.2, 2.3, 2.4); Alinari / Art Resource, NY (figs. 3.1, 8.1); Archaeological Museum of Florence, Italy (figs. 8.8, 9.7); *Art et Industrie* no. 8, August, 1930 (fig. 5.3); © 2001 Artists Rights Society (ARS), New York / ADAGP, Paris (fig. 5.5); Photo by Gilberte Brassai (fig. 6.2); Bündner Kustmuseum Chur (fig. 1.2); Egyptian Museum, Cairo (figs. 6.4, 6.9, 8.5); *Emporium* (Bergamo) XLVII 1928 (fig. 4.7); Courtesy of Pierre and Maria Gaetana Matisse Foundation / photo by Patricia Matisse (figs. 12.3, 12.4, 13.6); Magnum Photos / photo by Henri Cartier-Bresson (figs. 13.1, 13.7); Pierre Matisse Gallery Archives. The Pierpont Morgan Library, New York. MA 5020 (figs. 9.1, 10.1); Pierre Matisse Gallery Archives. The Pierpont Morgan Library, New York. MA 5020 / photograph by Patricia Echuarren Matisse (fig. 11.1); Pierre Matisse Gallery Archives. The Pierpont Morgan Library, New York. MA 5020 / photograph by Patricia K. Matisse (fig. 12.1); Pierre Matisse Gallery Archives. The Pierpont Morgan Library, New York. MA 5020 / photograph by Patricia Matta Matisse (figs. 11.2, 11.3); © 2001 Man Ray Trust / Artists Rights Society (ARS), NY / ADAGP, Paris (fig. 8.3); Copyright Réunion des Musées Nationaux / Art Resource, NY (figs. 4.1, 4.5, 6.5, 6.6, 6.8); Ernst Scheidegger / NZZ Pro Litteris (figs. 1.11, 6.11, 12.2, 12.5, 12.6, 12.7); © Schweizerisches Institüt für Kunstwissenschaft, Zurich (figs. 1.4, 1.5, 1.6, 1.7, 1.8, 1.9, 3.3); Staatliche Museen zu Berlin / photo by Margarete Büsing (fig. 2.1); Staatliche Museen zu Berlin - Preussischer Kulturbesitz, Aegyptisches Museum (fig. 8.2); Photo by A. Strasser (fig. 7.1); *Le surrealisme au service de la revolution*, no 3. (fig. 6.1); Swiss Institute for Art Research, Zurich (figs. 7.3, 7.4); Swiss Institute for Art Research, Zurich / Private Collection (fig. 13.2); Swiss Institute for Photography (figs. 4.2, 8.6); © 2001 Estate of Yves Tanguy / Artists Rights Society (ARS), NY / ADAGP, Paris / CNAC / MNAM / Dist. Réunion des Musées Nationaux / Art Resource, NY (fig. 6.10); Photo by Marc Vaux (figs. 4.8, 4.9, 4.10, 4.11, 4.12, 5.1, 5.2, 5.4, 8.4, 8.7, 9.3, 9.4, 9.5, 9.6, 11.4); Photo by Laurie Wilson (figs. 1.1, 1.3, 1.10, 3.2, 4.3, 6.3, 6.7, 9.2); Drawing by Laurie Wilson (fig. 4.4); Yanaihara Estate (figs. 13.3, 13.4, 13.5a, 13.5b).